ADVANCED
OUTCOMES

CENGAGE
Learning™

Australia • Brazil • Japan • Korea • Mexico • Singapore • Spain • United Kingdom • United States

WELCOME TO *OUTCOMES*

Outcomes will help you learn the English you need and want. Each of the sixteen units has three double-pages linked by a common theme. Each double page is an individual lesson – and each teaches you some vocabulary or grammar and focuses on a different skill. The first lesson in each unit looks at conversation, the next two at reading or listening.

WRITING UNITS

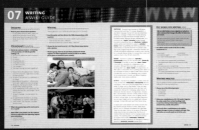

There are eight writing lessons in the Student's Book, which teach different styles of writing. Each one has a model text as well as speaking tasks to do in pairs or groups. There are also extra vocabulary or grammar exercises to help you write each kind of text. In addition, there is a lot of writing practice in the *Outcomes* Workbook.

REVIEW UNITS

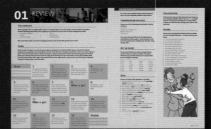

There are four Review units in this book. Here you practise the core grammar and vocabulary of the previous four units. The first two pages of each unit feature mini-presentations, a board game, a quiz and work on collocations and idioms. The next two pages feature a test of listening, grammar and vocabulary. This is marked out of 80 – so you can see how you are progressing.

Clearly stated communicative goals in the unit menu, supported by grammar and vocabulary.

Listening exercises provide examples of the conversations you try in Conversation practice.

Pronunciation activities are integrated with the communicative goals.

Interesting readings and listenings. Very varied contexts.

Further vocabulary points presented and developed through the unit.

Information on interesting bits of language common to native speakers of English.

02 CULTURE AND IDENTITY

In this unit, you learn how to:
- talk about different aspects of culture and society
- politely disagree with people's opinions
- express feelings and opinions more emphatically
- talk about useful objects in the home
- discuss your own personal / national identities

Grammar
- Emphatic structures

Vocabulary
- Society and culture
- Household objects
- Expressions with *thing*

Reading
- Foreign objects
- National and individual identity

Listening
- Society and culture in different countries
- Feelings about British culture

VOCABULARY Society and culture

A Work in pairs. Discuss how you feel about your country with regard to each of the categories below. Explain your ideas.

| bureaucracy | religion | crime |
| climate | cultural life | family / community life |

B Match each of the categories above to two sentences.
1 It's a very **close-knit** town. Everyone knows everyone.
2 Most people I met there seemed to be very **devout**.
3 A lot of companies are trying to **cut red tape** a bit.
4 They are **cracking down on** fraud.
5 The winters are incredibly **mild**.
6 We **got burgled** three times last year!
7 It's managed to remain a **secular** state.
8 Doctors are too busy **filling in forms** to do their job properly.
9 We get month after month of **damp** and **drizzle**.
10 There's a really **thriving** music scene.
11 It's still a very **male-dominated** society, in my opinion.
12 There's still a lot of **censorship** in the media.

C Which sentences in exercise B do you think describe positive things and which describe negative aspects? Why? What might be the possible causes and / or results of each sentence?

LISTENING

You are going to hear two conversations about society and culture in two different countries.

A ⊙2.1 Listen and take notes on what you hear about each place. Compare what you heard with a partner.

B Decide if these sentences are true or false. Listen again to check your ideas.

Conversation 1
1 She thinks it must be a dangerous country to visit.
2 People lead very isolated lives there.
3 The power balance in families perhaps wasn't what some people might expect.
4 He agrees that there's some truth in one of the stereotypes about the country.
5 He found the traffic absolutely infuriating.

Conversation 2
6 He was surprised at how quiet people were at concerts.
7 There's a healthy artistic community there.
8 The films are all heavily censored.
9 One recent film dealt with some controversial issues.
10 The economy is in recession.

C Work in groups. Discuss these questions.
- Do you think your country is similar to either of the two places discussed? In what way?
- What do you think are the common stereotypes of your area / country?
- How much truth do you think there is in these stereotypes?

14 OUTCOMES

SPEAKING

A Work in groups. Discuss these questions.
- In what ways do you think homes / rooms / household objects can reflect a person's culture or identity?
- Have you ever been in any homes in other countries? If yes, did you notice anything unusual about them?
- What do you think a foreigner might find unusual about your home or about other homes in your country?

VOCABULARY Household objects

A Check you know the objects in the box.

bucket	toilet	sink	nail
needle	cloth	ladder	tap
pin	string	oven	pan
glue	drill	dishwasher	

B Decide which objects in exercise A you usually do the actions in the box below to.

stick in	thread	climb	cut
cover	knot	hit	turn off
unblock	heat	load	plug in
spread	flush	run	wring out

C Take turns to act or draw the actions. Your partner should say the action and the noun.

D Discuss the difference between:
- **rope** and **string** / a **mop** and a **brush**
- **wire** and **cable** / a **nail** and a **screw**
- a **cloth** and a **sponge** / a **ladder** and **stairs**
- a **bucket** and a **bowl** / a **knee pad** and a **bandage**
- a **drill** and a **hammer** / **soap** and **washing-up liquid**

E Decide if the following are problems or solutions.

spill some water	protect yourself
rip your jeans	sweep the floor
soak your jeans	drop my glass
stain a shirt	rinse my glass
mend your shirt	wipe the table

F Work in groups. Take turns thinking of an object you want. Then say sentences like this:
I've spilt my drink. OR *I need to wipe the table.*

Your partner should offer the object:
Do you want a mop and bucket / cloth?

See who guesses the most objects correctly.

READING

You are going to read an article about objects people noticed when they travelled or lived in other countries.

A Read the introduction and discuss these questions.
- How far do you agree with the writer?
- Can you think of anything that:
  – you take for granted?
  – you've reacted to with bemusement or disgust?
  – your culture has adopted from abroad?

Foreign objects
In our globalised world, we can often take it for granted that the things that surround us are universal, sensible or normal. So when we travel or live abroad and discover new objects or the absence of things we're familiar with, it can be surprising. We may react with bemusement or disgust, but at such times we should bear in mind that visitors travelling to our country would no doubt have the same experience and that what we see as extraordinary or ridiculous today, we may adopt as our own tomorrow. Take an English aristocrat's comment on seeing a bizarre instrument in 17th century Italy: "Why should a person need a fork when God had given him hands?"

NATIVE SPEAKER ENGLISH
take for granted
If you take something (or someone) for granted, you assume it will never change and you don't value it as you should.

We often take it for granted that it's universal.
We take running water for granted and often waste it.
I don't take anything for granted.
My boss will realise he took me for granted when I leave.

16 OUTCOMES

GRAMMAR Emphatic structures

To emphasise a feeling or opinion, we often use these structures:

			that ...
What			the fact that ...
The thing that	verb	be	the amount of ...
One thing that	phrase		the lack of ...
			the number of ...
			the way that ...
			etc.

To show we don't share someone's opinion – and that we have a different opinion – we can use this structure:

A: Do they really drive as badly as the stereotype has it?
B: To be honest, *it wasn't that* that *really bothered* me. *It was more* just the total lack of any decent public transport.

A Look at audioscript 2.1 on page 161. Find examples of emphatic structures in conversations 2.

B Write full sentences using the ideas below.
1 thing / disturbs me / lack of democracy
2 worries / most / amount / censorship
3 thing / annoys / way / president talks to everyone
4 one / drives me mad / the traffic / the city
5 thing / scares / amount / money spent / weapons
6 bothers / lack / investment / art and culture
7 concerns me / power / judges have
8 one / gives / hope / future / fact / young people / so much more tolerant nowadays

▶ Need help? Read the grammar reference on page 137.

C Work in pairs. Take turns saying your sentences from exercise B.

If you agree with a sentence, respond by saying *I know* and then give an example. If you disagree, say *Really? It's not that that ... me. It's ... –* and explain your own ideas.

CONVERSATION PRACTICE

You are going to have a conversation about the place where you live now.

A Make a list of things that you like about the place and another list of things that annoy you.

B Work in groups. Explain your ideas. Agree or disagree with your partners. Use as much language from these pages as you can.

DEVELOPING CONVERSATIONS
Disagreeing

We use several different expressions to disagree. We usually then explain why we have a different opinion.

A: It's a very male-dominated society, isn't it?
B: *I don't know about that.* It may have that reputation, but that wasn't really my experience of the place.

A Put the words in the correct order to make expressions.
1 not that I'm about sure
2 exaggeration isn't that of a bit an?
3 far that I go wouldn't
4 isn't over that's a top the it bit?
5 looking well at way of things that's one
6 of that's overstatement a bit it an isn't?
7 really I see don't like it myself that

B 2.2 Listen and check your answers. Practise saying the expressions.

C Work in pairs. Take turns giving the opinions below and disagreeing with them. Explain why you disagree.
1 Films have a duty to tackle socially sensitive issues.
2 There should be no censorship of anything.
3 Income tax should be completely abolished.
4 Wars are often good for the economy.
5 Corrupt government officials should get life in jail.
6 The police don't do anything about most crimes!

Grammar taught in context, with natural examples of usage and clear practice tasks.

Many expressions and grammatical patterns in spoken english are similar to other languages. These exercises help you notice those.

Fuller explanations, more examples, and exercises are in the reference section at the back.

This section allows you to put together what you've learnt.

B Now read the four people's accounts and decide:
• if any of the things are usual in your country.
• if you think any of them will become common in the future. Why? / Why not?

C Read again and decide who:
1 expresses annoyance. ......
2 found something they liked a lot. ......
3 is impressed by someone. ......
4 couldn't adapt to something. ......
5 has adopted a foreign taste. ......
6 could be overstating how common something is. ......
7 felt restricted by something. ......
8 is reminded of something. ......
9 didn't agree with someone. ......

D Work in groups. Discuss the following.
• Which household objects do you think most reflect your national culture? In what way?
• Say three objects that remind you strongly of other countries or places.
• Have you seen anything in someone's house which you really liked? What? Why?
• What crazes did you have at school / when you were younger?
• Which objects would you miss the most if you went to live abroad? Why?

LANGUAGE PATTERNS

Write the sentences in your language. Translate them back into English. Compare your English to the original.
At times, it's not nearly as straightforward as it sounds!
It's far easier than it looks.
He's really not quite as laid-back as he seems.
It was nowhere near as bad as I expected.
It was miles better than I thought it'd be.

Cultural and cross-cultural contexts.

A translation exercise helps you think about how sentences work in your language compared to English.

IN-HA, SOUTH KOREA

I got used to many odd things I found in Britain, but one thing I still struggle to understand is why so many places still use separate hot and cold taps at the sink rather than a mixer tap. You have to fill the basin to get the water at the right temperature, but then you can't rinse your face properly because the soap stays in the water. It's much better with the mixer tap because you can leave it running. In fact, what drives you mad even more is if there's no plug. Then you end up either getting freezing hands, or burning them, or trying to move between the two. Useless!

...NADA

...e, of course, loads of things you notice in Germany, which are
...to back home like *steins*, litre jugs of beer which people drink, not
...on the waitresses that sometimes carry three or four in each hand.
...omen have wrists and forearms of iron. However, the thing which
...omes up sooner or later in conversation with foreigners is German
...nlike our traditional bowl with steep sides down to the water, most
...toilets have a shelf so that you can check everything is as it should
...hen flush it all away – something which at times is not nearly as
...orward as it sounds! I had a friend who used to really rant about
...ut they never bothered me.

ED, UK

I don't know how widespread some of these things are because Chinese people don't tend to invite you to their home that much – you arrange to meet out somewhere. The flat I rented when I lived there was furnished and there were a couple of things that struck me. The first was that there wasn't an oven, which somewhat reduced the scope of my cooking. I also found a massive meat cleaver, which was a bit disconcerting as I associate it more with a butcher or with serial killers! One thing I really took to, though, was the rice cooker. I should've brought one back.

MAGGIE, IRELAND

I was staying with a friend, Sheila, and she had this thing. It was like a tall mug, but without a handle, and made out of horn. It also had this metal straw. It was lovely. She told me she'd picked it up when living in Uruguay. You brew this tea called *mate* in it and then drink it together. She's fallen in love with the thing and has taken to using it quite a lot, but she didn't persuade me to have much, though – it was a weird taste. The other thing I saw while I was with her was her son playing with a spinning top. It really took me back. At school there was a mad craze for them. It only lasted about six months, but we were all really into it.

LEARNING

Research suggests words need lots of revision in context if you want to be able to use them with confidence. The authors of *Outcomes* have tried hard to make sure words reappear many different times in the course. Here are **nine** ways to learn the words *thrive / thriving*.

• see it and practise it in **Vocabulary** p. 10
• look it up in the **Vocabulary Builder** p. 10
• read it in **information file 1** p. 152
• meet it again in **Vocabulary** p. 14
• hear it in three different **Listenings** p. 14, p. 40 and p. 94
• read it in a **Reading** text p. 39
• write, read and listen to it in the **Workbook Unit 01**
• revise it in the quiz p. 33
• test it with **ExamView**

Outcomes VOCABULARY BUILDER

The *Outcomes Vocabulary Builder* provides lists of key vocabulary with clear explanations, examples of common collocations and exercises focusing on the grammar of the words.

MyOutcomes ONLINE

The pin code at the front of the Student's Book gives you access to a wide range of interactive, online exercises. We have created additional exercises to go with each unit from the book, so you can continue developing your English. Visit **www.cengage.com**

Grammar	Vocabulary	Reading	Listening	Developing conversations
• Perfect tenses	• City life • Changes • Binomials (*bits and pieces*, etc.)	• Cities that have overcome problems • Perpetuating the myths	• Two different cities • Recovering from disaster • Three urban myths	• Emphasising and reinforcing
• Emphatic structures	• Society and culture • Household objects • Expressions with *thing*	• Foreign objects • National and individual identity	• Society and culture in different countries • Feelings about British culture	• Disagreeing
• *would*	• Describing people • Divorce • Phrasal verbs	• The bitter end	• What're they like? • Relationships	• Giving your impression • *What's up?*
• Conditionals	• Consequences • Politicians • Elections and politics	• Beyond a joke! • The electoral system Swiss style	• Government proposals • Political jokes • Voting	• Giving opinions
• Noun phrases	• Feelings • noun + *of* • Describing books	• A *What's on* guide	• A night out • Book clubs	• *I bet / imagine*
• *I wish*	• Adverbs • War and peace • Social conflict	• Hope springs eternal • The Truth and Reconciliation Commission	• Two conflicts • Disputes in the news • The Truth and Reconciliation Commission	• Giving negative / private information
• Passives	• Talking about science • Statistics • Forming words	• Truth and statistics	• Discussing news stories about science • Five scientists discuss their jobs	• Expressing surprise and disbelief
• Auxiliaries	• Describing scenery • Communicating • Animals	• Why I love ... natural history programmes • Endangered animals	• Two different landscapes • A lecture by a linguistics professor • Animal habitats and features	• Emphatic tags

Grammar	Vocabulary	Reading	Listening	Developing conversations
• Continuous forms	• Company jobs and tasks • Adverb adjective collocations • The world of work	• *The Living Dead*	• The first day at work • Underemployment • Five news stories about work	• Deductions
• Modal verbs	• Operations • Body actions • Medical conditions	• East meets West • Two different medical conditions	• Two surgical procedures • A mindfulness experience • A miracle cure	• Vague language
• Linking words	• Doing and watching sport • Games • Sports and games metaphors	• Not just child's play	• Sports success and failure • A short lecture on playing cards • Stories about different games	• Irony and humour
• Dramatic inversion	• Personal histories • Presenting arguments and theories • Recent history	• Ancient history?	• An amazing life • Recent historical milestones	• Similes • Asking for clarification
• Reporting and verb patterns	• News headlines • Newspapers	• Popular papers	• *Did you see ...?* • Future of news publishing • The evening news	• Rhetorical questions and common opinions
• Relative clauses	• *How's business?* • Business situations	• Laughing all the way from the bank	• Two phone calls between colleagues • A business meeting in a footwear company	• Small talk
• Prepositions	• Style and design • Fashion and the media	• An extract from *Adorned in Dreams* • At a costume museum	• Four conversations about style • A lecture about fashion and society	• Backtracking and correcting
• Other future forms	• Accidents and injuries • Laws and regulations • Dangers and risks	• Bureaucrats back down on tan ban	• Scar stories • A health and safety officer • A radio phone-in programme	• Interjections

01 CITIES

In this unit, you learn how to:
- describe different aspects of cities and city life
- emphasise and reinforce ideas in different ways
- talk about urban problems and how to tackle them
- talk about changes in urban areas
- tell urban myths

Grammar
- Perfect tenses

Vocabulary
- City life
- Changes
- Binomials
  (*bits and pieces*, etc.)

Reading
- Cities that have overcome problems
- Perpetuating the myths

Listening
- Two different cities
- Recovering from disaster
- Three urban myths

SPEAKING

A Work in groups. Discuss these questions.
- What are the advantages / disadvantages of living in a city?
- Which is the best city in your country? Why?
- In your opinion, which is the worst city? Why?

VOCABULARY City life

A Match the adjectives in the box to 1–9.

well-run	congested	spotless
run-down	polluted	vibrant
dangerous	sprawling	affluent

1 The nightlife's wild. There's so much going on.
2 There are a lot of muggings and shootings.
3 Everything is very efficient and works very smoothly.
4 There's a permanent cloud of smog hanging over the city. You sometimes choke on the fumes.
5 People are obviously rolling in money.
6 There was no rubbish on the streets and no graffiti anywhere. It was amazing to see!
7 The transport system is non-existent and cars just crawl along bumper-to-bumper.
8 It just goes on for miles and miles. It's enormous.
9 The houses are crumbling and there are lots of derelict buildings, which seem to have been abandoned altogether.

B Spend two minutes reading and memorising the adjectives in the box. Then work in pairs.
Student A: say sentences 1–9.
Student B: without looking at the box, say the adjective that matches each sentence.

C Which adjectives in exercise A are opposites of the words in the box below?

filthy	deprived	dull	chaotic	compact	safe

D Work in groups. Think of different places that each of the adjectives in exercises A and C could describe.

The *Vocabulary Builder* at the back of this book has more information on what new words mean and how to use them. It also contains explanations and lists of common collocations.

LISTENING

You are going to hear two conversations about cities.

A 🔊 1.1 **Listen and take notes on what the two cities are like.**

B **Compare your ideas. Which place would you rather live in? Why?**

C **Listen again and complete the sentences.**
 1 a It's really wild. It ...., actually.
   b Honestly. The people there party ....
   c Actually, that was ...., the congestion.
   d .... Are you sure it's so great?
   e It does ...., but as I say, it just has a real buzz.
 2 a It is, if you like ....
   b It's more lively. There's ....,
     you know.
   c So you .... to live there?
   d Don't ...., it is a good place to live if you're bringing up kids.
   e So if I ...., I might move back. It's just not what I want right now.

D **Work in groups. Discuss these questions.**
 • What places, people, etc. have taken you by surprise?
 • Have you ever been out till four? Where? When?
 • What downsides are there to the place you live in?
 • What 'scenes' are there where you live?
 • Where's a good place to settle down in your country / region? Why?

DEVELOPING CONVERSATIONS
Emphasising and reinforcing

> **We can emphasise by:**
> • using extreme words: *appalling, packed, crawl, stink*
> • adding adverbs: *incredibly modern, ridiculously expensive*
> • using repetition: *really, really nice; miles and miles*
> • using *like*: *like crazy, like there's no tomorrow*
>
> **We often reinforce what we say using *honestly, seriously, I swear* and then adding a further description or example.**

A **Find at least one example of each of the ways of emphasising and reinforcing in the audioscript on page 160.**

B **Write a reinforcing sentence to follow each of 1–6.**
 1 The amount of building work is incredible.
 2 It's an absolutely huge sprawling city.
 3 The city's a complete dump.
 4 It's ridiculously cheap there.
 5 It's like a war zone in some parts of the city.
 6 It's an incredibly vibrant place.

C **Work in pairs. Have conversations like the one below, using the sentences you wrote. Take turns being student A.**
 A: The amount of building work is incredible.
 B: Really?
 A: Seriously. There are buildings springing up absolutely everywhere. You could see hundreds and hundreds of cranes from our hotel.
 B: Wow! That sounds amazing.

CONVERSATION PRACTICE

You are going to have similar conversations about cities to the ones you heard in *Listening*.

A **Write the names of two cities you've been to. Make notes about aspects of the cities, etc. and think of at least one thing that happened to you in each city. Use as much language from these pages as you can.**

B **Now have conversations starting *Have you been to ...?* Keep the conversation going by asking questions to get more details or by using comments like *Really?* or *Yeah?***

READING

You are going to read about places that have overcome serious problems.

A **Before you read, discuss these questions in groups.**
- Has your town or city ever been affected by any of the things in the box below? When? What happened?
- Which do you think is most damaging to a city?
- Which do you think is the most difficult to recover from – or which leaves the most lasting effects?

an economic downturn	a hurricane	a war
an earthquake	flooding	crime
severe pollution	terrorism	a fire

B **Divide the class into three groups.**
Group A: look at File 1 on page 152.
Group B: look at File 12 on page 156.
Group C: look at File 18 on page 159.

Read your text and answer these questions.
1 What problem did the city suffer from?
2 How did it affect the city?
3 What is the city like now?
4 What brought about its recovery?
5 Has the recovery had significance beyond the city?

C **With a person from your group, check your answers and discuss any vocabulary you are not sure of.**

D **Work with students from the other two groups. Discuss the three different cities, using the questions in exercise B and your own ideas.**

Decide which is the most remarkable and / or the most interesting story. Explain why.

E **Choose two new words from your text that you think are useful. Explain the words to your partners.**

VOCABULARY Changes

A **Replace the words in *italics* with the correct form of the verbs in the box.**

emerge	undergo	demolish	flourish
triple	decline	regenerate	overcome

1 The city has *gone through* huge changes since the war.
2 A strong community spirit *came out* from the disaster.
3 The city has *recovered from* a huge array of problems.
4 Many old buildings were *knocked down* in the 1960s.
5 The area has been *done up* – you might say gentrified.
6 Unemployment has *risen threefold* in the last year.
7 The whole area has *gone downhill* because of neglect.
8 Businesses are springing up and *thriving*.

NATIVE SPEAKER ENGLISH

gentrified

We use *gentrify* or *gentrification* to describe what happens when a poor area changes as more middle-class people buy the (cheap) properties and do them up to live there.

It used to be quite rough, but it's become quite gentrified.
The area's undergoing a process of gentrification.

B **Work in pairs. Discuss the questions below. Try to use some of the language in exercise A.**
- Do you know any places that have suffered any of the problems in *Reading* exercise A? What happened? What changes took place?
- What changes have taken place where you live over the last ten years?

GRAMMAR Perfect tenses

> Perfect forms are formed using *have* + past participle.
>
> There are past, present and future forms. We use perfect tenses to look back from a point in time and describe finished actions or continuing states. With finished actions, we often don't know exactly when they happened.

A **Work in pairs. Decide if one or both of the forms in italics is correct in the sentences below. If only one is correct, say why the other form is wrong.**
1. New York may *have been / always be* a major city for many years, but it has had to overcome many problems.
2. Murders *have fallen / fall* more than fourfold over the last 20 years and some believe the figure will *have dipped / dip* below 400 a year by the next election.
3. Tangshan *had been / was* a major industrial city until 28th July 1976.
4. Tangshan is now a symbol of that change, *having been / being* completely rebuilt since 1980.
5. The initial drop in crime is thought to *have contributed / contribute* to further reductions in crime rates over the last 20 years.
6. He said he'*d been / was* from Dortmund.

B **Which of the perfect forms above refer to finished actions and which to continuing states?**

▶ Need help? Read the grammar reference on page 136.

Mourners light candles to remember the victims of the Tangshan earthquake.

LISTENING

You are going to hear an interview with Lloyd Jones, an expert on disaster recovery.

A 🔊 1.2 **Listen and decide what the main point of Lloyd Jones' answers is.**

B **Work in pairs. Explain what Lloyd and the interviewer say about:**
1. the hurricane
2. rubble and shelter
3. an opportunity
4. fishing villages and the tsunami
5. Chicago.

C **Listen again and read the audioscript on page 160 to check your ideas.**

D **Work in pairs. Discuss these questions.**
- How far do you agree with Lloyd Jones?
- Think again about changes that have happened where you live. How far was the local community involved in the decisions? Who did the decisions benefit?
- How important is it to preserve a place's heritage?

SPEAKING

Oldbury is a small city of 150,000. There's a chemical works nearby which produces nasty fumes. The city has a number of deprived areas and high unemployment. The small historical centre, which is very run-down, dates back 300 years. It is to receive a £50 million regeneration grant.

A **Work in groups. Put the following in order of priority. Then decide how much should be spent on each project.**
- set up a recycling centre
- provide grants for people starting up new businesses
- renovate the historical centre and build a tourist centre
- provide low-interest loans to improve homes
- shut down the chemical works and relocate it on the coast
- set up youth centres to give young unemployed people something to do and to keep them off the street
- recruit more officers to police the poorer parts of the city
- plant trees in every street and increase the amount of green space available for public use

B **Compare your ideas with another group and create one proposal to present to the class.**

C **Work in pairs and say what you'd spend the money on if it was for your town / city.**

READING

You are going to read an article about urban myths.

A Before you read, discuss these questions in pairs.
- What do you think urban myths – or legends – are?
- What kind of things are they generally about?
- Why do you think people tell this kind of story?
- Do you think they are a purely modern phenomenon?

B Read the article on the right and answer the questions.
1 How is folklore generally defined in academic circles?
2 In what different ways can urban myths be analysed?
3 What kind of topics do urban myths generally tackle?
4 Why do we create these stories?
5 Why do popular urban myths spread so quickly?

C Discuss with a partner what the words in **bold** mean in the article. Then complete the collocations below.
1 ~ hope / ~ your congratulations / ~ advice
2 ~ changes / ~ surgery / ~ a radical transformation
3 ~ your opinion / ~ fears / ~ concern / ~ doubts
4 ~ possibilities / ~ solutions / ~ the issue in depth
5 ~ gossip / ~ the news / ~ like wildfire / ~ the word
6 ~ relevant / ~ confident / ~ a serious issue
7 ~ a message / ~ symbols / ~ dreams
8 ~ as a global power / ~ from recession / ~ from the shadows

D Can you remember which words in the article went with each of the verbs in exercise C? Look again to check.

LANGUAGE PATTERNS

Write the sentences in your language. Translate them back into English. Compare your English to the original.

Some people just spread the stories out of boredom.

How much was it, out of interest?

I did it out of curiosity, just to see what would happen.

No alcohol was served, out of respect for local traditions.

I only agreed to go on a date with him out of pity!

PERPETUATING THE MYTHS

What's the similarity between a story about children finding a house built of sweets and one about someone waking up in a bath of ice having had a kidney removed in their sleep? Academics argue that they are both examples of folklore, simply separated by time.

Throughout history, folklore has served complex social functions, and with the circulation of urban myths today, it **remains** meaningful, even if the stories themselves have changed dramatically. In academic terms, folklore means stories that are repeated by different individuals and that **undergo** variations over time, often becoming exaggerated or sensationalised.

Most scholars attempt to **decode** the meanings of stories in one of three main ways: firstly, there are those who focus on the structure and literary merits of stories; secondly, there's the more cultural approach, which **explores** historical, social and economic contexts; and finally, there's the more psychological approach, which concentrates on the reasons why people create and **spread** stories.

Many urban myths deal with topics such as crime, accidents and death, and seem to **emerge** from deep-rooted fears people have about the world and from the need to **offer** lessons about these anxieties.

While urban legends aren't necessarily true, the popular ones nevertheless have a ring of truth about them. Listeners then spread them for a whole range of different reasons: out of boredom, to **voice** personal worries, to get attention, to harm people or simply to make small talk.

LISTENING

You are going to hear three different people talking about urban myths they have heard in their countries.

A ⏣ 1.3 Listen to each person. You won't hear the end of each story yet. Take notes on what happened.

B Compare what you heard with a partner. Try to use all the words below.
1 reported – driveway – note – ill – concert – thrilled
2 collapsed – rushed – diagnosed – incident – the case
3 desperately sad – grabbed – freaked out – run out of – cashier – trolley – the spitting image – favour – good deed

C Listen again to check your ideas if you need to. Then discuss how you think each story will end.

D ⏣ 1.4 Listen to the end of each story. See if you guessed correctly. Explain what happened in each story.

E Work in groups. Discuss these questions.
• Which story do you like best? Why?
• What do you think of each of the people in the three stories? Why?
• Do you think the stories are true? Why? / Why not?
• What do you think the moral message of each story is?
• Do you agree with the messages?

VOCABULARY Binomials

> Binomials are pairs of words linked together by *and / or*. The two words are always used in the same order.
>
> He went to a supermarket to buy a few *bits and pieces*. They'll have to do something about it *sooner or later*.

A Work in pairs. Which four binomials are the wrong way round?

by and large	quiet and peace
take or give	long and hard
on and off	now and then
tired and sick	there and here

B Complete the sentences with the binomials in exercise A.
1 I've been studying Russian for about six years now, ...
2 Some buildings are crumbling a bit, but .... the old town seems very well preserved.
3 I still like to party ...., but I've calmed down a lot.
4 It can be quite hard to find .... in the city.
5 I thought .... about it before making a decision.
6 It's a fairly affluent area, but there are still pockets of deprivation ....
7 I can't take it any more. I'm .... of the constant noise.
8 The population's about ten million, ...

SPEAKING

You are going to tell your own urban myths.

A Work in groups. The pictures below are from urban myths. Discuss what you think happens in each one.

B Choose one of these stories – or a story you have heard yourself – to tell. Plan what you are going to say. Then tell your partners. Who has the best story? Why?

02 CULTURE AND IDENTITY

In this unit, you learn how to:
- talk about different aspects of culture and society
- politely disagree with people's opinions
- express feelings and opinions more emphatically
- talk about useful objects in the home
- discuss your own personal / national identities

Grammar
- Emphatic structures

Vocabulary
- Society and culture
- Household objects
- Expressions with *thing*

Reading
- Foreign objects
- National and individual identity

Listening
- Society and culture in different countries
- Feelings about British culture

VOCABULARY Society and culture

A **Work in pairs. Discuss how you feel about your country with regard to each of the categories below. Explain your ideas.**

bureaucracy	religion	crime
climate	cultural life	family / community life

B **Match each of the categories above to two sentences.**
1 It's a very **close-knit** town. Everyone knows everyone.
2 Most people I met there seemed to be very **devout**.
3 A lot of companies are trying to **cut red tape** a bit.
4 They are **cracking down on** fraud.
5 The winters are incredibly **mild**.
6 We **got burgled** three times last year!
7 It's managed to remain a **secular** state.
8 Doctors are too busy **filling in forms** to do their job properly.
9 We get month after month of **damp** and **drizzle**.
10 There's a really **thriving** music scene.
11 It's still a very **male-dominated** society, in my opinion.
12 There's still a lot of **censorship** in the media.

C **Which sentences in exercise B do you think describe positive things and which describe negative aspects? Why? What might be the possible causes and / or results of each sentence?**

LISTENING

You are going to hear two conversations about society and culture in two different countries.

A 🔊 **2.1 Listen and take notes on what you hear about each place. Compare what you heard with a partner.**

B **Decide if these sentences are true or false. Listen again to check your ideas.**

Conversation 1
1 She thinks it must be a dangerous country to visit.
2 People lead very isolated lives there.
3 The power balance in families perhaps wasn't what some people might expect.
4 He agrees that there's some truth in one of the stereotypes about the country.
5 He found the traffic absolutely infuriating.

Conversation 2
6 He was surprised at how quiet people were at concerts.
7 There's a healthy artistic community there.
8 The films are all heavily censored.
9 One recent film dealt with some controversial issues.
10 The economy is in recession.

C **Work in groups. Discuss these questions.**
- Do you think your country is similar to either of the two places discussed? In what way?
- What do you think are the common stereotypes of your area / country?
- How much truth do you think there is in these stereotypes?

DEVELOPING CONVERSATIONS
Disagreeing

> We use several different expressions to disagree. We usually then explain why we have a different opinion.
>
> A: It's a very male-dominated society, isn't it?
> B: *I don't know about that.* It may have that reputation, but that wasn't really my experience of the place.

A **Put the words in the correct order to make expressions.**
1 not that I'm about sure
2 exaggeration isn't that of a bit an?
3 far that I go wouldn't
4 isn't over that's a top the it bit?
5 looking well at way of things that's one
6 of that's overstatement a bit it an isn't?
7 really I see don't like it myself that

B 🔊 **2.2 Listen and check your answers. Practise saying the expressions.**

C **Work in pairs. Take turns giving the opinions below and disagreeing with them. Explain why you disagree.**
1 Films have a duty to tackle socially sensitive issues.
2 There should be no censorship of anything.
3 Income tax should be completely abolished.
4 Wars are often good for the economy.
5 Corrupt government officials should get life in jail.
6 The police don't do anything about most crimes!

GRAMMAR Emphatic structures

> To emphasise a feeling or opinion, we often use these structures:

What The thing that One thing that	verb phrase	be	that ... the fact that ... the amount of ... the lack of ... the number of ... the way that ... etc.

> To show we don't share someone's opinion – and that we have a different opinion – we can use this structure:
>
> A: Do they really drive as badly as the stereotype has it?
> B: To be honest, *it wasn't that* that really bothered me. *It was more* just the total lack of any decent public transport.

A **Look at audioscript 2.1 on page 161. Find examples of emphatic structures in conversation 2.**

B **Write full sentences using the ideas below.**
1 thing / disturbs me / lack of democracy
2 worries / most / amount / censorship
3 thing / annoys / way / president talks to everyone
4 one / drives me mad / the traffic / the city
5 thing / scares / amount / money spent / weapons
6 bothers / lack / investment / art and culture
7 concerns me / power / judges have
8 one / gives / hope / future / fact / young people / so much more tolerant nowadays

▶ Need help? Read the grammar reference on page 137.

C **Work in pairs. Take turns saying your sentences from exercise B.**

If you agree with a sentence, respond by saying *I know* and then give an example. If you disagree, say *Really? It's not that that ... me. It's ...* – and explain your own ideas.

CONVERSATION PRACTICE

You are going to have a conversation about the place where you live now.

A **Make a list of things that you like about the place and another list of things that annoy you.**

B **Work in groups. Explain your ideas. Agree or disagree with your partners. Use as much language from these pages as you can.**

SPEAKING

A Work in groups. Discuss these questions.
- In what ways do you think homes / rooms / household objects can reflect a person's culture or identity?
- Have you ever been in any homes in other countries? If yes, did you notice anything unusual about them?
- What do you think a foreigner might find unusual about your home or about other homes in your country?

VOCABULARY Household objects

A Check you know the objects in the box.

bucket	toilet	sink	nail
needle	cloth	ladder	tap
pin	string	oven	pan
glue	drill	dishwasher	

B Decide which objects in exercise A you usually do the actions in the box below to.

stick in	thread	climb	cut
cover	knot	hit	turn off
unblock	heat	load	plug in
spread	flush	run	wring out

C Take turns to act or draw the actions. Your partner should say the action and the noun.

D Discuss the difference between:

rope and **string**	a **mop** and a **brush**
wire and **cable**	a **nail** and a **screw**
a **cloth** and a **sponge**	a **ladder** and **stairs**
a **bucket** and a **bowl**	a **knee pad** and a **bandage**
a **drill** and a **hammer**	**soap** and **washing-up liquid**

E Decide if the following are problems or solutions.

spill some water	protect yourself
rip your jeans	sweep the floor
soak your jeans	drop my glass
stain a shirt	rinse my glass
mend your shirt	wipe the table

F Work in groups. Take turns thinking of an object you want. Then say sentences like this:
I've spilt my drink.   OR   *I need to wipe the table.*

Your partner should offer the object:
*Do you want a **mop** and **bucket** / **cloth**?*

See who guesses the most objects correctly.

READING

You are going to read an article about objects people noticed when they travelled or lived in other countries.

A Read the introduction and discuss these questions.
- How far do you agree with the writer?
- Can you think of anything that:
  – you take for granted?
  – you've reacted to with bemusement or disgust?
  – your culture has adopted from abroad?

> **Foreign objects**
> In our globalised world, we can often take it for granted that the things that surround us are universal, sensible or normal. So when we travel or live abroad and discover new objects or the absence of things we're familiar with, it can be surprising. We may react with bemusement or disgust, but at such times we should bear in mind that visitors travelling to our country would no doubt have the same experience and that what we see as extraordinary or ridiculous today, we may adopt as our own tomorrow. Take an English aristocrat's comment on seeing a bizarre instrument in 17th century Italy: "Why should a person need a fork when God had given him hands?"

NATIVE SPEAKER ENGLISH

take for granted
If you *take* something (or someone) *for granted*, you assume it will never change and you don't value it as you should.

We often take it for granted that it's universal.
We take running water for granted and often waste it.
I don't take anything for granted.
My boss will realise he took me for granted when I leave.

B Now read the four people's accounts and decide:
- if any of the things are usual in your country.
- if you think any of them will become common in the future. Why? / Why not?

C Read again and decide who:
1 expresses annoyance.
2 found something they liked a lot.
3 is impressed by someone.
4 couldn't adapt to something.
5 has adopted a foreign taste.
6 could be overstating how common something is.
7 felt restricted by something.
8 is reminded of something.
9 didn't agree with someone.

IN-HA
ED
BOB
MAGGIE
SHILA

ED
ED
MAGGIE?
BOB

D Work in groups. Discuss the following.
- Which household objects do you think most reflect your national culture? In what way?
- Say three objects that remind you strongly of other countries or places.
- Have you seen anything in someone's house which you really liked? What? Why?
- What crazes did you have at school / when you were younger?
- Which objects would you miss the most if you went to live abroad? Why?

LANGUAGE PATTERNS

Write the sentences in your language. Translate them back into English. Compare your English to the original.
At times, it's not nearly as straightforward as it sounds!
It's far easier than it looks.
He's really not quite as laid-back as he seems.
It was nowhere near as bad as I expected.
It was miles better than I thought it'd be.

IN-HA, SOUTH KOREA

I got used to many odd things I found in Britain, but one thing I still struggle to understand is why so many places still use separate hot and cold taps at the sink rather than a mixer tap. You have to fill the basin to get the water at the right temperature, but then you can't rinse your face properly because the soap stays in the water. It's much better with the mixer tap because you can leave it running. In fact, what drives you mad even more is if there's no plug. Then you end up either getting freezing hands, or burning them, or trying to move between the two. Useless!

ED, UK

I don't know how widespread some of these things are because Chinese people don't tend to invite you to their home that much – you arrange to meet out somewhere. The flat I rented when I lived there was furnished and there were a couple of things that struck me. The first was that there wasn't an oven, which somewhat reduced the scope of my cooking. I also found a massive meat cleaver, which was a bit disconcerting as I associate it more with a butcher or with serial killers! One thing I really took to, though, was the rice cooker. I should've brought one back.

BOB, CANADA

There are, of course, loads of things you notice in Germany, which are different to back home like *steins*, litre jugs of beer which people drink, not to mention the waitresses that sometimes carry three or four in each hand. Those women have wrists and forearms of iron. However, the thing which always comes up sooner or later in conversation with foreigners is German toilets. Unlike our traditional bowl with steep sides down to the water, most German toilets have a shelf so that you can check everything is as it should be. You then flush it all away – something which at times is not nearly as straightforward as it sounds! I had a friend who used to really rant about them – but they never bothered me.

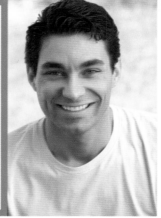

MAGGIE, IRELAND

I was staying with a friend, Sheila, and she had this thing. It was like a tall mug, but without a handle, and made out of horn. It also had this metal straw. It was lovely. She told me she'd picked it up when living in Uruguay. You brew this tea called *mate* in it and then drink it together. She's fallen in love with the thing and has taken to using it quite a lot, but she didn't persuade me to have much, though – it was a weird taste. The other thing I saw while I was with her was her son playing with a spinning top. It really took me back. At school there was a mad craze for them. It only lasted about six months, but we were all really into it.

SPEAKING

A Work in groups. Discuss these questions.
- What do you know about British culture? Think about: literature, theatre, music, broadcasting, visual arts, fashion, religion, cuisine, sport, buildings, monuments, etc.
- How much do you know about the things in the box below?
- How do you think each might be connected to British culture?
- How important is British culture in the world? In your country? For you personally?

God Save the Queen	Shakespeare
fish and chips	Islam
curry	punk
kilts	cricket
the Costa del Sol in Spain	Harrods
ballet	car boot sales
hip-hop	St George's Day
football	Easter
bowler hats	Jamaica

LISTENING

You are going to hear three people talking about their feelings about British culture.

A ✇ 2.3 Listen and find out which of the things in *Speaking* they mention – and what they say about them.

B Listen again and decide which speaker:
1 has a fairly global world view.
2 was surprised to find out what acquiring British nationality involved.
3 has sometimes had to deal with abuse.
4 seems a bit confused about the whole issue of cultural identity.
5 retains a sense of family roots.
6 is annoyed by a common false assumption.

C Work in pairs. Discuss these questions.
- Did anything the speakers said surprise / amuse / interest you? What? Why?
- Are there strong regional differences in your country?
- Do you think it's good for regions to have a lot of autonomy from central government?

VOCABULARY
Expressions with *thing*

> **In the listening, the speakers said:**
> *it's no big thing* **and** *it's a personal thing.*
> ···
> **There are many expressions with the word *thing* in English.**

A Translate the expressions with *thing*. Are any the same in your language?
1 Don't make a fuss. *It's no big thing.*
2 It's rude. *It's not the done thing* in our society.
3 I'd love to do it, but *chance would be a fine thing*!
4 *It's the furthest thing from my mind* at the moment.
5 I always do it *first thing in the morning.*
6 *It's the sort of thing* that makes you glad to be alive.
7 It's difficult, *what with one thing and another.*
8 I didn't plan it – just *one thing led to another.*

B Work in pairs. Discuss what 'it' could be in each of 1–8 above.

READING

You are going to read an extract from an article in a sociology journal about identity.

A **Before you read, discuss with a partner how far you agree with each of the statements below. Explain why.**
1 Globalisation has led to an increase in nationalism.
2 Individuals in any society are likely to share many common cultural characteristics.
3 Our cultural identities are not fixed; they change over time.
4 The Internet and big multinational companies have an influence on the kind of people we become.
5 The different kinds of roles we play and identities we have in life often lead us to feel conflicted.
6 National cultures are rooted in history and tradition.
7 All nations consist of a diverse range of peoples.
8 Nations are partly founded on negatives.

B **Now read the extract below and decide which four sentences above best summarise the points it makes.**

C **How would you summarise the main message of the extract? Compare your ideas with a partner – and discuss whether or not you agree with this message.**

SPEAKING

A **Work in groups of three. Choose ONE of the speaking activities below to do.**
1 Write down the top eight cultural icons from your country. They could be people, cultural / youth movements, kinds of food / drink, special days, places, sports, etc.
2 What eight things do you think people should know about your country as a minimum to gain citizenship? Think about:
   • history
   • the law
   • art, music and culture
   • facts and figures about the country
   • religions, traditions and special days
   • politics and the government
   • public services like schools, healthcare, etc.
3 Make a list of your own eight personal cultural markers. The list should include people, historical events, books, films, music, kinds of food / drink, places, sports and sporting events, etc. These can come from anywhere in the world, but should be important for you personally.

B **Work on your own. Spend a few minutes preparing for the activity. Then present your lists to your group and explain them. Your partners should comment or ask questions to find out more.**

The notion of a unified national culture which all those who inhabit a particular land share and participate in is a comforting one, especially in times of global uncertainty. It is, however, something of a myth.

The individual cultural identity of those living in any given society will vary so widely as to make the extraction of common features very difficult indeed. Furthermore, identity is not static: it emerges through our interactions with others, and in an increasingly globalised world driven by commerce, such interactions are becoming ever more complex and multi-layered.

Through our relationships with others, we grow into the many distinct roles we play in life. Each role may well be negotiated separately from the others, and may involve interacting only with those affected by the role in question. Given this, it is clearly quite possible for one person to be, say, a mother, a wife, a ballet lover, Welsh, British, Jamaican, black, and a marketing manager without any contradiction.

Where does all this leave national identity? Historian Eric Hobsbawn has argued that a nation's so-called traditions are not based in historical fact, but rather are propagated through certain kinds of education, public ceremonies and monuments, for the purposes of the ruling elite.

Perhaps the final word, though, should go to William Ralph Inge, a priest and Cambridge professor, who claimed that 'a nation is a society that nourishes a common delusion about its ancestry and shares a common hatred for its neighbours!'

03 RELATIONSHIPS

In this unit, you learn how to:
- talk about people you know
- give your impression of people you don't know well
- express opinions in more tentative ways
- discuss issues surrounding divorce
- share and talk through problems

Grammar
- *would*

Vocabulary
- Describing people
- Divorce
- Phrasal verbs

Reading
- The bitter end

Listening
- What're they like?
- Relationships

SPEAKING

A Spend two minutes noting down words that you feel describe your personality.

B Compare your ideas in pairs. Then discuss these questions.
- Do you think other people see you in the same way?
- Is there anything about your character you'd like to change? Why?

VOCABULARY Describing people

A Discuss whether you think the descriptions below are usually positive or negative. Explain your ideas.
1 She's completely incompetent.
2 She's very direct.
3 She's such a snob.
4 She's quite absent-minded.
5 She's quite hard work.
6 She's really bitchy.
7 She's very laid-back.
8 She seems very principled.
9 She's very strong-willed.
10 She's quite thick-skinned.

B Match the follow-up comments below to the descriptions in exercise A.
a She's prone to forget things from time to time.
b Once she's set her heart on something, there's no stopping her.
c She's one of those people who never worries about anything.
d She's not the easiest person in the world to talk to.
e She certainly stands up for what she believes in.
f She looks down her nose at everyone.
g She never seems that bothered by criticism or bitchy comments.
h Honestly, she hasn't got a clue what she's doing!
i She doesn't mince her words, I'll say that for her.
j I wouldn't trust her an inch. She'll stab you in the back the minute you're not there.

C Work in pairs. Test each other.
Student A: say the follow-up comments a–j.
Student B: close your book. Say the descriptions 1–10.

D Work in groups. Discuss which descriptions in exercise A are the best / worst. Then discuss which suit people you know, and why.

LISTENING

You are going to hear three short conversations about different people.

A ⬤ 3.1 Listen and answer these questions.
1 What kind of person is described in each conversation?
2 How is each person described?

B Work in pairs. Can you remember the missing verbs from each of the sentences below? Some are phrasal verbs.
1 a He's .... the rest of the team down with him.
  b He always just .... really defensive and .... this great big barrier.
  c Maybe you need to .... his head.
2 a I've always thought he .... as a really decent guy.
  b I just think you've .... him wrong.
  c He's done a lot to .... awareness of various different causes.
3 a We .... it .... straightaway.
  b The only problem is she kind of .... the bathroom.
  c He .... me as a bit of a slacker.

C Listen again to check your ideas.

D In groups, tell each other whether any of the people described remind you of anyone you know. In what way?

LANGUAGE PATTERNS

Write the sentences in your language. Translate them back into English. Compare your English to the original.

He's one of those people who'll just never accept they've done anything wrong.

She's one of those people who never worry about anything.

He's one of those people who is always willing to try new things.

DEVELOPING CONVERSATIONS

Giving your impression

To give our opinions about famous people or about people we haven't met many times, we often use these structures:

He / She seems really nice and bright and chatty.
He / She strikes me as a bit of a slacker.
He / She comes across as a really decent person.
I get the impression / feeling he's / she's very principled.

A Work in pairs. Together, think of five people currently in the public eye. Then spend two minutes thinking about your individual impressions of them and why you feel like this.

B Share your impressions of each person using the structures above. Start like this:

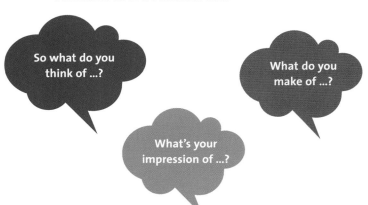

So what do you think of ...?

What do you make of ...?

What's your impression of ...?

GRAMMAR *would* 1

We often use *would* when giving opinions, to be polite or because we are uncertain or reluctant to say what we think. It makes our ideas sound more tentative. It's sometimes used with past tenses – even when talking about the present.

I'd say it was worse if anything, to be honest. (tentative)
It's worse, if anything. (more direct)

I'd have to agree with you on that. (tentative)
I completely agree with you. (more direct)

A Using the words in brackets, rewrite the sentences without *would* to make them more direct.
1 I'd imagine that they'll buy a new one. (probably)
2 I'd expect it to arrive sometime next week. (should)
3 I'd say it was your own fault, to be honest. (think)
4 I'd have to agree with you on that. (couldn't, more)
5 I would've thought that most people could see through the marketing. (surely, can)
6 I wouldn't have thought it'd be that hard to organise. (can't)

B Divide the sentences below into four groups of two to show different uses of *would*.
1 Would you mind just keeping the music down a bit?
2 He'd always hog the remote control and watch what he wanted to watch.
3 I'd like him more if he wasn't so self-centred.
4 Would you care to explain what you mean by that?
5 I wouldn't have said anything if I'd known he was going to react like that!
6 She promised she'd stop, but she never did.
7 I knew that would happen!
8 I wouldn't see him very often. He'd only visit during the holidays.

C Compare your ideas with a partner and explain the different uses of *would*.

▶ Need help? Read the grammar reference on page 138.

CONVERSATION PRACTICE

A On a piece of paper, write the name of someone:
• you find a bit annoying
• you don't get on very well with
• you get on really well with
• quite unusual or eccentric
• you admire.

B Swap pieces of paper with a partner and ask each other about the people on the lists. Explain who each person is, how you get on with them and what they're like.

VOCABULARY Divorce

A Check you understand the words in **bold**. Then discuss the questions with a partner.

1 Why do couples sometimes sign a **pre-nuptial agreement**?
2 What do you think are the most common reasons couples **file for divorce**?
3 What happens at the end of a **custody battle**?
4 What can happen during an **acrimonious divorce**?
5 Do you believe it's possible to have an **amicable divorce**? How?
6 What do you think of people who throw parties after their divorces **go through**?
7 What usually happens if a father (or sometimes a mother) refuses to **pay maintenance** for the children?
8 Which of the **grounds for divorce** below do you think are most / least understandable? Why?

unequal burden of housework	adultery	boredom
lack of physical intimacy	greed	physical abuse

READING

You are going to read an article about the history of divorce.

A Read the article on the opposite page and think about why the writer mentions each of the things below.

1 Sweden, Finland and Belarus
2 celebrity divorces and custody battles
3 Mesopotamia, the Greek Empire and Cairo
4 Emperor Charles the Fifth
5 the Church of England
6 1857
7 TV, junk food, social networking sites
8 a heated argument at a wedding reception

B Work in pairs. Cover the article and explain why the writer mentioned the things in exercise A.

C Complete the sentence starters about the article. Then explain your ideas to a partner.

- I was quite surprised to learn that …
- It didn't surprise me at all to read that …
- I honestly couldn't believe that …
- I wonder why / how / what / when …
- I'd like to know a bit more about …

D Look at the words in **bold** in the article. Underline the words that collocate with them. Some words will have more than one collocate. Compare your ideas with a partner.

E Look at the article again and find as many collocations for the word *divorce* as you can. The collocates could be adjectives, verbs, other nouns, etc. For example:
(One in every two marriages) *ends in divorce*

F Work in groups. Discuss these questions.

- Do you think the divorce rate in your country is high or low? Why do you think this might be?
- What do you think of the divorce laws in your country? Do you agree that it's too easy to get divorced?
- Is it easy for someone who has been divorced to remarry in your country?
- Have there been any high-profile divorce cases in the news recently? Do you know why the couples split up?
- Why do you think people continue to get married these days?

GRAMMAR *would 2*

> We can use *wouldn't* + verb to talk about things that people – or objects – refused to do in the past.
>
> … the Pope … *would not comply* with Henry's wishes. Her husband *wouldn't stop* eating junk food.

A Complete the sentences with *wouldn't* + a verb from the box below.

come	hear	leave	let
listen	put	start	stop

1 I tried to make him change his mind, but he ....
2 I slept really badly. My son just .... crying last night. I don't know why.
3 I realised things weren't going well when he .... to my mum's 60th birthday party.
4 I begged her father to open the door, but he .... me see her.
5 I'm not surprised she left him. He never lifted a finger round the house. I mean, he .... even .... the rubbish out!
6 Sorry I'm late. My car ....
7 I offered to pay for my share of the meal, but he simply .... of it.
8 It was so annoying! I was trying to work, but my little brother just .... me alone.

▶ Need help? Read the grammar reference on page 138.

B Tell a partner about two things that people you know wouldn't do – even if you asked them to.

The Bitter End

A recent survey found that slightly more than one in every two marriages in the United States now ends in divorce, with Sweden, Finland and Belarus sharing this dubious **distinction**. Given such news, coming as it does against a **backdrop** of endless high-profile celebrity divorces and custody battles, it would be easy to assume that chronically **high** divorce rates were a strictly modern phenomenon.

The truth, however, is rather more interesting. In fact, even in ancient times, divorce was commonplace. It is known to have existed in ancient Mesopotamia and certainly occurred during the Greek Empire. By the 15th century, around 30% of all

marriages in Cairo were ending in failure and many people were marrying two or even three times.

The concept arrived in England at around the same time, as a result of a rather unusual set of circumstances. In 1533, King Henry the Eighth decided he wanted to leave Catherine of Aragon, his wife of 18 years, due to her failure to provide him with a male **heir** to the throne. All divorces had to be officially **sanctioned** by the Pope, who would not **comply** with Henry's wishes for fear of offending Catherine's uncle, Emperor Charles the Fifth, then the most powerful man in Europe. Furious at this decision, Henry persuaded an English archbishop to grant him his divorce. There was a subsequent split from the Church of Rome and the Church of England was born.

However, it was not until 1857 that ordinary British people (which tended to mean just men!) were allowed to file for divorce through a court of law, and even then the only legal grounds were adultery and cruelty. Nowadays, around 70% of all divorces in the country are instigated by women and the grounds are much broader and include 'mutual separation' and 'unreasonable behaviour', which can cover **a multitude of sins**.

Indeed, many believe that divorce has now become too easy and point to the increasing number of divorces filed for ridiculous reasons. There was the English couple who went their separate ways because they could never agree what to watch on TV; then there was the Indian man who claimed he was allergic to his wife's sweat – and the Jamaican woman who claimed her husband wouldn't stop eating junk food and loved fried chicken more than he loved her! A remarkable number of divorce cases now also mention social networking sites such as Facebook.

What happens if you **follow** such trends to their logical extreme was recently demonstrated by the painfully short marriage of a young Polish couple who got into a heated argument while cutting the cake at their reception – and ended up seeking an annulment there and then! Given all this, it's amazing that people still want to get married at all!

King Henry the Eighth

SPEAKING

A Work in pairs. Discuss which items in the list below usually go with the people in the different age groups in the box. More than one person is possible. Explain your reasons.

a toddler	a thirty-something	a pensioner
a teenager	a middle-aged person	

- being frail and unsteady on your feet
- feeling very self-conscious
- being very affectionate
- fancying someone
- wetting the bed
- going into a home
- settling down
- being cheeky and answering back
- going bald
- going off the rails
- losing your faculties
- establishing a career
- paying off a mortgage
- having no commitments

B What else do you think is typical of these age groups? Which age do you think is the best / most difficult?

LISTENING

You are going to hear five conversations about different relationships.

A 🔊 3.2 Listen and decide which of the relationships below are being discussed.

- a couple
- a neighbour
- colleagues
- sisters
- teacher and pupil
- doctor and patient
- coach and player
- mother and baby

B Listen again and answer the questions.
1. a Why is the main speaker worried?
   b What shows the old lady is strong-willed?
2. a What two reasons does the woman give for the behaviour?
   b What solutions do they each give?
3. a What do they agree about?
   b What happened at the Open and why is it mentioned?
4. a What was sweet?
   b What was amazing?
5. a Why was the first speaker unhappy?
   b What does the second speaker advise and why?

C Discuss in pairs.
- Do you know anyone like the people in the conversations? In what way are they similar?
- What traits are there in your family?
- What relationships do you have with different professionals that you know? Are they good? Why? / Why not?

NATIVE SPEAKER ENGLISH

have a ... streak
We say someone *has*, for example, *a competitive streak*, to show an important part of their character, especially one which contrasts with their normal behaviour.

He has a strong competitive streak.
He has a vicious streak, if you get on the wrong side of him.
She seems easy-going, but she's got a stubborn streak.
You'd be surprised. He has an adventurous streak.

VOCABULARY Phrasal verbs

> As with normal verbs, it's important to notice collocations and expressions which go with phrasal verbs.
>
> They can form part of a fixed expression. (i.e. only the grammar of the verb can change):
> *He went off the rails* when he was young and got into drugs.
>
> They might be part of a semi-fixed expression (a word in the expression can vary it a little):
> *She's got no* family / money / experience *to speak of.*
>
> They may have a few very common collocations:
> I *took* time / a day / a week *off.*
>
> They may have more than one meaning:
> *Take off* your jacket. / The plane's *taken off.*

A Look at the underlined phrasal verbs in audioscript 3.2 on pages 162–3. Discuss which other words go with each one.

B Complete each sentence with one of the phrasal verbs from exercise A.
1 We had big plans, but nothing .... them.
2 He's .... I think he's in his mid-80s.
3 It'd be better if she .... her energy ....
   something useful, rather than sticking her nose into my business.
4 You shouldn't .... being treated like that. You should tell him to get lost!
5 They were really pleased with our work and they ....
   you .... for particular praise.
6 I really don't want to .... an ordeal like that again.

C Find six more phrasal verbs in audioscript 3.2 on pages 162–3 and think of your own examples of how to use them.

DEVELOPING CONVERSATIONS
What's up?

> We often use *What's up?* or *What's the matter?* if we think something's wrong. We often give a very short answer followed by details:
> It's (just) work. I'm completely snowed under.

A Decide what the problem could be in 1–6.
1 It's this .... I'm sick of this drizzle. It's depressing.
2 It's my .... She's always singling me out and she gives me bad grades.
3 It's my .... I don't seem to be making any progress.
4 It's my .... They keep me up all night partying.
5 It's my .... I twisted it really badly and I can hardly walk on it.
6 It's the .... She's teething at the moment and she doesn't stop screaming!

B Practise short conversations, starting *What's up? / What's the matter?*

SPEAKING

A Work in groups.
   Student A: look at File 2 on page 152.
   Student B: look at File 14 on page 157.
   Student C: look at File 17 on page 158.

   Read the problems and choose one which you think is the most interesting. You are going to talk about the problem as if it was really happening to you. Think about some details you could add.

B Role-play a conversation about each problem. Ask someone *What's up?* As they explain the problem, you should sympathise and share experiences / give advice / reassure. Use expressions such as:
   Oh dear!
   That must be difficult.
   How awful!
   I know exactly what you're going through!
   Something similar happened to a friend of mine.
   I'd talk it over with them (if I were you).
   Have you been in touch with the police?
   I'd have thought they could help.
   I'd imagine it'll all blow over.
   I wouldn't worry about it.
   What an idiot!

C When you have discussed one problem each, choose another one or invent your own relationship issue. Have another conversation.

© Mike Baldwin / Cornered

" I thought we agreed not to fight in front of the children."

04 POLITICS

In this unit, you learn how to:
- give opinions about politics
- talk about consequences of political proposals
- describe politicians and their qualities
- tell jokes
- talk about voting and elections

Grammar
- Conditionals

Vocabulary
- Consequences
- Politicians
- Elections and politics

Reading
- Beyond a Joke!
- The electoral system Swiss style

Listening
- Goverment proposals
- Political jokes
- Voting

DEVELOPING CONVERSATIONS
Giving opinions

A Find six pairs of sentences with a similar meaning.
12 1 I'm a huge fan of the idea.
5 2 I don't know where I stand, really.
10 3 I'm totally against it. F
8 4 I think the negatives far outweigh the positives. F
2 5 I can't pass judgement. I don't know enough about it.
9 6 It's a good idea in theory, just not in practice. F
11 7 I am in favour. I just have some slight reservations. F
4 8 I have some major doubts about it. F
6 9 It's OK in principle. I just think it's unworkable.
3 10 I'm completely opposed to it. F
7 11 It's not without problems, but on the whole I like it.
1 12 I'm totally in favour of it. F

B Work in groups. Give opinions about the following.
- a maximum wage
- nuclear energy
- globalisation
- US foreign policy
- free health care
- banning golf
- six-week school holidays
- hosting an international event
- a 30–hour working week
- allowing only electric cars

LISTENING

You are going to hear two conversations discussing topics from *Developing Conversations*, exercise B.

A 4.1 Listen and decide what the topics are and where each person stands on the issue.

B Choose the words that you heard. Then listen again to check. favour against
1 a Some of these salaries are *obese / obscene.*
  b It *puts / pushes* up prices.
  c They'd just *declare / detail* it as part of their income.
  d I'm sure they'd be able to find ways *round / through* it.
  e I did. I'm just playing devil's *advert / advocate.*
2 a Did you hear about this proposal to *bet / bid* to hold the Olympics here? women
  b Won't the games *earn / make* a lot of money?
  c They always talk about them leaving a good *facility / legacy.*
  d It's lucky we don't have a hope in *hell / earth.*
  e It'd be a *recipe / receipt* for disaster. men against

C Work in pairs. Discuss the following.
- Explain what the sentences in exercise B refer to.
- Which people do you sympathise with more? Why?

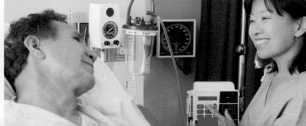

GRAMMAR Conditionals 1

A Match 1–5 to the best endings a–e.
1 If people don't have to pay for a service,
2 If they go ahead with the proposal,
3 If the New Party gets elected,
4 I think if we had a shorter working week,
5 What if you were on a low wage, though,

a what would happen then? You might not get by.
b they say they're going to end nuclear power.
c it could lead to energy shortages.
d they take it for granted.
e there'd be less unemployment.

> In *if*-clauses, we talk about general or likely conditions with a present tense, and unlikely conditions about now or the future with the past simple / continuous. This choice may be dependent on the speaker's point of view. The condition is sometimes implicit, so people don't say the *if*-clause but only refer to the consequence.
>
> ....
>
> We can talk about the consequences of a condition using present tenses or *will, going to, would, might* or *could* – depending on how certain we are of the result.

B Look at the sentences in bold in audioscript 4.1 on page 163 and answer the questions.
a What's the condition for each of the sentences?
b Does the speaker see the condition as generally true, likely or unlikely?
c Does the speaker think the consequence is likely?

▶ Need help? Read the grammar reference on page 139.

VOCABULARY Consequences

A Complete the sentences with the words in the box.

compound	trigger	devastate	curb	discourage
undermine	benefit	bankrupt	lead	boost

1 It might .... people from working.
2 It's a bad idea. If anything, it'll .... the existing social problems.
3 It might .... the rich, but it'll harm the poor.
4 It might .... an election earlier than they wanted.
5 It could .... the area and leave thousands dead.
6 It'll create division and .... to tension.
7 It'll .... the economy and create jobs.
8 It's bad. It'll .... relations between the two countries.
9 It might help to .... drug addiction.
10 It'd put an enormous strain on finances. It could .... the country.

B Can you think what conditions might be needed for each of 1–10 to happen? For example:

> **If they put up taxes, it might discourage people from working.**

C Use the verbs below to rewrite five sentences from exercise A so that they mean the opposite. You need to change more than just the verb!

encourage	strengthen	damage	sort out	delay

CONVERSATION PRACTICE

You are going to have similar conversations to the ones you heard in *Listening*.

A Think of two proposals in areas such as education, health, the economy, housing, culture or transport, one you would like to see happen (*Personally, I'm in favour of ...*) and one which you have heard is happening – good or bad (*Did you hear about this proposal to ...?*). Make notes about the consequences of each.

B Work in pairs. Take turns to start conversations and then discuss the proposals.

VOCABULARY Politicians

A In your view, which of the qualities below do politicians most need? Rank them from 1 (most important) to 10 (least important).

honesty	compassion
ruthlessness	flexibility
passion	bravery
charisma	excellent communication skills
self-confidence	the ability to compromise

B Explain your choices to a partner.

C Work in groups. Can you think of any politicians you would describe using the words below? Explain your ideas.

passionate	humble and down to earth
arrogant	sincere
shrewd	indecisive
no substance	hypocritical
charismatic	brave

READING

You are going to read a short article about the effect of humour on politics and politicians.

A Read and decide if 1–8 are true or false, according to the article. Underline the sentences in the article that help you decide.

1 The old saying teaches people not to use violence.
2 Professor Peterson claims comedians spend too much time mocking politicians' track records and theories.
3 The jokes on late-night comedy shows reaffirm rather than challenge the public's perception of politicians.
4 Some comedians like to suggest that politics is just a waste of time.
5 Ben Lewis suggests that humour helped to undermine the system in some totalitarian states.
6 The humour that emerged under these systems was racist.
7 People used to laugh at their own misfortunes as a way of voicing their frustrations.
8 Some dictators were very fond of telling jokes.

B Work in pairs. Discuss these questions.
- How far do you agree that comedy is bad for democracy?
- What satirical shows are on TV at the moment? Do you ever watch them? Why? / Why not?
- Have you seen any impressionists? Were they any good?
- Can you do any impressions of famous people? Who?

BEYOND A JOKE

The old saying claims that 'sticks and stones will break my bones, but words will never hurt me'. However, according to two new books, this might not quite be true for politicians.

In *Strange Bedfellows: How Late-Night Comedy Turns Democracy into a Joke,* Professor Russell Peterson argues that comedians are having a harmful effect on politics as a result of the way they constantly ridicule all politicians, irrespective of track records, theories or qualifications. Because the main target of most jokes is the character and personal qualities of politicians, audiences are left with the impression that all politicians are equally awful, a feeling which increases already widespread cynicism and frustration with the democratic process. 'The jokes play into the public perception of politics,' Professor Peterson explains, and so we come to believe that 'every candidate in every party is, has, and always will be the same: corrupt, inadequate or self-interested. They turn political engagement into a joke by implying that it's just a silly game and futile.'

In *Hammer and Tickle: A History of Communism Told Through Communist Jokes*, Ben Lewis argues that humour played a rather different role in totalitarian states. The black humour that emerged under such systems represented not just a release for people living in grim circumstances, but was an act of defiance against oppression. As such, the more extreme dictatorships tended to regard comedians as a threat and the telling of jokes was frequently banned or severely restricted.

LISTENING

You are going to hear three jokes.

A 🔊 4.2 **Listen and decide which book's argument each joke illustrates – Russell Peterson's or Ben Lewis's.**

B **Work in pairs. Compare your ideas. Which jokes did you find amusing? Why?**

> We often dramatise jokes by using the present tense instead of past forms. We also often use quite descriptive or exaggerated verbs and act them out at the same time.

C **Listen again and complete the sentences.**
1 a Two friends are .... down the road when one turns to the other.
  b 'Follow me.' And he .... down a side street.
  c 'Not here. It's not safe.' And they .... the stairs.
  d The other one .... nervously. 'Well' he ....
2 a The son arrives home and they .... to watch him.
  b He picks up the money, holds it up to the light and then .... it into his pocket.
  c He picks up the Bible, ... it and then pockets that as well.
  d Finally, he .... the bottle, opens it and .... it to check it's good quality, before sticking it into his bag.
  e He then happily .... the stairs to go for a nap.
3 a A man is walking down the street .... to himself, cursing the government.
  b They all suddenly .... him and .... him down to the station.
  c The man's scared stiff and .... in fear.

D **Take turns to say the sentences in exercise C and act them out at the same time.**

LANGUAGE PATTERNS

> **Write the sentences in your language. Translate them back into English. Compare your English to the original.**
> The boy seemed quite unable to decide on a career
> He seems utterly unable to give a straight answer!
> She seems unable to differentiate between right and wrong.
> They were just completely unable to cope with the situation.
> They're either unwilling or unable to spend more.

SPEAKING

You are going to tell each other jokes like the ones you heard in *Listening*.

A **Work in pairs.**
Student A: look at File 5 on page 153.
Student B: look at File 7 on page 154.
Read out your jokes and decide which you prefer.

B **Spend a few minutes trying to remember the joke you chose. Then tell the jokes to each other – from memory. Use present tenses. Act out some of the actions and the way the characters speak. Which joke do you like best? Why?**

C **Work in groups. Discuss these questions.**
- Do you know any other jokes about politics or politicians?
- Have you heard any funny – or crazy – anecdotes about politics or politicians? What happened?
- Do you know any funny books or films about politics or politicians? Tell your partner about them.
- What other things make you laugh?

"At last, a politician we can trust!"

"Think about it – if you were a politician, would *you* want more prison space available?"

READING

You are going to read a text about the Swiss electoral system.

A Read the text. In the margin, tick ✓ what you think is positive, and cross ✗ what you think is negative about the system.

B Work in pairs. Compare and explain your ideas.

C Work in groups.
1 Discuss what the words in **blue** mean.
2 Find the word forms based on these words.

elect	devolve
represent	normal

D Discuss what is similar too / different from the system in your country.

VOCABULARY Elections and politics

A Match a key word to its collocates. Two are extra.

election	victory	figure	vote	MP
consensus	scandal	strike	poll	party

1 she's a prominent ~ in the anti-war movement / a hate ~ / be seen as a ~ of fun / a divisive ~
2 the ~ takes place in May / call an ~ / trigger an early ~ / fix the ~ / what'll decide the ~? / the run-up to the ~
3 go to the ~s / carry out a ~ / conduct a ~ among students / in the latest ~ / have a low standing in the ~s
4 reach a ~ / establish a ~ / an emerging ~ / a broad ~
5 a bribery ~ / a sex ~ / expose a ~ / the ~ erupted / he's mixed up in a ~ / be hit by a series of ~s/ cover up a ~
6 stand as an ~ / a long-standing ~ / a prominent ~ / a right-wing ~ / an outspoken ~ / lobby ~s
7 a unanimous ~ / cast your ~ / a protest ~ / a no ~ / an overwhelming ~ in favour / alleged ~-rigging
8 a narrow ~ / a landslide ~ / a stunning ~ / a hollow ~ / claim ~ / ensure their ~ / pull off a surprise ~

B Underline the collocations which you hadn't heard before or needed to look up in the *Vocabulary Builder*.

C Compare the words you underlined with a partner. Say an example sentence for each.

THE ELECTORAL SYSTEM SWISS STYLE

Switzerland has a long tradition of democracy – some claim it dates back to the 13th century. It is also perhaps unique in the amount of power it **devolves** from central government to regional and local institutions. Parliament only sits 12 weeks a year and MPs are paid modest salaries compared to **counterparts** abroad. Most have second jobs in the community.

In fact, this devolution of power extends to individual citizens. Even when parliament decides to change federal law individuals can challenge the decision by collecting 50,000 signatures on a **petition**. This triggers an automatic **referendum**. Furthermore, anyone can propose laws by getting 100,000 signatures. Similar processes exist at a local level. People may vote on these single issues 15 times a year or more. Most of these votes are done via post rather than heading to a **polling station**.

The Swiss have a federal parliament with two bodies – the National Council and the Senate – which chooses the government. The Senate is formed by the individual states (cantons) electing two representatives each, **irrespective** of population size. The 200 MP's in the National Council are elected via a complex form of proportional representation. Each canton is allocated a number of seats according to population, ranging from 34 (Zurich) to one (Uri). The political parties provide lists of candidates for each canton, which are sent to the electorate. Voters can vote not only for the party, but for specific candidates. They can even make their own list.

The number of seats each party gains in any canton is determined by the percentage of party **ballot papers** returned. The specific people who are then chosen for each party depends on the individual votes cast for each candidate. Because of this system, individual representatives maintain a direct relationship with their voters, often rejecting **the party line**. Special interest groups often **lobby** voters to support MPs favouring their cause.

Coalitions are the norm in Switzerland as parties don't gain an absolute majority, with the result that a tradition of consensus has become established. This may partly explain why voter **turnout** is often only 40% of the electorate.

LISTENING

You are going to hear five people talking about votes.

A Before you listen, work in groups. Look at the words in the box and answer the questions.

a general election	an opinion poll
a local election	a strike ballot
a referendum	election for student council
a talent show vote	a parliamentary vote

- In which do you vote for a person or party? In which for a law or action?
- Who votes in each case?
- Which ones have you voted in and why? What was the outcome?
- Can you think of any other times you might vote?
- Have you ever stood for election or campaigned in a vote? When? What happened?

B ◉ 4.3 Listen and say which of the votes in exercise A they are talking about.

C Listen again. Decide in which extract someone does the following. One is extra.
- a mentions a broken promise
- b talks about vote-rigging
- c talks about voter turnout
- d talks about standing for parliament
- e expresses surprise at something
- f is defending an unpopular decision

D Compare and explain your choices.

GRAMMAR Conditionals 2

The past simple or continuous in an *if*-clause shows a real past event or an *imagined* present / future condition. Past perfect in an *if*-clause shows an imagined *past* condition. The consequences of the conditions may refer to now (*would be*) or to before now (*would've been*).

A Work in pairs. Try to write the missing parts of the sentences from *Listening*. Listen if you need to.
1 It .... if they had a kind of hate figure.
2 I might not have minded so much if ....
3 If it hadn't been for their intransigence, ...
4 I guess if ...., they'd be keener to bring about electoral reform.
5 On another day I ...., but I was at a bit of a loose end when the researcher called.
6 It's unlikely we .... if we didn't have a body like this.

B Compare your sentences with audioscript 4.3 on page 164. Explain the use of the verb forms in the six sentences.

▶ Need help? Read the grammar reference on page 139.

C Think about the effects of the following things. Write two conditional sentences about each.
- the result of the last election
- a famous figure in your country
- an important moment in your life

SPEAKING

A Work in groups. Discuss these questions.
- What's voter turnout like in your country? Why?
- How do you think you could improve democracy?
- Which elections were significant for you personally / your country / the world? Why?
- Have you heard of any scandals? What happened?
- Have you heard of any results that were fixed?
- Can you think of any examples of tokenism?
- What would be your proposals if you stood for a school body / a local election / parliament?

TWO MINUTES

Work in groups. You are going to give a short two-minute talk on one of the topics in the list below. Spend five minutes thinking about what you are going to say. Look back at your notes to check language if you like.

- A city that's changed
- Culture
- A political system
- Divorce
- Relationships
- A political party

Give each other marks out of ten for language, interest and clarity. Who got the most marks?

GAME

Work in pairs. Student A use *only* the green squares; student B use *only* the yellow squares. Spend five minutes looking at your questions and revising the answers. Then take turns tossing a coin: heads = move one of your squares; tails = move two of your squares. When you land on a square, your partner looks at the relevant page in the book to check your answers, but *you don't*! If you are right, move forward one square (but don't answer the question until your next turn). If you aren't right, your partner tells you the right answer and you miss a go. When you've finished the game, change colours and play again.

Start	**1** *Developing Conversations* p. 9: your partner will say sentences 1–6 in exercise A. You should say a reinforcing sentence.	**2** *Native Speaker English* note p. 10: if you can say what the *Native Speaker English* note was and give an example, throw again.	**3** *Grammar* p. 11: tell your partner five things about you or your city using four different perfect forms.	**4** *Vocabulary* p. 13: say six sentences using binomials.
5 *Grammar* p. 15: say five things about your family or your country using three different emphatic structures.	**6** *Developing Conversations* p. 15: your partner will say 1–6 in exercise C. Reply with a different expression each time.	**7** *Native Speaker English* note p. 16: if you can say what the *Native Speaker English* note was and give an example, throw again.	**8 Miss a go!**	**9** *Vocabulary* p. 18: say six expressions with *thing*.
10 *Grammar* p. 21 and 22: say five things about you or people you know using four different uses of *would*.	**11 Miss a go!**	**12** *Vocabulary* p. 22: say the eight phrases in **bold** connected with divorce.	**13** *Native Speaker English* note p. 24: if you can say what the *Native Speaker English* note was and give an example, throw again.	**14** *Developing Conversat[ion]* p. 25: your partner w[ill] ask *What's up?* six tim[es]. Each time, give a diff[erent] answer.
15 *Developing Conversations* p. 26: say eight of the expressions for giving your opinion.	**16** *Grammar* p. 139: your partner will read six conditional starters from the table. Complete the sentences in your own words.	**17** *Vocabulary* p. 30: your partner will say the eight key words. Give two collocations for each.	**18** *Native Speaker English* note p. 31: if you can say what the *Native Speaker English* note was and give an example, throw again.	**Finish**

For each of the activities below, work in groups of three. Use the *Vocabulary Builder* if you want to.

CONVERSATION PRACTICE

Choose one of the following *Conversation Practice* activities.
Cities p. 9
Culture and Identity p. 15
Relationships p. 21
Politics p. 27

Two of you should do the task. The third person should listen and then give a mark between 1 and 10 for the performance. Explain your decision. Then change roles.

ACT OR DRAW

One person should act or draw as many of these words as they can in three minutes. The others should try to guess the words. Do not speak while you are acting or drawing!

a pin	peer	sweep	curl up
drip	rinse	sneak	mutter
suck	wring	glance	demolish
knot	flush	a crane	shelter
leap	choke	drizzle	thread
soak	a pad	a straw	a stain

QUIZ

Answer as many of the questions as possible.
1 How would you describe an area with **crumbling** or **derelict** buildings?
2 What do you need to do if you **rip** your shirt?
3 If a situation is **grim**, is it very good or very bad?
4 What happens when an economy is **thriving**?
5 What's happened if you need to **clear rubble**?
6 How do you feel if you're **thrilled** with something?
7 What is **burgled** and who does it?
8 Why might an area **go downhill**?
9 Why might you **single** someone **out**?
10 What does **close-knit** describe?
11 What do politicians try to **cover up**?
12 What happens if there's a **craze**? Give an example.
13 If someone one is **bitchy**, what do they do?
14 What kind of things might be **cracked down on**? How?
15 Say four different **grounds** for divorce.

COLLOCATIONS

Take turns to read out collocation lists from Unit 1 of the *Vocabulary Builder*. Where there is a '~', say '*blah*' instead. Your partner should guess as many words as they can. Each time you change roles, move to the next unit.

IDIOMS

Discuss the meaning of the idioms and try to think of a real example about you – or about someone you know.
1   I'm just playing devil's advocate.
2   I'm at a bit of a loose end.
3   He can be very hard work.
4   She's really set her heart on it.
5   She didn't mince her words.
6   He stabbed me in the back.
7   I tend to take things in my stride.
8   You should put your foot down.
9   We didn't really hit it off.
10 He never lifts a finger in the house.
11 It came completely out of the blue.
12 Chance would be a fine thing!
13 They're rolling in money.
14 It's just not the done thing.
15 It spread like wildfire.

LISTENING

A ⟳ R 1.1 **Listen and choose one answer for each speaker. There are two extra. Decide which speaker is talking about:**
a a referendum
b falling out with a friend
c making a friend
d a historical perspective (on a current issue)
e an urban regeneration
f a politician
g doing up their house.

B ⟳ R 1.1 **Listen again and choose one answer for each speaker. There are two extra. Which speaker:**
a complains about losing their community?
b expresses uncertainty about what they're going to do?
c suggests a theory is not true?
d regrets something they did?
e shows sympathy with someone?
f reveals the reason for someone's behaviour?
g criticises a government policy?

[... / 10]

GRAMMAR

A **Complete with one word in each gap.**
1 The thing .... concerns me is the power they have.
2 It sounds great. I wish I .... seen it.
3 I .... imagine there might be some opposition to the demolition of the building.
4 I wouldn't buy a car without .... driven it.
5 When I was a teenager, I .... often sneak out at night to play with friends after I had 'gone to bed'.
6 What I hate is the .... of public transport at night.
7 It's the .... they've done nothing to curb pollution that bothers me.
8 If I wasn't worried, I wouldn't .... talking to you now.

[... / 8]

B **Complete the second sentence with 2–5 words and the word in bold so it has a similar meaning to the first.**
1 Debt was three times lower when they won the election.
since
Debt .... they came to power.
2 The policies they followed compounded the problem.
so
With a different policy, the problem .... bad.
3 Losing the vote, will definitely force an early election.
trigger
If they lose the vote it's .... early election.
4 There's a lot of red tape, which is infuriating.
mad
What .... of bureaucracy there is.
5 I wouldn't recommend it after the ordeal we underwent.
through
Having .... a terrible experience, I wouldn't recommend it.
6 We would've won, but they fixed the result.
rigged
If they .... election, we'd be in power now.

[... / 12]

LANGUAGE PATTERNS

Find the four sentences with a mistake and correct them.
1 She's one of those people that she's always moaning.
2 It's nowhere nearly as complicated as it sounds.
3 It was miles better than I thought it'd be.
4 He utterly unable to make up his mind.
5 He's one of those people who'll always play devil's advocate.
6 I read it three times out of disbelieving.

[... / 6]

PREPOSITIONS

Choose the correct preposition.
1 The whole region is prone *to / with* earthquakes.
2 Comedians mock politicians irrespective *to / of* their track record.
3 Once she's set her heart *at / on* something there's no stopping her.
4 He's very laid back. He takes everything *in / on* his stride.
5 The building does not comply *for / with* regulations.
6 The controversy comes *against / to* a backdrop of ethnic tension.
7 He's regarded *as / of* a very shrewd politician.
8 We should look into the issue *in / with* depth.

[... / 8]

OPPOSITES

Replace the words in *italics* with their opposite from the box.

deprived	sprawling	acrimonious	long-standing
vibrant	secular	filthy	thriving

1 It's a *compact* city
2 It was an *amicable* divorce
3 It's quite a *dull* area.
4 It's a *devout* community.
5 The place was *spotless*.
6 The industry is *struggling*.
7 It's a very *affluent* area.
8 It's quite a *recent* problem.

[... / 8]

MISSING WORDS

Complete each set of three sentences with one word.

1 I don't know where I ...... on the issue.
  He decided not to ...... again in the next election.
  She's principled. She'll ...... up for what she believes in.
2 The murder rate has fallen threefold and it is hoped the ...... will dip below 300 this year.
  She's a prominent ...... in the green movement.
  You don't need to diet. You have a lovely ....
3 It must've fallen through the hole in my trouser ....
  The city's flourishing now, but there is still the odd ...... of deprivation.
  I've never seen him give a receipt. I think he must just ...... the money.
4 It was a very ...... victory. They only won by two votes.
  There's a lot of prejudice and ......-mindedness here.
  The street's too ...... to get the car down.
5 I think she's seven months old. She's just started ....
  It took ages. The traffic was ...... along.
  I saw a cockroach ...... along the kitchen floor.

[... / 5]

NOUNS

Complete the collocations with a household object.

1 wring out the ~ / wipe the table with a ~ ....
2 switch on the ~ / load the ~ / empty the ~ ....
3 flush the ~ / clean the ~ / unblock the ~ ....
4 plug in the ~ / ~ a hole / hold the ~ ....
5 climb the ~ / hold the ~ steady / fall off a ~ ....
6 cut the ~ / knot the ~ / tie it up with ~ ....
7 a hammer and ~ / hit the ~ / ~ it together ....
8 rinse it under the ~ / leave the ~ running / turn the ~ on
  ....

[... / 8]

WORD FAMILIES

Complete the gaps with the correct form of the words in CAPITALS.

There's always this [1].......................... that | ASSUME
love will conquer all in marriage so
couples [2].......................... the stress that | ESTIMATE
basic things such as housework can put
on a relationship. The way you squeeze
the toothpaste tube can be [3].......................... | RIDICULE
divisive. So if you have any [4].......................... | RESERVE
about your partner, you should resolve
them before you make a [5].......................... | COMMIT
to marriage. Of course people have the
[6].......................... to change, but in practice we | CAPABLE
tend to be quite [7].......................... to change | WILL
if we perceive a habit as being part of our
personality.

[... / 7]

VOCABULARY

Complete the book review by choosing the correct words A–C.

Mariam is getting on. She's [1]...... and a little unsteady on her feet, but her mind is as sharp as ever. She [2]...... doubts that the new election will [3]...... old-age pensioners. "This country is undergoing a transformation, but [4]...... it's one driven by young people. I think they feel older generations have let them down, and they may be right!"

Certainly, Nigeria has [5]...... many difficulties with a number of the ruling elite being [6]...... bribery and corruption scandals. However, in the [7]...... to new elections there are signs of change. The country is emerging from recession and with a population that is predominantly under the age of 30, a new generation of politicians are [8]...... hope that the many remaining problems can be overcome. However, having seen it all, you can understand why Mariam may be a little cynical.

1 A grim   B frail   C thick-skinned
2 A voices   B instigates   C strikes
3 A flourish   B shelter   C benefit
4 A by and large B now and then C give or take
5 A got by   B devastated   C been through
6 A mixed up in B involved   C got away with
7 A leading   B aftermath   C run-up
8 A offering   B tackling   C granting

[... / 8]

[Total ... /80]

05 NIGHT IN, NIGHT OUT

In this unit, you learn how to:
- talk about feelings
- comment on what you hear
- change the subject
- understand and comment on a guide
- describe books

Grammar
- Noun phrases

Vocabulary
- Feelings
- noun + *of*
- Describing books

Reading
- A *What's on* guide

Listening
- A night out
- Book clubs

VOCABULARY Feelings

A Use the extra information in 1–10 to guess the meaning of the words in **bold**. Translate them.
1. We were **in stitches**. It was hilarious.
2. I was bored to death. I just couldn't stop **yawning**.
3. She was **in bits** – just in floods of tears.
4. I was **stuffed** after the meal. I thought I'd burst.
5. I'm exhausted. I was **tossing and turning** all night.
6. He was **off his head**. He was shouting loudly and he couldn't walk straight.
7. The film didn't **live up to the hype**. I was really disappointed.
8. I was a bit **overwhelmed**. I couldn't take it all in.
9. I'm feeling a bit **rough**. I think I overdid it last night.
10. Honestly, I was **mortified**. I went bright red and just wanted to curl up and die.

B Work in pairs. Take turns giving a reason for the feelings in 1–10. Your partner should say the expression. For example:
A: I was really stressed and couldn't get to sleep.
B: I'm exhausted. I was tossing and turning all night.

LISTENING

You are going to hear two conversations where people talk about a night out and something else.

A 🔊 5.1 **Listen and answer these questions.**
1. What did they do on the night out?
2. What is the other thing they talk about?
3. What phrases from *Vocabulary* do you hear?

B Compare the phrases you heard and discuss why the speakers used them. Then listen again and check.

C Complete 1–12 with the correct preposition / adverb. Then read the audioscript on pages 164–5 to check.
1. She actually burst ...... tears.
2. She's been ...... a lot recently.
3. She got ...... it pretty quickly.
4. He's so full ...... himself.
5. Anyway, talking ...... dancing, are you still going to those tango classes?
6. I'm still a bit prone ...... treading on toes.
7. It's all ...... hand.
8. I just couldn't switch ....
9. Tell me ...... it.
10. Thanks for being so ...... top of things.
11. ...... the way, how was your meal?
12. He just burst ...... shouting at a waiter.

SPEAKING

A **Work in groups. Discuss these questions.**
- Have you ever been to a surprise party? How was it?
- Explain a time when someone reacted unexpectedly.
- Do you know anyone who's a really good / bad dancer? In what way? Are you any good? What do you dance to?
- Do you ever take the mickey? Out of who? Why?
- How good are you at dealing with stress?

NATIVE SPEAKER ENGLISH

strut your stuff
We can say someone *struts their stuff* when they do something very well, but more commonly it is an ironic way to talk about dancing at a party or club.

You've never seen him strutting his stuff, then?
Are you ready to strut your stuff (on the dance floor)?
We were strutting our stuff all night.

DEVELOPING CONVERSATIONS
I bet / imagine

We often give our opinion about what someone says using *I bet / imagine* or *You must / must've.*
I bet she was pleased.
You must be getting quite good.
You must've been stuffed by the end.

A **Rewrite 1–6 using *must be / must've been.***
1 I bet that was pretty dull.
2 I bet you're glad you didn't go now.
3 I imagine he was a bit disappointed.
4 I bet you're feeling a bit rough now.
5 I bet you were mortified.
6 I imagine she was quite upset.

B 🔊 **5.2 Listen and check. Notice the responses.**

We usually respond to opinions like those in 1–6 by agreeing or disagreeing. We often also add a comment.

C **Take turns saying 1–6 in exercise A. Your partner should agree / disagree and comment.**

CONVERSATION PRACTICE

You are going to have similar conversations to the ones you heard in *Listening.*

A **Think of a night which resulted in at least one of the feelings in *Vocabulary*. Think about what happened.**

B **Work in pairs. First discuss the night out and then change the subject to something else. Use language from these pages.**

READING

You are going to read an online *What's on* guide for London on the opposite page.

A **Before you read, discuss these questions in groups.**
- Where do you get information about what's on?
- Do you ever read reviews of films, plays, etc.? How much attention do you pay to them?

B **Work in pairs. Read the *What's on* guide and decide:**
1 what you think of each event.
2 how much you'd be prepared to pay for each thing.

Use some of these expressions:
It sounds too weird / pretentious / gory, etc. *for my liking.*
It doesn't sound like my cup of tea / my kind of thing.
It sounds interesting / brilliant / dreadful, etc.
It sounds like a laugh / the kind of thing I'd like, etc.

C **Work in groups. Choose the three things you would all most like to go to. Then compare with the rest of the class.**

D **Which event(s) / person:**
1 aims to make you laugh?   ...... and ......
2 is an updated version of something old?   ...... and ......
3 is part of a public campaign?   ......
4 has already been successful?   ......, ... and ......
5 helps you get a better figure?   ...... and ......
6 offers suggestions on how to improve?   ...... and ......
7 is a bit scary in parts?   ......
8 is about space?   ......
9 can help you get rid of something you own? ......
10 overcame something?   ......

SPEAKING

Work in pairs. Answer these questions and explain your choices.
- What's the best museum you've ever been to?
- If you could re-release a film, what would it be?
- If you could put any art in Art Bin, what would it be?
- If you could put on an exhibition about someone, who would it be of and what would you display?
- If you had time to do any course, what would you do?

VOCABULARY Noun + *of*

Many nouns often go with *of*, such as these from the guide:

the secrets of surgery; *the format of* the classes; *a wealth of* hints; *the centenary of* his birth; *the loss of* both his legs; *the onset of* war; *the Battle of* Britain; *the existence of* ice; *a set of* questions; *the disposal of* works of art

A **Think of one more ending for each of the nouns in *italics* in the explanation box.**

B **Match the nouns + *of* to the possible endings.**

1	a bundle of	slavery / the death penalty / VAT
2	a fraction of	enquiries / complaints / people
3	a risk of	life / weakness / things to come
4	a flood of	my tongue / the island / the iceberg
5	a sign of	the cost / an inch / a second
6	the supply of	fun / measures / wood / clothes
7	the abolition of	water / drugs / blood to the brain
8	the tip of	accidents / cancer / failure

GRAMMAR Noun phrases

A basic pattern in English is subject–verb–object.
Rory McCreadie reveals secrets.

We can add extra information to the basic subject / object in different ways, to make noun phrases.
Rory McCreadie, a barber surgeon from the 17th century, reveals the gory secrets of surgery in the past.

A **Look at the underlined words in the guide and discuss these questions.**
1 What are they?
- adjective
- noun
- relative clause
- a participle clause
- a prepositional phrase
2 Which noun do they go with?
3 How many words are in the whole subject / object phrase?

▶ Need help? Read the grammar reference on page 140.

B **Work in pairs. Choose one of the sentences in 1–4. Add information to the subject and object. Which pair can write the longest sentence?**
1 Leona Hart won the award.
2 A policeman found a boy.
3 The exhibition presents sculptures.
4 Man seeks woman.

WHERE CAN WE GO?

Barber Surgeon: leeches, lancets and blood-letting
From trepanning (drilling a hole in the skull) to blood-letting with leeches, Rory McCreadie, a barber surgeon from the 17th century, reveals the gory secrets of surgery in the past. Audience participation encouraged!

Blues Brothers Banned Live at The 100 Club
Eleven young musicians deliver a twist on Blues Brothers' classics. The Banned packed London's legendary Hard Rock Cafe last year. A gig for everybody.

Can-Can Course
Polestars Can-Can course is a fun-filled, high-intensity dance class for legs, bums and tums. Each week you learn a routine that will have you in stitches!

Douglas Bader Centenary Exhibition
In this display, marking the centenary of his birth, we examine Bader's early career, the accident that led to the loss of both his legs and his legacy to the disabled community. Despite his disability, with the onset of war in 1939 Bader rejoined the RAF becoming a crack pilot in the Battle of Britain and a national hero.

Ice Worlds
Discover the important role ice plays throughout the Solar System in the fascinating Ice Worlds planetarium show. Take an awe-inspiring journey exploring Earth's frozen extraterrestrial neighbours and see how the existence of ice shapes the landscape.

London Treasure Hunt: Ideal Quirky Winter Trip Out!

Spitalfields is one of London's most vibrant areas: our exciting Treasure Hunt takes in the soaring 'Gherkin' building, passes Hawksmoor's stunning Christ Church, and then creeps down a creepy burial chamber before venturing along Brick Lane. Two sets of questions (easy/cryptic) for all ages.

Michael Landy: Art Bin
Michael Landy transforms the South London Gallery into Art Bin, a container for the disposal of works of art. Over the course of the six-week exhibition, the enormous 600m³ bin will gradually fill up as people discard their art works in it, ultimately creating, in Landy's words, 'a monument to creative failure'. Anyone can dispose of their art works.

Cupcake Decorating Classes
Learn how to make and decorate delicious cupcakes. The format of the classes will be demonstration and interactive participation. You will take home your own creations, recipes used during the class and a wealth of hints and tips relating to baking and decorating.

Odyssey UK Tour
Theatre Ad Infinitum reinvent Homer's timeless Greek myth with *Odyssey*. One actor. One hour. One man's epic quest to reunite with his family and seek his bloody revenge. This passionate retelling was an Edinburgh Fringe sell-out show, receiving four- and five-star reviews across the board.

Rainman
Re-release of the 80s film that follows the journey of Charlie Babbit and his autistic brother Raymond across America, to coincide with mental health awareness week. Funny and incredibly moving. Take a handkerchief.

Re/Landscape – Impossible Photographs
Re:Landscape presents illusory photographs of English rural scenes and coastlines. Using mirrors when photographing each landscape, Karen Grainger blurs the boundary between the reflected and the real, presenting an extraordinary take on the traditional landscape genre.

Richmond and Twickenham Jazz Club
This thriving weekly jazz club, featuring some of the finest names in jazz and hosted by saxophonist Kelvin Christiane and vocalist Lesley Christiane, has different guest artists each week and an outstanding rhythm section.

Weight Loss through Ayurveda
This two-day workshop looks at simple guidelines for quick and effective weight loss. It explores the cause of weight gain, and shows yoga and breathing exercises suitable for losing weight along with anti-aging therapies.

SPEAKING

A Work in groups. Discuss these questions.
- Which of the things in the box below do you ever read?
- Which do you enjoy reading most / least? Why?
- How often do you read in English? What kind of things do you usually read?
- Do you know anyone who's ever belonged to a book club? Would you consider joining one? Why? / Why not?

newspaper articles	poems	instruction manuals
academic books	novels	Internet forums
comics	blogs	

LISTENING

You are going to hear a radio programme about book clubs.

A ◐ 5.3 Listen and complete the summary below with your own notes.

Support from Oprah can have a big effect on
1...................................... .

Website features 2...................................... .

Britain now has around 3...................................... .
including specialist groups like
4...................................... .

Two main reasons for popularity of book clubs:
1   5......................................
2   6......................................

However, there's been some criticism on the grounds
that reading groups 7...................................... .
Fears also voiced about mass audience's taste for
8...................................... .

One popular book, 'Reading Lolita in Tehran', is
about 9...................................... .

Book Crossing also growing in popularity.
Main idea is to encourage people
10...................................... .

One City, One Book idea – started in Seattle.
Basic idea is everyone 11...................................... .
Can also involve 12...................................... .

B Work in pairs. Compare your notes.

C Match the verbs to the nouns they were used with in *Listening*.

1	endorse	a	a number of different factors
2	boast	b	the spread
3	share	c	over two million members
4	be down to	d	the movement of items
5	see	e	the trend in a positive light
6	halt	f	a book
7	track	g	free copies
8	fund	h	their thoughts

D Compare your answers with your partner. Discuss who or what each of the verb–noun collocations in exercise C is connected to.

E Listen again and read the audioscript on page 165 to check your ideas.

F Work in groups. Discuss these questions.
- Who do you think are the most influential tastemakers in your country? Why?
- Do you think tastemakers have a positive or negative influence? In what way?
- Do you think any of Brian Sewer's criticisms of book clubs are fair? Why? / Why not?
- Do you like the idea of Book Crossing? Would you consider taking part in it?
- Do you think the One City, One Book idea would work in your town / city? What book would work best?

VOCABULARY Describing books

A Complete the reviews by choosing the correct words.

1

Tove Jansson
Fair Play

This slim novel contains seventeen loosely connected chapters and ¹*centres* / *revolves* on the lives and loves of two elderly female artists. There is very little ²*plot* / *argument* as Jansson is far more interested in the minutiae of everyday life and in the way the relationship between her two ³*stars* / *protagonists* is realised through the sparse, minimal ⁴*dialogue* / *speech*.

'A book about love – tender, eccentric and fiercely independent. It feels a privilege to read it.' Esther Freud

Tove Jansson | fair play

INTRODUCED BY ALI SMITH

2

Anya Seaton
Katherine

This vivid portrayal of love and politics in medieval England is ¹*rooted* / *based* on a true story and manages to ²*bring* / *carry* its characters and era to life through its rich, vibrant language. If you believe that love conquers all and enjoy stories ³*held* / *set* in the past, then this uplifting ⁴*history* / *tale* may well be for you.

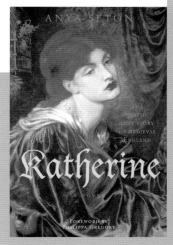

ANYA SEATON

Katherine

FOREWORD BY PHILIPPA GREGORY

5

Kaylie Jones
Lies My Mother Never Told Me

In this moving ¹*memoir* / *memory*, Jones confronts her childhood and her troubled relationship with her abusive mother, whose ²*conflict* / *struggle* to overcome her alcoholism is explored in heart-wrenching detail. The book ³*treats* / *deals* with the themes of acceptance and transcendence and is a real page-turner from start to finish. I can't ⁴*suggest* / *recommend* it highly enough.

3

Megan McDonough
Step By Step

This gripping non-fiction work ¹*traces* / *discovers* the history of the feminist movement in twentieth-century America and ²*explores* / *finds* the impact it had on women. ³*Basing* / *Revolving* around the lives of ten women, the book ⁴*sorts out* / *tackles* such issues as marriage and divorce, domestic violence and the civil rights movement.

4

Mil Millington
Things My Girlfriend and I Have Argued About

This comic novel is so frequently laugh-out-loud funny that you might not want to read it in public! Told in the ¹*main* / *first* person, the book explores the many arguments between the ²*narrator* / *commentator* and his German girlfriend – to hysterical effect! By ³*turns* / *episodes*, absurd, dark and full of ⁴*insight* / *judgement*, it's a must-read for anyone who's ever been in a relationship!

B Underline any new adjective + noun collocations in the book reviews in exercise A. Compare and discuss what they mean.

C Work in pairs. Discuss these questions.
- Would you recommend any of the five books to people you know? Which ones? Who to? Why?
- Which of the books would you most / least like to read? Why?
- Have you ever read anything similar to any of the books described?

SPEAKING

Imagine you and some of your classmates have joined a book club and you are going to decide what to read first.

A Think of the book you would most like other students to read. Who's it by and what's it called? Decide how to describe it. Use some of the language from *Vocabulary*.

B Work in groups. Try to persuade your partners to read your choice first – and explain why it's so good.

C Vote to decide which book to read first.

06 CONFLICT

In this unit, you learn how to:
- describe what people do during and after arguments
- give negative / private information
- talk about how you'd like things to be different
- discuss war and social conflict
- talk about peace and justice

Grammar
- *I wish*

Vocabulary
- Adverbs
- War and peace
- Social conflict

Reading
- Hope springs eternal
- The Truth and Reconciliation Commission

Listening
- Two conflicts
- Disputes in the news
- The Truth and Reconciliation Commission

SPEAKING

A **Check you understand the words in bold. Then tell a partner which of the things below you sometimes do.**
- lose your temper and scream and shout
- **storm off** and **slam** the door behind you
- throw things across the room – or at someone
- have a big **sulk**
- **hold a grudge** against someone after an argument
- apologise first and try to **make up**

B **Look at the list of things people often argue about in the box below. With a partner, discuss how each might lead to arguments and which you think cause the worst arguments.**

money	politics
religion	work
sport	homework
careers	kids
stress and tiredness	exes
time spent together	household chores
silly annoyances	in-laws

C **Which of the things above do you argue about most often? Who with? How do the arguments usually end?**

LISTENING

You are going to hear two conversations in which conflicts occur.

A ✪ 6.1 **Listen and answer these questions about each conversation.**
1 What's the relationship between the people?
2 What are the conflicts about?
3 What happens in the end?

NATIVE SPEAKER ENGLISH

I hasten to add

To clarify or comment on a previous statement, we can use *I hasten to add*. It can be used either formally or jokingly.

A: I do understand I made a mistake.
B: And not for the first time, I hasten to add.

I was absolutely furious about it – not that I'm normally an angry person, I should hasten to add!

DEVELOPING CONVERSATIONS
Giving negative / private information

When we give negative or private information, we often use sentence starters that warn the listener about what's to come.

To be frank with you, I'm really not sure there's a future for you here at all.

A **Work in pairs. Imagine the sentence starters below were all used in an office over the space of a week. Complete each one in a humorous or serious way.**
1 I don't mean to be rude, but
   ....
2 To be brutally honest, ... :
3 With all due respect, ...
4 To put it bluntly, ...
5 If you want my honest opinion,
   ....
6 Between you and me, and this shouldn't go any further, ...

B **Compare your sentences with another pair. Who has the best ideas?**

GRAMMAR *I wish*

A **Divide the sentences below into three groups of two according to the grammatical patterns.**

1 I just wish you were a bit less selfish, to be honest!
2 I wish I'd never started this conversation.
3 I wish I didn't have such a short temper!
4 I wish he'd understand that people do have exes!
5 I wish I'd told him what I thought of him earlier, to be honest!
6 I wish you wouldn't always make fun of me in front of all my friends.

B **Compare your ideas with a partner and explain the different uses of *wish*.**

▶ Need help? Read the grammar reference on page 141.

C **Complete the sentences below by adding the correct forms of the verbs in the box.**

be	can	have	leave	sent	think

1 I wish I .... longer to stop and talk, but I'm afraid I'm actually in a bit of rush.
2 I wish I .... her that e-mail! It just made everything worse.
3 I wish you .... your things lying around all over the place all the time. It's so annoying!
4 I wish I .... turn back time and start again.
5 You always talk such rubbish! I wish you .... sometimes before you open your mouth!
6 It's the fact that you lied to me that really hurts. I just wish you .... more honest with me!

D **Write down five things you wish using the patterns below. Explain your sentences to a partner.**

1 I wish I'd never ....
2 I wish I wasn't ....
3 I sometimes wish I could ....
4 I wish my .... wouldn't ....
5 I wish my .... would sometimes ....

VOCABULARY Adverbs

Some adverbs commonly go with particular verbs. We also use adverbs at the start of sentences to show our attitude towards the information that follows.

....

I *expressly asked* you to send that parcel recorded delivery.
I'm really sorry. *Honestly,* it won't happen again.

A **Complete the sentences with the adverbs in the box.**

bitterly	desperately	dramatically	expressly
freely	strongly	stupidly	vaguely

1 I ...~~expressly~~... told you never to contact me at home!
2 He's a real snob – and to make it worse, he ...~~freely~~... admits it!
3 I ...~~strongly~~... recommend that you try it before you buy it.
4 I ...~~desperately~~... need to find a job! I'm really short of money.
5 I ...~~vaguely~~... remember him saying something about it last time we spoke, but I might be wrong.
6 I'm such an idiot. I ...~~stupidly~~... left my bag on the bus!
7 I ...~~bitterly~~... regret what I did. It was totally wrong of me.
8 The number of ongoing civil wars has increased ...~~dramatically~~... over the last 20 years.

B **Work in pairs. Think of one more verb that goes with each of the adverbs in the box.**

C **Choose the correct adverb in each sentence.**

1 ~~Apparently~~ / Evidently, I'm wasting my breath here. You're clearly not listening to me.
2 ~~Personally~~ / Hopefully, we'll just be able to make up and put it all behind us.
3 Realistically / Theoretically, it's possible, but let's see how it works in practice.
4 Presumably / Ideally, you think that's funny!
5 Surprisingly / Technically, you're not supposed to be using that phone to make personal calls.
6 Frankly / Luckily, I think that's totally ridiculous.

CONVERSATION PRACTICE

You are going to have two conversations similar to the ones you heard in *Listening*.

A **Student A:** read File 3 on page 152.
Student B: read File 10 on page 156.

B **Prepare for both conversations. Try to use some of the new language from these pages. Then role-play each one.**

VOCABULARY War and peace

A **Read the short editorial from a newspaper and discuss these questions.**

- Are the examples given also true for your language?
- In what other areas of life might war vocabulary be used in English (or in your language)?
- Do you agree with the points made in the final two sentences?

We must be violent people by nature. Just consider the way the language of war invades all sorts of aspects of our lives. Advertisers *bombard* target groups; politicians get involved in *wars of words* as they *attack* plans and *defend* policies; lobby groups want to *combat* poverty; companies might *join forces* to *gain ground* in the market, they might *fight off a hostile takeover* or engage in *a price war*. Patients might *battle* cancer or *surrender* to a disease.

Much less common seems to be the language of peace and negotiation. Is this reflected in other languages? If so, perhaps this is why conflict resolution is so difficult. People find it difficult to forget about aggression because so much of our lives is framed in terms of victory and defeat. We need to find a new language if we are to work together.

The peace talks collapsed when the dogs insisted the sandbox had to go out in the hall.

B **Put each group of verbs into the most likely order that they happen, starting with the words in bold.**

1 a truce is called / conflict escalates / **tension rises** / some fighting breaks out / war rages
2 have a row / fall out / **take offence** / get in touch / make amends
3 defend yourself / **be invaded** / join forces / defeat the enemy / gain ground / lose ground
4 restart negotiations / sign a peace agreement / **declare a ceasefire** / begin negotiations / talks break down / reach a settlement.
5 return to democracy / seize control of the country / **plot to overthrow the president** / suffer sanctions / stage a coup / undermine the economic stability
6 be under siege for weeks / **be surrounded** / run out of food / become a prisoner of war / surrender
7 seek a UN resolution / **receive reports of human rights violations** / withdraw troops / send in international troops / re-establish security
8 put on trial / arrest / cause casualties and fatalities / track down / claim responsibility / **plant a bomb**

C **Try to memorise the words in exercise B. Then test each other.**
Student A: say an expression in bold.
Student B: try to say the rest of the verbs in order.

D **Work in groups. Try to think of an example of each of the following and explain what happened – and what the causes and results of each were.**

- an invasion
- a civil war
- a terrorist attack
- a siege
- a coup
- a falling-out
- an international intervention
- a peace process

LISTENING

You are going to hear four news stories about different issues, all using vocabulary of war and peace.

A 🔊 6.2 **Listen and decide which issue is the most serious.**

B **Work in pairs and explain your choices.**

C **Listen again and decide which sentences are true.**
1 a Dan Craddock has been found guilty of spying.
  b Mr Craddock was a manager for Pit-Pots.
  c Jazz Drinks has a bigger market share now.
2 a Jonas Bakeman is in danger of losing his job.
  b Bakeman spoke to the press and fully apologised.
  c Ms Campbell claims she didn't initiate the affair.
3 a A court decided people didn't have to submit to body scans at airports.
  b One lobby group funded the woman's defence.
  c The government has accepted the ruling.
4 a Pig farming is an important industry in Paulston.
  b Both sides in the dispute inflicted some kind of damage.
  c The sides agreed a settlement between themselves.

D **Match the words from the listening. Then check in the audioscript on page 166.**

1	a fierce	a	wrongdoing
2	deny	b	invasion of privacy
3	a lapse of	c	symbol
4	claim	d	eyesore
5	a gross	e	battle
6	split	f	victory
7	a hideous	g	into two camps
8	a proud	h	judgement

E **Discuss any stories that you have heard which are similar to those in *Listening*.**

LANGUAGE PATTERNS

Write the sentences in your language. Translate them back into English. Compare your English to the original.
They've been pouring money into ever more extravagant advertising campaigns.
Last year was Jazz Drinks' best ever.
It comes against a backdrop of ever-increasing tension.
There are more weapons than ever on our streets.
As ever, she managed to calm things down.
The government is, as ever, committed to peace.

SPEAKING

A **As a class, choose two of the following statements to debate. Then divide into groups – half the class will agree with the two statements and the other half will disagree.**
- You should never negotiate with terrorists.
- There should never be international intervention in a country's internal affairs.
- Wars are a necessary evil.
- You can't win a war on drugs.
- Peaceful protests are the only ones that work.
- Companies are too concerned with market share or growth.
- There should be more restrictions on advertising.

B **In your group, spend ten minutes preparing your ideas and think how you might attack your opponents. Choose a spokesman for your group.**

C **One group should speak for two minutes, presenting their ideas *agreeing* with one statement. Another group should then speak against. When they have finished, anyone can comment or ask questions.**

D **Repeat exercise C with the other statement.**

SPEAKING

In groups, discuss what you know about South Africa.

VOCABULARY Social conflict

A Match the nouns in the box to their collocates.

oppression	support	condemnation	dissent	boycott
unrest	sanctions	segregation	march	massacre

1 a policy of racial ~ / strict ~ of men and women
2 call for a ~ / a consumer ~ / a mass ~
3 a ~ of innocent civilians / carry out a cold-blooded ~
4 draw widespread international ~ / issue an official ~
5 ~ of non-whites / suffer racial ~ / battle ~
6 impose ~ on the country / lift economic ~
7 go on a pro-democracy ~ / break up a protest ~
8 express ~ / crush ~ / growing ~ / tolerate political ~
9 growing popular ~ / a wave of social ~ / spark fresh ~
10 strengthen ~ for the resistance / enjoy popular ~

B Work in pairs. Test each other.
Student A: say the nouns in the box.
Student B: close your book. Say at least one collocate.

C With a partner, discuss how the nouns in the box in exercise A might be connected to the history of South Africa. Try to use some of the collocates in your discussion.

READING

A Read the article about South Africa's recent history and see if your predictions were right.

B With a partner, discuss how the ten nouns in **bold** are connected to South Africa's recent history.

HOPE SPRINGS ETERNAL

As the eyes of the world focused on South Africa at the start of the 2010 football World Cup, national pride was at an all-time high. The new stadiums glittered, the national anthem was sung as never before and the multiracial team took to the pitch fully aware of what their presence on the global stage meant to their nation, for behind the choice of location for the tournament lies one of the most remarkable transformations undergone by any nation in recent times.

A mere twenty years before, the man who was to become the country's first black president, Nelson Mandela, was released from jail after 27 years, having initially been imprisoned for his role as leader of the banned African National Congress and for planning acts of sabotage against the state. The road to freedom had been littered with obstacles, and for a long time it had seemed as if the destination would never be reached.

The system of apartheid that was formalized in the 1940s, and which lasted until 1994, had its roots in the racial **segregation** introduced during colonial times, when the British and Dutch battled for control of the country's riches. The policy of **oppression** and relocation of non-whites initially reaped huge rewards for the ruling white minority and by the 1960s the country had economic growth second only to Japan. At the same time, however, the effort to maintain the rigid social structures imposed upon the majority of the nation was becoming ever more costly and complicated.

Internationally, calls for **boycotts** were growing, and the country was becoming increasingly isolated. Pressure was also growing for **sanctions** to be imposed. Internally, popular **unrest** was growing. The government faced wave after wave of strikes, **marches**, protests and sabotage by bombing and other means.

The repeated **massacres** of demonstrators drew widespread international **condemnation** and, of course, served to strengthen **support** for resistance organisations. By the 1970s, the country was also embroiled in a number of military missions in neighbouring countries in an attempt to crush all **dissent**, while internal repression and censorship reached new levels. By the mid-80s, South Africa's economy was one of the weakest in the world and the writing was clearly on the wall.

Following Mandela's release and the dismantling of the apparatus of apartheid, the issue of how to move the country forward peaceably loomed large. The establishment of The Truth and Reconciliation Commission was a major step in this direction.

C **Work in pairs. Discuss these questions about the article.**
1 In what ways was the 2010 World Cup significant?
2 Why was Nelson Mandela sentenced to jail?
3 When – and why – did the apartheid system begin?
4 What seems to have been the main factor in its collapse? What other factors played a part?
5 What do you think the goals and working methods of The Truth and Reconciliation Commission were?

D **Read the Wiki about The Truth and Reconciliation Commission and see if you guessed correctly.**

Wiki:
The Truth and Reconcilliation Commission

Following the abolition of apartheid, a court-like body entitled The Truth and Reconciliation Commission was established. The main aim of the Commission was to establish the truth about human rights violations by giving both victims and perpetrators the chance to describe their experiences. The Commission had no explicit power to prosecute, but in exchange for the truth about their actions, those who had committed crimes in the past could request amnesty from prosecution, provided their actions had been politically motivated and proportionate.

Despite this, the Commission explicitly set out to focus primarily on the victims. It was hoped that through the process of revealing their stories they would reach some kind of closure. Compensation was also offered in some situations.

E **Decide if these sentences are true or false.**
1 The Truth and Reconciliation Commission aimed to punish those who had committed atrocities.
2 It did not have the power to sentence people to prison.
3 It had the power to exempt people from prosecution.
4 Anyone wanting a pardon had to show remorse.
5 The Commission sometimes gave money to victims.

F **Work in groups. Discuss these questions.**
• How do you feel about the idea of The Truth and Reconciliation Commission?
• What do you imagine its main strengths and weaknesses would be?
• How successful do you imagine the Commission was when it came to establishing the truth? Why?
• How successful do you imagine it was at bringing about reconciliation between people? Why?

LISTENING

You are going to hear three people discussing their experiences of The Truth and Reconciliation Commission.

A ✆ 6.3 **Listen and decide how each speaker feels about the Commission and why.**

B **Listen again and decide which speaker:**
1 speaks the most highly about the Commission.
2 found telling the truth did not lead to reconciliation.
3 had a minor crisis of faith.
4 feared the worst when apartheid was abolished.
5 turned down compensation.
6 found listening to testimony traumatic.
7 wants a different solution to the problems of the past.
8 complains about a delay.
9 feels the country's standing in the world has been boosted.

C **Work in pairs. Discuss these questions.**
• Did any of the speakers mention any pros / cons that you didn't think of in *Reading*?
• What seems to have been the biggest problem with the Commission? And what about the biggest strength?
• Did the three speakers leave you feeling that the Commission was more a good or a bad idea? Why?
• Have you heard of any similar processes anywhere else in the world?

SPEAKING

A **Discuss in groups how far you agree with each of the ideas about justice below.**

Mercy bears richer fruits than strict justice.

An eye for an eye; a tooth for a tooth.

It is better that ten guilty escape than one innocent suffer.

The more laws there are, the less justice there is.

In seeking justice, we must ensure we do not become as evil as that which we oppose.

Injustice anywhere is a threat to justice everywhere.

In this unit, you learn how to:
- explain and discuss news stories about science
- express surprise and disbelief
- discuss the uses and abuses of statistics
- talk about what different kinds of science entail

Grammar
- Passives

Vocabulary
- Talking about science
- Statistics
- Forming words

Reading
- Truth and statistics

Listening
- Discussing news stories about science
- Five scientists discuss their jobs

VOCABULARY Talking about science

A **Replace the words in *italics* with the correct form of the synonyms in the box.**

underlying	impaired	devise	adverse
slippery slope	undertake	insert	lead to
step forward	duplicate	disorder	due

1 It's a major *breakthrough* in the fight against AIDS.
2 No-one knows the *root* cause of the phenomenon.
3 The huge noise left many with *diminished* hearing.
4 They *stuck* probes into the skin.
5 The experiment represents a *thin end of the wedge*.
6 Researchers *carried out* the survey to establish a link between attitudes and health.
7 The findings could *pave the way for* new techniques.
8 Other scientists are yet to successfully *reproduce* the results under laboratory conditions.
9 The lack of funding was *down* to the radical nature of the theory.
10 There are concerns about *negative* side effects to the procedure.
11 The study found that the genetic *condition* was more prevalent than first thought.
12 Scientists have *created* a way to detect seismic waves before earthquakes hit.

B **Test each other.**
Student A: say the words in italics in 1–12.
Student B: say the synonyms.

Note that the words and phrases above will not always be synonymous. It will depend on context or register, typical collocations or changes in meaning. For example:

Can you just ~~insert~~ stick this in your bag?
It's the law of ~~impairing~~ diminishing returns.
The next bus is ~~down~~ due in two minutes.

LISTENING

You are going to hear two conversations about science-based stories in the news.

A **Work in pairs. Look at the newspaper headlines and discuss what you think each story is about.**
a Researchers clone glow-in-the-dark dogs
b Hormone inhaler may help autism
c Cat owners are more intelligent
d Backing for space sun shield ✓
e Gay penguins adopt chick
f DNA fragrance with the smell of Elvis Presley
g Mind-reading a step closer
h Scientists breed see-through frogs and fish
i Scientist gets funding for time-reversal experiment
j Scientists successfully transplant mosquito nose ✓
k One in five scientists on performance-enhancing drugs

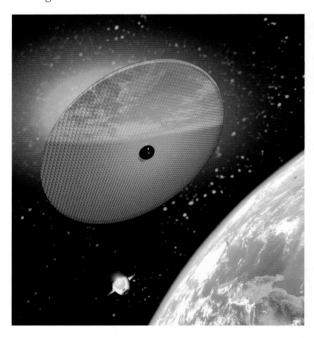

B 🔊 **7.1 Listen and take notes on the news stories the speakers talk about.**

C **Listen again and decide if 1–9 are true or false.**

Conversation 1
1 The mosquito receptors are transferred to a frog. *f*
2 The research is connected to preventing disease. *T*
3 The researchers are going to produce a perfume. *f*
4 The speakers are both concerned about the
  implications of the research. *f*

Conversation 2
5 The shield is to stop the earth heating up. *T*
6 They also want to build a stadium in space. *f*
7 The 'cloud' could be finished ten years from now. *T*
8 The researcher has received funding for the proposal. *f*
9 One of the speakers thinks all the talk about climate
  change is really only for the benefit of big business. *T*

D **Work in pairs. Discuss these questions.**
• What do you think of the two stories you heard?
• Do you have any concerns about genetic research?
• Do you know anyone who is sceptical about climate
  change or other scientific theories? What are their
  reasons?

LANGUAGE PATTERNS

**Write the sentences in your language. Translate them
back into English. Compare your English to the
original.**
It's hardly the same thing!
Hardly an instant solution, then!
It's hardly surprising people are concerned about it.
Hardly a day goes by without hearing one of these
stories.
I hardly know anyone who agrees with it.
There's hardly any funding available for research into it.

DEVELOPING CONVERSATIONS
Expressing surprise and disbelief

**You can show surprise or disbelief by adding *on earth*
to questions.**
How *on earth* do they do that?
How *on earth* are they going to build something
that big?

A ♫ **7.2 Listen and repeat the questions. Pay attention
to the stress and intonation.**

B **Write questions in response to 1–6 using *on earth*.**
1 We're developing a Nanobridge. *What*
2 They've managed to grow a human ear on a rat's back. *Why*
3 Their head office is in Flitwick. *Where*
4 They're planning to send farm animals into space. *Why*
5 I'm going to take part in a drugs trial. *Why*
6 Apparently, they've bred see-through frogs to sell.
  widoozhle *Who or Why*

C **Take turns saying 1–6 above. Your partner should
respond with their question from exercise B.
Continue each conversation for as long as you can.**

CONVERSATION PRACTICE

You are going to read some articles and talk about
them in a similar way to the conversations in
Listening.

A **Work in groups.**
Student A: look at File 8 on page 155.
Student B: look at File 15 on page 157.
Student C: look at File 19 on page 159.

Read the articles quickly and choose one to talk about.
Read it again and make sure you understand it.

B **Close your books and take turns starting
conversations by saying *Did you read that thing
about ...?* Your partners should ask questions
and make comments to find out more. Finish by
discussing your opinions on the subject.**

C **When you have discussed one article each, choose
another one you read or a similar one you've heard
about. Have further conversations.**

VOCABULARY Statistics

A Use the extra information in 1–9 to guess the meanings of the phrases in **bold**. Translate them.

1 The data showed **a negative correlation** between income and birth rate: the richer the country, the lower the birth rate

2 The research didn't come up with the 'right' result so the company **twisted the figures to suit its own ends**.

3 With the run-up to the election, the government **has a vested interest** in removing people from the unemployment figures.

4 The figures **don't stand up to scrutiny** when you look at them closely. They're full of holes.

5 **Contrary to popular belief**, the latest statistics show crime has been falling, and not getting worse as the papers suggest.

6 The **research is seriously flawed**. The sample group wasn't chosen at random: they were self-selected.

7 Because a number of variables weren't covered by the data, it's difficult to **establish a causal link** between gaming and bad behaviour.

8 It's too early to say if these two figures are part of a new upward trend or whether they are **a statistical anomaly**.

9 There is **conflicting evidence**. Some data show a correlation, some don't.

B Work in pairs. Choose five of the phrases in **bold** and give a true example of them.

READING

You are going to read an article about statistics.

A Before you read, discuss why it might be important to ask these questions about research.

1 Who was the research commissioned by?
2 How was data collected?
3 How big was the sample?
4 Are the numbers in their full context?
5 Does the data explain the conclusions?
6 Has the data been reviewed by peers?

B Read the article and find out why it claims the questions in exercise A are important.

C Work in pairs. Discuss these questions.

- Do you react to statistics in the ways the author says?
- Was there anything you didn't understand? Can your partner explain?
- Say two things you agree / disagree with in the article.
- Do you think there is anything else about statistics people should know?
- Agree on three new words you want to remember from the text. What are the collocations?

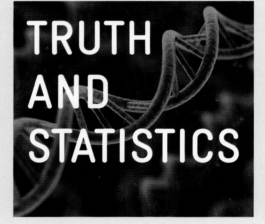

TRUTH AND STATISTICS

We are bombarded by statistics every day – from opinion polls to government figures on crime, from measures of what is a healthy weight or what our salt intake should be, to product claims in advertising: 'eight out of ten owners said their cats preferred it', and so on! What is more, where there is a statistic, there is also bound to be an argument with counter statistics.

Faced with this onslaught of figures, it is easy to run and hide or alternatively to simply respond with cynicism. However, both responses are probably born out of a fear of maths. Statistics is simply a way of interpreting data and, as in other walks of life, the truth can be fuzzy.

Even so, different interpretations have lesser or greater validity. A survey with a sample of 5,000 chosen at random will be more valid than if you just asked five friends who think the same way as you. A study which has been checked by other experts is more likely to be accurate than one which is published anonymously on the Internet. Without any truth in statistics, we have no science, no policy developments, no progress. So part of every responsible citizen's armoury should be a basic understanding of how statistics work and a certain scepticism which looks for underlying problems with the data and research we are presented with.

For example, differences between absolute and relative figures can be manipulated. Company A could report it had increased production 100% more than a rival, by comparing *relative* increases. Company A may have started producing 1,000 TVs and increased it to 1,400 (40%) while Company B started from 10,000 and increased it to 12,000 (only 20%). Furthermore, the absolute increase may disguise inefficiencies, because Company A employed more people to get the increase whereas Company B achieved it while reducing staff. Nor does one year make a trend. Something unusual could have happened that year.

In the case of probabilities, we also need to ask whether variables are independent of each other and the sample group. For example, the chances of being involved in a train crash are the same each time you board a train: in terms of the passenger, it is essentially a random event, like winning the lottery. So experiencing a train accident will not increase your risk the next time you take the train. The probability of having a heart attack, however, may be dependent on various things including whether you have had one before. If you have, the risk of another is very much increased.

Finally, once you have checked the figures, you still need to assess the conclusions drawn: the fact that TV sales increased in line with crime does not prove that one affected the other. The *choice* of statistics and conclusions may be the result of cynical self-interest if the researcher is not independent.

GRAMMAR Passives

A Work in pairs. Look at the sentences from the texts you read in *Conversation Practice* and:
1 underline the passive construction(s).
2 decide who / what the doer of the actions is.
3 decide how you would write it without a passive.
4 decide why an active sentence wasn't used.

1 The frogs, which will be sold for around $100 each, were bred for educational purposes.
2 Rather than getting killed for dissection in class, the transparent frogs allow students to see all the internal organs in action.
3 The fish, which are genetically similar to humans, have cancerous cells inserted in their bodies.
4 The so-called 'love' hormone is thought to be responsible for encouraging bonding.
5 This is just one finding of a census undertaken by the Department of Clinical Veterinary Science
6 The two male penguins are rearing a chick after they were given an egg to look after.
7 The research is seen as a step towards finding cures.
8 The DNA has been extracted from locks of hair.

▶ Need help? Read the grammar reference on page 142.

B Work in groups. Discuss these questions.
• Have you heard of any scientific discoveries or developments recently? How were the breakthroughs achieved?
• Do you know anyone who's had an operation? What did they have done?

C Complete the research reports by putting the verbs in brackets in the correct active or passive form.
1 Whenever there was heavy snowfall, a journalist would call the headquarters of the traffic police, and ask how many car crashes [1].......................... (report). The news would then [2].......................... (lead) with a story like 'A fierce winter storm [3].......................... (dump) a foot of snow on the south today, [4].......................... (cause) huge tailbacks and 28 accidents.' One day, the journalist asked how many crashes were typical for clear, sunny days. The answer? 48!
2 A study [5].......................... (publish) in a child education journal [6].......................... (find) that the toddlers in pre-school were more aggressive than the kids who [7].......................... (keep) at home with mum. In the study, 'aggression' [8].......................... (define) as stealing toys, pushing other children and starting fights.
3 A small study conducted after motorcyclists [9].......................... (oblige) by law to wear helmets discovered that the actual number of injuries [10].......................... (treat) in hospital leapt suddenly.
4 A poll in a magazine, where readers phoned in to vote, revealed that 85% of people felt that rules around experiments [11].......................... (involve) live animals ought [12].......................... (tighten).
5 The government claimed that the murder rate in the city [13].......................... (plunge) by 30% in just eight years as a result of their policies, falling from 130 a year at the beginning of the period to just 91 last year.

LISTENING

A Work in groups. Discuss these questions.
• What problems do you think there might be with the statistics in Grammar, exercise C above?
• What lessons can be learned from each story?

B 🔊 7.3 Listen and see if you were right about the problems.

SPEAKING

A **Read the short text below. Then discuss the questions that follow in groups.**

> Scientists are often seen as a homogenous bunch of geeky men in white lab coats and protective glasses, hunched over some kind of bubbling test tube while muttering to themselves or frantically scribbling equations on a scrap of paper. Such stereotypes not only fail to represent the full diversity of activities that scientists (of both sexes!) engage in, but also serve to dissuade the young from contemplating a career in science. It's time for this to change!

- Does this text reflect your own view of scientists?
- Do you agree that negative stereotypes of scientists may well put young people off entering the field?
- Do you know anyone who works in the field of science? What do they do?

NATIVE SPEAKER ENGLISH

geeky

If we think someone is boring or socially inept because they're only interested in computers / science / academic study, we might call them *geeky / a geek* or *nerdy / a nerd*.

A homogenous bunch of geeky men in white lab coats.
My brother is a complete science geek.
He's a nice guy, but he looks a bit nerdy, if you ask me!
He's such a nerd! He only talks about computers and has no social skills whatsoever.

LISTENING

You are going to hear five different kinds of scientists talking about their jobs.

A **Work in pairs. Discuss these questions.**
- What do you know about each of the different kinds of scientist in the box?
- What's the main point of each job?
- What do you think their working lives involve on a day-to-day basis?

agricultural scientist	hydrologist
anthropologist	immunologist
astronomer	marine biologist
neurologist	military scientist
geologist	educational psychologist

B **7.4 Listen and match each speaker to one of the different kinds of scientist in the box. What does each job involve?**

C **Listen again and decide which speaker:**
1 studies the possible harm that drought can do.
2 sometimes makes recommendations about living environments.
3 says their line of work involves making policy recommendations.
4 finds their job immensely satisfying.
5 says their line of work is more boring than is commonly believed.
6 feels the stereotype about their job is out of date.
7 has done research on the global spread of a particular phenomenon.
8 notes a way in which their field is unusual.
9 is quite secretive about what their job involves.

D **Work in pairs. Discuss these questions.**
- Which of the five jobs do you think sounds most interesting? Why?
- Which do you think is likely to be best / worst paid? Why?
- Can you think of any jobs where the stereotype may well be more glamorous than the reality? In what way?

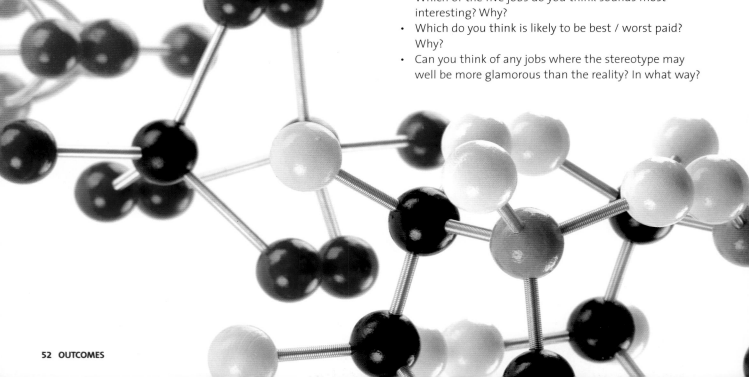

VOCABULARY Forming words

A Complete the sentences below by adding the correct noun forms of the adjectives in brackets.

1 Continuing to invest in space .... is a total waste of money! (exploratory)
2 There are too many .... to be able to say for sure what causes crime. (varied)
3 There's not much .... in my country. (diverse)
4 Learning about statistics is beyond my .... (capable)
5 One of the main causes of depression is the .... of human needs and desires by advertising. (manipulative)
6 .... plays an important and useful role in both business and sport. (aggressive)
7 When it comes to health, ... is far better than cure. (preventative)
8 It's healthy to have a large degree of .... (cynical)
9 There's currently an .... of employment opportunities in my town / city. (abundant)
10 We're not doing enough to reduce the number of .... on the road. (fatal)
11 In all ...., I'll end up working overseas at some point in my career. (probable)
12 The desire of scientists to explore the limits of what is possible has serious .... for both human and animal rights. (implied)

B Which six of the adjectives in brackets in exercise A can be made into verbs? What are the verb forms? Compare your ideas with a partner.

C Work in groups. Discuss the degree to which you agree with each of the statements in exercise A. Explain your ideas.

SPEAKING

As a class, choose one of the two activities below.

1 Work in groups of four or five. Look at the different kinds of scientists in the box in *Listening* exercise A. Choose a different one each. Make sure you choose ones not featured in *Listening* exercise B.

Working individually, use the Internet to find out as much as you can about what the job involves, what qualifications you need, what the career opportunities are, etc.

Report back to your group on what you found. The others in your group should ask questions. Once you have all finished, vote to decide which job sounds best.

2 Work in groups. Discuss these questions.
- What do you think are the most important scientific discoveries of recent times? Why?
- What future scientific breakthrough would have the most positive impact on the world? Why?
- Did / Do you enjoy science subjects at school? Why? / Why not? What was the most useful thing you learned?
- How many examples of scientific developments that we take for granted in our daily lives can you think of?
- Which would you miss the most if you had to live without it?

08 NATURE

VOCABULARY Describing scenery

A Label the picture with the correct numbers in the box.

| 1 a mountain range | 2 plains | 3 a peak | 4 a crater | 5 the mouth of the river | 6 a glacier |
| 7 wetland | 8 a stream | 9 cliffs | 10 a bay | 11 a gorge | 12 woodland |

B Work in pairs. Decide if both or only one of the words in *italics* is correct.

1 It's a beautiful area – *rolling / barren* green hills, winding *lakes / streams* and *thick / dense* woodland.
2 It's very *arid / deserted*. We passed through all these little villages on the *edge / fringes* of the desert – and then we hit the sand *dunes / hills*.
3 The *countryside / landscape* is very lush and green. The land's very *fertile / barren*.
4 We drove along this bumpy dirt *track / road*, through an *industrial / rugged* landscape of mountain peaks and deep *cliffs / gorges*.
5 The scenery was *breathtaking / stunning*. Around every bend were views of *sandy / rocky* beaches and crystal *clear / coastal* seas.

C Work in pairs. Discuss these questions.
· Which parts of your country do you think are the most beautiful? Which are the worst? Why?
· Have you been to these areas? When? Why?
· Which of the features in exercises A and B do you have in your country? Whereabouts?

LISTENING

You are going to hear two people talking about the scenery in places they have visited.

A 🔊 8.1 **Listen and answer these questions about each conversation.**
1 Where have they visited?
2 What were they doing there?
3 What was the scenery like?

B **Work in pairs. Do you remember what the speakers said about the following?**

Conversation 1	Conversation 2
a a border	f all over the place
b vineyards	g the other day
c the Internet	h global warming
d being fit	i snow-capped mountains
e her hometown	j conclusive

C **Listen again to check your ideas.**

D **Work in pairs. Discuss these questions.**
• Had you heard of either of the two places they visited?
• Which of the two visits sounds better to you? Why?
• Have you ever been hiking? Where did you go?
• Do you think climate change is affecting your country at all? If yes, in what way?

LANGUAGE PATTERNS

Write the sentences in your language. Translate them back into English. Compare your English to the original.

It's really mountainous, with all these gorges dropping down into the valleys.
We rented one of those foot pedal boats.
Our HQ was right on the edge of all this dense woodland.
We stayed in that hotel you recommended.
I haven't felt this fit in years.
It wasn't that bad.

DEVELOPING CONVERSATIONS
Emphatic tags

We often add tags to emphasise our opinions. We usually begin with a pronoun + *really* and we then repeat the auxiliary if there is one (or add *do / does / did* if there isn't).

A: So how was your holiday? Did you have a good time?
B: Yeah, it was amazing, *it really was*.

A **Add emphatic tags to the sentences below.**
1 I wouldn't drive it if I were you.
2 The views were just stunning.
3 The scenery takes your breath away.
4 I just love it there.
5 It made no difference whatsoever.
6 He'll never change.
7 I've never been anywhere like it.
8 That sounds amazing.

B 🔊 8.2 **Listen and check your ideas. Then practise saying the sentences with the added tag. In the tag, stress *really*.**

CONVERSATION PRACTICE

You are going to have conversations like the ones you heard in *Listening*.

A **Think of two places you have visited that had interesting scenery. Think about what you were doing there, how you travelled around and what the place was like. If you want, you can use your imagination and pretend you have been to a place that you know of.**

B **Have conversations with other students about your places.**

C **Which was the best place you heard about? Why?**

SPEAKING

A Read the short text below. Then discuss the questions that follow in groups.

When it was first published in 1992, John Gray's *Men are from Mars, Women are from Venus* shot to the top of the best-seller lists – and has since gone on to sell over 30 million copies. The book has spawned a mini-industry of copycat self-help books and Gray himself not only has published numerous follow-ups but also runs seminars, residential retreats, a telephone helpline and a dating service.

At the heart of the book lies the notion that men and women communicate in fundamentally different ways; that, indeed, they are hard-wired to process the world differently and that, consequently, there are tips that can help to bridge this vast divide.

Have you ever read *Men are from Mars, Women are from Venus* – or any other self-help or relationship books?

- If yes, what did you think of it / them?
- If no, would you like to? Why? / Why not?
- Why do you think such books are so popular?
- Do you agree that men and women are 'hard-wired to process the world differently'? Why? / Why not?
- How far do you agree with the statements below?
  - Women talk more than men.
  - Women know and use more words than men.
  - Women talk about their feelings more.
  - Men interrupt more than women.
  - Men use language more competitively than women.

LISTENING

You are going to hear a lecture about language and gender by a professor of linguistics.

A 🔊 8.3 Listen and complete the summary below with your own notes.

Stereotypically, men deal with stress by
¹.., while women

prefer to ².. .

Self-help books have perpetuated

³.. and have

had ⁴.. .

Hardly any of these books are actually

⁵.. !

It's a myth that women talk more and have larger

vocabularies. In reality, ⁶..

and use around ⁷..

a day while doing so. Similarly, how much

someone interrupts has more to do with

⁸.. than gender. Appeal

of Mars–Venus concept due to:

(a) fact it matches ⁹..

and therefore we remember ¹⁰..

while forgetting contradictory examples.

(b) popular fear of changing ¹¹.................................. !

Proof that nurture more important than

nature seen in Papua New Guinea village,

where men speak more indirectly, and women

¹².. !

B Work in pairs. Compare your notes.

C Match the adjectives to the nouns they were used with in *Listening*. Then compare with a partner.

1	common	a	inspection
2	a negative	b	research
3	valid scientific	c	generalisations
4	a cursory	d	changes
5	sweeping	e	effect
6	the continuing	f	gender roles
7	unsettling	g	knowledge
8	traditional	h	appeal

D Work in groups. Discuss these questions.
- Was there anything in the lecture that surprised you?
- Was there anything you strongly agreed or disagreed with? What? Why?
- Do you agree that nurture is more important than nature in determining how people act? Why? / Why not?
- How have gender roles changed in your country over the last 30 years? How do you feel about this? Why?

NATIVE SPEAKER ENGLISH

the slightest

We often use *the slightest* to mean '*any at all*' or '*the smallest*'.

The male of the species retreats into a cave to brood at the slightest sign of stress.
Even the slightest noise will make it run for cover.
Watch out! He'll bite at even the slightest provocation.
I haven't got the slightest idea what that is.

GRAMMAR Auxiliaries

A Complete the sentences by adding the correct auxiliaries. You will need to use negatives.

1 a It's common knowledge that men and women do things differently, ... it?
   b Women are better communicators, ... they?
2 a It's easy to assume these books must be based on valid scientific research, but in reality very few ....
   b Both sexes tend to talk equally as much and use as many words per day while .... so.
3 a While some men .... interrupt far more than the vast majority of women, this is atypical.
   b That guy certainly .... like to talk!
4 a A: You'll find the research backs me up on this.
      B: .... it? OK. I'll have to read more about it, then.
   b A: It was awful. She just kept interrupting me!
      B: .... she? That's so rude!
5 a A: I wish he'd get to the point!
      B: So .... I. This is taking forever!
   b A: I've never really believed in that kind of thing.
      B: No, neither .... I, to be honest.

B Compare your ideas with a partner. Discuss the five different uses of auxiliaries shown in the pairs of sentences.

▶ **Need help? Read the grammar reference on page 143.**

VOCABULARY Communicating

A Complete the sentences with the pairs of words in the box.

articulate + struggle	manners + butting into
bush + point	mince + blunt
gossip + rumours	shuts up + word
listener + shoulder	twisting + words

1 He's a terrible .... – and he's always spreading .... about everyone in the office.
2 He's never less than 100% honest. He certainly doesn't .... his words. He can be very .... sometimes.
3 Once he starts talking, he never .... No-one else can get a .... in edgeways!
4 He's always .... what I say and trying to put .... into my mouth.
5 He's got no .... ! He's always .... other people's conversations.
6 He's a great .... – always good to go to if you need a .... to cry on.
7 He's not very .... I mean, he seems to find it quite a .... to express himself.
8 I wish he'd stop beating around the .... and get to the .... This is taking forever!

B All the sentences in exercise A are about men. Do you think any of the ways of communicating mentioned really are more common among men than women? Tell a partner.

SPEAKING

A Work in groups. Discuss these questions.
- Do any of the sentences in *Vocabulary* exercise A remind you of people you know? In what way?
- Which do you think describe you?
- Do you know any men / women who completely defy gender stereotypes? In what way?
- Do you know any men / women who completely conform to traditional gender stereotypes? In what way?
- Do you know people who are very different to the stereotype that exists of them (age, gender, nationality, etc.)?
- Why do you think people stereotype others? Do you think it's useful in any way? What harm might it cause?
- What stereotypes do you think other people might think you fit in with? To what degree do you think you conform to these stereotypes?

READING 1

A Before you read, discuss these questions in pairs.
- Do you ever watch natural history programmes on TV? Why? / Why not?

B Read the opinion piece below and list the reasons the writer gives for watching and making natural history programmes.

Simon Dawkins
Why I love ... natural history programmes.

I absolutely adore natural history programmes. Watching them from the comfort of my sofa on my super widescreen high-definition TV with surround sound, they make me marvel at the ingenuity of the human race. I find myself thinking that humans truly are the masters of our universe as we are able to capture the tiniest details of nature and transport them around the world through these invisible forces. Then at the same time, I start to realise that there are vast expanses of earth totally deserted in terms of mankind, but teeming with other life: huge **herds** of caribou roaming over arctic plains; **flocks** of migrating birds in their millions, taking hours to pass overhead; bizarre fish drifting in the dark depths of the ocean. It's awe-inspiring and I soon feel humbled.

Next up, you get the details of each animal's life – hunting their **prey**, defending themselves against predators, **foraging** for food in the trees and shrubs, putting on displays to attract a partner, **mating**, giving birth, **rearing** their young, dying. It's like watching six films rolled into one: a thriller, a tragedy, a comedy, a costume drama, a feel-good movie and an 18-certificate film!

Finally, what it all brings home is that we humans really have little more than these animals: we are born, we eat, we reproduce, we die. And it is us who have evolved and diversified in the most bizarre ways. Take these documentary programmes: why do we make them? We may think of them as entertainment or education, but really they are no more than an elaborate way of attracting a partner and / or getting food. We may be at the top of **the food chain** with no real **predators**, we may have miracles of technology like nature documentaries, but in the end it is the universal laws of nature that master us.

C Work in pairs. Discuss the following.
- Think of an example from the natural history world for each of the six types of film that the writer mentions.
- How far do you agree with the last paragraph of the article?
- What did you think of the article in general – is it depressing, silly, funny or what? Explain why.

D Complete the sentences below with the correct form of the words in **bold** in the article.
1 Its body is covered in sharp needles to protect itself from ....
2 It catches its .... by making a sticky web.
3 They swim back upstream to .... and reproduce.
4 I get really depressed seeing the old homeless guys .... for food in the rubbish bins.
5 It exists in a delicate ecosystem in the middle of the ....
6 There was a huge .... of seagulls on the beach.
7 We saw a .... of elephants when we were on safari.
8 The male incubates the eggs before they hatch and .... the young.

VOCABULARY Animals

A Look at the photos of animals on the left and find examples of the words in the box.

a hoof	legs	nostrils	a horn	a toe
scales	fur	a claw	teeth	a hump
a tail	feelers	a beak	a wing	a breast

B 🔊 8.4 Listen to two short descriptions and decide which of the animals in the photos are being described. What are the different parts of their bodies for?

C Match 1–10 to the correct endings.
1 It builds   a through the bark.
2 It can sense   b a high-pitched squeal.
3 It digs   c reserves of fat.
4 It blends   d its chest.
5 It can withstand   e a nest.
6 It gnaws   f into the background.
7 It puffs up   g the slightest movement.
8 It leaps out   h and snatches its prey.
9 It stores   i freezing temperatures.
10 It lets out   j down into the earth.

D Look at the photos again. Discuss these questions in pairs.
- Which of the animals look cute / horrible to you?
- Do they look like anything else – or remind you of anyone?
- Where do you think they live – in what kind of landscape and in what part of the world? Explain why.
- Why do you think they have adapted as they have?
- What do you think they might eat? Explain why.

READING 2

You are going to read about two of the animals shown opposite.

A Divide the class into two groups.
Group A: look at File 6 on page 154.
Group B: look at File 11 on page 156.

B Read the texts and find out about:
- the animal's habitat
- the animal's behaviour
- its unique features
- any threats it is facing
- conservation efforts.

C With someone from your group, check your answers and discuss any vocabulary you are not sure of.

D Work with a student from the other group. Discuss the two different animals, using the topics in exercise B. Decide which animal you prefer. Explain why.

SPEAKING

A Work in pairs. Decide which speaking activities below you prefer.
1 Discuss these questions.
- Have you seen any nature documentaries about animals recently? What animals did they show? Report everything you remember about what was said.
- What animal life did you study at school? Why? What aspect of nature did they illustrate?
- What animals do you know that:
  - are endangered species? Why are they endangered?
  - are unusual predators? How do they catch their prey?
  - are protected in your country? In what ways? Do you agree with this?
  - have unusual behaviour? Explain what they do.
  - look funny / cute / ugly / scary? Describe them.
  - make an unusual noise?
  - have a symbolic significance?
2 Do a web search for unusual animals. Choose an animal that looks interesting or strange. Find out more about it on the Internet. Tell your partner what you learnt.

B Work on your own. Spend a few minutes preparing for the activity. Then compare and discuss your ideas with your partner.

TWO MINUTES

Work in groups. You are going to give a short two-minute talk on one of the topics in the list below. Spend five minutes thinking about what you are going to say. Look back at your notes to check language if you like.

- A favourite book or film
- Lies and statistics
- War: what is it good for?
- Arguments I have had
- A weird animal
- What's on

Give each other marks out of ten for language, interest and clarity. Who got the most marks?

GAME

Work in pairs. Student A use *only* the green squares; student B use *only* the yellow squares. Spend five minutes looking at your questions and revising the answers. Then take turns tossing a coin: heads = move one of your squares; tails = move two of your squares. When you land on a square, your partner looks at the relevant page in the book to check your answers, but *you don't*! If you are right, move forward one square (but don't answer the question until your next turn). If you aren't right, your partner tells you the right answer and you miss a go. When you've finished the game, change colours and play again.

Start	**1** *Developing Conversations* p. 37: your partner will say sentences 1–6 in exercise A. You should agree / disagree and comment.	**2** *Native Speaker English* note p. 37: if you can say what the *Native Speaker English* note was and give an example, throw again.	**3** *Grammar* p. 38: write five different kinds of addition to the nouns in: *Bob Martin has written a book.*	**4** *Vocabulary* p. 38: say eight 'of' expressions.
5 *Native Speaker English* note p. 42: if you can say what the *Native Speaker English* note was and give an example, throw again.	**6** *Grammar* p. 43: say five things starting with *I wish* using three different structures.	**7** *Developing Conversations* p. 42: give five pieces of negative / private information starting with a different phrase each time.	**8 Miss a go!**	**9** *Vocabulary* p. 44: you partner will say six o the phrases in **bold**. Each time, say two more of the phrases i the same group.
10 *Vocabulary* p. 48: your partner will say the words in italics. You need to say nine of the synonyms.	**11 Miss a go!**	**12** *Developing Conversations* p. 49: your partner will say 1–6. You must respond with a question showing surprise or disbelief.	**13** *Vocabulary* p. 50: your partner will read sentences 1–9 apart from the words in **bold**. You need to say seven of the expressions.	**14** *Native Speaker Englis* note p. 52: if you can what the *Native Spea English* note was and an example, throw ag
15 *Vocabulary* p. 54: say ten of the words to describe scenery in exercise A.	**16** *Grammar* p. 143 [*Auxiliaries*]: your partner will read six sentences. in exercise 3. You should say the correct auxiliary.	**17** *Native Speaker English* note, p. 57: if you can say what the *Native Speaker English* note was and give an example, throw again.	**18** *Vocabulary* p. 59: say 12 of the body parts for different animals in exercise A.	**Finish**

For each of the activities below, work in groups of three. Use the *Vocabulary Builder* if you want to.

CONVERSATION PRACTICE

Choose one of the following *Conversation Practice* activities.

Night in, Night out p. 37
Conflict p. 43
Science and Research p. 49
Nature p. 55

Two of you should do the task. The third person should listen and then give a mark between 1 and 10 for the performance. Explain your decision. Then change roles.

ACT OR DRAW

One person should act or draw as many of these words as they can in three minutes. The others should try to guess the words. Do not speak while you are acting or drawing!

storm off	slam	yawn	a web
disguise	sulk	a herd	fuzzy
winding	grip	waves	tread
overlap	bark	a flock	insert
dispose	gory	snatch	hatch
plunge	dense	a siege	pluck

QUIZ

Answer as many of the questions as possible.
1 Why might you feel **rough**?
2 How do you feel if you are **mortified**?
3 Who's paid **royalties**?
4 Why might someone hold a **grudge**? What might they do?
5 What might be described as **cold-blooded**?
6 What happens if fighting **escalates**?
7 Who might **seize power**? How?
8 If something is **prevalent**, is there a little or a lot?
9 Say three things you might **devise**.
10 Who might have a **vested interest** in a war continuing?
11 Give an example of a **positive** and **negative** correlation.
12 Say three things you could **manipulate** and explain why.
13 What kind of landscape is **rugged**?
14 When might someone **butt in** and how would you feel?
15 What kind of animals **gnaw**?

COLLOCATIONS

Take turns to read out collocation lists from Unit 5 of the *Vocabulary Builder*. Where there is a '~', say '*blah*' instead. Your partner should guess as many words as they can. Each time you change roles, move to the next unit.

IDIOMS

Work in pairs. How many of these idioms can you explain? For how many can you give a true example?
1 He was off his head.
2 I was tossing and turning all night.
3 We were in stitches.
4 He was in bits.
5 We need to draw a line under it.
6 The writing's on the wall.
7 It was something else, it really was.
8 The research is full of holes.
9 You're putting words into my mouth.
10 I couldn't get a word in edgeways.
11 Don't beat about the bush.
12 Can you get to the point?
13 I got into the swing of it in the end.
14 I think he was taking the mickey.
15 We're on a slippery slope.

LISTENING

You are going to hear an interview with a photographer, Leila Flannagan, about her new book.

A ⟳ R 2.1 **Listen and complete the notes with 1–3 words.**

1 Her new book is called ....
2 She's found the response to the book quite ....
3 The book is a blend of wildlife photography and ....
4 By challenging and mixing different genres she believes you can ....
5 She started out photographing ....
6 The dam project caused unrest because it .... where a number of tribes lived and worked.
7 She found big projects were often corrupted by ....
8 She started taking photos of wildlife because it was also threatened by projects and as a means ....
9 Leila was frightened by a .... when she was photographing it.
10 She compares the iguana's behaviour to .... against projects.

B **Listen again to check.**

[... / 10]

GRAMMAR

A **Correct the mistake in each sentence.**

1 I do go to several shops, but the books I wanted weren't on sale anywhere.
2 It's an adventure story basing on his travel experiences.
3 I occasionally wish I'm doing something else, but generally I like my job.
4 The disease is believed that it has a genetic component.
5 We won't be gone that long, are we?
6 They're building a 35-storeys office block in the city centre, which is due to open next year.
7 I wish I'd said something, but I hadn't.
8 The device can withstand high temperatures after treated with the special paint.

[... / 8]

B **Complete the second sentence with 2–5 words and the word in bold so it has a similar meaning to the first.**

1 In the end, we threw out the toys as no-one used them.
   ended
   The toys .... as no-one used them.
2 The share price has shot up so it's a shame I sold them.
   only
   .... the shares – I might be rich!
3 Both Steve and I would love to visit India some day.
   so
   Steve's keen to visit India some day and ....
4 There are days I regret moving to this part of town.
   live
   I sometimes wish .... this part of town.
5 The dentist said he'd have to extract two teeth.
   taken
   Apparently, I'll have to ....
6 Paul Krugman, who's a professor of economics from the United States and has won a Nobel prize, is speaking.
   economist
   The Nobel .... Professor Paul Krugman is speaking.

[... / 12]

LANGUAGE PATTERNS

Complete the sentences with one word in each gap.

1 There is more violence than ...... on our streets.
2 I ...... know anyone who hasn't been affected by it.
3 With ...... this crime, I don't want to go out at night.
4 ...... ever, the government's failing to help.
5 I went to see ...... film you told me about.
6 It's so moving, it ...... me in floods of tears.

[... / 6]

PREPOSITIONS

Complete 1–8 with a preposition from the box.

around	from	of	out	for	into	on	to

1 They burst ...... laughter when I told them.
2 The book revolves ...... three main characters.
3 Their reaction was largely born ...... of fear.
4 The Queen is exempt ...... paying taxes.
5 It was a minor lapse ...... judgement. That's all.
6 They've imposed sanctions ...... the country.
7 Several businesses may be prosecuted ...... offering bribes to get planning permission.
8 The reduction in crime has been attributed ...... the improvement in the economy.

[... / 8]

OPPOSITES

Replace the words in *italics* with their opposite from the box.

stuffed	elaborate	flawed	adverse
sparse	fierce	arid	fertile

1 The soil is *barren*.
2 There's *abundant* information about it.
3 The army met with *minimal* opposition.
4 The findings are essentially *valid*.
5 I'm absolutely *starving*.
6 It's a *lush* landscape.
7 It has a number of *positive* effects.
8 It quite a *simple* process.

[... / 8]

MISSING WORDS

Complete each set of three sentences with one word.

1 The two warring factions ...... a truce over Christmas.
  The US has ...... for a boycott of all goods.
  I was ...... a geek at school just for wearing glasses!
2 The book tackles the ...... of domestic violence.
  He should ...... a clear condemnation of the attack.
  Have you seen the latest ...... of *Vogue* magazine?
3 The film has a very complicated ....
  They'd hatched a ...... to overthrow the government.
  If you ...... the points on a graph, you see the correlation.
4 There have been ...... of unrest because of the proposals.
  The device detects radio ...... from objects in space.
  My son always ...... goodbye to me from the window.
5 Their house is at the end of a dirt ....
  The president has a poor ...... record in government.
  We must ...... down the perpetrators of this atrocity and
  bring them to trial.

[... / 5]

VERBS

Match the verbs in the box with the collocations in 1–8.

carry out	claim	grasp	gain
diminish	draw	express	establish

1 ~ a commission / ~ a causal link / re-~ security
2 ~ dissent / ~ disbelief / struggle to ~ yourself
3 ~ conclusions / ~ condemnation / ~ a line under the past
4 ~ ground / ~ weight / ~ greater autonomy
5 ~ responsibility for the bombing / ~ victory / ~ innocence
6 ~ a census / ~ a massacre / ~ an investigation
7 ~ anxiety / her hearing's ~ed / the numbers are ~ing /
8 ~ in its claws / difficult to ~ / ~ the main idea

[... / 8]

FORMING WORDS

Complete the gaps with the correct form of the words in CAPITALS.

Over the years of the conflict, there have
been hundreds of [1].......................... as well   FATAL
as many injured. Many have also had to
[2].......................... flee their homes because   FRANTIC
of death threats, so it is very welcome
news to hear that [3].......................... talks   EXPLORE
aimed at bringing about peace have
been successful and a ceasefire has been
established. There's a long way to go
before a final [4].......................... is reached   SETTLE
and previous [5].......................... have failed,   RESOLVE
but it seems that this time things really
might be different. The new President
is already dealing with some of the
[6].......................... problems such as police   UNDERLIE
[7].......................... .   HARASS

[... / 7]

VOCABULARY

Complete the book review by choosing the correct words A–C.

Marjorie Spackman is a legendary figure in the world of
publishing. At the height of her powers, the company
she set up [1]...... sales of over a billion dollars in books
and magazines, before she was pushed out by a
hostile takeover and amid rumours of alcoholism. *Full
of Spine* [2]...... her life from its humble beginnings in
Queensland, Australia, to wealth and riches as a global
businesswoman, with surprising humour. She also has
great [3]...... into an industry which changed immensely
over her 50-year career. In one amusing episode she
recounts how far she went to persuade a top TV host
to [4]...... one of her books for a reading club. Although
Spackman [5]...... admits her personal life was at times
'chaotic', she claims the boardroom difficulties she
suffered were far more [6]...... to dissent about future
policy and the fact she was a woman in a world still
dominated by men. This is a fascinating [7]...... which will
undoubtedly [8]...... to a broad range of readers .

1 A grew   B raised   C boasted
2 A traces   B centres   C treats
3 A findings   B insight   C breakthrough
4 A endorse   B recall   C condone
5 A desperately B highly   C freely
6 A down   B up   C in
7 A remembrance B memory   C memoir
8 A enjoy   B appeal   C spark

[... / 8]

[Total ... /80]

09 WORK

In this unit, you learn how to:
- describe what people do at work
- signal that you are making deductions
- talk about the nature of work
- discuss terms and conditions of employment
- discuss issues related to dismissal and tribunals

Grammar
- Continuous forms

Vocabulary
- Company jobs and tasks
- Adverb–adjective collocations
- The world of work

Reading:
- *The Living Dead*

Listening
- The first day at work
- Underemployment
- Five news stories about work

VOCABULARY Company jobs and tasks

A Work in groups. Discuss these questions.
- Do you know anyone who works for a company? What do they do?
- Do they enjoy it? Why? / Why not?

B Discuss what people do in a company if they are:
- a rep / a CEO / a PA.
- in HR / in IT / in R&D / in admin.

C Complete the tasks in 1–10 with the words in the box.

troubleshoot	draw up	place	schedule	oversee
come up with	process	input	network	liaise

1 I have to .... information into the database.
2 We maintain the network and .... any problems.
3 Shall we .... a meeting for tomorrow?
4 I .... closely with designers to implement our strategy.
5 I .... ads in different magazines and organise product launches – that kind of thing.
6 Any invoices or expense claims, I'll .... them.
7 I .... any contracts and deal with all contractual issues.
8 I have to .... and entertain a lot to attract new business.
9 I .... everything, making sure everyone meets their deadlines and stays on budget.
10 I .... the strategy and provide leadership and then delegate the work to others.

D Work in pairs. Discuss these questions.
- Which tasks from exercise C would you be good / bad at? Why?
- Which things have you done at work (or elsewhere)?

LISTENING

You are going to hear a conversation with someone being shown around on their first day in a new job.

A 🔊 9.1 Listen and take notes on what you find out about:
- Tasneem
- Bianca
- Mary
- Harry
- the photocopier
- the company

B Work in pairs. Compare your notes.

C Listen again and try to write down four new words or expressions. Compare what you wrote with a partner and then check in the audioscript on page 170.

D Work in pairs. Discuss these questions.
- What was your first day at work / school like?
- Can you remember what you did?
- Do you like the way Tasneem shows Harry around? Why? / Why not?
- Do you think it's OK to jokingly make negative comments about colleagues? Do you ever do it? What about?
- What's good / bad about open-plan offices?

NATIVE SPEAKER ENGLISH

raring to go

If we say we're *raring to go*, it means we're ready and very eager to start doing something. We also use *raring* with some other verbs.

So, raring to go, then?
He was raring to get back to school.
I'm raring to have a go.

DEVELOPING CONVERSATIONS
Deductions

> We often indicate we are making a deduction based on what someone says by adding *then* at the end. The intonation often sounds like we're asking a question and needs a reply.

You were eager to get here, then.
I'm not the only one who's being taken on now, then.
She's not in the office that much, then.

A Can you remember from *Listening* why the speakers made the deductions in the explanation box above? What were the replies? Check in audioscript 9.1 on page 170.

B Take turns saying 1-6 below. Your partner should make deductions with *then*. You should reply.
1 I was in Bulgaria with work last week.
2 My boyfriend says I should slow down.
3 You don't want to get on the wrong side of him.
4 I'm going to have to cover for him again.
5 I'm going to be rushed off my feet all week.
6 I liaise closely with our reps in Russia.

GRAMMAR Continuous forms

> Continuous forms use *be* + *-ing*. We can use them to talk about the past, present or future. They can combine with perfect forms (*have been doing*), passives (*is being done*), *is supposed to* and modals (*will be doing*, *should be doing*, etc.).

A Complete the sentences from *Listening* with the correct continuous forms.
1 I .... actually .... in the coffee bar over the road for the last hour. (hang around)
2 I should've said, we .... alongside each other. (work)
3 I .... just .... one of them to schedule a time for us all to meet when you arrived. (email)
4 I'm not the only one who .... now, then. (take on)
5 Three or four more .... in the next couple of weeks. (join)
6 She .... probably .... all kind and helpful now, but wait till you get started. (be)
7 To be honest, you .... that much to do with them in your day-to-day dealings. (not have)
8 I .... about moving out there for a while and I happened to get the house just before I got this job. (think)

B 🔊 9.2 Listen and check your answers.

C Work in pairs. Discuss why you think the continuous form is used in each sentence.

▶ Need help? Read the grammar reference on page 144.

CONVERSATION PRACTICE

You are going to have similar conversations to the one in *Listening*.

A Draw a rough plan of the place where you work / study. Then work in pairs and:
- explain who works where and what they do.
- explain what the people are like.
- explain any rules or things workers need to have.
- explain any machines you might need to operate.
- warn about anything odd or temperamental.

B Now choose one of your places and work with another pair. Welcome the other pair and 'show them around' your place. Introduce them to different people (role-played by your partner). The other pair should ask questions and make deductions.

VOCABULARY Adverb–adjective collocations

A Look at the adverbs in *italics*. They are all possible. In each sentence, choose the one you think is most true.
1 Most jobs are *mind-numbingly / largely / pretty* boring.
2 Gardening is *technically / physically / not terribly* demanding.
3 Nursing is *financially / immensely / fairly* rewarding.
4 Teaching kids is *emotionally / utterly / quite* draining.
5 You have to be *fiercely / very / quite* competitive to get ahead in business.
6 IT is not *remotely / mildly / inherently* interesting.
7 The public sector is *highly / reasonably / not particularly* efficient.
8 I'm *blissfully / relatively / not entirely* happy with what I'm doing now.

B Work in pairs and compare your choices. Discuss any differences.

C Use each of the eight adjectives from exercise A plus a connected adverb of your choice to tell a partner about things you have done – or something you believe to be true.

READING

You are going to read a true story from a book on management called *The Living Dead* by David Bolchover.

A Before you read, discuss what you think the theme of the book might be, given the title.

B Read Part 1 of the story on the opposite page and discuss these questions with a partner.
1 What has happened to David (the author)?
2 How does his friend feel about it?
3 Why do you think David feels the system (of work) has cheated him? Would you feel that way in his shoes?
4 How do you think the situation came about?

C Read Part 2 and find out:
1 how the situation came about.
2 how it ended.
3 who 'the living dead' are.

D Match the words from the text in 1–10 to the endings they were used with.
1 my vitality   new skills
2 acquire   the question
3 sponsor   to someone else
4 spark   my interest
5 get the most   out of its investment
6 his mind   was drifting off
7 set   me
8 pass this on   me redundant
9 which begs   drained away
10 make   the wheels in motion

E Work in pairs. Re-tell the story using the expressions in exercise D and your own words.

F Work in pairs. Discuss these questions.
- Do you think what happened was a freak occurrence?
- Who was most to blame for the situation? Why?
- What lessons can you take from the story?

LISTENING

You are going to hear a very brief summary of the lessons David Bolchover takes from his experience.

A 🔊 9.3 Listen and answer the three questions in *Reading* exercise F.

B Listen again. Then discuss these questions.
1 What statistics are connected to the numbers below?
- one in three
- nine million
- two-thirds
- 8.3 hours a week
- 14.6%
- up to 20 personal e-mails a day
- 24%
2 Why does he say small companies are better?

C Work in groups. Discuss these questions.
- Do you agree with David Bolchover's ideas? Why? / Why not?
- What would you have done in his situation?
- Have you heard of any instances of incompetence in the workplace? What happened?
- How do people get to the top at work? Does it depend on the industry? In what way?
- Which person you know has the best work–life balance?

PART 1

I'm sitting in a café with my friend Paul. He lives in the States now and I haven't had the chance to chat with him for months.

"Now let me get this straight" – he leans forward on the edge of his seat. "Your company has forgotten about you? You're on the payroll, but you've got nothing to do. And how long did you say this has been going on?"

"Six months."

Paul leans further forward. It's clear he's not going to drop the subject.

"They pay you a full salary for sitting on your backside at home, apart from the times when you're not at home, but out and about with your mates or travelling round Europe to watch Man United play in the Champions League?"

"No, you've missed a bit; you've forgotten the rugby and the …"

"You bastard!"

All the conversations I've had about this period of my life contain those two words. There's a depressing inevitability about it, even though I always enjoy the underlying admiration which I perceive in their voice for having screwed the system. Except I wasn't screwing the system; the system was screwing me.

PART 2

I'd joined Giant – a big multinational insurance company – in June of 1997. The job was financially rewarding, but I quickly started to feel restless as some days I did nothing apart from make the occasional call. The Internet still hadn't taken off, so I spent hours staring at the wall, drifting off into my own little world, while all my vitality slowly drained away. Every morning, I'd get up full of life, and every evening, I'd return with my shoulders slumped, my head bent and my mind numb. I was joining the terrible world of the living dead.

I decided that if I was going to get ahead, I needed to acquire new skills. It was clear that in my current post I wasn't exactly going to race to the top of the insurance world, so I decided to persuade Giant to sponsor me to take a year off to do an MBA in return for me committing to the company afterwards. I presented the idea to my boss. He was about to retire and was looking for an easy life so he quickly agreed and, with his backing, the process was a formality.

The MBA filled me with renewed energy and optimism. After six months, I went back to the office to see my boss in readiness for my return on October 4th. I explained how the course had sparked my interest in management and business strategy. I suggested it was pointless me going back to what I had been doing and that instead Giant might think about a suitable post that would get the most out of its investment. It was a good speech full of common sense, but from the dull look in my boss's eyes, I could've been talking to an Italian about cricket. You could tell his mind was drifting off to another place rather than focusing on a job which could benefit both me and the company. As a result, I consulted human resources. The woman I spoke to nodded and sounded interested and said she'd set the wheels in motion.

However, months past and I heard nothing. I was beginning to worry, not to say get angry, at the lack of communication so I arranged an appointment with someone higher up in HR. It didn't go well and on reflection I can imagine what he was thinking. "I've got this guy who's a pain in the neck. We owe him a job, but he doesn't want to go back to his old post and there's no point in him going there on a temporary basis. It'd be better if I just passed this on to someone else to sort out before he makes me look like a fool."

The 4th of October came. Nothing. A few days later, the guy from HR put me in contact with a guy in finance, for whom I worked on a project at home, but which he quickly dropped. A few weeks went by. Nothing. Well, nothing, apart from October the 26th when a nice big juicy pay cheque dropped through my letterbox.

In mid-November, the finance guy rang and told me to see this guy Nick, who was brilliant at assessing people and placing them in the post which would enthuse them most. It sounded impressive, but the results weren't. After scheduling some meetings that didn't go anywhere, he came to the conclusion that basically people with MBAs didn't fit into the insurance sector, which rather begs the question: why on earth did Giant – an insurance company – agree to fund me!

The months passed and I decided I should find a job elsewhere. Ironically, I was just about to phone my department to let them know I was leaving when HR called, inviting me to a meeting with the big boss. They were going to make me redundant! Of course! It's only fair that after being with the company for over two years and having done nothing for the previous ten months, I should get a redundancy payment and one-month's notice to leave. As I left the meeting, the big boss accompanied me to the lift. He uncomfortably tried to start some small talk. "So … er … what have been doing for the last few months?"

All I could think of was a variety of football matches, sunny days walking round London zoo, afternoons in the cinema. However, instead I heard myself saying "Obviously, it's been a difficult time for me and my family."

SPEAKING

A **Read the Fact File below. Then discuss these questions.**

- Which facts surprise you? Why?
- Is there anything you don't find surprising? Why not?
- How do you think your country compares in terms of all the facts and figures below?

> **FACT FILE**
> - A large majority of British workers don't consider taking stationery home from work to be stealing.
> - Nearly one in 20 British workers confessed to taking valuable items such as mobile phones or computer hardware.
> - 37% of American workers prefer to work in a uniform. Even more – 85 %– prefer a precise dress code, as opposed to just 16% who feel unaffected by their work clothes.
> - German women get 14 weeks' maternity leave at full pay, six weeks of which can be taken before birth; they also get a further 12 months at 67% of pay.
> - In Spain, men and women get 15 days' paid leave when they get married.
> - Japanese companies spend approximately 40 billion dollars a year entertaining clients. That's almost the national GDP of Bulgaria!
> - Retirement age in Malaysia is 55 for private sector workers and 58 for those in the civil service. The government is planning to raise the age substantially.
> - The average monthly salary of employed people in Guinea Bissau, West Africa, is around $15.
> - There are between 15 and 30 million people around the world working in forced labour and slavery.
> - Turks work the most hours per week in Europe – an average of 54 – while the Swedes work fewest hours – 38.5 per week.

VOCABULARY The world of work

A **Complete the sentences with the pairs of words in the box. You may need to change the order of the words.**

> | | |
> |---|---|
> | crèche – childcare | compassionate leave – grateful |
> | opposition – raise | voluntary redundancy – cuts |
> | perk – subsidised | early retirement – pension |
> | tribunal – dismissal | collective bargaining – union |
> | quit – notice | crackdown – absenteeism |

1 If I want to _quit_, I basically just have to give my boss a week's _notice_.
2 We all get _subsidised_ travel, which is a nice _perk_ of the job.
3 When my father died, I was granted a week's _compassionate leave_, which I'm eternally _grateful_ for.
4 We have a _crèche_ at work where I can leave my daughter, which makes _childcare_ much easier.
5 My dad was planning to take _early retirement_, but he basically can't afford to live on the state _pension_.
6 We're losing so much money because of _crackdown_ that we've decided to launch a bit of _absenteeism_ and start demanding sick notes.
7 He was sacked last year, but he took his employers to a _tribunal_ and was awarded compensation on the grounds of unfair _dismissal_.
8 The government promised to _raise_ the legal minimum wage, but they're facing a lot of _opposition_ from business leaders.
9 We were facing swingeing _cuts_ across the department and in the end I just decided to take _voluntary redundancy_ instead.
10 I'm a _union_ member, so any pay rises or whatever are always negotiated through _collective bargaining_.

B **Cover the sentences in exercise A. With a partner, see if you can remember the verbs that were used with these nouns**

> | | |
> |---|---|
> | • a week's notice | • compassionate leave |
> | • early retirement | • the state pension |
> | • a crackdown | • a tribunal |
> | • compensation | • the legal minimum wage |
> | • a lot of opposition | • voluntary redundancy |

C **Look back at exercise A to check your ideas. Can you find any other new collocations?**

D **Work in groups. Discuss these questions.**

- What other perks can you think of for different kinds of jobs?
- Under what circumstances do you think it's OK to grant workers compassionate leave?
- Are crèches common in workplaces in your country? Do you think they're a good idea?
- What's the state pension like in your country?
- Why do you think there is so much absenteeism? What's the best way to tackle the problem?
- Do you think things like pay rises are best negotiated individually or through collective bargaining?

LISTENING

You are going to hear five news reports related to work.

A 🎧 9.4 **Listen and match one of the statements in a–f to each report. There is one extra statement you will not use.**
   a Someone neglected to pass on relevant information.
   b Traditional ways of working are under threat.
   c Someone went to prison.
   d A perk has been cut.
   e Someone reported a colleague.
   f Statutory rights have been enthusiastically embraced.

B **Compare your answers with a partner.**

C **In pairs, re-tell as much of the five stories as you can, using these words.**
   1 call centre – CCTV footage – £150 – retraining
   2 mourn – 137 days – tribunal – injuries – compensation
   3 full entitlement – divorce rate – birth rate – role models
   4 seats – a thousand pounds – uniforms – theft – fares
   5 a burden – retirement – society – leisure – incentives

D **Listen again and read the audioscript on page 171 to check your ideas.**

E **Work in groups. Discuss these questions.**
   • How do feel about what happened to the call centre worker and the postman? Why?
   • Do you agree that men taking more paternity leave is socially beneficial? Why? / Why not?
   • What do you think of the budget airline's decision to ban the charging of mobile phones?
   • Does your country have an ageing population?
   • Do you think there's much ageism in society?

LANGUAGE PATTERNS

Write the sentences in your language. Translate them back into English. Compare your English to the original.

They insisted he be awarded compensation,
The CEO demanded that he be kept up-to-date on the issue.
They've asked that they be given more time to look into it.
The judge insisted that he repay the cost of the biscuits.
The firm requested that she pay for all her training.

SPEAKING

A **Read about the three cases that came before an employment tribunal below. Decide what you think should be done in each case.**

> A young woman who did voluntary work experience for an accountancy firm run by a multi-millionaire businessman is demanding a million euros' compensation after – as she sees it – being forced out of her job. The 25-year-old claims she was the victim of sexual harassment after she was bombarded with obscene text messages and e–mails from the boss, all of which she has kept. The boss of the firm claims the woman was a willing recipient of his attentions.

> A man is claiming unfair dismissal after he was fired from the branch of the supermarket chain he had worked in for nine years for using his discount card in another branch. The man claims he had been off work sick and was unaware that changes had been made to the use of the card. Shortly after breaking the news of his sacking to his family, his wife suffered a stroke and died. The company insists the man was guilty of deliberate abuse of staff privileges.

> A 54-year-old nurse claims her employers had discriminated against her on grounds of her faith, after she was taken off front-line duties for refusing to remove the cross she wears around her neck. The woman feels her bosses tried to prevent her from expressing her religious beliefs. The hospital, however, says its actions were motivated by health and safety concerns and that its dress code prohibits staff wearing any type of necklace.

B **Work in groups. Discuss what you think should be done in each case. Try to reach unanimous decisions.**

C **Have you heard any other stories involving employment tribunals? When? What happened?**

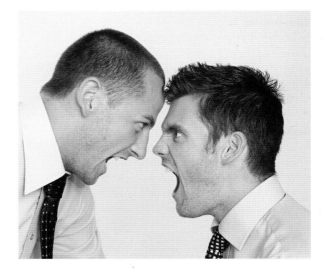

10 HEALTH AND ILLNESS

In this unit, you learn how to
- describe different medical and surgical procedures
- show you are not being exact when describing things
- describe medical conditions and their symptoms
- make comments about past and present situations

Grammar
- Modal verbs

Vocabulary
- Operations
- Body actions
- Medical conditions

Reading:
- East meets West
- Two different medical conditions

Listening
- Two surgical procedures
- A mindfulness experience
- A miracle cure

SPEAKING

A **Work in pairs. Discuss these questions.**
- What do you know about the different kinds of surgery in the box below? What's each one for and when might each be used?

reconstructive surgery	exploratory surgery
cosmetic surgery	keyhole surgery
experimental surgery	laser surgery

- Have you heard of any surgical innovations in recent years? What do they involve?
- Do you know of any other recent medical advances?

LISTENING

You are going to hear two conversations about surgical procedures.

A ◐ **10.1 Listen and answer these questions.**
1 What kind of procedures do they discuss?
2 What did each procedure involve?
3 Is any further treatment required?

B **Listen again and decide if 1–10 are true or false.**

Conversation 1
1 Part of his eye had to be cut open.
2 He was given an injection to anaesthetise him.
3 He took further medication to ease the pain.
4 His eyes feel completely fine now.
5 She is not tempted to have the operation herself.

Conversation 2
6 The pain in her jaw a week ago was very severe.
7 She's sure her daughter damaged her tooth.
8 Measures were taken to ensure the tooth doesn't get infected.
9 She was unconscious during the whole procedure.
10 It's going to cost her over £500.

C **Add the verbs in the box to the nouns they were used with in the conversations. Then look at the audioscript on page 171 to check.**

administer	drill	recover	take
change	numb	slice	thrash

1 .... your eyes
2 .... a flap in the front of the eye
3 .... the anaesthetic
4 .... from the operation
5 .... a knock
6 .... her arms and legs around
7 .... her nappy
8 .... a hole in the back of the tooth

D **Work in pairs. Discuss these questions.**
- Which of the two procedures described would you rather undergo? Why?
- Which aspect of each procedure sounds worst to you?
- Have you ever heard of any side effects or complications that can occur with either procedure?

NATIVE SPEAKER ENGLISH

in a matter of
When we are talking about periods of time, we often use *in a matter of (seconds, minutes,* etc.) instead of *in only a few.*

It's over in a matter of minutes.
The operation gets rid of all your fat in a matter of hours!
He went from feeling slightly unwell to being critically ill in a matter of days.

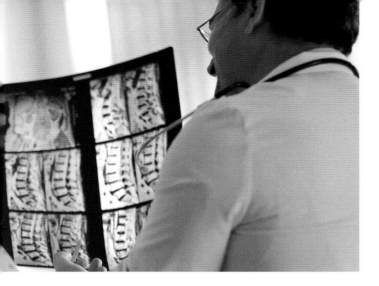

VOCABULARY Operations

A Put each group of words into the most likely order they happen, starting with the words in **bold**.

1 **suffered third degree burns** / had to wait for the scarring to heal / was rushed to hospital / had a skin graft / was put on a drip

2 **had to fast for twelve hours** / was given an anaesthetic / had stitches removed / gums bled a lot and cheeks swelled up / had my wisdom teeth removed

3 **was diagnosed with kidney disease** / had a transplant / was put on a waiting list / took part in a rehabilitation programme / finally found a donor

4 **severed three fingers** / regained feeling in the fingers / underwent extensive physiotherapy / had the fingers sewn back on / lost a lot of blood

5 **broke his leg in three places** / got a prosthetic limb / had part of the leg amputated / got an infection / had an operation to insert metal pins

6 **found a lump** / had a relapse / the cancer went into remission / had an operation to have it removed / had it diagnosed as malignant / underwent chemotherapy

B Try to memorise the words. Then test each other.
Student A: say an expression in bold.
Student B: try to say the rest of the words in order.

C Work in pairs. Discuss these questions.
- What might have caused each of the six situations in exercise A?
- Which of the six kinds of operation / procedure do you think is the most remarkable? Why?

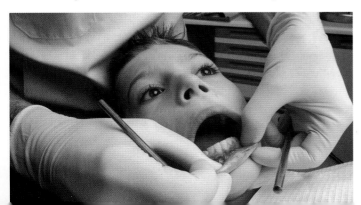

DEVELOPING CONVERSATIONS
Vague language

> We use *kind of / sort of* before verbs to show we can't find the exact word we want and are using the next closest word.
> You *kind of* have to watch as the whole thing happens.
> ....
> We add *or so* to numbers and periods of time to show we are not being exact.
> About a week *or so* ago
> ....
> We use *somehow* before some verbs and after others to show we do not really know how something happened.
> He told me that one of my teeth had died *somehow*.
> ....
> We use *some kind of* before nouns to show we're not sure what kind exactly. We can add *or something* after the noun.
> He stuck *some kind of* temporary filling in.
> Is it an injection *or something*?

A Make the sentences less exact using words from above.

1 I asked for a second opinion, but they just ignored me.
2 He used bleach solution on my teeth.
3 It should cost about 100 euros.
4 They told me that a build-up was damaging blood vessels in my brain.
5 He managed to slice the end off one of his fingers!
6 They use a tiny little knife to make the incision.
7 It was quite a traumatic birth, but they managed to deliver her after about an hour.
8 They just glued the skin back together again using clear plastic tape.

B Work in pairs. Use vague language to describe what you know – or imagine – about how the following work.
- surgery to relieve lower back pain
- hip replacement
- liposuction
- tooth whitening

CONVERSATION PRACTICE

A Think of some medical or surgical experiences that you – or people you know – have had. Plan what you want to say about them.

B Discuss your experiences with some other students.

SPEAKING

Work in pairs. Discuss the questions below. Choose one of the answers or give your own. Ask each other one more additional question.

1 How well do you deal with pain and illness?
   a I tend to get quite grumpy and moan a lot.
   b By and large, I just get on with things and don't complain.
2 How would you describe your general demeanour?
   a I'd say I'm pretty cheerful most of the time.
   b I have a tendency for mood swings.
3 How well do you deal with stress?
   a To be frank, not so well. I have a tendency to blow up.
   b Generally speaking, I'm pretty cool under pressure.
4 What do you do if you have negative feelings?
   a I will often dwell on things and it sets off depression.
   b I shrug them off quite quickly.
5 How fit are you?
   a I have a bit of a belly, and I get out of breath easily.
   b I'm quite fit, but not supple. I find it difficult to bend and crouch down.
6 How does diet affect your mood?
   a A lot. I take dietary supplements so my body's always in balance
   b I don't think about it. I eat whatever I like.

READING

You are going to read an article about 'Eastern' and 'Western' medicine.

A **Before you read, discuss what you know about any of the following**
   - mindfulness and meditation
   - depression
   - life expectancy and well-being
   - the worried well
   - Traditional Chinese Medicine

B **Now read the article and compare your ideas with what it says about the topics.**

C **Use as many of the following sentence starters about the article as you can to write sentences that are true for you. Then discuss your ideas with a partner.**
   - I already knew this bit about ...
   - I was interested in the fact that ...
   - I was surprised that ...
   - I find it difficult to believe that ...
   - It's very true that ...
   - If this was in my country, ...
   - I didn't really understand this bit about ...

East meets West

Mindfulness is a meditation therapy that has been gaining ground in mental health circles as evidence builds up of its potential in dealing with a range of health problems, from reducing recurrent bouts of depression and anxiety to possibly strengthening immune systems.

When people suffer from depression, negative moods become accompanied by negative thoughts such as "I am a failure" as well as physical symptoms such as fatigue. While these usually all disappear once the episode has passed or a patient takes medication, an association has been established in the brain between the various symptoms. As a result, a mood swing caused by something relatively trivial such as miserable weather or being laid up in bed can actually trigger the same combination of symptoms leading to a recurrence of the depression. The more this happens, the more likely it is to recur, making it more resistant to drug treatment.

Mindfulness-based therapies allow sufferers to break this downward spiral by getting them to first notice these patterns of thought, but to then refocus and anchor their minds in the present instead of dwelling on the past or worrying about the future. Furthermore, it has physical effects: the heart beats slower, muscles loosen and it can even change the structure of the brain. Mindfulness is believed to spark new neural connections and studies have shown that areas of the brain associated with emotional regulation were bigger in people who had practised meditation regularly over five years.

Mindfulness, which is drawn from Eastern Buddhist philosophy and practice, is an example of the increasing interest being taken by so-called "Western" medicine in "Eastern" medical practices. Western medicine has been incredibly successful in improving mortality. Over the course of the 20th century, life expectancy doubled in developed countries. In Austria, for example, in 1900 females at birth could expect to die before they were 40, whereas now they typically live past 80. We have eradicated many infectious diseases and survival rates for chronic degenerative diseases are ever increasing. However, these figures can also hide a truth: while we are successfully putting off death, we are living longer in sickness rather

than in health. And Western medical practice is often less effective at dealing with long-term illness and well-being. Unless you are in excruciating pain or have something life-threatening, Western doctors often have little to offer. Indeed, many dismiss patients with low-level complaints as "the worried well". Eastern medicine such as Traditional Chinese Medicine (TCM), on the other hand, is much more focused on maintaining good health and, apparently, through acupuncture, herbal remedies and massage is more successful in relieving conditions such as eczema, back pain, migraine and stress.

TCM is underpinned by a philosophy that there exists a harmony between mind, body and the environment. It aims to "rebalance" patients and unblock natural energy flows called "chi". Such quasi-religious descriptions can often be met with scepticism within a science-based medical profession wanting evidence from randomised trials. The experience of mindfulness proponents highlights how hard that scepticism can be to break down. Firstly, research can be costly with little financial incentive to drug companies if the results prove positive. Secondly, the results can be difficult to quantify or randomise: how do you measure well-being or have a "blind" control group for meditation? Finally, even when positive results are gained, there remains resistance and training issues. Recently, a leading mental health charity had to run a campaign to raise awareness of mindfulness and to demand greater access to courses, which remains very limited, some six years after it was approved as a treatment in the UK.

Write the sentences in your language. Translate them back into English. Compare your English to the original.

The more this happens, the more likely it is to recur.
The longer you leave it, the more difficult it'll be.
The richer the country, the healthier the people tend to be.
The older people get, the more prone they are to high blood pressure.

VOCABULARY Body actions

A **Why might the following actions happen / be done?**
- your mind drifts or wanders
- your belly rises and falls
- your heart beats fast
- your body shudders
- wipe your forehead
- raise your eyebrows
- raise your hand
- clutch your chest
- click your fingers
- drop your head
- shrug your shoulders
- clench your fist
- support your back
- stretch your legs
- flutter your eyelashes

B **Work in pairs. What part of the body do you use for the actions in the box?**

kick	stroke	clap	pat	scratch
sniff	blink	hug	spit	crouch
glare	frown	grin	nod	punch

C **Test each other. Take turns acting out the different actions in exercise A and B. Your partner should say the word(s).**

LISTENING

You are going to hear a mindfulness exercise.

A 🔊 10.2 **Listen and do what the speaker tells you to do.**

B **Work in groups. Discuss these questions.**
- How well did you follow the instructions?
- Did you like the experience? Why? / Why not?
- Can you think of anyone it might help? Who? Why?
- What other alternative / complementary therapies do you know about? Are they popular where you live? Why? / Why not? What do you think of them?
- Is your healthcare free or subsidised? Does it include complementary healthcare? Are treatments rationed in any way?

SPEAKING

Work in groups. Discuss these questions.
- Which of the conditions in the box below have you heard of?
- What do you know about each one? Think about: causes, symptoms and the problems they cause sufferers.
- What do you know about the ways they are treated?

autism	narcolepsy	migraines	Tourette's syndrome	leprosy	bulimia nervosa
diabetes	post-traumatic stress	vitiligo	gluten intolerance	asthma	eczema

READING

You are going to read about two of the conditions in the box above.

A **Divide the class into two groups.**
Group A: read the text below.
Group B: read the text in File 13 on page 157.

B **As you read, try to find out:**
- what the symptoms are
- what problems it causes sufferers
- how many people it affects
- what causes the condition
- how it is treated.

THE COLOUR OF PREJUDICE

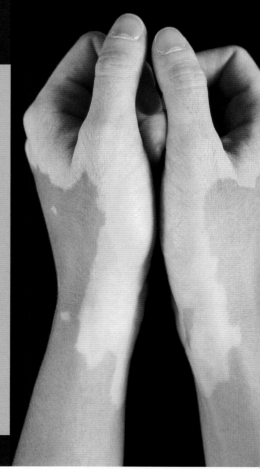

Vitiligo is a chronic skin condition that affects pigmentation, frequently resulting in the development of white patches on the body. These are most commonly found on areas that receive a lot of sunlight, such as your hands, face, neck and so on. The disease affects at least one person in every hundred in countries throughout the world. For obvious reasons, the disorder is more visible — though no more common — in those with darker natural skin tones.

For the most part, the symptoms themselves are the most serious aspect of the condition, though there are often attendant psychological pressures stemming from sufferers seeing their bodies as unhealthy, unattractive or in some way disabled.

The causes of vitiligo are still the subject of much research and debate, but it is generally classified as an auto-immune disorder, which means that the body mistakes it own cells as intruders and declares war on "enemy" cells. In this case, the malfunctioning immune system attacks melanocytes, the cells which produce the pigment responsible for skin colour.

There is currently a wide variety of treatments available, ranging from light therapy to oral medication and strong sunscreen. More recently, skin grafts have also started to be used. To counter the psychological side effects of the disease, people are generally encouraged to see a psychologist to help with feelings of depression or isolation.

C **With a person from your group, check your answers and discuss any vocabulary you are not sure of.**

D **Work with a student from the other group. Discuss the two different medical conditions, using the topics in exercise B. Decide which condition you think is worse. Explain why.**

E **Choose two new words from your text that you think are useful. Explain the words to your partner.**

VOCABULARY Medical conditions

A Replace the words in *italics* with synonyms in the box.

block up	passed on	stick to
exacerbated	relieved	swollen
genetic	long-term	tiredness
fail	shortage	triggered

1 It causes your motor skills to *deteriorate* over time.
2 It can be *aggravated* by forceful and repetitive use of the hand.
3 She suffers from *chronic* pain in her lower back.
4 If you don't treat it, it can lead to extreme *fatigue*.
5 Most of the symptoms can be *eased* by avoiding caffeine and cutting down on alcohol.
6 It's usually only *transmitted* to other people as a result of direct person-to-person contact over a period of time.
7 It runs in the family. It's a *hereditary* disorder.
8 Sufferers are supposed to *maintain* a strict diet.
9 They think it's probably *set off* by stress.
10 He's basically suffering from a *lack* of red blood cells.
11 It basically causes the belly to become *bloated*.
12 It causes the arteries in the heart to slowly *clog*.

B With a partner, discuss what conditions you think sentences 1–12 above might describe.

LISTENING

You are going to hear a news extract about a young child who has been suffering from a rare medical condition.

A 🎧 10.3 Listen and answer these questions.
1 What problems did the condition cause the child?
2 How did the doctors respond to his problems?
3 How did his parents respond?
4 What was the result of their research?
5 What implications might their research have?

B Can you remember which nouns in the extract these adjectives were used to describe? Work in pairs to compare your ideas. Then listen again to check.

dedicated	rare	permanent
painstaking	painful	weak
vulnerable	countless	alternative
vital	successful	average

C Work in pairs. Discuss these questions.
- Why do you think it was left to Dexter's parents to find a cure?
- How would you feel now if you were them and what would you do next?
- Have you heard any similar stories? What happened?
- Do you know anyone who uses alternative therapies? What kind? What for? How do you feel about these kinds of therapy?

GRAMMAR Modal verbs

> We often use the modal verbs *should, could, might / may, must, can't* and *would* to comment on the past. The form is modal verb + *have* + past participle (or + been -ing).

A Complete the sentences from this unit by choosing the correct form.
1 I *should've / might've* got it done years ago, really!
2 He said I *must've / should've* taken a knock.
3 I'm not sure, but I think it *must've / might've* been my daughter, actually, thrashing her arms and legs around.
4 That *mustn't / can't* have been much fun!
5 The doctors *can't have / should've* considered Dexter's condition as thoroughly as they *would've / should've* done.
6 They clearly *should've / might've* looked into other options.
7 We *could've / can't have* come to our own conclusions sooner and that way Dexter *wouldn't / shouldn't* have had to go through all this trauma.

B 🎧 10.4 Listen to the extracts and check your ideas.

C Work in pairs. Discuss the differences in the pairs of sentences below, and why different forms are used.
1 a That must've been nice.
   b That can't have been very nice.
2 a It must've been because of all the fatty food.
   b It might've been because of all the stress.
3 a I couldn't have done anything about it even if I'd tried.
   b The doctors couldn't have tried that hard.
4 a He shouldn't have driven off after the crash.
   b He shouldn't have been driving so fast!
5 a It must've been hurting for him to go to the dentist!
   b It must've hurt, having those teeth out.
6 a She must've picked up the infection in hospital.
   b She picked up the infection in hospital.
7 a He can't have been feeling well or he would've come.
   b He can't be feeling well or he'd come.

▶ Need help? Read the grammar reference on page 145.

SPEAKING

A Work in groups. Discuss these questions.
- Do you know anyone who suffers from a medical condition? What kind?
- What causes it and how does it affect their life?
- Can you think of any famous people who have had to struggle against a particular condition or against disability?
- How are doctors and nurses generally thought of in your country? Are they fairly treated?

11 PLAY

SPEAKING

A **Work in groups. Ask each other these questions to find out.**
· Who's the fittest person in your group?
· Who's the best swimmer / runner / tennis player?
· Who's the biggest sports fan?
· Who's completed the biggest physical challenge?

VOCABULARY Doing and watching sport

A **Work in groups. Discuss these questions.**
1 Why would a crowd **go wild**? Why would they **boo**?
2 Does a team **get knocked out** of a league or out of a tournament?
3 Why does the referee **send** someone **off**?
4 What's the difference between being **suspended**, being **substituted** and being **dropped**?
5 Name two sports that have **a keeper**.
6 What happens if someone makes a **reckless tackle**?
7 What's the opposite of the **underdog** in a game?
8 What's the difference between a **tight** game, an **open** game and a **dirty** game?
9 If a player **challenges a decision**, do they hope the decision will be upheld or **overturned**?
10 What happens if you **blow your chance** at the end of a game or season?
11 Say five ways people could **cheat** in various sports.
12 Why might you begin to **fade** in a race?
13 What happens if a player or team gets **thrashed**?
14 What's the opposite of getting **relegated**?
15 If you **scraped through** to the next round, what happened in your match?

B **Choose five of the words in bold and say something true that happened to you or a team / player you know. It could be a non-sporting situation. For example:**
I scraped through my French exam at school. I got 51%.

LISTENING

You are going to hear conversations about playing tennis, a mountain walk and a football match.

A **Before you listen, decide which four words in the box go with each of the three activities.**

draw	a penalty	rallies
return game	double fault	trudge
clouds broke	the crossbar	stunning
hypothermia	deuce	fade

B ⚡ **11.1 Listen and find out how good an experience each activity was for the main speakers – and why.**

C **Work in pairs. Re-tell what happened in each conversation using the words from exercise A. Listen again if you need to.**

DEVELOPING CONVERSATIONS
Irony and humour

> Irony can be quite common in conversation. If we are being ironic, we say the opposite of what we think, or exaggerate the difference between the example we use and the reality.
> I'm not exactly Picasso when it comes to painting.

A Work in pairs. Look at each of the underlined expressions in the audioscript for track 11.1 on page 172–3 and discuss these questions:
1 Is the speaker being ironic or not?
2 Where they're being ironic, what's the reality?
3 Do you say similar ironic comments in your language?

B Match 1–5 to the ironic comments.
1 So you're starting at high school next week.
2 What did you think of the poems he wrote?
3 He's a bit absented-minded, then?
4 I'm not exactly the best at tennis.
5 Did you see that goal he scored? It was amazing.

a You could say that! He's managed to lose his passport three times.
b It wasn't bad. I didn't exactly go wild though.
c Yeah. I can't wait – all that lovely homework!
d Well, it's not exactly Shakespeare.
e Come on! You only made about 20 double faults!

> We often use *manage to* ironically when we 'succeed' in doing something stupid.
> I once *managed to* break my leg making a cup of tea!

C Complete each of the sentences below in two ironic ways that are true for you.
a I once managed to …
b I'm not exactly …

D Tell a partner your sentences and discuss them further.

CONVERSATION PRACTICE

You are going to have similar conversations to the ones you heard in *Listening*.

A Think about something sporty you have seen or done. Think of one 'success' and one 'failure' and make some notes. Write two questions to start the conversation and give them to a partner.
For example:
How was the match you went to see last week?
How was your skiing holiday?

B Start the conversations with the questions you were given. Your partner will explain what happened.

D Work in pairs. Discuss the following.
- Are there any sports events that you regularly watch?
- Can you give an example of when a team / someone should've won, but didn't? Why didn't they?
- Give an example of when you had to bite your tongue or 'could've killed someone'.
- Give an example of something that was a cock-up.
- Give examples of overrated people or things.

NATIVE SPEAKER ENGLISH

a cock-up

A *cock-up* is a very big mistake. The term is usually used between people who have an informal relationship, although it is also sometimes used in journalism or even in politics.

The Arsenal keeper made a right cock-up to let them score.
The hotel made a complete cock-up with our booking.
I think the failure was more cock-up than conspiracy.
I completely cocked up the last question of the exam.

SPEAKING

A Work in groups. Discuss these questions.

- Which of the games in the box have you played?
- Did you enjoy them?
- Are you any good at them?
- What's good / bad about them?

poker	dominoes	Scrabble ™	The Sims™	chess	backgammon	Monopoly™	Call of Duty™

VOCABULARY Games

A Decide whether 1–12 are said during a board game, a computer game or a card game.

1. You didn't **shuffle** these very well. I have almost exactly the same as last time.
2. Hurry up and throw the **dice**!
3. You're moving my **counter**! You're red.
4. There's something wrong with the **controller**? Maybe it needs **resetting**.
5. You've **dealt** me eight instead of seven.
6. A friend told me **a cheat** to get to the next level.
7. If you **land** on that square, you have to miss a go.
8. How do I get him to **punch**?
9. This is a terrible **hand**! I'm not going to win anything.
10. You're running low on **ammunition**.
11. I think you're **bluffing**. You haven't got any aces.
12. You have to **take my piece** if you can.

B Work in pairs.

Student A: explain, act or draw the words in **bold**. **Student B:** guess the words.

LISTENING 1

You are going to hear a short talk on playing cards.

A 11.2 Listen and take notes on:

1. the origin of playing cards
2. the three different types of playing cards
3. different types of games.

B Compare the notes you made. Whose are easiest to follow? Discuss what you could add to them to make them better.

C What are the things below? Listen again to check.

- deck
- suits
- clubs
- a jack
- trumps
- a joker

D Work in pairs. Discuss these questions:

- Can you name the different cards in the pictures?
- Which kind of cards are most common in your country? Do you know any other types of playing cards?
- Can you give examples of the different types of card game mentioned? What's your favourite game?
- What restrictions are there on gambling in your country?
- Do you think banning gambling is a good idea? Why?

GRAMMAR Linking words

> When we talk about games and explain rules, we use a lot of linking words. These may show (1) contrasts, (2) conditions, (3) the purpose or result, or show (4) the order or time things happen.
>
> They may join two parts of a sentence or show the relation between two separate sentences.

A Match the words in the box to the four different categories in the explanation above.

even though	although	then	so
otherwise	provided	unless	if
whether	so as to	until	even if

B Complete 1–10 with the words in exercise A.

1 Shuffle the cards. ...., deal six to each player and leave the rest of the deck face down. To start, the player to the dealer's right takes the top card off the deck and decides .... to keep it.

2 Put four of your cards face up on the table .... that everyone can see them.

3 You can leave two counters on one square .... block your opponents.

4 You have to declare that you have your last card. ...., you can't finish.

5 You can move your counter in any direction, ... that there's a free space.

6 .... you can't play the same suit or a card of the same rank, you have to pick up from the deck. .... you have an ace, in which case you can use that as a joker.

7 You can't go on to the next level without completing the task, ... you can find cheats on the Internet in order to bypass some tasks.

8 He keeps trying to bluff, ... he's rubbish at it!

9 You keep playing .... only one person is left.

10 You won't win now, ... you take that piece, because I can take all your other ones.

▶ Need help? Read the grammar reference on page 146.

C Think of one or two card games – preferably ones your partner doesn't know. Explain how to play to your partner.

LISTENING

You are going to hear five people talking about games.

A 🔊 11.3 Listen and decide which speakers talk about:
a playing for money ......
b being injured because of a game ......
c the social nature of the game ...... and ......
d hitting someone ......
e the game sounding worse than it is ...... and ......
f parent(s) stopping a computer game being played ......

B Compare your answers with a partner and explain your choices.

C Listen again and complete the sentences.
1 a The aim .... a particular kind of car.
   b You knew they could get .... at any moment.
2 a My brothers used to .... me.
   b My brothers all burst out laughing and teased me and I just .... the board and stormed out of the room.
3 a The problem lies when .... involved.
   b I kept thinking I'm .... next time.
4 a It felt like I'd ....
   b I guess I'm just not .... those muscles.
5 a You can choose the .... you undertake.
   b I guess he distinguishes .... OK.

SPEAKING

A Work in groups. Discuss these questions.
- Did you ever make up games when you were younger? What were the aims and the rules?
- Did / Do you ever get upset when playing games? Why?
- Did / Do you ever play games as a family? Which ones? Explain the aim of the game and the rules.
- What can you learn through playing games?
- Do you think computer games influence behaviour?
- What's your favourite computer game?
- Do you think children should have limits on playing computer games? What limits? Why? / Why not?

READING

You are going to read an article about different kinds of language play.

A Before you read, work in groups. Discuss which of the different kinds of playful uses of language in the box you are already familiar with.

advertising slogans	riddles
puns	metaphors
word games	idioms
comic insults	alliteration
tongue twisters	nursery rhymes

B Read the article and find examples of each of the above. Then think of one more example of each different kind of language play.

C Work in pairs. Discuss these questions about the article.
1 What other kinds of language play are mentioned?
2 What reasons are put forward to explain language play?
3 What social functions do you think banter and the kind of word play the writer encountered in the office serve?
4 What do you think the answer to the riddle is?
5 How do you feel about the kind of insults mentioned? Why?

LANGUAGE PATTERNS

Write the sentences in your language. Translate them back into English. Compare your English to the original.
There are all sorts of word games – from crosswords to TV game shows.
The software ranges from fun games with no educational value to some really powerful training programmes.
Language play encompasses everything from kids' nursery rhymes to sophisticated advertising slogans.

SPEAKING

A Work in groups. Discuss these questions.
• Do comic insults exist in your language? Do they translate well into English?
• Is language play important when it comes to learning a foreign language? Why? / Why not?
• Do you know any riddles in your language? Do they work in English?
• Which of the tongue twisters below is hardest for you to say?

> A really weird rear wheel.

> She sells seashells on the seashore.

> A big black bug bit a big black bear.

> A cheap sheep is cheaper than a cheap ship.

> Three free throws

VOCABULARY
Sports and games metaphors

Many words connected to sports and games have literal and metaphorical meanings. The literal meaning of a word is its basic sense. A metaphorical meaning is when a word is used to refer to something other than its basic sense.

A Decide what sport or game the metaphors in *italics* originate from, and what you think they mean in the contexts they are in.
1 I think that comment was *a bit below the belt*, to be honest. It was a hurtful thing to say.
2 Currency trading is *a very high stakes game*.
3 All we're asking for is *a level playing field* when we compete with local companies.
4 Recent events have forced the president to *show his hand* sooner that he would've wanted.
5 For months, the two main parties were *neck and neck* in the polls.
6 I can't believe I actually managed to *bluff my way through* the interview.
7 The city has been a *pawn* in regional power games for hundreds of years.
8 You never know what he's really thinking. I mean, he *keeps his cards close to his chest*!
9 I've said all I have to say about the matter. *The ball's in your court* now.
10 Phew! *Saved by the bell*. I would've died if that meeting had gone on much longer!
11 I've had to overcome a lot of *hurdles* to get to where I am today.
12 Don't get too excited. We're not finished yet. It's *a marathon, not a sprint*.

B Work in pairs. Discuss these questions.
• Are you good at bluffing your way through interviews, meetings, presentations, etc.?
• Have you heard or said any comments that you think were a bit below the belt? What was the reaction?
• What hurdles have you had to overcome in your life?
• Are you good at keeping things close to your chest? Do you know anyone who's better at it than you are?
• Can you think of any examples of people / things that have been pawns in a bigger game?

NOT JUST CHILD'S PLAY

The desire and ability to play with linguistic forms and functions in order to entertain both oneself and others is innate in the majority of humans. Indeed, it is now widely accepted that children who do *not* participate in language play are in some way abnormal. From around the age of one, children start playing with the sounds of their mother tongue, a phenomenon which feeds into a later love of tongue twisters such as *We surely shall see the sun shine soon*. This is followed by chants, songs and other noises made to accompany motor activities, and by the age of three or four kids are able to use the language of their peers as a springboard for their own creativity. Among other things, they start adding rhymes and nonsense words. Naturally, this is encouraged by exposure to nursery rhymes, many of which feature nonsensical elements like:

> *Hey diddle, diddle,*
> *The cat and the fiddle.*
> *The cow jumped over the moon.*
> *The little dog laughed to see such fun,*
> *And the dish ran away with the spoon.*

Before long, children start grappling with more complex riddles (*What gets wetter the more it dries?* for example). As we grow, we develop an ever more sophisticated grasp of language, and become increasingly adept at processing idiomatic and metaphorical usage. Without such abilities, we would be unable to deal with such concepts as a boss *moving the goalposts* or sport being *war minus the shooting*! Through high school encounters with literature, we become more familiar with playful language in poetry and prose too.

We also start learning how to banter, an art which, when carried to an extreme, can involve insults directed at physical and personal characteristics, such as "Your mum"s so fat, people jog round her for exercise'" and the response: "Yeah? Well, YOUR mum's so stupid, she puts lipstick on her head just to make up her mind!"

In the adult world, language play is still widespread. Newspaper headlines, especially the tabloid variety, rely heavily on puns. There was, for instance, the article about the leader of the new government in Iraq looking to boost his country's military capacity that drew readers in by proclaiming *IRAQI HEAD SEEKS ARMS*! Pop lyrics and movie dialogue are packed with witty lines and there are also all sorts of word games – from crosswords to TV game shows to *TABOO*, where you have to define words like *coffee* without using words like *drink*.

Then there's the advertising industry, which is heavily dependent on copywriters being able to forge memorable slogans out of limited means. This may be achieved through the use of alliteration (*Don't dream it – drive it*, for example), puns (such as the slogan used to sell a perfume called Impulse – *Men can't help acting on impulse*) and so on.

The degree to which such playful attitudes to language are commonplace was made painfully clear to me earlier this year, when I returned to work after a disastrous skiing holiday, during which I managed to break my arm. Once my colleagues had spotted the arm in a cast, the fun began. As I ordered a coffee, I was asked if I needed a *hand*! Next, a new employee being given a guided tour of the office was told not to mind me as I was armless! And on it went: during the course of the day, I was asked if the injury meant I now had more free time on my hands, whether or not I'd got a hand-out from my insurance company, and finally I was congratulated for putting my finger on a key problem in a brainstorming session! Ouch!

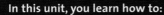

12 HISTORY

In this unit, you learn how to:
• describe key events in people's lives
• talk about how people have built success
• use similes to make descriptions more interesting
• ask for clarification
• discuss key historical events

Grammar
• Dramatic inversion

Vocabulary
• Personal histories
• Presenting arguments and theories
• Recent history

Reading
• Ancient history?

Listening
• An amazing life
• Recent historical milestones

VOCABULARY Personal histories

A Work in pairs. Say what you think the key moments in your life have been so far. Explain why.

B Read the sentences below. Check the meaning of any words you don't understand in the *Vocabulary Builder*. Then discuss the positive and / or negative effects that each situation might have on someone's life.
1 He had a very **sheltered upbringing**.
2 She's from quite a **deprived** background.
3 They had to **flee** the country after the military **coup**.
4 He was very involved in **radical** politics in his youth.
5 She was **evacuated** during the war.
6 He saw **active service** during the war.
7 She's always had a real **lust for life**.
8 He comes from a **broken home**.
9 He grew up in a very **close-knit** community.
10 She's from a very **privileged** background.
11 She won a **scholarship** to study in the States.
12 He was **orphaned** when both his parents died in a plane crash.

C Do you know anyone who any of the sentences in exercise B could describe? Tell a partner.

LISTENING

You are going to hear a conversation in which someone describes the amazing life his girlfriend's father has had.

A Before you listen, discuss with a partner how you think the words in the box could be connected to the man's personal history and life.

first generation	poverty	drop out
ice cream	textiles	the capital
outboard motors	the States	a peasant

B ♪ **12.1 Listen** and see if your guesses were correct. Then discuss with a partner the connection between the words in exercise A and the girlfriend's father's life.

C Listen again and complete the sentences below with the missing phrasal verbs.
1 The whole visit .... far better than I'd dared to hope it would.
2 It .... his bark is much worse than his bite.
3 When he was 13, his dad ....
4 He had to .... of school and start working.
5 He .... selling ice creams ... and then .... to selling textiles door-to-door.
6 He decided that if he really wanted to ...., he'd have to move to the capital, and .... to make his fortune.
7 He got there, somehow managed to .... his own company ... and then just slowly .... things ....
8 His eyes .... when I told him how much I got for that portrait I sold last year.
9 I didn't .... that fact too much.

NATIVE SPEAKER ENGLISH

get your head round it

If you try to *get your head round* something unusual or unexpected, you try hard to understand it or accept it.

Well, he's still trying to get his head round it all.
I'm still trying to get my head round my new Smartphone.
She still can't get her head round what happened!
I'm still struggling to get my head round the whole thing!

D   Work in groups. Discuss these questions.
- Can you think of anything that passed off far better than you'd hoped it would?
- What do you think are the pros and cons of coming from a very large family?
- Do you know anyone you'd describe as a self-made man or woman? How did they build their success?

DEVELOPING CONVERSATIONS
Similes

A simile is a phrase that describes something by comparing it to something else. The comparison is introduced using *like* or *as*. Similes are often intended to be humorous.

He eats *like a peasant* still and burps after dinner and everything.

A   Make common fixed similes by matching 1–5 to the correct endings a–e.

1	I've got a memory	a	like the plague.
2	He smokes	b	like a fish out of water.
3	I felt	c	like a sieve.
4	I avoid him	d	like chalk and cheese.
5	They're	e	like a chimney.

B   Now match 6–10 to f–j.

6	He's as hard	f	as a dodo.
7	It's as dead	g	as the hills.
8	She went as white	h	as nails.
9	That joke is as old	i	as mud!
10	That's as clear	j	as a sheet.

C   Work in pairs. Discuss what you think each simile means – and whether or not you have similar expressions in your language.

D   Test each other.
Student A: read 1–10 in exercises A and B above.
Student B: close your books and say the correct endings.

E   Complete these sentences with your own ideas. You can be as poetic, funny or serious as you want to be.

1   Once he'd started up his business, he had to work like
....
2   She was the only teacher I ever had who treated us like ....
3   I come from a very argumentative family. Dinner at our house was usually like ....
4   Once I started university, I was as happy
....
5   He emerged from his childhood as tough
....
6   She's an amazing woman. She's got a voice as
.... and she looks like
....

CONVERSATION PRACTICE

A   Think of someone you know – or know of – that you think has had an incredible life. Make notes on what you know about their personal history. Think of at least one simile you can use when telling their story.

B   Work in groups. Tell each other as much as you can about the people you have chosen.

SPEAKING

A **Work in groups. Discuss these questions.**
- How much do you know about your country's history?
- Do you know much about ancient history?
- Are there any ruins near where you live? What of?
- Are there any World Heritage sites in your country? Have you been to them? Why are they preserved?
- How important do you think it is to preserve historical sites? Why?

READING

You are going to read an article about the fall of the Roman Empire.

A **Read the article and answer these questions.**
1 What reasons are mentioned for the empire's collapse?
2 Why are so many theories put forward?
3 Why do theories change over time?

B **What evidence, if any, is given to support each of the statements in 1–6? How strong is the evidence? What else would you want to know to believe each statement?**
1 Life was worse after the end of the Roman Empire.
2 Thatching was an inferior building technique.
3 People were happy with Roman rule.
4 There's a lot of academic interest in the fall of Rome.
5 Lead poisoning brought down the empire.
6 Historians' theories are influenced by contemporary concerns.

C **Work in pairs. Discuss the meaning of the words in bold.**

D **Work in pairs. Discuss these questions.**
- What empires have you heard of? When did they exist? Do you know why they ended?
- Do you think we learn lessons from history? Give an example of when we did or when we didn't.

Ancient history?

There is a sketch from a historical comedy called *The Life of Brian*, where a meeting of a small revolutionary group is taking place under Roman occupation. Their leader is trying to **whip up** anger at the oppressive Roman Empire. 'What,' he growls, 'have the Romans ever done for us?' A moment's silence. 'The aqueduct.' 'OK, the aqueduct …' 'And sanitation.' 'All right. Apart from aqueducts and sanitation, what have they ever done for us?' There then follows a series of suggestions ranging from roads to public order to wine, **culminating** with the leader's exasperated cry, 'Oh, shut up!'

The joke may be closer to reality than we imagine. The Romans were not defeated by popular **uprisings** for independence – in stark contrast to the end of more modern empires. Furthermore, some scholars, such as Bryan Ward-Perkins, suggest that once the Western Roman Empire had collapsed, many of their civilised advances were lost. Not only did coins largely disappear, but also pottery stopped being manufactured so widely, and sophisticated constructions such as tiled roofs were replaced by inferior techniques such as thatching, which was prone to fire and sheltered insects that bred disease.

So if things were so good and what followed so dreadful, why did the Roman Empire **crumble**? It is a question that continues to attract huge interest in academic circles. Hardly a year goes by without a book on the subject coming out and, **to date**, over 200 theories have been put forward. In part, this is because of the relative **scarcity** of evidence available for the period of Rome's fall, so when new facts are discovered, they quickly become the basis of whole new theories. For example, the analysis of bones from the Roman period revealed a high content of heavy metals, which gave rise to the theory that lead poisoning brought down the empire. More recently, agricultural degradation has been blamed following new archaeological findings.

Most scholars, though not all, agree that the decline took place over a long period of time, rather than there being a single collapse in AD 476, when Rome was **sacked** by the Barbarians. Most also suggest that a number of contributing factors led to its demise. The causes tend to divide into five main areas: decadence, economic problems, external pressures, division and infighting, and Christianity and cultural change.

It is the relative importance given to different factors that sparks debate. Again, the lack of evidence means historians are freer to fill in the gaps with guesswork and interpretation. As a result, they may attach different resonances according to the times they live in. For example, Edward Gibbon, writing during the new rigorous, scientific age of the Enlightenment, tended towards blaming Christianity and decadence. Some say historians who **contended** that there was a smooth transition between the fall of Rome and invading Germanic tribes were influenced by drawing parallels with Germany's smooth integration into a European union following the Second World War. Finally, ideas on environmental causes, it is argued, are about the **outlook** of modern green movements rather than real problems in Roman times.

DEVELOPING CONVERSATIONS
Asking for clarification

> When you ask for clarification after a lecture or reading, you usually need to give a short context then the question.
> You quoted from a film. Could you give me the reference?

A 🔊 **12.2 Listen and complete the questions asked to the author of the article.**

1 You cited .... Could you .... ?

2 When you were talking about changes in construction techniques, you .... Could you just .... ?

3 You referred to a theory that lead poisoning .... Could you .... ?

4 You mentioned some findings that suggested .... Do you .... ?

B Write three more similar questions you could ask about the reading article.

C Work in pairs.
Student A: read the information in File 4 on page 153.
Student B: read the information in File 9 on page 155.

D Ask your partner questions from exercise A and the questions you wrote in order to find out more information that wasn't covered in the *Reading* text. Your partner should reply using the information they learned, apologise for being unable to reply or try to make up an answer!

VOCABULARY
Presenting arguments and theories

A **Work in pairs. Decide if the words in *italics* have the same meaning in the context. If not, what's the difference?**

1 Fukuyama *put forward / advanced* the theory of the end of history. He *established / claimed* that the arrival of democracy following the Cold War was the endpoint for political development and conflict.

2 Heather *asserts / demonstrates* that the Roman Empire's decline *stemmed from / gave rise to* invasions.

3 St Catherine's monastery is *allegedly / supposedly* the site where Moses received the Ten Commandments, although archaeologists have *questioned / cast doubt on* the claim.

4 Zinn *challenged / accepted* the status quo by *highlighting / emphasising* the importance of ordinary people in American history.

5 Paul *argues / contends* that the governments tend to play a *significant / minor* role in the economy.

B **Use some vocabulary from exercise A and your own ideas to prepare a short presentation on one of these topics.**

- One of the historical figures below and their ideas.
  – Marx
  – Archimedes
  – Galileo
  – Einstein
- A person or a theory you have studied.

SPEAKING

A **Work in small groups. Give the presentation you wrote in *Vocabulary* exercise B. After each of you finish, the others should try to ask questions like those in *Developing Conversations*.**

SPEAKING

A Work in groups. How much do you know about the recent historical milestones below? Discuss what you think happened – and what the causes and results were.

- the fall of the Berlin Wall
- the September the 11th attacks
- the Iraq conflicts
- the Asian tsunami of 2004
- the creation of the euro
- the genocides in Rwanda and Sudan

VOCABULARY Recent history

A Complete the sentences with the correct form of the verbs in the box.

abolish	call	gain	massacre
assassinate	declare	go	overthrow
carry out	dent	issue	push

1 After years of fighting, the two sides finally .... a truce last month.
2 About 20 years ago, one of our former presidents .... by his bodyguard, and that sparked a civil war.
3 We .... independence in the 1970s, but we didn't actually .... full independence until 2002.
4 Our national airline .... bust a few years ago, which very much .... our pride.
5 Capital punishment .... back in the 1960s.
6 Our government .... in a military coup last year.
7 A few years ago the government finally .... a formal apology for our involvement in the slave trade.
8 In about 1996, around a hundred civilians .... in cold-blood by government forces during a demonstration.
9 A terrorist organisation .... a series of bombings on civilian targets over the last few years.
10 We .... for accession to the European Union for several years now.

B Work in pairs. Discuss these questions.

- Can you think of any high-profile people who have been assassinated? Do you know why?
- Can you think of any high-profile firms or organisations that have gone bust recently? Do you know why?
- Can you think of any countries which have gained independence in the last two or three decades? How well has it gone?

LISTENING

You are going to hear four people talking about milestone events in the recent history of their different countries.

A ⏷ 12.3 Listen and answer these questions.
1 What event does each person describe?
2 Why do they claim these events were significant?

B Listen again and decide which sentences are true.
1 a Anna Lindh's career was on the up.
  b It was a politically motivated attack.
  c She died instantly.
2 a The speaker thinks joining the EU helped heal old wounds.
  b Only a slim majority voted for EU membership.
  c The speaker puts some of his recent success down to the time he spent abroad.
3 a The new pipeline passes through Russia.
  b Thus far, it hasn't brought in much revenue.
  c It has had positive political ramifications.
4 a Children with one aborigine parent were often forced into care.
  b These children now have excellent job opportunities.
  c The speaker thinks an apology should have been issued earlier.

C Match the words from the listening. Check in the audioscripts on page 174–5. Then discuss with a partner who or what did each of the things below.

1	take a strong	a	a rite of passage
2	sound	b	the old trade routes
3	symbolise	c	the mistakes of the past
4	draw	d	the stain
5	bypass	e	stand
6	give	f	the death knell
7	acknowledge	g	a line under the past
8	remove	h	greater geo-political clout

D Work in groups. Discuss these questions.

- In global terms, which of the four events from the listening do you think is most significant? Why?
- How much impact on world events do you think the oil trade has? Why? Which other trades are very important?
- Do you think countries should apologise for past mistakes? How far back should this go? Should compensation ever be offered? Why? / Why not?

LANGUAGE PATTERNS

Write the sentences in your language. Translate them back into English. Compare your English to the original.

All of that can only be for the good.

The city's changed a lot, but not necessarily for the better.

I'm not happy about it, but I guess it's probably for the best.

I think it was a change for the worse.

He's in hospital. He took a turn for the worse last night.

GRAMMAR Dramatic inversion

We can invert sentences by putting the auxiliary before the subject. This is more common in writing, but is sometimes used in speech to make descriptions more dramatic.

No sooner had we been granted full membership *than* literally hundreds of thousands of young Poles headed off abroad.

This structure emphasises the fact that the second action happened very quickly after the first.

A **Rewrite these sentences using *No sooner*. There are some words in each sentence you will not need to re-use.**

1 It was a terrible time. The President was overthrown and then civil war broke out the next day.

....

2 We adopted the euro about 12 years ago, and almost immediately prices went up!

....

3 It was depressingly predictable. The looting began almost as soon as the earthquake struck.

....

4 Brazil equalised and then 30 seconds later, we went up the other end of the pitch and scored the winner!

....

There are several other ways to invert sentences. All are more common in writing and formal speech.

Not only did coins largely disappear, *but also* pottery stopped being manufactured so widely.

B **Complete the sentences with the words in the box.**

never before	nowhere else	not until
at no time	not only	only

1 They were exciting times. .... were we as a society on the map again, but we felt as if we'd come of age.

2 I surprised even myself because .... whatsoever did I panic. I remained remarkably calm throughout.

3 It was a time of tense industrial relations. .... had the unions been quite so militant or quite so well organised.

4 .... it was too late did people begin to realise what was really going on.

5 .... in the world could anything quite as ridiculous as this happen! Seriously! .... in Britain could school kids gaining exposure to other languages be seen as negative!

▶ **Need help? Read the grammar reference on page 147.**

SPEAKING

A **Think of three major historical events from your country in recent decades. These could be related to politics, economics, sport, society, law and order, etc. Make notes about each one and think about why they were significant.**

B **Work in groups. Explain as much about each of the events as you can to the rest of the group. (If you come from the same country, see if you agree on which events were the most important and why they were significant. Then discuss how you would explain these events to a foreigner.)**

03 REVIEW

TWO MINUTES

Work in groups. You are going to give a short two-minute talk on one of the topics in the list below. Spend five minutes thinking about what you are going to say. Look back at your notes to check language if you like.

- A job that interests you
- An operation
- Mental health
- A major sporting event
- The rules of a game
- An incredible life

Give each other marks out of ten for language, interest and clarity. Who got the most marks?

GAME

Work in pairs. Student A use *only* the green squares; student B use *only* the yellow squares. Spend five minutes looking at your questions and revising the answers. Then take turns tossing a coin: heads = move one of your squares; tails = move two of your squares. When you land on a square, your partner looks at the relevant page in the book to check your answers, but *you don't*! If you are right, move forward one square (but don't answer the question until your next turn). If you aren't right, your partner tells you the right answer and you miss a go. When you've finished the game, change colours and play again.

Start	**1** *Native Speaker English* note p. 64: if you can say what the *Native Speaker English* note was and give an example, throw again.	**2** *Developing Conversations* p. 65: your partner will say sentences 1–6 in exercise B. You should make deductions using *then*.	**3** *Grammar* p. 65: say six things people might say at work using six different continuous forms.	**4** *Vocabulary* p. 66: you partner will say the adjectives from exer A. Say two adverbs t collocate with each.
5 *Native Speaker English* note p. 70: if you can say what the *Native Speaker English* note was and give an example, throw again.	**6** *Developing Conversations* p. 71: your partner will choose six sentences from exercise A. Add vague expressions to make them less exact.	**7** *Vocabulary* p. 73: your partner will say the 15 actions from exercise B. Say which part of the body you use for each one.	**8** **Miss a go!**	**9** *Grammar* p. 75: mak four comments abou illnesses people you know have had usin different modal verb
10 *Vocabulary* p. 76: your partner will keep asking questions from exercise A until you have answered six correctly.	**11** **Miss a go!**	**12** *Native Speaker English* note p. 77: if you can say what the *Native Speaker English* note was and give an example, throw again.	**13** *Developing Conversations* p. 77: say two ironic things about your life using *managed to* and two using *not exactly*.	**14** *Grammar* p. 79: give eight rules for games using eight different linking wor
15 *Native Speaker English* note p. 83: if you can say what the *Native Speaker English* note was and give an example, throw again.	**16** *Developing Conversations* p. 83: your partner will say the first half of the ten similes in exercises A and B. You should say the endings.	**17** *Vocabulary* p. 85: say six things that have happened recently using six different verbs from exercise A.	**18** *Grammar* p. 87: your partner will say the sentences from exercise A. Invert each one to make it sound more dramatic.	**Finish**

For each of the activities below, work in groups of three. Use the *Vocabulary Builder* if you want to.

CONVERSATION PRACTICE

Choose one of the following *Conversation Practice* activities.
Work p. 65
Health and Illness p. 71
Play p. 77
History p. 83

Two of you should do the task. The third person should listen and then give a mark between 1 and 10 for the performance. Explain your decision. Then change roles.

ACT OR DRAW

One person should act or draw as many of these words as they can in three minutes. The others should try to guess the words. Do not speak while you are acting or drawing!

drift off	a flap	a tackle	evacuate
lean	on a drip	trudge	textiles
nod	excruciating	shuffle	a portrait
a crèche	shrug	a sword	pottery
mourn	clench	tease	a bodyguard
anaesthetise	shudder	a sprint	assassinate

QUIZ

Answer as many of the questions as possible.
1 Why do people **network**?
2 What's the opposite of **upholding** a decision?
3 What kind of jobs might be **emotionally draining**?
4 Why do people sometimes **bluff**?
5 Say three things that can be **temperamental**. Explain how.
6 Is it good or bad if cancer **goes into remission**?
7 Can you think of three reasons why people **flee** an area?
8 When might you need a **skin graft**?
9 What can **clog** – or **clog up**? What with?
10 What happens if a town or city is **sacked**?
11 Say three things you could **confess to**.
12 Can you think of an example of a **chant**?
13 What happens if a team is **relegated**? What's the opposite?
14 Why might you **glare at** someone?
15 What kind of places might get **looted**? When?

COLLOCATIONS

Take turns to read out collocation lists from Unit 9 of the *Vocabulary Builder*. Where there is a '~', say '*blah*' instead. Your partner should guess as many words as they can. Each time you change roles, move to the next unit.

IDIOMS

Discuss the meaning of the idioms and try to think of a real example about you – or about someone you know.
1 We're all in the same boat.
2 He's just pulling your leg.
3 I've been rushed off my feet all day.
4 Maybe you can show me the ropes?
5 It was a bit below the belt.
6 His bark is worse than his bite.
7 I just don't think he's pulling his weight.
8 I just had to bite my tongue.
9 It's a kind of rite of passage.
10 She keeps her cards close to her chest.
11 They keep moving the goalposts.
12 Let me just get this straight.
13 The ball's in your court.
14 She comes from a broken home.
15 We're just a pawn in the game.

LISTENING

You are going to hear five speakers talking about different things.

A ♪ R 3.1 **Listen and choose one answer for each speaker. There are two extra. Which speaker is:**
a   putting forward a theory?
b   discussing a football match?
c   giving evidence to a tribunal?
d   talking about a car race?
e   describing a journey?
f   complaining about discrimination?
g   discussing a tennis match?

B **Listen again and choose one answer for each speaker. There are two extra. Which speaker:**
a   wanted to get back in touch with their cultural heritage?
b   has undergone a kind of rehabilitation?
c   discusses a military coup?
d   disagrees with conventional wisdom?
e   recognises their opinions may not be popular?
f   describes a comic accident?
g   blew a chance?

[... / 10]

GRAMMAR

A **Correct the mistake in each of 1–8.**
1   Under no circumstances you're to leave your post unattended.
2   If it wasn't for my old Chemistry teacher, I wouldn't be work here now!
3   Only after a full inquiry were we understanding the full horror of the incident.
4   That shouldn't have been much fun. I would've gone crazy if it'd happened to me.
5   I wouldn't work for that firm even though the money was amazing!
6   It was awful. My phone was going off while I was being interviewed.
7   I can't believe he failed. He might be feeling dreadful now.
8   I don't mind you answering the call in class unless it's quick.

[... / 8]

B **Complete the second sentence with 2–5 words and the word in bold so it has a similar meaning to the first.**
1   It's her own fault. She was texting while she was driving.
    shouldn't
    It's her own fault. She .... while she was driving.
2   She was probably feeling ill. She wouldn't have cancelled otherwise.
    can't
    She .... or she would've come.
3   The boss resigned a couple of days after I started there.
    No sooner
    .... than the boss resigned.
4   He never asked me for any help whatsoever.
    at no time
    .... ask me for any help.
5   I still think about him almost every day.
    goes by
    Hardly .... me thinking about him.
6   I find computers very hard to deal with!
    adept
    I .... with computers.

[... / 12]

LANGUAGE PATTERNS

Complete the sentences with one word in each gap.
1   The boss has demanded that he ...... kept informed of any developments.
2   You should get that tooth looked at it. The ...... you leave it, the worse it'll get.
3   It's certainly changed, but not necessarily for the ....
4   The course covers everything ...... an overview of the basics to far more sophisticated areas.
5   The doctors are very worried. Apparently, he took a turn for the ...... last night.
6   The ...... pressure we put on them, the more likely they are to reverse their decision.

[... / 6]

PREPOSITIONS

Choose the correct preposition.
1   Experts have cast doubt *towards / on* the authenticity of the finds.
2   We got knocked out *of / from* the competition in the second round.
3   I've got real admiration *towards / for* the work you do.
4   Having a company car is one of the perks *of / with* the job.
5   Stop ganging up *to / on* me. It's not fair.
6   The policy hasn't really impacted *to / on* our business yet.
7   He fell ill following exposure *to / of* toxic chemicals.
8   There's no point dwelling *about / on* it. It won't help.

[... / 8]

OPPOSITES

Replace the words in *italics* with their opposite from the box.

substantial	malignant	privileged	quick
conservative	civilian	significant	good

1 They bombed *military* targets.
2 She has some fairly *radical* views.
3 Tests showed the lump was *benign*.
4 She played a *minor* role.
5 The signs are pretty *ominous*.
6 They carried out a *thorough* search.
7 He's from a *deprived* background.
8 There's been a *slight* rise.

[... / 8]

MISSING WORDS

Complete each set of three sentences with one word.

1 Poverty has a terribly negative ...... on life expectancy.
 The measures have had little ...... thus far.
 Failure to pull your weight can directly ...... on colleagues.
2 She has an excellent ...... of French language and politics.
 I didn't really ...... the main idea, I don't think.
 You have to ...... every opportunity that comes your way.
3 She won an ...... for best director last year.
 They decided to ...... the contract to our main rivals.
 I don't get why they ...... bankers such obscene sums.
4 It's hard to get out of a downward ...... once you're in one.
 The whole situation is starting to ...... out of control.
 The country is locked in a ...... of decline.
5 You don't want to show your ...... too soon, do you?
 If you know the answer, raise your ....
 I'm not going to win anything with this ....

[... / 5]

VERBS

Match the verbs in the box with the collocations in 1–8.

administer	bypass	forge	cite
exacerbate	put forward	retain	draw up

1 ~ contracts / ~ guidelines / ~ plans / ~ a list
2 ~ its old charm / ~ your best staff / ~ a sense of humour
3 ~ an argument / ~ a proposal / ~ two main reasons
4 ~ a problem / ~ an already bad situation / ~ an issue
5 ~ the old trade routes /~ the lawyers / ~ the city centre
6 ~ a test / ~ an anaesthetic / ~ a project / ~ an injection
7 ~ an alliance / ~ trade links / ~ a memorable slogan
8 ~ a recent survey / ~ statistics / ~ personal reasons

[... / 8]

FORMING WORDS

Complete the gaps with the correct form of the words in CAPITALS.

According to the [1].......................... of a recent report, an ever-increasing number of people now feel that having to go through [2].......................... is the most stressful event of their lives. Mass lay-offs have become a common [3].......................... in all types of organisation and many report that their [4].......................... with HR departments are profoundly unsatisfactory. In addition, once unemployed, they then often face a [5].......................... of redeployment opportunities, which can have a serious effect on their mental well-being.

FIND
REDUNDANT
OCCUR
DEAL
SCARCE

For companies themselves, one [6].......................... problem is motivating staff that remain. The vacuum created by job losses is best filled by direction. There is a need to focus the [7].......................... on what will be achieved in the long term.

RECUR
WORK

[... / 7]

VOCABULARY

Complete the email by choosing the correct words A–C.

I'm coping OK in my new post, I guess, but I've had to overcome a few more [1]...... than I would've liked! I guess I've been going through a period of [2]...... .

The interview was more stressful than I'd been expecting, I have to say. I'd been led to believe that the job was mine and that the whole thing would be little more than a [3]......, but it was actually all very [4]...... . They carried out [5]...... checks on all applicants and assessed our [6]...... skills. Anyway, I got it in the end and here I am!

I've got a PA for the first time in my life and she's amazing – very [7]...... and easy to get on with, as well as being very easy to [8]...... stuff to, which is great.

	A	B	C
1	proponents	relapses	hurdles
2	accession	transition	remission
3	procedure	schedule	formality
4	decadent	rigorous	reckless
5	brutal	troubleshoot	painstaking
6	leadership	statutory	merchant
7	sheltered	innate	witty
8	delegate	liaise	subsidise

[... / 8]

[Total ... /80]

13 NEWS AND THE MEDIA

In this unit, you learn how to:
• understand news programmes better
• comment on news stories
• recognise and use rhetorical questions
• talk about the media
• report what people said

Grammar
• Reporting and verb patterns

Vocabulary
• News headlines
• Newspapers

Reading
• Popular papers

Listening
• *Did you see ...?*
• Future of news publishing
• The evening news

VOCABULARY News headlines

Newspaper headlines in English use short synonyms such as *blast* instead of *explosion* or *slash* instead of *cut heavily*. They also miss out a lot of grammar words.

Girl stabbed at birthday party =
A girl's been stabbed at a birthday party she was attending.

A Look at the headlines below and check any words in **bold** you don't know in the *Vocabulary Builder*.
1   Bomb **blast toll** reaches 20
2   President **hails** breakthrough in peace process
3   Club **bars** fans in **crackdown** on hooliganism
4   Sanders **cleared** of bribery charges
5   Police **seize** $10 million drugs haul in house **raid**
6   Win brings Boca to **brink** of league title
7   Email **leak** reveals secret plan to **slash** jobs
8   Kirov **ups** stake in Mac in takeover **bid**
9   Police **clash** with protesters at union rally
10 Teachers **rule out** strike action to **halt** pay cuts
11 Kohl **pulls out of** Open over sex scandal
12 Safety fears deal **blow** to car company's recovery
13 Hector **vows** to continue despite outburst

B   Work in pairs. For each headline, discuss:
a   what happened
b   if you think it is good news or bad news
c   if you would want to read more.

C   Work in pairs. Discuss these questions.
1   Give an example of a real blast. What caused it?
2   Have there been any crackdowns in your country / city recently? On what?
3   Have you heard of any police raids? What happened? Did they seize anything?
4   Why do people leak information? Can you give any real examples?
5   Have you heard of any bids to break a record / win something / take over a company? Do you think they'll be successful?
6   Have you heard of any clashes between political colleagues, work colleagues, a player and coach?
7   Is there anything you would rule out doing in your life?

LISTENING

You are going to hear five short conversations about some of the headlines in *Vocabulary*, exercise A.

A 🔊 **13.1 Listen and decide:**
1   which headline story they are talking about.
2   whether the speakers in each conversation agree or disagree.

B Complete each of the sentences from the conversations with a noun. Then listen again and check.
1   a   It was so obvious he's been lining his own
        ....
    b   The case was dismissed on some kind of
        ....
2   a   There's an .... coming up in just over a year.
    b   Maybe the opposition is just stirring up
        ....
3   a   It's such a .... about nothing.
    b   It's all to do with money and ...., isn't it?
4   a   It undermines our .... in the world.
    b   It's just a storm in a .... It'll all blow over quickly enough.
5   a   A whole load of them have had their ....
        confiscated.
    b   I know. They're .... They should be locked up.

NATIVE SPEAKER ENGLISH

all over

All over means *everywhere* or *in lots of different places.*

I don't see how having it all over the papers will help.
The pictures were all over the front pages.
The story's being covered all over the world.
I've been looking all over for him.

DEVELOPING CONVERSATIONS
Rhetorical questions and common opinions

When people talk about news stories, they often put their point of view as a rhetorical question (questions that don't require an answer) or use expressions that show common opinions.

What did you expect? (= I'm not surprised)
It's one rule for us and another for them.

A Work in pairs. Look at the audioscript 13.1 on page 175. Decide which questions are real and which are rhetorical. What opinion do the rhetorical questions show?

B Work in groups. Which of these common opinions could you yourself imagine saying? In what situation?
1   It's one rule for the rich and another for the poor.
2   They should lock them up and throw away the key.
3   They're just in it for the money.
4   Young people today! They have no respect.
5   They haven't got a hope in hell.
6   It's all about oil.
7   It's about time they did something about it.
8   If you live by the sword, you die by the sword.

CONVERSATION PRACTICE

You are going to have similar conversations to the ones you heard in *Listening*.

A Think of three different stories you have heard in the news recently. Write a question to start a conversation about each one.

B Have conversations with different students in the class. Start by asking questions. Use as much language from these pages as you can.

"Why can't newspapers run more good-news stories?"

SPEAKING

A Read the short text below. Then discuss the questions that follow with a partner.

> The seemingly unstoppable rise of the Internet has posed serious questions for the newspaper industry, with such prominent figures as Bill Gates himself predicting the imminent demise of paper-based publishing. Why continue to waste money on printing and distribution costs, the argument goes, when you could simply focus all your energies on providing an online newspaper instead?

- Do you (or does anyone in your family) regularly read a printed newspaper or news magazine? If so, which one?
- Do you ever read news online? What kind? Where?
- Do you think Bill Gates is right about printed newspapers being on the way out?
- Why do you think newspaper companies persist with print-based versions?

LISTENING

You are going to hear an extract from a radio programme about the future of newspaper publishing.

A ◔ 13.2 Listen and answer these questions.
1 What is the main reason given for the continued existence of print-based newspapers?
2 What other reason is given – and why is it described as ironic?

B Listen again and decide which sentences below the speaker claims are true.
1 Newspaper owners are not paying enough attention to technological developments.
2 In many ways, recent technological developments have not really altered traditional ways of gathering news.
3 Plenty of successful online news sites now use only self-generated items.
4 Reduced delivery and printing costs mean online journalism will soon be more profitable than print-based.
5 The failure of news websites to become profitable in one sense has made them appealing to investors.

LANGUAGE PATTERNS

Write the sentences in your language. Translate them back into English. Compare your English to the original.
Advertisers are keen to hit as wide a range of potential customers as possible.
It still has as wide a circulation as it's always had.
It's not as depressing a story as it might initially appear.
This is as stern a test as we have ever had to face.
It may not be as widespread a problem as we first thought.

VOCABULARY Newspapers

A Use the extra information in 1–8 to guess the meaning of the words in **bold**. Translate the words.
1 The cheaper **tabloids** generally sell better than the more serious **broadsheets**.
2 On Sundays, most papers come with all kinds of **supplements** like a sports section and a business section.
3 The **circulation** of most papers is falling as more and more people turn to the web for their news.
4 A lot of the tabloids are very **sensationalist**. They'll print absolutely anything so as to sell papers! It's all designed to appeal to the **lowest common denominator**.
5 Most papers display a clear left- or right-wing **bias**, and this is usually reflected in their **editorials**.
6 Celebrities always say that stories about their private lives are an **invasion of privacy**, while the papers claim they're **acting in the public interest**.
7 The papers are sometimes forced to r**etract** claims they have made if they're unable to **substantiate** them.
8 We're still a long way off having a **free press**. There's a lot of censorship and **harassment** of journalists.

B Work in groups. Discuss how far you think each of the sentences in exercise A are true for your country.

READING

You are going to read about three popular newspapers from different countries.

A Read and decide which of the newspapers:
1 have been accused of disseminating propaganda.
2 have attempted to diversify their brand.
3 has been criticised for its attitudes towards gay people.
4 shows the least bias.
5 has had to defend itself in court.
6 has been prevented from printing certain things in the past.
7 tends to feature a narrow range of news stories.
8 has developed a reputation for linguistic playfulness.
9 frequently includes extra, separate sections.
10 has been accused of meddling in financial affairs.
11 does not attract many casual readers.
12 has changed its basic format.

B Compare your ideas with a partner and explain how you made your decisions.

C Work in pairs. Discuss these questions..
- Which of the three papers described would you most / least like to read?
- What are the nearest equivalents in your country? How do you feel about them?
- Which newspapers in your country do you think hold most political influence?
- Do you think censorship of the press can ever be a good thing? If yes, under what circumstances?

Despite having started life as a broadsheet in 1964, *The Sun* has become not only the premier tabloid in the United Kingdom, but also the biggest-selling paper of any kind, with a daily circulation of over three million. Owned by Rupert Murdoch, an Australian who now holds US citizenship, and who does not pay tax in the UK, the paper has traditionally been to the right of the political spectrum.

Much of its rise in popularity has been attributed to its introduction of topless models on page three in 1970 and of bingo in the 1980s. Loved and loathed in equal measure, the paper's staple diet is celebrity gossip and exposés, and it is also renowned for its way with catchy, punning headlines.

Over the years, the paper has frequently been sued for libel and has had accusations of sexism, homophobia, jingoism and vicious personal attacks on public figures levelled against it, yet little seems to dent its popularity!

Rupert Murdoch

Helsingin Sanomat is the most popular newspaper in Finland, with a daily circulation of over four hundred thousand, 97% of which is subscription-based. The broadsheet also provides readers with a monthly and weekly supplement as well as an online edition, plus a radio station.

Founded in 1889, when Finland was under the control of the Russian Tsar, the paper was initially subject to considerable censorship and as a result became a leading advocate for freedom of the press and eventually for outright national independence.

Hasari, as it is popularly known, has been politically independent since the 1930s and has long been a family business, being owned as it is by the influential Erkko clan. Nevertheless, over the years its editorials have held considerable political influence, such as when the paper strongly advocated Finnish entry into the EU.

Beckham's move to Real Madrid

With an estimated readership of over two million, *Marca* can claim to be the most widely read daily newspaper in Spain. Its website receives over three million hits a month and it now has its own 24-hour-a-day radio station – not bad for a sports paper that is essentially the unofficial mouthpiece of Real Madrid and that focuses predominantly on football.

Founded in 1938, at the height of the Spanish Civil War, the paper has often been criticised for its clear Madrid bias and for its role in initiating several of the major football transfers of recent years, such as David Beckham's move away from Manchester United to the Spanish capital, a move which prompted his former manager, Sir Alex Ferguson, to claim that *Marca* was nothing more than "a vehicle to unsettle players on behalf of Real Madrid".

Office of *Helsingin Sanomat*

SPEAKING

A **Think about news stories you have heard in the last year or so. Which was:**
- the funniest?
- the most surprising?
- the longest-running?
- the most horrifying?
- the most stupid / irrelevant?

B **Discuss your choices in pairs. See if you agree, or explain the stories if your partner hasn't heard of them.**

LISTENING

You are going to hear a news bulletin.

A 🔊 **13.3 Listen to the headlines for the bulletin once. Then work in pairs and write down what each story is about.**
1 ....
2 ....
3 ....
4 ....
5 ....
6 ....

B **Before you listen to the full bulletin, discuss which two nouns or noun phrases you think go with each story.**
- a thigh strain
- inflation
- a private matter
- bomb disposal
- tear gas
- the base rate
- sham marriage
- health grounds
- bravery
- an appeal
- petrol bomb
- good form

C 🔊 **13.4 Listen and find out what happened in each story and how the words in exercise B were connected.**

D **Work in groups. Discuss if each statement is definitely true, definitely false or still unclear – and why.**
1 Carol Dixon had argued over government policy.
2 She is suffering from heart problems.
3 Bodge works for the police.
4 The two men were killed in a blast.
5 The president has the support of most people.
6 Interest rates may rise again before the year's end.
7 Johnson was injured in training.
8 The team can afford to draw the match.
9 The couple said they wouldn't keep the compensation.
10 The payout may cause the newspaper to go bust.

E **Now listen again and read the audioscript on page 176 to check.**

BREAKING NEWS

GRAMMAR Reporting and verb patterns

When we report what someone said, we often summarise the content using a reporting verb. These verbs are followed by a number of different patterns, most commonly:

1 verb + (that) clause
2 verb + object + (that) clause
3 verb + to-infinitive
4 verb + object + to-infinitive
5 verb + noun phrase
6 verb (+ object) + preposition

Some verbs can be followed by more than one pattern.

A Work in pairs. Discuss which patterns followed these reporting verbs from the news bulletin in *Listening*.

acknowledge	claim	express	reject
assure	confirm	praise	urge
blame	deny	refuse	vow

B Now check your ideas in audioscript 13.4 on page 176.

C Write five sentences about things you have heard in the news recently, using verbs from exercise A.

D Compare what you have written and discuss the stories.

▶ Need help? Read the grammar reference on page 148.

SPEAKING

A Work in groups. You are the editors of your regional paper. Discuss and reach agreement about which five of the following stories you would publish.

1 An ex cabinet minister has launched a scathing personal attack on one of her former colleagues.

2 A graphic photograph has been sent to your office showing the aftermath of a bombing abroad and an accompanying update on investigations.

3 A foreign clothing company has been taken over by its rivals. The company has a factory in the region.

4 Unemployment figures for the region have been released, showing a 1% fall in unemployment.

5 A famous actress, who grew up in a local town, has announced she is divorcing her husband of six months.

6 The government has announced the introduction of education reforms.

7 A local TV presenter has been caught on camera taking drugs at a party.

8 The region's main football team is in danger of relegation and its star player has put in a transfer request.

9 A woman was killed in a traffic accident in the region's main city.

10 A local businessman has been accused of offering bribes to politicians in property deals. There is no evidence at the moment.

11 A family in the region has won the equivalent of $500,000 in a lottery.

12 A police dog has been awarded a medal for bravery.

B Now put the stories you chose in order of importance and decide on a headline for each.

"Right, we'll lead on 'Environmental Armageddon' followed by the bird flu 'End of Humanity' story, and the main feature will be questioning the reasons for increases in depression."

In this unit, you learn how to:
- discuss different aspects of running a firm
- talk about how your business is doing
- network and make small talk
- talk about problems with banks
- take minutes and hold meetings

Grammar
- Relative clauses

Vocabulary
- Business situations

Reading
- Laughing all the way from the bank

Listening
- Two phone calls between colleagues
- A business meeting in a footwear company

SPEAKING

Work in groups. Discuss these questions.

1 Do you know anyone who runs their own business? What kind? How big is it? How's it doing at the moment?
2 Do you like the idea of running your own business? Why? / Why not?
3 How good at business would you be? Give yourself a mark of 1–10 for each of the following (1= absolutely useless, 10 = exceptional) and explain why.
- raising start-up funds
- developing and implementing a business plan
- hiring and firing
- providing leadership
- building team morale
- networking and developing new contacts
- bookkeeping and managing your cash flow
- assessing and taking risks
- dealing with stress and long working hours

VOCABULARY *How's business?*

A **Work in pairs. Discuss whether the words in *italics* mean basically the same thing or something different. Explain any differences in meaning.**

1 We've been *inundated / flooded* with orders.
2 We're actually going to be *relocating / moving* to a smaller town, where *rents / overheads* are cheaper.
3 We've seen a definite *upturn / decline* in sales over recent months.
4 We're lucky in that we have a *solid client base / loyal customers*.
5 We've had to *lay off / employ* about 30 people.
6 We're actually thinking of *floating / launching* the firm on the stock market.
7 If things don't *pick up / get better* soon, we're going to *end up going under / have to make serious cutbacks*.
8 Times are tough, but we're just about *hanging in / surviving*.
9 We're having to *diversify / consolidate* the range of services we provide.
10 We've had *to take on staff / make staff redundant* this year.
11 There's been a definite *downturn / drop* in sales this quarter.
12 We're in the middle of *terminating / pitching for* a big contract in Russia.

B **Discuss what you think each of the possible options in 1–12 above are the result of. For example:**

> Maybe they're inundated with orders because they've launched a new product.

> Yeah, or it might be down to a successful advertising campaign.

LISTENING

You are going to hear two telephone calls between colleagues.

A 🔊 14.1 **Listen and answer these questions about each conversation.**
1 Why is the second speaker calling?
2 How's business?
3 What else do they talk about?

B **Work in pairs. Do you remember what the speakers said about the following?**

Conversation 1
1 panicking
2 this quarter
3 taken on
4 crawling
5 a bit of a pain

Conversation 2
6 the European Championships
7 chickens
8 overheads
9 half the staff
10 Thursday

C **Listen again to check your ideas.**

DEVELOPING CONVERSATIONS
Small talk

In many business contexts, it is common to engage in small talk before or after more serious conversations. It is also a central part of networking.

A **Work in pairs. Discuss these questions.**
- Do you like making small talk? What kind of things do you usually ask or talk about?
- Do you think men and women make small talk about different kinds of things? If yes, give examples.
- Do you think small talk is important when doing business in your country?
- What would you recommend foreign business people make small talk about in your country?

B **Work in pairs. Decide what questions produced these answers.**
1 We can't complain. We're weathering the storm, which is more than many companies can say!
2 Pretty dire, to be honest. It just seems to be sinking further and further into recession.
3 They're doing well. Johan's in his second year of secondary school now and Eva turned three last month.
4 I know. It's beautiful, isn't it? It was minus two and snowing when I left Malmö last night as well!
5 Oh, it's been really hectic. I'm glad it's the weekend tomorrow!
6 Don't ask! We're actually on the brink of relegation!
7 I'm having dinner with a client at seven, but after that I'm not sure, actually. Do you fancy maybe meeting up later on?
8 It was great. We stayed with friends down on the coast for ten days. It was much needed, I can tell you!

C **Work in pairs. Ask each other your questions from exercise B, but give different answers.**

CONVERSATION PRACTICE

You are going to role-play similar conversations to the ones you heard in *Listening*.

A **Work in pairs. Look at the six reasons for making telephone conversations below. Choose four that you want to have – and decide which roles to take in each case.**
1 chase up an order that hasn't arrived yet
2 arrange a convenient time and place for a meeting
3 apologise for the delay in sending an order out
4 check whether or not a delivery has been received
5 discuss sales / marketing strategy for the next quarter
6 cancel a meeting

B **Spend five minutes planning what you are going to say. Then role-play the phone calls. Make sure you engage in plenty of small talk.**

SPEAKING

Look at the problems connected to banks below. Then discuss in groups the questions that follow.

1 A cash machine has eaten your card.
2 You're unable to open a bank account.
3 Money has left your account without your authorisation.
4 Your bank has overcharged you on your overdraft.
5 Extra money has somehow been added to your account.
6 You've defaulted on your mortgage or loan payments.
7 Your bank has gone out of business.
8 Every time you try to call your bank, you get put on hold – and even when you do get through, it's to a machine!

- Which problems do you think are the most / least serious? Why?
- What do you think could be the cause of each problem?
- What would you do in each situation?
- Have you ever had any of these problems?

READING

You are going to read a blog entry about banks and banking.

A Read the main blog entry and answer these questions.

1 What do you think the title means?
2 What seems to have prompted this blog entry?
3 How does the writer feel about this news? Why?
4 Why do you think the writer mentioned each of the things below?
   - her parents' relationship with their bank manager
   - the 1980s
   - pensions and life insurance
   - the £30 billion profit British banks made
   - taxpayers

B Complete these sentences with nouns from the blog.

1 The new website is a real .... to the business.
2 Throughout the 1990s, the economy went through a .... of extraordinary instability.
3 The bank made a huge .... last year.
4 The new model is a completely different .... to the old one – faster and much more powerful.
5 Hundreds of small firms are facing .... due to soaring inflation and a weak currency.
6 The national airline needed a government .... to prevent bankruptcy.

C How would you summarise the main message of the blog entry? Compare your ideas with a partner and discuss whether or not you agree with this message.

GRAMMAR Relative clauses

A Without looking at the blog entry, correct the mistakes in each of these sentences.

1 Banks went through a period which deregulation allowed them to expand.
2 Banks became places which you went to pay money in or to take out loans.
3 They also worked out that they could charge loyal customers large amounts of money for services had once been provided for free.
4 The local branch became simply a tiny part of a much bigger beast, a beast that it fed off your hard-earned cash.
5 The ways to which bankers have learned to extract money knows no end.
6 When it comes to the bailout, it's the national government most directly concerned that takes the lead, that means us – the national taxpayers – picking up the bill.

B Compare your ideas with a partner. Then check by looking at the blog entry again.

▶ Need help? Read the grammar reference on page 149.

> Several abstract nouns often occur with clauses introduced by *where, when* or *why* – or as part of a prepositional phrase with *which*.
>
> ....
>
> Banks went through *a period in which* deregulation allowed them to expand.
> There are a number of *situations where* I've considered changing career.

C Complete the sentences with one word in each gap.

1 There is no reason .... we shouldn't consider this.
2 There have been a number of cases .... customers have refused to pay their bank charges.
3 I'm in a situation .... I require money fairly soon!
4 The amount we can loan you obviously depends on the extent to .... you are able to meet your repayments.
5 We just got to the point .... either we started laying people off or else faced up to the risk of bankruptcy.
6 I don't understand the way .... which you've reached these figures.

SPEAKING

A Read the comments which have been added in response to the blog. In pairs, discuss how far you agree with each person. Explain why.

B Discuss what you think the words in dark blue mean in the context they are in.

LAUGHING ALL THE WAY FROM THE BANK!

When I was growing up, my local bank was seen as an asset to the community. It was small-scale and friendly. My parents knew the clerks by name and occasionally dined with the manager. Deposits you made helped fund loans for others in your neighbourhood to buy new cars or start their own businesses. The bank needed you – and you needed them.

During the 1980s, though, things started to change as banks went through a period in which deregulation allowed them to expand and add a seemingly endless range of new services. Banks became places you went to not only to pay money in or to take out loans, but also to get life insurance, set up pensions and even buy shares on the stock market. They also worked out that they could charge loyal customers large amounts of money for services that had once been provided for free. Profit became all-important and the local branch became simply a tiny part of a much bigger beast, a beast that fed off your hard-earned cash.

In light of all of this, the news that the National Bank is on the brink of bankruptcy and may now need to be bailed out, while depressing, is not particularly surprising. The ways in which bankers have learned to extract money from the general public they are supposed to be serving know no end. Banks in Britain made over £30 billion last year, and while the big private banks may be global in life, they are sadly national in death. When it comes to the

bailout, it's the national government most directly concerned that takes the lead, which means us – the national taxpayers – picking up the bill. Again!

COMMENTS

Fatcatsam: I blame the bonus culture and the reckless pursuit of short-term gain. It's totally irresponsible to award bankers such **obscene** sums of money for taking risks that actually **jeopardise** the interests of their shareholders and the long-term health of the banks themselves!

2True: There are obviously many reasons why banks fail, but it would be wrong of us to ignore the role we play. Anyone who has spent money they did not have, encouraged by soaring house prices, **lax** mortgage lending and **seductive** advertising, should **bear a share of** the responsibility.

ChicagoRed: Banking is **legitimised** theft. They offer 2% interest when you have money in the bank, and yet charge anything from 8% to 20% when you borrow from them. It's **daylight robbery**. And it's even worse if you go over your limit. You're charged for that, and then they write to inform you of the fact you've **exceeded** your pre-arranged figure – and charge for the letter as well!

Indeep: Banks have ruined my life. If they hadn't been so keen to lend me money, I wouldn't be in the **hole** I'm in today! They **threw** credit at me! I used to get endless letters from different banks asking me if I'd like to take out a loan or get a new credit card and of course in the end I got to the point where I just gave in to temptation.

Dropthedebt: The big western banks make a **killing** by loaning money to poorer countries. It may be legal, but it's also deeply immoral and we've now got a situation where many countries spend so much **servicing** their debt that they're no longer able to invest in healthcare, education and so on.

DaveC: Stop whingeing and grow up!

VOCABULARY Business situations

A Match the groups of words in 1–6 to the situations in the box and explain the possible connections.

sales	a new product
an industrial dispute	a takeover
cutting costs	business taxes

1 target / projected sales / launch / gap in the market / a prototype / conduct focus groups / good feedback
2 ongoing negotiations / pay demands / hold firm / have a contingency plan / union threat / make concessions
3 be a good fit / recommend it to shareholders / up their offer / a hostile bid / raise their stake / share price rises
4 undertake restructuring / scale down / outsource / back office / lay people off / buy in bulk / switch suppliers
5 exceed targets / push a product hard / seal a major deal / increase fourfold / a low base / be dropped by a client
6 lobby / affect our bottom line / less competitive / fund government programmes / win concessions

B Work in pairs. Discuss these questions.
- What new products have come out recently? Who are they targeted at? Are they selling well? Why? / Why not?
- Do you think business taxes are good? Why? / Why not?
- How much do you think companies influence politics? Is it a good or a bad thing?
- Have you heard of any takeovers? Were they successful?
- Have you (or a place you worked in) ever had to cut costs? Why? How?
- If you could 'outsource' something you do in your life, what would it be?

LISTENING

You are going to hear a business meeting in a footwear company. They discuss a financial loss and a new product.

A Before you listen, work in pairs and discuss these questions.
1 What is an **agenda**?
2 What does **the chair** of a meeting do?
3 What does a **minute taker** do?
4 What meetings do you go to? What are they like? How are they run?

B 🔊 14.2 Listen to each of the speakers below and decide who has which role in the box.

sales	product development	chair	finance

1. Katrin:	operations
2. Peter:	
3. Henry:	
4. Rachel:	
5. Alex:	

> When you take minutes, you summarise what people say in note form. You may use reporting verbs such as *voice concerns*, *question*, etc. but not full grammatical sentences. Don't record irrelevant things such as joking comments.

C 🔊 14.3 Listen and take minutes of the meeting.

D Work in groups and compare the minutes you took. Whose were most accurate?

E Work in pairs. Discuss these questions.
- What do you think of the Shoe Saver? Why?
- Do you think it'll make the company a lot of money? Why? / Why not?
- What do you think the company should do to improve its situation?

F Using the minutes you took, discuss whether 1–12 are accurate. Make changes where necessary.

1 Henry stated the loss was down to state of the economy.
2 Rachel mentioned poor sales in Eastern Europe.
3 Katrin expressed doubts about ability to cut costs.
4 Henry denied there'd be redundancies.
5 Everyone v impressed by results of demonstration.
6 Alex said unit costs €35–45 and will retail at €100–130.
7 Cost €35 if outsourced.
8 Proj. sales: Y4 250,000.
9 Henry questioned if proj. sales achievable.
10 Alex estimated shoes last 50% longer so would pay for machine. Main market rich homes. Said initial sales v good.
11 Katrin asked about patents.
12 Alex said technology not protected, but some parts of manufacturing process patented. Still gap in the market.

G Look through the audioscript on page 177. Check your answers to exercise F and underline any useful expressions for managing a meeting.

LANGUAGE PATTERNS

Write the sentences in your language. Translate them back into English. Compare your English to the original.
That's also very much erring on the side of caution.
Who's speaking on the side of the workers?
Fortunately, my boss saw the funny side of the situation.
On the plus side, sales in Eastern Europe were up.
Their stuff is a bit on the expensive side.

SPEAKING

You are managers in an electronics company and are going to have a meeting like the one you heard in *Listening*.

A Divide into pairs or groups. Each group should take one of the points on the agenda below. Prepare a short proposal or update on your point. Under AOB ('Any Other Business'), you can write about anything – complaints, events, etc.

Meeting agenda
1 New products
2 Cost-cutting measures
3 Proposed takeover
4 Possible strike
5 AOB

B Now have the meeting. One person in the class should chair the meeting and another should take minutes. Each point should start with the proposal / update from the relevant points on the agenda. Anyone may interrupt and ask questions at any point.

15 FASHION

SPEAKING

A **Work in pairs. Discuss these questions.**
- What are the current trends in clothes and hairstyles? Do you like them? Why? / Why not?
- Do you ever look at the fashion pages in newspapers or magazines? Which ones?
- What do you think of the styles of the people on these pages? Explain your opinions.

VOCABULARY Style and design

A **Work in pairs. Match 1–8 to a–h and decide which word in each group is the odd one out.**
1. collar / pocket / lining / lapel / sleeve / laces
2. blouse / ribbon / bangle / beads / shades / purse
3. a bob / a ponytail / a shawl / permed / spiked / highlighted
4. summery / sturdy / low-cut / strapless / knee-length / slinky
5. flowery / checked / linen / tartan / pinstripe / spotted
6. greasy / thick / frizzy / baggy / red / wavy
7. open-toed / flats / heels / flared / wedges / strappy
8. ripped / frilly / faded / skinny / bootcut / designer

a. They're all hairstyles except ....
b. They all describe dresses except ....
c. They're all kinds of accessories except ....
d. They all describe jeans except ....
e. They all describe hair except ....
f. They're all patterns except ....
g. They're all parts of a jacket except ....
h. They all describe kinds of shoes except ....

B **Which words are illustrated in the photos? Who can find the most?**

C **Work in pairs. Discuss these questions.**
- What are your favourite clothes at the moment?
- Do you remember any clothes or hairstyles that you had in the past and really liked? What?
- Do you remember any that you had but wouldn't wear now? What?

WEIRDO!

Joseph Farris

LISTENING

You are going to hear four conversations about style.

A 🔊 **15.1 Listen and decide if the sentences are true or false.**

1 a They both have short hair now.
  b They both like each other's look.
2 a She is trying on some jeans.
  b The accessories improve the outfit.
3 a The girl they're talking about has followed a fashion.
  b They agree on the boots she's wearing.
4 a The man doesn't look good in the suit he's wearing.
  b The woman wants him to change.

B **Look at the audioscript on page 178. With a partner, discuss what the underlined expressions mean and how you would say them in your language.**

C **Work in groups. Discuss these questions.**

- Have you ever failed to recognise someone? Why?
- What clothes or hairstyles don't work for you?
- Do you know anyone with quite a 'different' style? What's it like? Do you think they pull it off well?
- Have you ever stuck out? When? Why?

NATIVE SPEAKER ENGLISH

funky

We say something is *funky* if it is stylish in an unusual way.

It's quite a funky look.
It's quite over-the-top, but she looks quite funky.
She was wearing these really funky shades.

DEVELOPING CONVERSATIONS
Backtracking and correcting

When people misunderstand what we say or take it the wrong way, we have to backtrack and correct the misunderstanding.

A: You don't like it?
B: No, you look fantastic. It's just that it's so different.

A **Complete the second sentence to repair the misunderstanding.**

1 A: You don't like my shirt?
  B: It's not that it's not nice. It's just
  ....
2 A: You think I'd look silly if I dyed it blonde, then?
  B: No, I didn't say that. All I meant was
  ....
3 A: What's wrong with the clothes I'm wearing?
  B: They do suit you. It's just that
  ....
4 A: So you don't like him?
  B: I do! It's just that ....
5 A: You don't think I'm good enough for the job?
  B: No, that's not what I meant. I just think
  ....
6 A: So you're saying it's a waste of money, then?
  B: No, it is nice. It's just that
  ....

B **Work in pairs. Take turns to say the first sentences in 1–6. Your partner should reply using their completed sentences.**

C **Write three 'misunderstandings'. For example:**
Sorry. Am I boring you?
Then read your sentences in pairs. Your partner should repair the misunderstandings.

CONVERSATION PRACTICE

A **Work with a new partner. Look at the photos in File 16 on page 158, or find photos in a magazine or on the web. Discuss:**

- if you like the look or not – and why.
- if the clothes / hair, etc. would suit you or your partner.
- if the photos remind you of anyone or of clothes / things you have.

READING

You are going to read the opening of *Adorned in Dreams;* a book on fashion by Elizabeth Wilson.

A Read the opening and answer the questions.
1 How does the author feel? Why?
2 Why does she compare the gallery to an Egyptian tomb?
3 Why does she see the clothes on display as 'sinister' and 'in limbo'?

There is something eerie about a museum of costume. In the dusty silence that surrounds the old gowns and the dim light that helps preserve the fragile clothes, the deserted galleries seem haunted. With a mounting sense of panic, the living observer moves through the world of the dead. May not these relics, like the contents of the Egyptian tombs, bring bad luck to the people who have been in contact with them? There are dangers in seeing what should have been sealed up in the past. We experience a sense of the supernatural when we gaze at garments that had an intimate relationship with human beings long since gone to their graves, for clothes are so much part of our living, moving selves that, frozen on display, they hint at something only half-understood, sinister and threatening: the degeneration of the body, the short-lived nature of life.

These clothes are congealed memories of times past. Once they inhabited the noisy streets, the crowded theatres and glittering events of the social scene. Now, like souls in limbo, they wait poignantly for the music to begin again.

B Work in pairs. Discuss these questions.
- Do you like the description of the museum of costume? Why? / Why not?
- What museums have you been to? When?
- What's the last exhibition you saw? Was it any good?
- Are there any exhibitions on near you now? What are they about? Are you planning to go? Why? / Why not?

You are going to read five information cards from a costume museum.

C Read and match the short texts opposite to five of the pictures 1–8.

D Work in pairs and discuss which of the items illustrated:
1 was a marketing ploy.   ...... and ......
2 took on a social significance.   ......
3 showed a hierarchy.   ......
4 had a practical purpose.   ......
5 was inspired by other clothes.   ......
6 had a ban on it.   ......, ... and ......
7 continued a trend.   ...... and ......
8 made use of something new.   ...... and ......

A

The Ottoman style of dress was made up of a pair of baggy silk trousers or *pantaloons*, a long short-sleeved jacket or *caftan,* and a turban. It was typical among the upper classes and military, and status was often shown by extra jewels added to the headdress. However, early in the 19th century, this military dress was replaced by Western style uniforms on the orders of Sultan, Mahmud II. Ironically, though the turban was abolished as a sign of modernisation, its replacement, the *fez*, was made illegal for the very same reason some hundred years later.

B

The ruff was widespread throughout the 15th and 16th centuries until it was gradually replaced by long, flat, falling collars. It evolved from a frilly piece on a drawstring shirt and was developed as a detachable section that could be washed separately. This avoided wear and tear at the neckline to the *doublet*, which was often ornate. With the discovery of starch, ruffs could be made stiffer, allowing them to be shaped into elaborate folds. Over time, they became increasingly broad – often up to 30 centimetres wide when reinforced with wire frames.

C

Mary Quant's design is seen as defining a generation and was embraced by the feminist movement. It symbolised freedom and sexual liberation and the style was widely frowned on when it first appeared, being banned in certain quarters. In fact, although Quant took the fashion to new lengths and popularised it, hemlines had been moving upwards for some time, and in sporting contexts above-the-knee wear was acceptable. Furthermore, the popularity of the style owed something to the development of tights, which meant women did not have to go bare-legged. Tights were often dense black, white or golden brown.

D

The gown is French and is made of silk and lace. Napoleon prohibited the use of British fabrics in an effort to boost the French textile industry, which had suffered because of the fashion for English cloth. The policy also influenced design, with the long trains requiring more material. Napoleon demanded that ladies in court did not wear an outfit twice and supposedly had the fires in the palace blocked in order to encourage the wearing of extra layers. His wife was held up as a fashion icon and the new styles spread, which had the desired effect on industry as production rose tenfold.

E

The fashion for sagging jeans originated from prison uniforms in the States. Prison trousers are often ill-fitting and inmates are refused belts because of the risk of suicide. The style, along with the hooded top or *hoodie*, was first adopted by rap artists selling a 'gangsta' image. Wearing the hood up was a way of avoiding identification by security cameras. In fact, some stores and shopping malls began to refuse entry to anyone wearing a *hoodie* for that very reason.

SPEAKING

A **Work in pairs. Discuss these questions.**
- Can you think of any garments or accessories which have been used to show status?
- Which other fashions have been banned? Why?
- Do any trends now have a social significance or is it all just marketing?
- What groups of people can you think of that are defined by lifestyles or the clothes they wear?
- Do you think technology has influenced any recent fashions? In what way?
- Can you think of any other fashions that were shocking when they first appeared?
- Does your country have a national dress? What does it look like? What do you think of it?

GRAMMAR Prepositions

> **Prepositions can be followed by nouns, pronouns or -*ing* forms and may show time, direction, possession, style, cause, etc.**
> We experience a sense *of* the supernatural when we gaze *at* them.
> ... a way *of* avoiding identification *by* security cameras
>
> ···
>
> **A preposition may collocate with a noun verb or adjective.**
> frozen *on display*
> *in* the dusty *silence*
> added *to* the headdress
>
> ···
>
> **They may be used to link two parts of a sentence.**
> The policy also influenced design, *with* the long trains requiring more material. (*with* = because)

A **Choose the correct prepositions.**
1 They hint *at / on* something half-understood.
2 The turban was abolished *as / like* a sign of modernisation.
3 It was widespread *for / throughout* the 15th century.
4 *By / With* the discovery of starch, ruffs could be made stiffer, allowing them to be shaped *into / to* elaborate folds.
5 They were up *to / until* 30 centimetres wide.
6 It symbolised freedom *of / from* conservative society.
7 The style owed something *to / from* the development *of / with* tights.
8 Skirts had been getting shorter *for / during* some time and *in / on* sporting contexts were acceptable.
9 The styles soon spread, *with / by* them having the desired effect *on / of* industry.
10 *On / At* gaining power, Napoleon introduced new dress codes in the court.

B **Compare your answers in pairs.**

▶ Need help? Read the grammar reference on page 150.

LISTENING

You are going to hear a lecture about the influence of the fashion industry on society.

A Before you listen, work in groups and discuss these questions.
- Which of the images below do you think are most typical of the fashion industry? Why do you think this might be?
- What impact on audiences do you think each image might have? Why?
- Which images do you respond most / least positively to? Why?

B 🔊 15.2 Listen and note the order in which the five different kinds of image shown below are mentioned. Think about these questions.
- What points does the lecturer make about each one?
- How would you summarise the main point of the talk?

C Work in pairs. Discuss why you think the lecturer mentioned the things below.
1 developed countries
2 our political representatives
3 the big fashion houses
4 teenage girls
5 Botox
6 extreme cosmetic procedures
7 *Dove* and the singer Beth Ditto
8 swimming against the tide

D Listen again to check your ideas.

E Try to match the words from *Listening*.

1	penetrate	a	the world as it really is
2	depict	b	images
3	disseminate	c	market
4	cut-throat	d	a chord
5	nigh-on	e	for procedures
6	opt	f	extreme procedures
7	undergo	g	every corner of the world
8	become	h	impossible
9	strike	i	publicity
10	attract	j	the norm

F Compare your ideas with a partner. Discuss who / what did the things in exercise E or who / what the words describe. Check in the audioscript on page 178.

G Work in pairs. Decide which of the statements below you think the lecturer would agree with. Explain why and discuss how far you agree with each statement.
1 It's completely unfair to blame the fashion industry for choices made by individual women.
2 Men these days are almost as vain as women!
3 Whether conscious or not, there's a degree of racism inherent in the fashion industry.
4 Fashions change over time. Sooner or later, larger female models will be back in again.
5 The fact that firms are using older or bigger models is healthy and it shows real changes are occurring.
6 No one wants to see overweight people modelling nice clothes. It's off-putting!

LANGUAGE PATTERNS

Write the sentences in your language. Translate them back into English. Compare your English to the original.

It seems to me to be no coincidence that this has coincided with a huge rise in eating disorders.
It is no great surprise that the fashion industry refuses to accept responsibility.
There is no real demand for larger models.
I'm no expert, but it can't just be coincidental, can it?
The impact images have is obviously no small matter.

VOCABULARY Fashion and the media

A Complete 1–10 with the correct form of the words in **bold**.
1 I don't know what all the fuss is about. Most photography is purely ...., isn't it? **represent**
2 The .... image of women that we see in the media is unrealistically narrow. **dominate**
3 It's really offensive when advertisers use religious .... to help sell their products. **image**
4 The appeal of designer brands has .... considerably in recent years. **broad**
5 Most models don't realise how incredibly .... they are. **influence**
6 The conditions under which many high street fashion items are made are totally .... **exploit**
7 The media is guilty of the .... of racial stereotypes. **perpetual**
8 The press really should do more to curb the .... of unhealthy models. **depict**
9 Most fashion advertising is both .... and .... It treats older people as invisible and women as objects. **age, sex**
10 The lack of .... of women in politics is directly linked to the way women are .... in the media. **represent, portrayal**

B Choose two sentences from exercise A you strongly agree with and one you strongly disagree with. In pairs, compare your choices and explain your feelings.

C How many other forms of the words in **bold** in exercise A can you think of? With a partner, write example sentences for each.

SPEAKING

A Work in groups. Discuss how far you agree with each of the quotations about fashion below. Say why.
1 A fashion is nothing but an induced epidemic.
2 There is no fashion for the old.
3 Nothing is as hideous as an obsolete fashion.
4 Fashion is what you adopt when you don't know who you are.
5 Fashion for the most part is nothing but the ostentation of riches.
6 Fashion is very important. It is life-enhancing and, like everything that gives pleasure, it is worth doing well.
7 Fashion as we once knew it is over; people now wear exactly what they feel like wearing.
8 As soon as a fashion is universal, it is out of date.

16 DANGER AND RISK

In this unit, you learn how to:
- describe accidents
- use and understand a range of interjections
- talk about risk and safety
- talk about laws
- think critically about texts
- discuss the pros and cons of Internet use

Grammar
- Other future forms

Vocabulary
- Accidents and injuries
- Laws and regulations
- Dangers and risks

Reading
- Bureaucrats back down on tan ban

Listening
- Scar stories
- A health and safety officer
- A radio phone-in programme

SPEAKING

A **Work in pairs. Look at the places and activities in the box. Discuss what kind of accidents might be connected to each.**

an ice rink	a beach	a nightclub
a football pitch	a campsite	a mountain
cooking dinner	cycling	doing DIY
driving	jogging	gardening

B **Which of the above do you think is most risky? Why?**

LISTENING

You are going to hear two conversations about accidents that resulted in scars.

A 🔊 **16.1 Listen and answer these questions about each conversation.**
1 Where are the scars?
2 How did the speakers get them?

B **Decide if 1–10 are true or false. Listen again to check your ideas.**

Conversation 1
1 One speaker is much better at tennis than the other.
2 The first speaker used to be a model.
3 She was ill when the accident happened.
4 The seriousness of the accident didn't sink in at first.
5 The accident ruined the whole of the following day.

Conversation 2
6 The accident happened during the holidays.
7 His initial assessment of the injury was optimistic.
8 He had to have several stitches the following day.
9 They both remember the news stories about the very strong winds.
10 The speaker hit his chin against the side of a car.

> When telling stories, it is common to use relatively informal expressions and more idiomatic language. It is also common to exaggerate and use irony.

C **Work in pairs. Discuss what you think the following words in *italics* from each conversation mean in the context.**
1 a That's *one hell of* a scar!
  b It was about four in the morning and I was *more dead than alive*.
  c I was so *out of it* that I was just staring at this gaping great hole.
  d I just wiped the blood off with a tissue, tried to super-glue it all together and *crashed out*.
2 a I was *smart* enough to somehow walk straight into a head-height shelf .
  b I'd been out to a party with some friends one night, *stumbled* home and *whacked* myself.
  c It was unstitchable the following day! *Just my luck*.
  d My wisdom teeth *weren't too happy either*!

D **Work in groups. Discuss these questions.**
- Which of the three injuries mentioned do you think sounds the most painful / serious? Why?
- What would you have done in each of the three situations? Why?
- Have you ever heard of any weather-related injuries or accidents? When? What happened?

LANGUAGE PATTERNS

Write the sentences in your language. Translate them back into English. Compare your English to the original.

I managed to cut a huge great big slice out of my thigh.
I've got a tiny little scar on my left thumb.
When we finally got to the hospital, it was filthy dirty.
I managed to knock boiling hot water all over myself.
It was dark and freezing cold and I had nowhere to sleep.

DEVELOPING CONVERSATIONS
Interjections

> Interjections are single words or noises made to show strong emotions such as anger or surprise.

> A: ... and when I came to, I found my chin completely split open ... and my wisdom teeth weren't too happy either!
> B: Woah!

A 🔊 16.2 **Listen to 12 interjections. After each one, discuss with a partner what you think it means – and in what kind of context it might be used.**

B 🔊 16.3 **Now listen to some short exchanges. See if you guessed the meaning and context correctly.**

C **Work in pairs. Discuss these questions.**
- Are any of the interjections the same in your language? Which ones?
- Do you use any of them in English already?
- Do you think it's important to use interjections when speaking a foreign language? Why? / Why not?
- What interjections would you recommend someone studying your language should learn?

NORMAN BORING WAS VERY PROUD OF HIS OPERATION SCAR

VOCABULARY Accidents and injuries

A **Replace the words in *italics* with synonyms in the box.**

banged	came to	heavily	ripped
break	cut	panicked	sliced
burnt	fainted	pouring	terrible pain

1 The machine almost *tore* one of my fingernails off!
2 When I *regained consciousness*, I realised I couldn't feel my hands.
3 It was horrible. Blood was *streaming* down my face.
4 I totally *freaked out* and started screaming.
5 I *whacked* my head on the ceiling and nearly knocked myself out.
6 I was bleeding quite *profusely* from the wound.
7 I *cut* my finger open when I was chopping onions.
8 I fell onto a nail and ended up with a huge *gash* on my arm.
9 I somehow managed to pour boiling water all over my hand and *scalded* myself really badly.
10 It was so crowded and hot and stuffy that I actually *passed out* on the train.
11 I heard the bone *snap*. It was horrible.
12 I was in *agony*. I was screaming my head off.

B **Test each other.**
Student A: say the words in the box in exercise A.
Student B: close your book. Say the synonyms in 1–12.

C **Decide which of the pairs of synonyms in each of 1–12 in exercise A you prefer. Compare your choices with a partner.**

CONVERSATION PRACTICE

A **Think of any scars you have – and how you got them. Spend five minutes planning how to describe what happened. Try to use as much new language from these pages as you can.**

If you don't have any scars, either use your imagination or talk about someone else you know.

B **Now tell some other students about how you got your scars.**

SPEAKING

Work in groups. Discuss these questions.
- What health and safety regulations do you know about in these areas?
  - – schools   – construction sites
  - – offices   – traffic
- Are there any health and safety rules that you think go too far? Why?
- Are there any that you think should be tightened? Why?
- Look at the pictures below. Which do you think is the craziest safety hazard?
- Have you seen or heard of anyone doing dangerous things at work / school?

READING

You are going to read a short newspaper article connected to health and safety.

A **Read the first two paragraphs. Then discuss these questions with a partner.**
1 Can you explain the headline?
2 Is the article objective or biased? Explain your view.
3 Why do you think the officials wanted to include sunlight in their directive?

B **Read the eight further examples of health and safety 'madness' and mark the examples with:**
- a tick ✔ if you agree that they are mad
- a cross ✗ if you disagree
- a question mark **?** if you are not sure.

C **Work in pairs. Discuss these questions.**
- How would you describe the general politics of the paper?
- Are there any newspapers in your countries that might have similar views?

BUREAUCRATS BACK DOWN ON TAN BAN

The European Union has bowed to pressure and excluded sunlight from its health and safety directive on protection against bright light sources such as lasers. Opponents of the measures had said the directive would have forced builders to wear shirts all year round and prevented barmaids in places like the Munich Oktoberfest from wearing traditional low-cut tops.

It seems that EU officials have now seen sense and the new regulation will only focus on people working with artificial light. It is a shame health and safety rules don't use common sense more often. Here are just a few examples of the madness:

- Employees at the office of the health and safety executive aren't allowed to shift any chairs or furniture and must give 48 hours notice to a porter who'll then do it for them.
- A school had to fill in a 40-page risk assessment before taking students to a local sports field for an athletics competition.
- Pupils have been banned from throwing snowballs.
- There's been a massive rise in the use of speed cameras.
- Bowling alleys have been told to employ an expensive safety system to make machines automatically cut out if customers walk down the lanes to knock the pins down by hand.
- Warning signs have appeared on packets of nuts for people suffering from nut allergies.
- A clown has been stopped from blowing bubbles for children to chase after.
- A family is suing the police for one million dollars after their daughter was handcuffed and taken to a police station for scribbling on a school desk.

D Now read the following short reports from the same newspaper. Discuss what an editorial from the paper might say about each one.

IN BRIEF

A report by the union APEC says workers are being put in danger because companies are failing to comply with safety regulations or are exploiting **loopholes** that go against the spirit of the law. The union wants to see laws tightened and tougher punishments for **non-compliance**.

An amendment to the Human Rights Act has been accused of risking British jobs. Opponents of the **legislation** say it would mean businesses would effectively be held **liable** for absolutely any accident at work and be forced to pay excessive compensation.

Litigation has increased by 35% according to new statistics. The report suggested that the wider availability of no-win, no-fee offers – along with the success of a number of high-profile **lawsuits** – was encouraging more people to sue.

A man has been awarded $200,000 in **damages** after a hospital admitted medical **negligence** in an operation that left the man in a wheelchair.

A court has overturned the film star Glen Brook's driving ban for speeding following **an appeal**. Lawyers for Brooks successfully argued that he would be at risk from invasions of privacy if he could not drive. They also added that he had posed no danger when caught exceeding the limit by 20km/h as the road was empty. He was given a fine.

VOCABULARY Laws and regulations

A Look back at the words in **bold** in the short reports and translate them into your language.

B Complete 1–8 with the correct forms of the verbs in the box.

admit	exploit	hold	oppose
award	file	sue	overturn

1 The company was .... liable for the accident.
2 They were .... a lot of money in damages.
3 They were .... for libel.
4 His conviction was .... on appeal.
5 The group have .... a class-action lawsuit.
6 They .... negligence and agreed to pay compensation.
7 It's a loophole in the law which people ....
8 A lot of people .... the legislation.

C Work in pairs. How many of 1–8 can you think of real examples for? Explain what happened.

LISTENING

You are going to hear an interview on a radio programme with a health and safety officer, Eva Chakrabati.

A Before you listen, discuss these questions in pairs.
- What do you think a health and safety officer does?
- What do you think they would say about the eight examples given in *Reading*, exercise B?

B 🔊 16.4 Listen and tick ✓ the arguments Eva gives.
1 Teachers shouldn't do experiments with flammable materials.
2 Risk is an essential part of life.
3 The paperwork that's asked for is not excessive.
4 Safety standards can sometimes be legitimately ignored.
5 The media exaggerates and makes up stories.
6 Snowballs usually contain stones or hard ice.
7 The clown had been successfully sued after someone slipped and fell.
8 There's some truth in the story about the office.
9 There's a financial benefit in health and safety.

C Compare and explain your choices.

D Work in pairs. Discuss these questions.
- Does Eva's interview alter your opinion of the news articles in *Reading*? Why? / Why not?
- How trustworthy are the following sources of information? What would it depend on?

a webpage	a school textbook	a newspaper
an academic article	a friend	TV

- Have you ever discovered that a story or information you read wasn't true? What? How did you find out?

SPEAKING

A **Work in pairs. Discuss these questions.**
- How much do you use the Internet?
- What do you usually use it for?
- What websites do you look at most often? Why?
- What do you think the benefits of the Internet are?
- What risks do you think the Internet brings? Make a list of all the dangers you can think of.

B **Compare your list of risks and dangers with another pair. Do they have any you didn't think of? Together, decide which of the risks is the most serious – and why.**

VOCABULARY Dangers and risks

A **Choose the correct words.**
1 The future of a lot of small businesses is under *danger / threat* because of increased online competition.
2 If you're a parent, you ignore the websites your kids are visiting at your *danger / peril*.
3 The Internet poses a health *peril / hazard* as so many people now order prescription drugs online.
4 They really should do more to combat the *menace / peril* of spam e-mails!
5 Cyber hackers pose a grave *threat / peril* to global security.
6 People talk about hackers like they're some kind of *menace / peril* to society, but they're mostly pretty harmless.
7 If we impose too many controls on Internet use, we run the *danger / risk* of restricting civil liberties.
8 Internet dating is fraught with *threat / danger*.
9 Every time you shop online, you're putting yourself at *risk / danger*.
10 A lot of people are in serious *danger / risk* of becoming completely addicted to the Internet.

B **Underline the verb–noun / adjective–noun collocations in 1–10 above. Which are new for you?**

C **How far do you agree with each of the sentences in exercise A? Why?**

LISTENING

You are going to hear a radio phone-in programme about the Internet.

A 🔊 16.5 **Listen and see how many of the problems you thought of are mentioned. Are any other risks mentioned?**

B **Listen again and answer these questions.**
1 What two recent news stories about the Internet does the presenter mention?
2 What are Joyce's plans for the future and how is she feeling about them?
3 How has access to the Internet affected her students' study skills?
4 Five different kinds of websites that students get drawn into are mentioned. What are they?
5 What's Nigel's first suggestion?
6 What flaws with this idea does the presenter point out?
7 What alternative proposal does Nigel put forward?
8 What does the presenter make of this idea?

C **Work in groups. Discuss these questions.**
- What do you think the Internet penetration rate in your country is like?
- Do you know anyone who's not connected? Why aren't they?
- Do you think it's a good idea to treat kids for Internet addiction? Why? / Why not?
- Do you use the Internet when studying or writing essays? If so, in what way? Do you ever cut and paste?
- Have you heard any stories of people getting drawn into dubious websites such as those mentioned?
- Do you think making an example of a few spammers or fraudsters would be a sufficient deterrent to others?

NATIVE SPEAKER ENGLISH

and the like / and what have you
We use *and the like* or *and what have you* to mean *et cetera* or *and so on*.

I'm guessing you're talking about pornography and the like here, Joyce?
Lots of people mainly use the web to participate in online games such as chess, role-play games and the like.
Like spammers and online fraudsters and what have you.
She spends half her life on Facebook and Twitter and what have you.

GRAMMAR Other future forms

A Try to complete the sentences by putting the verbs in brackets into the forms they were used in *Listening*.
1 The Internet penetration rate .... 80% sometime in the next month. (reach)
2 If the show ...., we need *you* to call up and tell us what's on your mind. (work)
3 I .... work in the summer. (stop)
4 I honestly don't think things .... any better in the foreseeable future. (get)
5 The Internet basically dangles all manner of temptation in front of young people, and that .... problems. (cause)

B Now try to complete these sentences with the nouns that were used in *Listening*.
6 I'm on the .... of retiring.
7 The .... of it helping are pretty slim, I'd imagine.
8 In all ...., most offenders are actually pretty harmless.
9 Hit them with the toughest sentences we can ... do that and the .... are you'll put the others off.
10 Do that and there's a distinct .... you'll end up embroiled in a lengthy legal dispute.

C Compare your answers with a partner.

D 🔊 16.6 Listen and check.

E Work in pairs. Discuss which form in exercise A:
1 is usually used to talk about timetables / things planned to happen at a particular time.
2 is used when you are sure something will happen.
3 is often used in the media to show something is fairly certain to happen.
4 is often used in the media to talk about scheduled / officially arranged events.
5 is commonly used for making predictions.

▶ Need help? Read the grammar reference on page 151.

F Rewrite the sentences below using the words in **bold** so they have a similar meaning.
1 In all probability, the situation will deteriorate. **bound**
....
2 There's a distinct possibility that our jobs will be at risk. **likely**
....
3 They're almost ready to finalise the deal. **verge**
....
4 Gamble online and the odds are you'll lose. **likelihood**
....
5 The work should be finished by May. **due**
....
6 Inflation will probably rise above 10% next month. **set**
....

SPEAKING

A Work in pairs. Look at the newspaper headlines below. Discuss what risks and dangers could be connected to each situation and decide which you think is the riskiest.

Daily Star wins case to block paper publishing celebrity revelations

Key witness in mafia trial 'not being fully protected'

SECRET PEACE TALKS WITH TERRORIST GROUP LEAKED

Government set to continue with cuts as unemployment reaches record high

State of emergency to be declared as rioting continues

B Work in a new group of three or four. You are going to role-play a radio phone-in programme about the issues of the day.

Student A: you are the presenter. Introduce the show with an overview of today's talking points. Use the headlines above and pose a few questions for callers to respond to.

Manage the 'calls' from other students, summarise their main ideas, and challenge them where appropriate in order to move the debate forward.

Students B–D: you are callers. Decide which of the headline stories above you want to comment on and what you want to say about it. Try to comment on what you think may happen in the future. You can also comment on previous callers' opinions.

04 REVIEW

TWO MINUTES

Work in groups. You are going to give a short two-minute talk on one of the topics in the list below. Spend five minutes thinking about what you are going to say. Look back at your notes to check language if you like.

- A story in the news
- The state of the economy
- Style
- My favourite newspaper
- A successful business
- The future of the Internet

Give each other marks out of ten for language, interest and clarity. Who got the most marks?

GAME

Work in pairs. Student A use *only* the green squares; student B use *only* the yellow squares. Spend five minutes looking at your questions and revising the answers. Then take turns tossing a coin: heads = move one of your squares; tails = move two of your squares. When you land on a square, your partner looks at the relevant page in the book to check your answers, but *you don't*! If you are right, move forward one square (but don't answer the question until your next turn). If you aren't right, your partner tells you the right answer and you miss a go. When you've finished the game, change colours and play again.

Start

1
Native Speaker English note p. 93: if you can say what the *Native Speaker English* note was and give an example, throw again.

2
Developing Conversations p. 93: say five sentences from exercise B. Explain the situations they could be used in.

3
Vocabulary p. 94: say six things about newspapers and the media in your country using words in **bold** in exercise A.

4
Grammar p. 97: your partner will say eight verbs in exercise A. Give examples of patterns which can follow each one.

5
Native Speaker English note p. 99: if you can say what the *Native Speaker English* note was and give an example, throw again.

6
Developing Conversations p. 99: say six questions often used when making small talk and give examples of possible answers.

7
Grammar p. 100: your partner will say the six sentences from exercise A. Correct the mistake in each one.

8
Miss a go!

9
Vocabulary p. 102: your partner will say the six situations from exercise A. Say four things connected to each one.

10
Vocabulary p. 104: describe the photos on page 158, using at least eight words from exercise A.

11
Miss a go!

12
Native Speaker English note p. 105: if you can say what the *Native Speaker English* note was and give an example, throw again.

13
Developing Conversations p. 105: your partner will read three exchanges from exercise A. You should repair the 'misunderstandings'.

14
Grammar p. 107: your partner will read the sentences from exercise A, saying 'blah' instead of the preposition. Say the correct prepositions.

15
Developing Conversations p. 111: say ten interjections and give examples of when they could be used.

16
Vocabulary p. 111: your partner will read 1–12 in exercise A, stressing the words in italics. Give synonyms.

17
Native Speaker English note p. 114: if you can say what the *Native Speaker English* note was and give an example, throw again.

18
Grammar p. 115: say eight things about the future, using eight different forms / noun phrases.

Finish

For each of the activities below, work in groups of three. Use the *Vocabulary Builder* if you want to.

CONVERSATION PRACTICE

Choose one of the following *Conversation Practice* activities.
News and The Media p. 93
Business and Economics p. 99
Fashion p. 105
Danger and Risk p. 111

Two of you should do the task. The third person should listen and then give a mark between 1 and 10 for the performance. Explain your decision. Then change roles.

ACT OR DRAW

One person should act or draw as many of these words as they can in three minutes. The others should try to guess the words. Do not speak while you are acting or drawing!

a raid	whinge	a lapel	a gash
a tabloid	relocate	permed	scald
a spreadsheet	crush	flared	stumble
chair a meeting	loathe	low-cut	handcuff
a focus group	a sleeve	a tomb	snap
the stock market	lining	vain	pass out

QUIZ

Answer as many of the questions as possible.
1   Why might someone **pull out of** a race or competition?
2   Can you think of three things that are now **obsolete**?
3   What's the opposite of **denying** an allegation?
4   When might someone make a **prototype**?
5   Can you think of three things that could **ruin** your day?
6   How could you **libel** someone?
7   Say two things companies can **outsource**. Explain why.
8   Where can you find **loopholes**? Who might look for them?
9   What happens when people **rampage** through the streets?
10   When might people **freak out**?
11   What might a government need to **bail out**? Why?
12   Say two things that are sometimes **frowned on**. Say why.
13   Where do you usually find **inmates**?
14   What kind of **overheads** do most companies have?
15   When might you decide to give someone a **head start**?

COLLOCATIONS

Take turns to read out collocation lists from Unit 13 of the *Vocabulary Builder*. Where there is a '~', say '*blah*' instead. Your partner should guess as many words as they can. Each time you change roles, move to the next unit.

IDIOMS

Discuss the meaning of the idioms and try to think of a real example about you – or about someone you know.
1   He's in a bit of a hole.
2   They're just lining their own pockets.
3   I crashed out as soon as I got home.
4   It's daylight robbery!
5   It's been on the cards for quite some time.
6   We're caught between a rock and a hard place.
7   They make a real killing.
8   It really struck a chord with me.
9   It's just a storm in a teacup. It'll soon blow over.
10   It's a classic example of the nanny state!
11   I wouldn't count my chickens if I were you.
12   It's a complete invasion of privacy.
13   It just appeals to the lowest common denominator.
14   I could maybe squeeze you in on Friday.
15   He's always swum against the tide.

LISTENING

A ☞R 4.1 **Listen and decide if these sentences are true or false.**

1 The report comes live from a major fashion industry event.
2 The economy has been in a fairly bad state.
3 Lady Za-Za was subverting a traditionally male outfit.
4 She was looking very thin.
5 The crowds were unimpressed by her new hairstyle.
6 Kyleen McClose faces accusations from a former colleague.
7 She's admitted there's some truth in the accusations.
8 The reporter didn't feel that Ms McClose was visibly affected by the pressure in any way.
9 The model who fell over wasn't hurt at all.
10 She's quite likely to be taking someone to court.

B **Listen again to check.**

[... / 10]

GRAMMAR

A **Complete the sentences with one word in each space.**

1 We got ourselves into a situation ...... our overheads were just far exceeding our turnover.
2 ...... being a very efficient worker, she's also a very nice woman.
3 The person to ...... all enquiries on this matter should be directed is now based at a different address.
4 The next train is ...... in a couple of minutes.
5 He claims to have been threatened ...... instant dismissal.
6 I'm afraid this cream is quite ...... to aggravate your skin condition.
7 I pleaded with them ...... stop, but they wouldn't listen.
8 The news of the sale came through ...... our trip to Cadiz.

[... / 8]

B **Complete the second sentence with 2–5 words and the words in bold so it has a similar meaning to the first.**

1 Of our 3,500 employees, 93% are bilingual.
vast
We employ three and a half thousand workers, the .... speak at least two languages.
2 I told them they'd be crazy to sign that contract!
urged
I .... sign that contract!
3 I don't really get how you've structured your argument in this essay.
way
I'm not sure I understand the
.... you've organised your ideas.

4 I'm writing about your ideas for improving sales over the next three months.
regard
I am writing .... your proposal for improving sales over the next quarter.
5 This recession has basically been caused by government incompetence.
blame
Personally, I ....
mismanagement.
6 We're expecting to sign a major new deal in the next couple of days.
verge
We are .... a major new deal.

[... / 12]

LANGUAGE PATTERNS

Find the four sentences with a mistake and correct them.

1 On the down side, the gown is extremely fragile.
2 This isn't an exercise as hard as might be imagined.
3 There's not demand for that kind of fabric any more.
4 At least he saw the funny side in the situation.
5 She made it quite clear it was no laughing matter!
6 He's got this great big huge scar on his face.

[... / 6]

PREPOSITIONS

Complete 1–8 with a preposition from the box.

on	with	of	at
for	throughout	in	from

1 All of the feedback we've been getting ...... the markets suggests there's a definite demand for the product.
2 We've been absolutely inundated ...... orders recently.
3 Stories of brutality and barbarism are common ...... the whole of human history.
4 I'm not convinced that the pursuit ...... fame and fortune makes anyone any happier.
5 He's threatening to sue them ...... negligence.
6 I can honestly say, with my hand ...... heart, that I never meant any harm.
7 There's been a real downturn ...... the economy since the last budget.
8 The CEO was hinting ...... some kind of cutbacks, I thought.

[... / 8]

OPPOSITES

Replace the words in *italics* with their opposite.

simple	volatile	lax	specific
final	mainstream	positive	off-putting

1 It was a very *bleak* appraisal.
2 What was the doctor's *initial* verdict?
3 It's a very *tempting* thought.
4 That's a very *ornate* necklace.
5 The market's very *stable* at present.
6 Security at the event was very *tight*.
7 I agree with the *broad* point he made.
8 She's a very *subversive* writer.

[... / 8]

MISSING WORDS

Complete each set of three sentences with one word.

1 We're going to ...... to host the 2026 World Cup.
   There was a hostile takeover ...... last year.
   I ...... $100 on it, but didn't win the auction.
2 The dates of the meetings ...... with the big matches.
   The red and the orange really ...... !
   There was a bit of a ...... in the meeting today.
3 Personally, I just can't see the ...... of things like that.
   The advertising is clearly designed to ...... to kids.
   He's said to be unhappy about the tribunal's decision and is considering an ....
4 We have an office in Bonn, but our main ...... is Rome.
   We've managed to build up a fairly solid client ....
   I wanted to ...... the book on my early childhood.
5 A ...... has revealed the government plans to raise taxes.
   There must be a ...... in the pipe somewhere.
   It was a huge decision to ...... this information.

[... / 5]

VERBS

Match the verbs in the box with the collocations in 1–8.

implement	switch	jeopardise	retract
enhance	regain	confirm	slash

1 ~ rumours / ~ my booking / ~ my suspicions
2 ~ the claim / ~ accusations / ~ the statement
3 ~ a business plan / ~ our strategy / ~ a law
4 ~ prices / ~ jobs / ~ production / ~ our budget
5 ~ sides / ~ lanes / ~ suppliers / ~ languages
6 ~ consciousness / ~ feeling in my hands / ~ my appetite
7 ~ her reputation / ~ your performance / ~ the experience
8 ~ the whole deal / ~ the company's interests / ~ the plan

[... / 8]

FORMING WORDS

Complete the gaps with the correct form of the words in CAPITALS.

The fact that such an infamous criminal has got off on a ¹......................... will mean endless hysterical press ²......................... and the usual claims that standards of ³......................... aren't what they used to be. This kind of media frenzy really isn't helpful, but I guess it boosts the newspapers' ⁴......................... . Obviously, we're not happy about the verdict, but the fact remains that his lawyer found a legal loophole and exploited it. It's ⁵......................... of the way things work nowadays.

TECHNICAL
COVER
POLICE

CIRCULATE

SYMBOL

I wish I had full ⁶......................... to explain what goes on behind the scenes during a high-profile trial like this, but head office issued a new ⁷......................... recently, forbidding us from making such information publicly available.

AUTHORISE

DIRECT

[... / 7]

VOCABULARY

Complete the two news stories by choosing the correct words.

A man who foiled an armed gang's ¹...... to hold up a security van is today being ²...... as a hero. Jo Lee, 53, was on his way to work when he chanced upon a masked man wielding a rifle. Without thought for his own safety, he then proceeded to ³...... the gun. ⁴...... say this action seemed to scare off the other two members of the gang, thus preventing their planned raid.

Newtown United will today announce they are planning to ⁵...... the contracts of more than half of their team. The shock news comes only months after the club was ⁶...... on the stock market. A statement released claims the move is designed to ⁷...... the team's current position. However, it is widely rumoured that it is actually the result of having ⁸...... on a recent loan.

1	A appeal	B menace	C bid
2	A hailed	B depicted	C idealised
3	A detach	B confront	C seize
4	A observers	B witnesses	C lookers
5	A terminate	B deregulate	C lay off
6	A flooded	B floated	C picked up
7	A consolidate	B legitimise	C liberate
8	A failed	B cut out	C defaulted

[... / 8]

[Total ... /80]

SPEAKING

A **Work in pairs. Look at the table and chart and discuss these questions.**
- What trends and facts do the table and chart show?
- Why do you think these trends are happening?
- Can you see similar trends in your country?
- How do you feel about these changes? What is good / bad about them?

Table 1
World's biggest cities by population (in millions)

2007			2025		
1	Tokyo	35.6	1	Tokyo	36.4
2	New York	19.1	2	Mumbai	26.4
3	Mexico City	19	3	Delhi	22.5
4	Mumbai	18.9	4	Dhaka	22.0
5	São Paulo	18.8	5	São Paolo	21.4
6	Delhi	15.9	6	Mexico City	21.0
7	Shanghai	14.9	7	New York	20.6
8	Kolkata	14.7	8	Kolkata	20.5
9	Dhaka	13.4	9	Shanghai	19.4
	Buenos Aires	12.8	10	Karachi	19.1
	Los Angeles	12,5	11	Kinshasa	16.7
	Karachi	12.1	12	Lagos	15.8

▓ city located on coast or major river

Chart

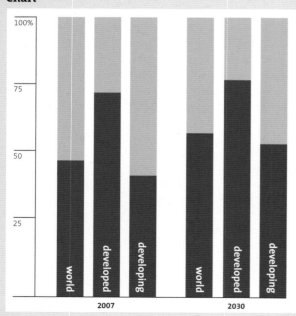

rural ▓   urban ▓

WRITING

A **Read the description of the data in the table and the chart, and find six factual mistakes.**

B **Work in pairs and do the following:**
- Compare the mistakes you found and correct them.
- Discuss one other feature of the table and chart you would draw attention to.

The table shows the 12 largest cities in the world by area in 2007 and projected figures for 2025. As can be seen, all the main cities are set to grow as might be expected given the continued shift from urban to rural living illustrated in the chart. Already two out of every three people live in cities in the richer countries, and urban populations in the whole world are projected to rise by 25% over the period, the bulk of which will occur in developing countries in Asia and Africa. This is also reflected in the table. It shows that the populations of cities such as Tokyo, New York and Mumbai will be relatively stable, rising only slightly, while Los Angeles and Buenos Aires are projected to drop out of the top 12. In contrast, Dhaka in Bangladesh is going to nearly triple in size and by 2025 African cities (Kinshasa and Lagos) will have entered the top 12 for the first time.

VOCABULARY Describing percentages

A **Replace the words in *italics* with the words in the box.**

a tiny percentage	four out of five
the vast majority	almost a fifth
a significant minority	more than halved
slightly higher	fourfold

1 The chart shows there were around 20,000 immigrants, *91%* of whom came from other European countries.
2 The graph illustrates that urban sprawl increased by *19%* over this period.
3 As is illustrated in figure 1, mortgage interest rates *fell from 5% to 2%* while inflation increased *from 1.5% to 6%*.
4 As can be seen in the pie chart, *80% of* customers were satisfied with the service, which was *6% more* than last year.
5 This is illustrated in figure 3, which shows that only *0.1%* of household income is spent on books.
6 The survey indicated that *43%* of respondents were concerned about the effects of the proposals.

GRAMMAR Describing changes

We often use passive constructions to describe future predictions instead of *will* or *going to*. Note the adverbials.

All the main cities *are set to grow* over the next 20 years.
Urban populations *are expected to rise* by 10% over the period.
Los Angeles and Buenos Aires *are projected to drop* out of the top 12 in the next few years.

If we look back, we may use a perfect infinitive.
Kinshasa *is expected to have entered* the top 12 by 2025.

A Rewrite these changes using the verb in brackets.
1 By 2025, the population of Dhaka will have risen to 22 million. (**project**)
2 In the next 20 years, the rural population is going to fall. (**set**)
3 African cities will grow rapidly over the next few years. (**expect**)
4 China will become the world's largest economy in the next ten years. (**predict**)

Remember other tenses describe past and present trends:
Between 2000 and 2005, Internet usage *rose* dramatically.
Since 2000, overall crime *has fallen* steadily.
The number of bilingual schools *is* currently *increasing*.

See also the grammar reference on page 136 (perfect tenses)

B Work in pairs. Think of an example of 1–3. Discuss why they are happening / have happened and predict how they will develop in the future.
1 an upward trend
2 a downward trend
3 a general shift from one thing to another

KEY WORDS FOR WRITING
of whom / of which

We can give information about a part of a group or statistic we have just mentioned using *of whom* or *of which*. Of whom refers to people and *of which* to things.

Urban populations are expected to rise by 10% over the period, the bulk *of which* will occur in developing countries.

There were around 20,000 immigrants, 91% *of whom* came from other European countries.

A Join the sentences in 1–8 using *of whom / of which*.
1 The government donates 0.6% of GDP as aid. The bulk of that money goes to countries in Africa.
2 There were 2,650 fatalities from car accidents last year. The vast majority of the accidents were caused by driver error.
3 University entries are set to increase. 12% of the new students will come from deprived backgrounds.
4 There was a significant fall in crime in the last decade. A large part of the drop was put down to rising living standards.
5 The survey interviewed 950 people altogether. The interviewees were mostly 18–25 years old.

WRITING PRACTICE

You are going to write a short description of the main trends illustrated in the table and graph below.

A Work in pairs and discuss:
- what the table and graph generally show
- the main trends
- key statistics that illustrate the trend
- any surprising aspects you would highlight.

B Write your description in 150–180 words.

Fig 1. The languages of international education

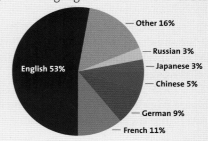

Fig 2. Millions of adults learning English

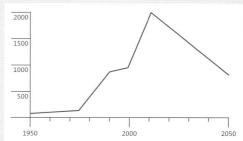

SPEAKING

A Work in groups. Discuss these questions.
- What do you think are the strengths and weaknesses of the health care system in your country?
- If you could change one thing about the system, what would it be? Why?
- Do you know anyone who works in health care? Who? What do they do? Do they enjoy it?

WRITING

You are going to read a response to the essay title: *'The government should provide free health care for all. Discuss.'*

A Think of three reasons why someone might agree with the statement in the title, and three reasons why they might disagree.

B Work in pairs. Compare your ideas. Then discuss which of the reasons you thought of in exercise A you actually agree with. Explain why.

> When writing introductions to opinion essays, it is common to structure the opening paragraph like this:
> - Show the reader you know why the subject is important (why it's being discussed).
> - Introduce what you regard as a 'weak view' on the title – one you disagree with.
> - Query the weak view and introduce your own opinion.

C With your partner, discuss how a writer could show that the subject of free health care is important – and what you might expect someone who *disagrees* with the essay title to follow this up with.

D Compare your ideas with the following introduction. Divide it into the three parts mentioned in the box above.

> The health of the nation is clearly of paramount importance. Economic growth depends on it, as do social cohesion and unity. Given this, it might seem logical to conclude that the state has a duty to provide universal health care. While there is some sense in this line of thought, it would, however, be dangerous to follow this argument to its logical end-point.

E There are four more paragraphs in the essay. In pairs, discuss what you expect the function of each of these paragraphs to be. Then read and check.

F Complete the essay with the words in the box.

as such	such	indeed	while
however	in short	so	secondly

> It is often argued that any civilised state has a responsibility to provide health care for all its citizens, especially the most vulnerable, and that failure to do [1].......................... is symptomatic of a deeper malaise in society. [2]..........................., it has been claimed that a society that allows its own citizens to fall sick is, by definition, a sick society.
>
> [3]..........................., it may seem that to argue against universal health care is a perilous task. [4]..........................., firstly, it should be remembered that in reality the government does not pay for anything – the taxpayers do. [5]..........................., it is important to recognise the fact that a small but sizeable minority of people in any given society abuse their bodies and damage their own health willingly. Why should the rest of society subsidise such disregard for life and limb?
>
> [6].......................... I do believe that a basic level of free health care should be provided for all, especially in times of great need, the notion of extending this beyond the minimum is potentially problematic in the extreme. Where would free health care stop? With treatment for depression? With gender-reassignment operations? With tattoo removals? I could go on.
>
> [7]..........................., while it is clearly desirable to ensure all members of society receive essential health care without having to worry about financial matters, it would be financial suicide to expand any [8].......................... service.

G Work in pairs. Discuss these questions.
- Did you predict the function of each paragraph correctly? If not, what differences were there?
- Which words / phrases does the writer use to draw attention to what they see as 'weak' arguments?
- Which words / phrases does the writer use to highlight their own (stronger) arguments?
- To what degree does the writer's opinion reflect your own? Where do you agree / disagree? Why?

Key words for writing *indeed*

A **Divide the sentences below into three groups of two – to show different uses of *indeed*.**
1 After much questioning, he was eventually forced to admit that there was indeed something wrong.
2 There are those in society who do not pay sufficient attention to their own health. Indeed, many actively abuse it.
3 Following repeated accusations, it was later proven that the test results had indeed been falsified.
4 The final results of the experiment were very strange indeed.
5 Putting such a theory into practice would be hard. Indeed, you might say almost impossible.
6 Cultural identities in any society vary so widely as to make the extraction of common features very difficult indeed.

B **Compare your ideas with a partner and explain the different uses of *indeed*.**

C **Now compare your ideas with the explanation below.**

> There are three main uses of *indeed* in written English:
> 1 for emphasis – after *very* + an adjective or adverb
> 2 to introduce a sentence that exemplifies or expands on a previously made point
> 3 to emphasise that something there was some doubt about is actually true.

D **Write sentences to exemplify or expand on 1–4 below.**
1 The government simply cannot afford to expand health care any further. Indeed, ...
2 Governments can always find money to fund things when it suits them. Indeed, ...
3 Every election brings new pledges to increase spending on the health service. Indeed, ...
4 In countries where free health care for all is the norm, the system does not always function as well as we might imagine. Indeed, ...

E **Compare your ideas with a partner. Who wrote better follow-up sentences?**

Writing practice

A **Work in pairs and discuss possible reasons why people might agree or disagree with each of the following statements – and then discuss your own opinions.**
1 'Nuclear energy is the most realistic long-term option we have.' Discuss.
2 'Rather than bringing countries closer together, globalisation has led to increased nationalism.' Discuss.
3 'There should be a maximum working week for all of 35 hours.' How far do you agree?

B **Write short introductions for each of the three essay titles, using the model in *Writing* (exercise B).**

C **Compare your introductions with a partner. Can you see any ways in which your partner's work could be improved?**

D **Write an essay of around 300 words in response to one of the titles above. You should aim for five paragraphs, as in the model provided. Try to use *indeed* at least once.**

SPEAKING

A **Work in groups. Discuss these questions.**
- How often do you do the things in the box below? Are there any things you never do? Why not?
- Can you remember the last time you did each thing? What was it like?

see plays at the theatre	read novels
go to exhibitions	go to the ballet
go to small gigs	go to big concerts
see films at the cinema	go to the opera
see musicals	read poetry

VOCABULARY Reviews

A **Complete the sentences with the pairs of words in the box.**

abstract + sculptures	production + plot
album + encores	rhyme + collection
based + set	sets + choreography
orchestration + role	symphony + finale
prose + multi-layered	technique + partner

1 ...... on a true story and ...... in 1940s Texas, the new release by director Jackie Lee tackles issues of violence and sexism that remain highly relevant today.
2 Generally avoiding such conventions as ...... and punctuation, this ...... contains some wonderful, albeit challenging, pieces of poetry.
3 This intimate setting really allowed the bulk of the latest ...... to breathe, and no-one was surprised when the enthusiastic crowd demanded three ....
4 The ...... are amazing, the songs wonderful and the ...... is just out of this world.
5 Featuring both representational and ...... work, this collection spans five decade's of Morton's life and also features some of her rarely seen ....
6 This is the fourth ...... of this classic that I've seen, and it's undoubtedly the best. The cast are excellent and the ...... gripping from start to finish.
7 With her superb classical ...... and witty intelligence, Dorothy Gilbert outshines her ...... in this new work by quite some distance.
8 Don't let the deceptively simple ...... fool you, for this is a complex, ... work that can be interpreted on many levels.
9 With wonderfully sympathetic ...... and with tenor Richard Hamilton making his debut in the leading ......, this staging is one of the season's must-sees.
10 Whilst not my favourite ......, the orchestra's performance was nevertheless gripping and the grand ...... even brought tears to my eyes.

B **Match sentences 1–10 to the ten activities in the box in *Speaking*.**

C **Choose at least six words from exercise A that describe things you've seen / read. Tell a new partner as much about each thing as you can.**

WRITING

You are going to read a review of a British musical.

A Read the review. Then discuss these questions.
- How many stars out of five do you think the reviewer gave the musical? Why?
- Does *Billy Elliot* sound like the kind of thing you'd enjoy? Why? / Why not?
- What do you learn about the plot? Does it remind you of any other films / books, etc.?
- What's the function of each of the five paragraphs?

Given that it has been adapted from the film of the same name, it is no surprise that the musical version of *Billy Elliot* is full of cinematic suspense. Set against the backdrop of the miners' strike in 1980s Britain, the plot revolves around a young boy who rejects his father's moves to push him into boxing in favour of ballet lessons, a decision which initially causes conflict in his family, but which eventually leads him to fame and fortune.

The beautifully choreographed drama unfolds in a tense, gripping manner and the stage is exploited to the full. The scenes that alternate between Billy's ballet lessons and his father's battles against the police on the picket lines at the mine are particularly powerful. The sets are incredibly evocative and capture the mood of social unrest excellently, transporting the audience to another time and place.

When one stops to consider the extreme youth of its main star – Liam Mower, who plays Billy, is only twelve years old – the show becomes even more remarkable. Liam is dazzling and I found myself unable to take my eyes off him for the whole performance. He brings a vulnerability and tenderness to the role that left many in tears.

If I do have a criticism then I suppose it would be the music, written by pop legend Sir Elton John. Whilst it is often uplifting and anthemic, it does start to feel somewhat formulaic after a time. Therein lies the other slight problem – at just over three hours, the show is perhaps thirty minutes too long. By the time the excellent cast had received three standing ovations, I'd been in my seat for almost 200 minutes!

Regardless of these minor flaws, this is nevertheless an outstanding spectacle and a must-see for anyone keen on contemporary musicals.

KEY WORDS FOR WRITING
nevertheless / given

> **Given means 'considering'. It shows you are taking account of a fact when you give an opinion.**
>
> *Given* that it has been adapted from the film, it is no surprise that the musical version of Billy Elliot is full of cinematic suspense.
>
> **Nevertheless is used with *despite, while, regardless* etc. to emphasise that something is true despite what you first said. It is also used like *however* to refer back to a previous sentence.**

Regardless of these minor flaws, this is *nevertheless* an outstanding spectacle.
The film lasts four hours. *Nevertheless*, the time flies by.

A Match the sentence halves.
1 While Caine only plays a minor role,
2 Given that Caine only plays a minor role,
3 The play received very poor reviews,
4 The play received terrible reviews,
5 Irrespective of the band's refusal to give an encore,
6 Given that the concert was quite short and the band refused to give an encore,

a but nevertheless, went on to be hugely popular.
b it's remarkable that he won an Oscar.
c even given the low expectations surrounding it.
d it was unsurprising there were boos and complaints as the audience left the auditorium.
e it was nevertheless an amazing concert.
f he nevertheless outshone everyone with his remarkable performance.

B Complete 1–4 below. Then compare your ideas.
1 While her recent collection has been badly received by the press, I nevertheless found it …
2 Despite a huge budget, the film nevertheless …
3 Given the length of the novel …
4 This is a very young orchestra. Nevertheless …

WRITING PRACTICE

A Write a review of a concert, album, exhibition, ballet, musical or novel, etc. It should be between 250 and 300 words. Try to use as much language from these pages as you can.

WRITING

A Work in pairs. Look at the two diagrams on these pages and discuss these questions:
- What are the processes shown? What happens in each case?
- Why do you think they are important these days?

B Read the text that describes the process of concentrating solar power and decide what 1–6 are.

C Complete the description with the linkers in the box.

> meanwhile   whereby   thus   which   as

D How does the writer avoid using personal pronouns (*I, we, me, us*) in the text? Would you avoid such pronouns in similar texts in your language?

The diagram shows a process known as Concentrating Solar Power (CSP) [1].......................... solar energy is used to create steam to power electrical generators.

Large parabolic troughs are directed at the sun. The mirrored surfaces of the troughs reflect the sun's rays and concentrate them onto pipes carrying a fluid which is [2].......................... heated up. This heated fluid passes through a heat exchanger, where it boils water and creates steam, before returning in a loop back to the parabolic trough. The steam [3].......................... is conveyed through pipes at high pressure to a generator where it drives turbines, to create electricity. [4].......................... the steam goes through the turbine, it loses heat and is then further cooled in a tower, converting it back into water. The water then continues in a loop back to the heat exchanger where it is again boiled to create steam. In the absence of sunshine, the steam is generated by supplementary gas-powered heaters.

CSP offers a number of benefits: it provides clean sustainable energy; it can make use of large tracts of unused desert land; and it can be adapted to make use of sea water, [5].......................... can be easily desalinated at the cooling-tower stage, thereby providing much-needed fresh water in arid zones.

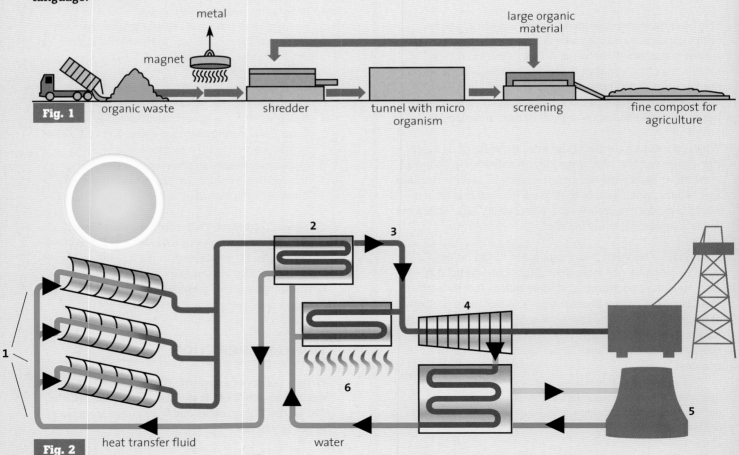

Fig. 1   organic waste — magnet — metal — shredder — tunnel with micro organism — large organic material — screening — fine compost for agriculture

Fig. 2   heat transfer fluid   water

MONEY

SPEAKING

A **Work in pairs. Discuss the questions and do the task.**
- What energy-creating or energy-saving schemes or processes are there in your country?
- Is there any opposition to these schemes? Who from? Why? What benefits do these types of schemes have?
- Draw a flow chart or diagram of one of the processes you thought of. Then explain it to another pair.

VOCABULARY Processes

A **Rewrite the sentences in the passive and replace the words in *italics* with a word from the box.**

insulate	categorise	assemble	screen
discard	deliver	break down	box
power	remove		

1 They *take out* plastic from the rubbish manually.
2 They *wrap* the pipes with foam to minimize heat loss.
3 They *check* the final product for impurities.
4 They *sort* the tea leaves into different grades according to size and quality.
5 They don't *throw away* anything during the process, to maximise efficiency.
6 The raw materials *arrive* in a container ship.
7 They *put together* the parts in a central plant.
8 They *package* the oranges and load them onto lorries.
9 They *drive* the turbines by forcing water through them.
10 They use microbes to *decompose* the oil into droplets.

B **Work in pairs. Discuss why different processes may use:**

a filter	a conveyor belt	a pump
a magnet	a hammer	a furnace

KEY WORDS FOR WRITING
whereby, thereby and *thus*

> ***Whereby*** explains the way something is done according to a method, agreement, rule etc.
> ....
> ***Thereby*** and ***thus*** both show the result of a particular process previously mentioned.

A **Complete the following sentences with *whereby* or *thereby*.**
1 Glassblowing is the process .... glass is heated and then shaped.
2 The milk is heated to around 70%, ... killing the vast majority of microbes.
3 We have to comply with strict regulations .... our machines are inspected weekly, ... ensuring total safety.
4 There's a trade-in scheme .... any car over 15 years old can be scrapped for $3,000 dollars when buying a new car.

B **Work in groups. How many of these natural, industrial and legal processes do you know? Explain them using *whereby* and possible results using *thus / thereby*.**

desalination	Gaia	hydroelectric power
metamorphosis	a veto	photosynthesis
osmosis	auditing	distillation
landfill	an embargo	a high court appeal

WRITING PRACTICE

You are going to write a similar description to the one in *Writing*.

A **Choose either the diagram of the composting process, or the diagram you did in Speaking.**

B **Write a description of the process in 150–200 words.**

SPEAKING

A Work in pairs. Discuss the following questions.
- What's the difference between a CV and a covering letter? What kind of information might you typically include in each?
- Do you have a CV? Are you happy with it?
- Have you ever had to write a covering letter? In which language? When? Do you think it was effective?

B Read the short text below and compare it with your ideas. Does it contain anything you didn't mention?

> **When applying for jobs, it is standard to include two important documents:**
> - a **CV** (sometimes also known as a résumé)
> - a **short covering letter**
>
> The covering letter is meant to encourage the company you're applying to to take a closer look at your CV. It should clarify why you want to work for the firm – and why you would be a good fit. Highlight key information from your CV, but don't just repeat what is listed. Match your skills, interests and experience to the needs of the company and sell your qualities to the reader. The aim of a covering letter is to get you invited for an interview.
>
> **Content**
> Your letter should be concise and relevant.
> It should:
> - state why you are writing and what post you are applying for
> - explain where you learned about the job vacancy
> - say why you want the job
> - say why you would be a benefit to the company
> - request an interview.

C In light of the text above, discuss how you would angle your covering letter if you were applying for the job below. What kind of 'sell' might be needed?

> **JOBS**
>
> We are a leading online tourism agency looking for a full-time CUSTOMER SERVICE AGENT.
> We require:
> - an ability to listen attentively and hear important information and to provide clear information in excellent English
> - proven ability to deal with customer enquiries
> - previous customer service or call centre experience – desirable, but not essential
> - basic IT skills
> - ability to work flexible (and sometimes long) hours.

WRITING

You are going to read a covering email sent by an applicant for the job in *Speaking*.

A Choose the correct forms.

> To whom it may concern,
>
> I ¹*write / am writing* to apply for the post of customer service agent, ²*as / which* advertised on www.jobseekers.com recentl[y]
>
> I feel I ³*would / will* be suitable for the post for several reasons. Firstly, I speak excellent English, ⁴*spending / having spent* the last year living and working in Canada. Secondly, I feel I possess the relevant customer service experience, having ⁵*worked / been working* in a range of service industry positions, many of ⁶*them / which* necessitated considerable interaction with the general public. My inter-personal skills and ability to communicate also benefited from having to deal with frequent customer complaints in my places of work. I am now keen to ⁷*implement / put* these skills into practice and to continue to develop myself and extend my range of abilities.
>
> In addition to all this, I am a dedicated, motivated worker, able to act both independently and as part of a team. In my last job, I was responsible for setting up a new system for the collection and compilation of customer feedback, a process that exemplified my listening and communication skills as well as my competence with computers. I enjoy new challenges and never give less than my ⁸*everything / all*. I trust you will agree that my track record so far – as detailed in my CV – shows this.
>
> I am available for interview at any time and would be happy to provide references, ⁹*should / when* you require them.
>
> Please do not hesitate to contact me should you require any further information.
>
> I look forward to ¹⁰*hear / hearing* from you soon,
>
> Yours faithfully,
> Karim Nourani

B Compare your choices with a partner and discuss any differences. Then discuss whether or not you would interview this applicant for the post. Why?

VOCABULARY Achievements at work

> It's common in covering letters to detail your previous achievements at work or in the field of education. After detailing achievements, we often go on to explain the skills these achievements demonstrated or developed.

> *I was responsible for* setting up a new system for the collection and compilation of customer feedback, *a process that exemplified my listening and communication skills as well as my competence with computers.*

A **Complete the sentences with the verbs in the box.**

achieved	conducted	implemented
advised	dealt with	negotiated
arranged	devised	promoted
budgeted	diagnosed	represented

1 I booked flights and .... accommodation for colleagues who had to go away on business trips.
2 I .... a variety of up-and-coming musicians and DJs at a club night I co-ran with two friends.
3 I .... my colleagues on a wide range of personal and professional matters.
4 I .... above-average grades in the majority of my end-of-school exams.
5 I .... a survey of staff attitudes.
6 I .... some remarkably abusive customers during my time at the call centre.
7 I .... a new system for filing all the office paperwork.
8 I .... the successes and failures of the business and thus helped determine the path we subsequently took.
9 I .... a script for new teleworkers, but unfortunately my boss was unwilling to implement it.
10 I .... my money carefully during my time at university and was thus able to meet all my financial commitments.
11 I successfully .... my own debt reduction by 50%.
12 I was elected as an official spokesperson and .... my colleagues in meetings with the management.

B **Work in pairs. Discuss the skills or abilities you could reasonably claim that sentences 1–12 in exercise A show or develop.**

KEY WORDS FOR WRITING *should*

> In formal writing, *should* is often used to mean *if*.

> I am available for interview and would be happy to provide further references, *should* you require them.

A **Put the words in the correct order to make common sentences using *should*.**
1 further please contact require hesitate any do you should not information me to
2 available request references should them on are you require
3 please the possible vacancies become any opportunity contact at should earliest available me
4 test after days you should retake can so the 60 you wish to do
5 wish matter phone appointment should discuss to please an you this further to make

B **Work in pairs. Decide how the sentences in exercise A might be worded in informal spoken English.**

WRITING PRACTICE

A **Look at the three job advertisements below and decide which one most appeals to you.**

1 ART GALLERY ASSISTANT
Busy modern art gallery seeks full- or part-time administrative assistant to work with gallery directors. Fluent English essential. You are a calm, intelligent, flexible, curious person who likes to get things done.

2 ASSISTANT SALES MANAGER
Large European hotel chain seeks assistant sales manager. You are degree qualified (or equivalent) sales experience and good communication and administrative skills. Must be driven, able to work under pressure and happy to travel 15–20 weeks per year.

3 OFFICIAL GUIDES WANTED
We are looking for guides with a keen interest in history or archaeology as well as excellent English skills to join our association. We organise high-quality cultural guided tours of historic sites.

B **Compare your choice with a partner. Discuss what experience or abilities applicants for each post need.**

C **Write a covering letter to accompany an application for one of the posts above.**

06 WRITING
A MAGAZINE ARTICLE

SPEAKING

A Put the inventions below in order:
- of usefulness to you.
- of their impact on the world.

> **First vending machine** (dispensing holy water)
> invented by Hero of Alexandria (Egypt) in AD50
> **Pressure cooker**
> invented by Denis Papin (France) in 1679
> **Mercury thermometer**
> invented by Daniel Fahrenheit (Holland / Poland) in 1714
> **Lawnmower**
> invented by Edwin Beard Budding (UK) in 1827
> **Dynamite**
> invented by Alfred Nobel (Sweden) in 1866
> **Automatic teller machine** (ATM)
> invented by Luther Simjian (Armenia) in 1939
> **Soft contact lenses**
> invented by Otto Witcherle (Czechoslovakia) in 1961
> **CD-ROM**
> invented by Phillips / Sony (Holland / Japan) in 1985

B Work in pairs. Compare your lists and explain your choices. Did you find anything surprising about the original list or your partner's choices?

WRITING

A magazine has set a competition where people write to nominate an inventor and invention to be displayed in a museum of design.

A Read the article and then answer these questions in pairs.
1 Which picture shows the invention being described.
2 Do you think it is a better choice than those in *Speaking*. Why?

B Work in pairs and do the following.
1 Divide the text into three paragraphs. What does the writer do in each one?
2 Find examples of these ways of creating interest and persuasion.
   - Revealing the main topic of the paragraph in the last sentence of the paragraph
   - Rhetorical questions
   - Pairs of contrasting facts
   - Quotations
   - 'Tripling' – giving lists of three things or three related statements
   - Using *surely*, *yet* or *besides*
3 Think of a title for the article.

His invention has saved thousands of lives, yet you probably take it for granted. It made its inventor millions of pounds, yet few people know his name. I believe Percy Shaw is a great inventor and his cat's eye should be displayed in the Design Museum. Despite coming from a deprived background and leaving school at 13, Percy always showed inventiveness. He allegedly came up with the idea of the road reflector when he almost crashed into a wall. His headlights reflected in the eyes of a cat which directed him back onto the road. Thinking how the cat's eye could be placed on the road itself, he devised a hard rubber casing for four small glass reflectors and set them in a metal shoe. When cars ran over the cat's eye it pressed the rubber over the glass wiping it clean with the aid of rainwater that collected in the metal shoe. It therefore needed little maintenance. Since its invention the cat's eye has been fitted to roads throughout the world in order to make them safer. No doubt we can all think of things with apparently more impact – telephones, cars, computers, etc – but how many of these were really invented by one man? Their inventors "stood on the shoulders of giants" as Newton once said. Shaw's creation was different: it solved a real problem, it was unique, and it was beautifully simple. Besides, few inventions can claim to have prevented so many deaths. Surely, therefore, Percy Shaw and his cat's eye deserve a prominent place in the new museum.

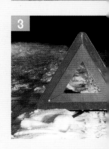

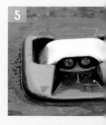

KEY WORDS FOR WRITING
surely, yet, besides

We use *surely* to mean 'without doubt', or to emphasise something is true, especially when you think people may disagree.
Surely, therefore, [they] deserve a prominent place ...
It is *surely* one of the greatest designs of the 20th century.

We use *yet* to emphasise that a fact is surprising given what you have just said.
It made its inventor millions of pounds, *yet* few people know his name.

Besides gives an additional reason and often emphasises the final decisive argument.
... and it was beautifully simple. *Besides*, few inventions can claim to have prevented so many deaths.
Besides being cheap to produce, it needed little maintenance.

Notice the punctuation in the sentences above.

A **Rewrite the sentences replacing the words in italics with *surely, yet* or *besides*.**
1. There was enormous interest in the new device. Actual sales were sluggish, *though*.
2. *Quite apart from* the fact that it was cheap to produce, it was beautiful to look at.
3. *There can be little doubt that* this is the greatest achievement of the 21st century so far.
4. Some may argue that many others were working on the problem, but *it seems clear to me that* his was the biggest and most decisive contribution.
5. The train was fast and comfortable and, *what's more*, it was the cheapest option.
6. *Despite* making millions from his invention, he died in poverty.

GRAMMAR *few / a few, little / a little*

We use *few* with plural nouns and *little* with singular, uncountable nouns. *A few / a little* means 'some', but *few / little* (without the article) means 'hardly any'.

... *few* people know his name. (Remember *people* is plural!)
It therefore needed *little* maintenance.

(A) few and *(a) little* can also be used as pronouns:
Thousands of *inventions* are patented, but *few* are produced.
We asked for *help*, and we got *a little*.

A **Complete the sentences with *a few, few, a little* or *little*.**
1. They raised most of the investment from friends and family. They got relatively .... from banks.
2. He had .... friends and died a lonely man.
3. She received .... education, yet she became a best-selling author.
4. After they made .... improvements to the original design, sales took off.
5. We need .... more time to develop the prototype – maybe a couple of months
6. There can be .... inventions that have done so much for so many people.
7. We received hundreds of suggestions and quite .... have been implemented.

B **Complete these sentences using *(a) little / (a) few* and your own ideas.**
1. Many people have tried, but ....
2. The government has promised a lot, yet ....
3. It was a groundbreaking invention, and yet ....
4. The mobile phone is a fantastic invention: ....

WRITING PRACTICE

You are going to write an article for the same competition as in *Writing*.

A **Work in pairs. Choose an invention which you think should go into the museum.**

B **Individually, make a list of reasons why the invention is so good and some unusual or interesting facts about the inventor. Then compare your lists.**

C **Write a three- or four-paragraph article about the invention and inventor. Use some of the language you've learned on these pages.**

SPEAKING

A Work in pairs. Discuss these questions.
- Do you watch much TV? Why? / Why not?
- What's your favourite channel? Why?
- What's your favourite programme? Why?
- What do you think of your national and local TV?

VOCABULARY Evaluating

A Match the sentence starters – evaluating a TV channel in 1–8 with the possible endings a–h.
1 Our local TV station compares ...
2 It ranks ...
3 Its output ...
4 It is generally seen ...
5 It has been praised ...
6 It is often criticised ...
7 One strength is ...
8 The news coverage has been singled out ...

a third in terms of audience share / bottom out of 50 companies / high when it comes to entertainment.
b for praise / for criticism / as a weakness in its output.
c favourably to competitors / unfavourably to its rivals / well to the national average
d for its bias / for its lack of depth / for the length of the advertising breaks.
e for its involvement in the community / for making the most of a small budget / for its drama output.
f its sports coverage / its soap operas / its sitcoms.
g as a government mouthpiece / as being independent / as a symbol of the region.
h is very varied / has improved / has been dumbed down.

B Why is the passive form of the verb used in 4, 5, 6 and 8?

C Work with a new partner. Use the sentence starters to talk about the following. Explain your evaluations.
- a local TV channel
- a national TV channel

WRITING

You are going to read a Wiki entry for a guide to TV channels.

A Read the guide and then discuss the following questions with a partner.
- Are there any channels of a similar nature in your country? How are they the same / different?
- Would you watch this channel? Why? / Why not?

B Choose the best word to use in 1–10. Then discuss your choices with a partner.

C Work in groups. How far do you think parliament should regulate TV? What regulations would you like to see either put in place or removed in your country?

OVERVIEW   Channel 4 was founded in 1982 when it became the fourth free TV channel. Alongside it, a new Welsh-language channel S4C was also established following a campaign in Wales that included lobbying government and even the threat of hunger strike by one Welsh leader. Although the two channels were, and continue to be, [1]**largely / somewhat** funded through commercial advertising, they are [2]**effectively / relatively** publicly owned and Channel 4's output is [3]**partially / merely** limited by guidelines laid down by parliament. The parliamentary act requires Channel 4 to provide varied, high quality programming with a distinctive character that includes educational programmes as well as ones catering for a culturally diverse society. It is ranked third in terms of audience share in the UK with around 8%.

BRAND   Channel 4's audience is [4]**explicitly / predominantly** young (16–34) and educated. [5]**Eventually / Essentially** in line with its remit (see [6]**above / below**), it has built up a reputation for independence and innovation. Although there have been accusations of dumbing down (see [7]**above / below**), its programmes are often seen as provocative and as creating public debate. It has expanded its brand on cable TV with *Film4* (Channel 4 funded films such as *Four Weddings and a Funeral*), *E4* (an entertainment channel), and *More4* (targeting a slightly older, more serious audience).

OUTPUT   Channel 4 has pioneered a number of formats in the UK that have [8]**deliberately / subsequently** become mainstream. It was one of the first broadcasters to launch reality TV shows such as *Big Brother*. It has also been connected with groundbreaking drama and been both praised and criticised for challenging certain taboos. It introduced stranded seasons of programmes, including films, documentaries and even comedy shows on topics of social and political concern such as ageing, the war on terror, and gay rights. Its hour-long news programme has also been singled out for its in-depth and unbiased coverage. It shows little sport apart from horse racing.

In recent years some people have voiced concerns that the channel overuses American shows, albeit award-winners such as *Desperate Housewives* and *Ugly Betty*. There has also been criticism of an excess of low-brow reality-show formats and programmes that focus on middle-of-the-road interests such as buying property and cookery. This dumbing down is in contrast to previous accusations that it made [9]**deliberately / deliberate** attempts to provoke controversy, for example by showing a season of [10]**previously / previous** banned films.

KEY WORDS FOR WRITING *albeit*

> We use *albeit* before a noun, adjective or adverb to add a comment that changes the effect of what was just stated.
>
> ....
>
> [It] overuses American shows, *albeit* award-winners …
> The film was very well made, *albeit* rather lightweight.
> They agreed, *albeit* unwillingly, to pay compensation.

A   Use *albeit* and the words in the box to add a comment to 1–5.

very slowly	conservative
an academic expert	funny sometimes
one I didn't wholly agree with	

1   He is seen as an independent commentator.
2   The experiments they do on the show are really stupid.
3   The peace process is progressing.
4   It was a fascinating documentary that passionately argued its case.
5   The newly appointed head of the channel has never worked in the commercial sector.

WRITING PRACTICE

You are going to write a similar contribution to a wiki guide to the one in *Writing*.

A   **Choose one of the following topics:**
   • a TV channel
   • a magazine
   • a newspaper
   • a business

B   **Write your contribution in 250–350 words. Organise the entry under three or four headings such as *overview, history, brand, output, ownership, controversies, awards, stars, future*.**

C   **Read each other's contributions to the guides. Suggest changes in terms of content and style. Give each other an overall mark out of 10 for each.**

SPEAKING

A **Work in groups. Discuss these questions.**
- Do you enjoy going to museums? Why? / Why not?
- Which museums do you have in your town / city? Which would you recommend? Why?
- Which social functions do you think museums serve?
- Which ethical issues connected to museums may sometimes arise? Give examples.
- What's the strangest museum you've ever heard of / been to?
- Which of the unusual museums below would you like to visit? Why?

The Currywurst Museum, Berlin
This uniquely interactive museum is dedicated to the much-loved national sausage and allows you to see, hear, smell and take part in the *currywurst* experience!

Parasite Museum, Tokyo
This museum boasts over 300 different kinds of parasite, with the highlight being a 30-foot worm pulled out of an unsuspecting woman's stomach!

Museum of Funeral Carriages, Barcelona
Located in the strangely silent basement of the city's Municipal Funeral Services, the museum is home to many ornate carriages, some of which date back to the 18th century.

Paris Sewer Museum
Bored with the Louvre? Already seen the Eiffel Tower? Why not take a walking tour of the network of tunnels underneath the city? Not for those with sensitive noses!

WRITING

You are going to read a web page giving information about a famous museum of art and design in London.

A **Before you read, write five questions you would expect the web page to answer.**

B **Complete the text with the correct form of the verbs in the box.**

enter	follow	house	walk
feature	found	situate	

[1]...... a permanent collection of over four and a half million objects, the Victoria and Albert Museum is the world's largest museum of decorative arts and design. [2]...... in 1852, the museum now consists of 145 different galleries, and features, among other things, pottery, glass, textiles, costumes, silver and ironwork, jewellery, sculpture and photographs. It is particularly celebrated for its East Asian and Islamic collections.

[3]...... within walking distance of both underground and bus stops, the museum is easily accessible and lies at the heart of London's museum district, with the Science and Natural History museums both nearby. The nearest tube station is South Kensington, which is on the Piccadilly, Circle and District Lines.

[4]...... in a similar vein to other national UK museums, entrance to the museum has been free since 2001. Opening hours are 10am to 5.45pm daily, with a late opening on Fridays, when the doors do not close until 10pm. The building does not open between Christmas Eve and Boxing Day.

The main entrance is on Cromwell Road and on [5]...... visitors will find cloakrooms and the main museum shop, which offers a huge range of books, stationery and gifts. [6]...... straight on, you come to the delightful John Madejski Garden, and eventually to the café, which provides hot dishes, salads, sandwiches, pastries and cakes, as well as hot and cold drinks, wine and beer.

In addition to the permanent collection, there are frequent temporary exhibitions. Currently running is Grace Kelly: Style *Icon*, [7]...... the Hollywood star's spectacular wardrobe. Entrance for the exhibition is £6 or £4 for concessions.

C **How many of your questions were answered?**

GRAMMAR
Participle clauses with adverbial meaning

> In more formal writing, we often use *-ing* forms or past participles in clauses that function as adverbs. *-ing* forms give an active meaning, past participles give a passive.

> Sometimes these clauses talk about reasons or results.
> *Situated within walking distance of both underground and bus stops*, the museum is easily accessible.
> (= because it is situated near underground and bus stops)

> Sometimes the clauses talk about conditions.
> *Walking straight on*, you come to the delightful John Madejski Garden. (= if you walk straight on)

> We can also use these clauses to talk about time.
> *Entering the museum*, I was struck by how modern it was. (= as / when I entered the museum)

> Note that we always use a comma to separate the clauses.

A Rewrite the sentences in a more formal manner, using active or passive participle clauses.
1   As we walked into the museum, we were greeted by a vast dinosaur skeleton in the entrance hall!
2   During our walk round the museum, I started to realise just how amazing ancient Persia must've been.
3   The Elgin Marbles were removed from Greece at the start of the 19th century and have been controversial ever since.
4   If they were redecorated, the galleries would surely attract many more people.
5   Because we didn't have long before closing time, we decided to just look round the Egyptian room.
6   Because I'm a regular visitor to the city, I'm quite familiar with all the museums there.
7   As it's about ten miles outside of town, the museum is quite difficult to get to.
8   A new law was introduced about ten years ago and the result was that all entrance fees were scrapped.
9   If you visit the museum during the morning, it's much less crowded.
10 The guide just pretended not to hear her questions and carried on with the tour!

KEY WORDS FOR WRITING
among and *within*

> *Among* shows something is included in a larger group or list or is situated in the middle of a group.

> *Within* shows something is inside a place, limit or range, or is situated close enough to walk, see etc.

A Match the sentence starters to the pairs of possible endings below.
1   The hostel is situated among
2   Smoking is not permitted within
3   The museum is among
4   The new wing of the museum is within
5   Visitors are free to handle the artwork within
6   The museum runs competitions among
7   The campsite lies within

a   schools / other ways of boosting participation.
b   one month of completion / sight of the river.
c   the grounds / 100 metres of the hospital.
d   the pine trees / several skyscrapers that dominate it.
e   earshot of a motorway / easy reach of the centre.
f   reason / the rules set down.
g   several that open at night / the largest in the world.

B Complete these sentences in ways that are true for you. Then compare your sentences with a partner.
1   I live within …
2   Sometime within the next few years, …
3   Among the things I like about living here is …
4   … is among the best …

WRITING PRACTICE

You are going to write a page of information about a museum – or other cultural amenity – that you know.

A Find out and make notes about the following.
•   its history
•   what's special about the place
•   its size and contents
•   its location and how to get there
•   opening times and entrance fee
•   any noteworthy facilities
•   any special exhibitions / current events

B Write 250–300 words about the place you chose.

01 CITIES

PERFECT TENSES

Perfect forms

Perfect forms are formed using *have* + past participle. There are past, present and future forms. Use perfect tenses to look back and describe finished actions or continuing states. With finished actions, we often don't know exactly when they happened.

Tenses

Compare the simple forms of the perfect tenses.
They invest a lot of money in the area. (generally)
They have invested a lot in the area. (from the past to now)
I have a car. (now)
I've had a car for six years. (from six years ago to now)
He went when I arrived. (He went the same time I arrived)
He had gone when I arrived. (He left before I arrived)
He said *he was* a teacher. (When we spoke, he still taught)
He said *he'd been* a teacher for six years. (before then)
He said *he'd been* a teacher. (He no longer taught then)
I'll do it on Friday. (start and finish on Friday)
I'll have done it by Wednesday. (finish before Wednesday)

Use the past simple to talk about hypothetical situations now, and the past perfect to look back.
I wish I *knew* one. (I want to know now but I don't)
I wish I *hadn't done* it. (I did it before, but I regret it)

Other forms

We may *arrive* late. (future)
We may *have arrived* too late. (We arrived before now)
He seems *to lose* things all the time. (generally)
I seem *to have lost* my wallet. (before now)
Being here, I don't recommend it. (I'm here now)
Having been there, I don't recommend it. (before, not now)

Time phrases and other patterns

Some patterns and adverbials often go with perfect tenses.

Present perfect

It's the first / second time I've done it.
It's the best thing I've *ever* seen.
It's changed a lot *in / over the past / last* few years, etc.
Once / After / As soon as I've finished, I'll call.
I haven't seen him yet.   I've *already* done it.

Don't use past time phrases *(e.g. ages ago, last year, when I was younger)* with the present perfect.

Past perfect

By the time he got there, I'd left.
Once / after / as soon as I'd said it, I regretted it.
Over the previous six years, things *had improved*.

Future perfect

I'll have left *by Friday* / 2020 / etc.
I'll have finished *before the weekend / I'm 60* / etc.

Exercise 1

Use the verbs in bold to complete each pair of sentences – one sentence with a perfect form, one not.

1 **call**
  a If I .... by six, it means I'm not coming.
  b As a rule, I .... anyone after nine at night.
2 **be done up**
  a It .... a few years ago, but the plaster's already crumbling.
  b It used to be very run down, but ....
3 **be struck**
  a It was the second time the city .... by an earthquake.
  b Our house .... by lightning last year.
4 **curb**
  a The government is introducing radical measures .... congestion and pollution.
  b The economic downturn doesn't appear .... investment yet.
5 **change**
  a I doubt anything .... by this time next year.
  b I think things .... with the new government.
6 **see**
  a .... what smoking did to my grandfather, I'd never take it up.
  b I'll have a drink too, ... as you're having one.
7 **pump**
  a I wouldn't swim there. They .... sewage into the sea!
  b They .... huge amounts of money into regenerating the area and it's beginning to pay dividends.
8 **be**
  a I wish he .... here now.
  b It sounds like you had a great time. I wish I .... there.

Exercise 2

Find the five sentences with mistakes and correct them.

1 I bet you he won't of finished by the time we get back.
2 I've been amazed at how sprawling the city is.
3 In the past year, the country's emerging from the economic downturn.
4 I think they may have won, if they play well tonight.
5 He wasn't against the idea, he just wanted to play devil's advocate.
6 Considering it's only the second time you play this game, you're doing very well.
7 It was disappointing to see things so run down, investing all that money before.
8 Once the rumour had started, it spread like wildfire.

02 CULTURE AND IDENTITY

EMPHATIC STRUCTURES

To emphasise a feeling or opinion, we often use these structures:

What The thing that One thing that	verb phrase	be	that … the fact that … the amount of … the number of … the way that … etc.

In the sentences below, the information we want to focus special attention on is in *italics*.

What bugs me is that *the expense is unnecessary*.
What bothers me is the fact that *he's not elected*.
One thing that worries me is *the amount of money wasted*.
The thing that really concerns me is *the lack of jobs*.
What has surprised me is *the number of applications*.
The thing that most annoys me is *the way he talks to people*.

Sentences starting with *What* can also be followed by verb clauses. This emphasises the action performed by someone.

What happened was *I decided to research my roots*.
What we did was *we booked our tickets well in advance*.
What they did next was *write to the government directly*.
(OR   What they did was *they wrote to* …)
What they should do is *increase the basic rate of tax*.
(OR   What they should do is *they should increase* …)

To show we don't share someone's opinion – or to correct wrong information – we can use this structure:

It wasn't me that said that. *It was* Brian!
OR
It was Brian *who / that* said that – not me!

The information we want to focus on comes after the verb *be* and is followed by a clause, usually starting with *that*. This structure is also known as a **cleft sentence**.

> ## Glossary
>
> **bugs:** if something bugs you it annoys you
> **sheer:** we use *sheer* before lots of nouns to emphasise the amount or degree of something
> **capital punishment:** the state killing people because of crimes they have committed
> **a caution:** a warning from the police
> **tone:** the tone of a speech or piece of writing is the general attitude it shows
> **divisive:** if something is divisive, it's likely to cause arguments between people

Exercise 1

Complete the sentences with the pairs of words in the box.

frustrates + lack	concerns + number
disturbs + stance	upset + seeing
amazes + amount	angers + not
drives + way	worries + level

1 What ……………… me is the sheer ……………… of wealth those at the top of society possess.
2 What ……………… most people is the ……………… of investment in basic health care and education.
3 What ……………… me the most while I was there was ……………… all the kids sleeping on the streets.
4 What ……………… me is the government's ……………… on law and order – and their emphasis on capital punishment.
5 What ……………… me crazy is the ……………… in which the police often let first-time offenders off with just a caution.
6 What ……………… me – and lots of other company directors – is the sheer ……………… of kids leaving school unable to read and write properly.
7 What ……………… me most is the alarming ……………… of ignorance that most people display about the whole issue.
8 What ……………… me most is ……………… their policies. It's more just their general tone.

Exercise 2

Rewrite the sentences so they start with *What* and a verb to emphasise how you feel.

1 The city is very cosmopolitan, which surprised me.
   What ………………………………… .
2 He can be very nationalistic! It's very disturbing.
   What ………………………………… .
3 The growing wealth gap is a concern.
   What ………………………………… .
4 The whole society is ageing at an alarming rate. That's the really scary thing.
   What ………………………………… .
5 People assume that I must love football just because I'm Brazilian. I get really angry about it.
   What ………………………………… .

Exercise 3

Complete the sentences with one word in each gap.

1 ……………… isn't the traffic that bothers me. It's the heat!
2 It's not the cold that's making you ill. It's ……………… you've been working too hard!
3 It's Michael you need to talk to about this – ……………… me.
4 It's not the openly racist people ……………… scare me, to be honest. It's the polite, middle-class ones!
5 It's the ……………… that people stereotype me all the time that really annoys me.

03 RELATIONSHIPS

WOULD

Would has several different uses.

1 **To make statements sound more tentative**
I'd call it a bit of an overreaction, personally.
I'd have to say no to that offer, though it's very kind of you.
I'd expect them to arrive sometime around five.
I wouldn't say it's a great film or anything.

We can make the last sentence above sound even more tentative like this:
I wouldn't have said it was a great film or anything.

2 **To make polite requests and offers and to ask for permission**
Would you mind passing me that book?
Would you care to try our house speciality?
Would you mind if I left early today?

Notice the verb patterns we use with these structures.

3 **To talk about actions that happened regularly in the past**
We used to go to Wales every summer. *We'd stay* with my uncle and aunt and *we'd go swimming* in the sea every day. It was great!

4 **To talk about imaginary or hypothetical situations in the past or present**
I would've gone crazy if that had happened to me.
It's lucky you weren't there. *You wouldn't have enjoyed* it.
I wouldn't have done that if I'd known she was going to get upset.
I would help you if I was free, but I've got a lot on today.
I wouldn't be where I am today if it hadn't been for her.

5 **To report speech / thoughts / ideas**
I knew that would happen.
I thought they'd probably *end up* getting married.
I didn't know he'd start crying, did I?
He promised he'd pay me back, but he hasn't done yet!
I think *we both realised we would have to compromise.*

6 **Use *wouldn't* to talk about the refusal of people or things to do what we wanted them to do in the past.**
I begged her to stop crying, but *she wouldn't.*
The window just *wouldn't open.*

7 **Use *I wish you / he / she would(n't)* + verb to complain about annoying things people regularly do – or don't do.**
I wish he'd just call me when he's going to be late.
I wish you wouldn't say things like that!

Exercise 1

Rewrite the sentences below in a less direct way, using *would* and the words in brackets.
1 I'm completely with you on that. (agree)
2 I think it was your own fault, to be honest. (say)
3 They'll probably buy a new one. (imagine)
4 It should arrive sometime next week. (expect)
5 Surely he was just trying to lighten the mood. (thought)
6 It can't be done! (not / thought)

Exercise 2

Find the five mistakes and correct them.
1 I hadn't realised I would have to work this much overtime.
2 I would have really long hair when I was a teenager.
3 Would you care to elaborate on that?
4 I wish my nose wouldn't be so big!
5 Would you mind me to sit here?
6 I wouldn't be here if I wouldn't have had the surgery.
7 I wouldn't have said it was a big problem.
8 I tried to talk him out of it, but he wouldn't listen.
9 It doesn't surprise me. I knew he'll say that! He's so predictable!

Exercise 3

Complete the sentences with the correct forms of the verbs in the box.

add	be	bother	explain	get
react	take	think		

1 My dad would always .... really annoyed if we walked in front of him when we were kids.
2 Your grandfather would've .... so proud of you!
3 Would you mind if I .... a link to your site on my web page?
4 I wouldn't .... seeing it if I were you. It's rubbish!
5 I wouldn't have .... he'd mind if you borrowed it.
6 I honestly didn't know that he would .... as badly as he did! It was only meant to be a joke.
7 Would you mind just .... a quick look at my essay?
8 Would you care .... what you meant by that last comment?

Glossary

overtime: if you work overtime, you work extra hours. You usually get overtime – extra money – for this
elaborate: if you elaborate, you give more information or details about something
talk him out of it: to persuade him not to do something stupid or dangerous

04 POLITICS

CONDITIONALS

Conditionals often have two parts / clauses. The *if*-clause may refer to real / generally true situations and actions (present or past simple / continuous) that happen(ed).

If-clauses may also refer to a *planned or possible* future situation (present tenses), or an imagined / impossible present, future or past event (past and past perfect tenses).

The second part of the sentence may show the normal (real) consequence (present, past tense); a certain opinion about the consequence (*will / going to, bound to, would*); or an uncertain opinion (*may, might, could,* etc.).

The second part of the sentence may also be an order (*don't*), advice (*should, would*), suggestion (*could / how about ...?,* etc.), possibility (*can*), promise (*will*), etc.

Remember the perfect infinitive (*would have done*) refers to before now or a point in time in the future / past.

Study the table. Find examples for the explanations above.

Generally true	
If they're late,	I don't let them in the class.
If they're late,	don't let them in.
If you're going to be late,	you should phone.
Possible future	
If they're late,	we can have a coffee there.
If I'm going to be late,	I'll call you.
If I'm late,	please don't wait.
If you're late again,	you're going to get the sack.
If they cut the budget,	there are bound to be job cuts
If you have time,	I'd go to the museum.
If I get there early,	I might do some shopping.
Unreal general truth / possible future	
If they raised taxes,	there'd be a riot.
If I could,	I'd quit my job tomorrow.
If she wasn't so busy,	she could help.
If people were kinder,	it would never have happened.
If he wasn't worried,	I wouldn't be talking to you.
Real past	
If we were late,	we always phoned home.
If you knew it was true,	you should've told me.
Unreal past	
If I'd told the truth,	he wouldn't have been sacked.
If he'd told the truth,	the press wouldn't care.
If the economy hadn't been doing so badly,	they might've won.

Exercise 1

Decide which option is not possible.
1. If the parliamentary vote goes against the government next week, *it could trigger / it'll trigger / it triggered* an election.
2. The government should've done more for the middle classes, if they *want / wanted / would've wanted* to win the election.
3. If anyone complains, *tell / I wouldn't tell / I told* the boss.
4. If I'd heard something, *I'd told / I would tell / I would've told* you.

Exercise 2

Complete with ONE word in each gap. (contractions = one word)
1. If it all goes wrong, ...say I didn't warn you.
2. If they clamp down on petty crime, it's .... to have a knock-on effect on more serious crimes.
3. If you go there, I .... take someone with you. It's a rough area.
4. Maybe they .... take a harder stance, if the softer approach is failing.
5. People here would .... put up with a law like that – there'd be a riot.
6. People complain about services, but there's always an outcry if the government .... putting up taxes.
7. If they .... what they were doing, I'd have more faith, but they obviously ....
8. You're very calm. I'd .... furious if that .... happened to me.

Exercise 3

Rewrite 1–5 with an *if*-clause and the word in **bold**.
1. We won't achieve anything without support.
   we
   .... we won't achieve anything.
2. I'm running late, otherwise I'd stop and talk.
   hurry
   ...., I'd stop and talk.
3. They would've won by a landslide with a better leader.
   changed
   They would've won by a landslide
   ....
4. I'd vote for them, but I don't like their stance on education.
   different
   I'd vote for them .... education.
5. He might still be president, but for his implication in that scandal.
   mixed
   He might still be president, ...

05 NIGHT IN, NIGHT OUT

NOUN PHRASES
Read below how this basic sentence can be expanded by adding information to make noun phrases.
John Moffit **stars in** 'The Dying'.

Names and categories
We often explain what a name is. No linker or relative clause is needed.
John Moffit, *the actor*, **stars in** *the movie* 'The Dying'.

Adjectives
Compound adjectives have hyphens between the two parts. Compound adjectives with number + noun are not plural.
John Moffit, the *award-winning* actor, **stars in** the *action-packed* movie 'The Dying'.
John Moffit, *the 37-year-old*, award-winning actor, **stars in** the *three-hour*, action-packed movie 'The Dying'.
John Moffit **stars in** the three-hour, action-packed movie 'The Dying', *now available on DVD*.

Compound nouns
Nouns can define other nouns.
John Moffit, the 37-year-old, award-winning *character* actor, **stars in** the three-hour, action-packed *road* movie 'The Dying'.

Relative clauses
If relative clauses add extra information that doesn't define the noun, put commas round the clause.
John Moffit, the 37-year-old, award-winning character actor, *who plays in his first lead role*, **stars in** the action-packed road movie 'The Dying', *which is based on the book*.

Participle clauses
We often shorten relative clauses by using participles. *-ed* forms replace passives and *-ing* forms replace active forms.
John Moffit, the 37-year-old, award-winning character actor, *playing* in his first lead role, **stars in** the three-hour, action-packed road movie 'The Dying', *based* on the book.

Prepositional phrases
Many nouns can be followed by prepositional phrases. It's also another way to reduce relative clauses.
John Moffit, the 37-year-old, award-winning character actor *from Canada*, *in his first lead role*, **stars in** the three-hour, action-packed road movie 'The Dying' based on the book *by Tom Daley*.

Noun phrases beginning with a participle or preposition may also precede the main clause.
Following his success on the stage in the musical 'StreetCar', John Moffit, the 37-year-old award-winning character actor from Canada, playing in his first lead role, **stars in** the three-hour, action-packed road movie 'The Dying', based on the book by Tom Daley.

Exercise 1
Underline the most basic subject, verb and object in 1–3.
1 The Oscar-winning director Joel Riley, whose latest documentary *Sick Life* is currently on release, gives a talk at the Barbican tonight, explaining his take on the current state of the film industry in the UK.
2 From the first tentative 'drawings of shadows' produced in the mid 1830s to its universal acceptance as a leisure pursuit, photography was swept along by a tide of entrepreneurial activity throughout the 19th century.
3 The parents of two troubled teenagers who were caught at the scene of a robbery in Georgetown, supposedly after listening to subliminal messages in the music of their favourite band, *Death House*, are seeking an as-yet unspecified amount of damages in compensation from the thrash metal group concerned and their record label.

Exercise 2
Shorten all the relative clauses as much as possible. You may need to use an *-ing* participle.
1 Visit the awe-inspiring cathedral which was designed by the architect Antonio Gaudi.
2 I read a fascinating article in the paper by the novelist whose name is Anne Tyler.
3 The exhibitions which are held in the centre are accompanied by workshops which are suitable for all ages.
4 There is a wealth of exhibits which are on show, which date back thousand of years.
5 The number of people who go to the cinema is far fewer than the number that currently attend theatre performances.

Exercise 3
Rewrite 1–4 using noun phrases.
1 The course lasts six weeks and teaches a number of guidelines. If you follow them, you will be able to lose weight quickly and effectively.
.... provides guidelines for
....
2 When they want to dispose of nuclear waste, the matter often causes controversy.
The .... is a
....
3 They want to abolish car tax, but a lot of people are opposed to the idea.
There's .... to the
....
4 The statue was erected to celebrate the fact he had been born a hundred years earlier.
The .... celebrated the
....

06 CONFLICT

I wish

We use *I wish* to talk about hypothetical situations – things we want, but which are impossible.

To talk about things in the present that we would like to be different, use *wish* + the past simple or *could*.

I wish we were closer as a family. (but we're not)
I wish I could help you. (but I can't)
I wish I didn't have this exam tomorrow. (but I do)
I wish you were a bit more thoughtful. (but you're not)

To talk about how we would like the past to be different, use *wish* + the past perfect or *could've* + past participle.

I wish I hadn't asked you now. (but I did)
I wish I'd never met him, I really do! (but we did meet)
I wish I'd chosen my words a bit more carefully. (but I didn't)
I wish I could've helped in some way. (but it was impossible)

To show how you want other people to behave differently, use *wish* + *would / wouldn't*.
I wish you wouldn't always *shout* when you get angry.
I wish my boss wouldn't keep calling me on my days off.
I wish my flatmates would stop stealing my food!
I wish you'd learn to control that temper of yours!

If only

We also use *If only* to talk about things we want to be different. It means the same as *I wish* and works in the same way.

Use *If only* + past tenses to talk about things we would like to be different now. Look at these patterns.
If only we spent more time together. Then we might get on better.
If only you weren't so bad with money. Then I wouldn't need to chase you up all the time!

Use *If only* + past perfect to talk about how we would like the past to be different.
If only I'd known. I would've come over and helped you.
I feel awful! *If only I hadn't had* that second slice of cake!

Use *If only* + *would / wouldn't* + verb to talk about how we want other people to behave differently.
If only you'd actually *try* and talk instead of sulking all the time! Then we might actually be able to sort things out.
If only you wouldn't always *turn* everything into such a big deal! It drives me mad the way you exaggerate things!

Exercise 1

Complete the sentences with the correct forms of the verbs in brackets.

1 I wish I .... say it was good, but it really wasn't. (can)
2 I'm enjoying my new job, but I wish I .... so busy all the time! (be)
3 I wish I .... never .... it to her! She's told half the office about it now! (mention)
4 I wish you .... and listen to yourself sometimes. (stop)
5 I wish I .... something to her, to be honest. I regret letting the chance pass me by. (say)
6 I wish I .... come with you, but at least you had a good time. (can)
7 My mum's so passive! I wish she .... actually .... angry about things and lost her temper more! (get)
8 I wish you .... that! It's really annoying! (do)
9 I wish I .... a bit more bothered, but I honestly couldn't care less! (be)

Exercise 2

Rewrite the sentences using *If only*.

1 I just can't stop smoking.
    If only ....
2 I can't believe I didn't give him my mobile number!
    If only ....
3 He keeps taking things from my room without asking.
    If only ....
4 You're so selfish!
    If only ....
5 You never listen to me when I'm trying to talk to you.
    If only ....
6 I stupidly forgot to lock the front door when I left.
    If only ....

Exercise 3

Complete the sentences by adding the correct auxiliary verbs (*do, did, had*, etc.).

1 A: Didn't you sort this out at the meeting last week?
    B: Sadly not, no. I wish we ...., but we didn't get round to it.
2 A: Are you coming to the sales meeting next week?
    B: I wish I ...., but I can't, unfortunately.
3 A: Did you go to that new Lebanese place in the end?
    B: Yes, but I wish we .... The food was dreadful.
4 A: Are you good with money?
    B: If only I ....! I'm hopeless – always in debt!
5 A: You know I'm leaving tomorrow, don't you?
    B: I do. And I wish you .... I'll miss you.

07 SCIENCE AND TECHNOLOGY

PASSIVES

Passive structures use a form of the verb *be* + a past participle. We use them when the subject of the verb is not the doer or cause of the action. This is because the doer is either unimportant or is unknown.

The genes *are then cloned* and *implanted* into the mother.

The DNA *has been extracted* from locks of hair.

The penguins *were given* an egg to look after.

They *had* previously *been seen* mimicking others.

If the process could *be repeated* in humans, it could save lives.

The perfume will *be sold* at around $100 a bottle.

They want the research *to be funded* by government.

Rather than *being used* for good, it could *be abused*.

Sometimes *get* is used instead of *be*, although this is unusual in scientific writing.

Thousands *get killed* every year in avoidable accidents.

Participle clauses

Participle clauses are passive or active.

The study ~~that was~~ *conducted* last year was flawed.

The numbers of people ~~that own~~ *owning* dogs have fallen.

Reporting

In academic writing / journalism, we often use reporting verbs in the passive form where the source is unimportant. Note the patterns that follow.

The chemical *is thought to be* carcinogenic.

The disease *is believed to have* a genetic component.

The government *is said to be considering* an enquiry.

It is argued that the research could provide a breakthrough.

It is hoped the research will result in new treatments.

Other passive structures

We sometimes use *have / get something done*. The subject of these sentences is the 'owner' of the thing that receives an action. Again, *get* is not usually used with scientific language or reports.

The fish *have cancerous cells inserted* in their bodies.

My uncle *had a kidney removed*.

I *got my legs waxed* the other day.

I *got my jacket caught* in the closing door.

Need + -ing is a passive (= *need / have to be done*).

The phenomenon *needs investigating* further.

My house desperately *needs repainting*.

We often use *you* or *they* in speech to avoid passives.

You can buy tickets online. (Tickets can be bought online.)

They've demolished the pub. (The pub's been demolished.)

Exercise 1

Rewrite the sentences with a passive construction.

1 They've achieved a breakthrough in nanotechnology.
   A breakthrough in nanotechnology ....
2 They gave me an injection before they stitched it up.
   I .... they stitched it up.
3 Scientists believe this technique is the way forward.
   This technique .... the way forward.
4 The dentist took one of my wisdom teeth out.
   I .... out.
5 The government should fund our research.
   Our research needs .... government.
6 It's important thorough research underpins policy.
   Policy should always .... thorough research.
7 In the end, he got employment as a researcher with the FBI.
   He ended up .... the FBI as a researcher.
8 Some believe a mineral deficiency causes the disorder.
   The disorder .... deficiency.

Exercise 2

Complete with a passive or active form.

1 The research, which is due to be completed sometime next year, ... by Tokyo University. (carry out)
2 The government says that since the outbreak started, those .... have received full treatment, while all those in vunerable groups .... (affect, vaccinate)
3 Scientists .... the research are confident it will lead to clean renewable energy that can .... at a competitive price. (undertake, produce)
4 The results can't .... by anything other than the people .... radiation in the area for a number of years. (cause, expose)
5 After .... from the organ, the sample tissue .... for the disease and the results came out negative. (extract, test)
6 While the failure of the initial probe .... the exploration of Mars, it .... that the lessons learnt will .... other problems further down the line. (set back, hope, prevent)

Glossary

carcinogenic: carcinogenic things can cause cancer
deficiency: if you have a deficiency, you don't have enough
probe: a machine or tool used to examine something
tissue: a collection of cells
outbreak: if there's an outbreak, a disease suddenly becomes widespread
set back: if something is set back, it's delayed or postponed

08 NATURE

AUXILIARIES

Tags
We use auxiliaries to make question tags. We add question tags to statements to get responses, to check things and to make polite requests. For positive sentences, use negative tags:
It's very industrial there, *isn't it*?

With negative statements, use a positive tag:
The hike won't be too strenuous, *will it*?

Positive tags are commonly used to make polite requests:
You couldn't lend me your phone for a minute, *could you*?

To express surprise or anger, we can use a positive tag with a positive sentence.
You can speak Thai, *can you*? How did you learn that?
Oh, you've got a son, *have you*? Why didn't I know that?
You want to borrow some money, *do you*? You haven't paid me back from last time yet!

Avoiding repetition
Auxiliaries help us to avoid repeating verbs already used.
I've never read it, but I think my sister *has*.

We sometimes need to change tense, but we still only use the auxiliary if it avoids repeating the same verb.
A: I'm not coming tomorrow.
B: Aren't you? I thought you *were*.
A: Yeah, I thought I *might*, but I've got to work.

Emphasising
Auxiliaries can add emphasis. In speech, we usually stress the auxiliary. If there's no auxiliary, add *do, does* or *did*.
I *HAVE* been there. I just can't remember much about it.
I *DO* love the scenery here!
We use auxiliaries like this to introduce contrasting ideas.
I *DO* like the landscape. It's just that it's a bit barren.

Showing interest / responding
Use auxiliaries to respond to people and to show interest.
A: I spent a month in Mongolia.
B: *Did you*? I bet that was interesting.

A: I speak pretty good Arabic.
B: *Do you*? Where did you pick that up?

Showing agreement
Use auxiliaries to show agreement with someone.
A: I can't stand those kinds of books.
B: No, neither *can I*.

A: I'd love to see a bit more of the rainforest there.
B: Oh, so *would I*.

Exercise 1
Write responses that contradict the statements in 1–5.
1 A: You never told me you'd been to Venezuela.
   B: .... You must have forgotten.
2 A: It looks a bit like a chicken.
   B: .... It looks more like a swan or something.
3 A: There's no way we'll get there on time.
   B: .... – if you just start driving a bit faster!
4 A: It never really gets that cold there.
   B: .... It actually snowed the year before last.
5 A: I don't think it's an endangered species.
   B: .... I read there were only 400 left in the wild.

Exercise 2
Rewrite the sentences below, adding an auxiliary in the correct place to emphasise the opinions.
1 That fish looks weird!
2 Don't get me wrong. I liked the country. I just found it a bit arid.
3 My son really enjoys going to the zoo.
4 The female of the species participates in the raising of the young, but it's predominantly a male job.
5 Tigers used to be quite common in the area, but they've been hunted to the verge of extinction.
6 He interrupts a bit, but his wife is worse!

Exercise 3
Add the correct auxiliaries. You will need to use negatives.
1 I'm not keen on zoos, but my kids ....
2 I .... hope you enjoy your time here.
3 I .... warn you it might bite!
4 That fish really .... look very strange indeed!
5 He's always butting in! I really wish he ....
6 The car should be OK on the dirt roads, ... it?
7 We spent a fortnight there, but I wish we .... I hated the place, I really ....!
8 My car's at the garage at the moment. If it ...., I'd come and get you from the airport, but I ...., I'm afraid.
9 A: I think we'll probably book in advance.
   B: You .... It gets very busy at this time of year.
10 A: Have you fed the dog?
   B: No, I ...., but I .... in a minute, OK?
11 A: Make sure you drive safely on the roads up there.
   B: Don't worry. I ....
12 A: I thought you were going to Poland this summer?
   B: I ...., and I still .... It's just all a bit up in the air at the moment.

09 WORK

CONTINUOUS FORMS

Continuous forms are formed using *be + -ing*. When we use continuous forms to talk about the present and past, they show something is unfinished and / or temporary (*not generally true or complete*). They may also emphasise the activity rather than the finished result. Compare the pairs of sentences using simple and continuous forms below.

Take no notice. He's *being silly*. (only now / temporary)
I don't like him. He's *stupid*. (his general quality)
The car's *being repaired*. (unfinished)
The car's *been repaired*. (complete)
The economy's *improving*. (at the moment / temporary)
The economy *improves*. (always!)
Call back later. I'm *working*. (now / unfinished, temporary)
I *work* for the government. (generally true / not temporary)
I *was skiing* when I broke it. (the skiing trip was unfinished)
I *skied* when I broke my leg. (I broke my leg – then skied!)
I've *been writing* some emails. (activity / maybe unfinished)
I've *written* some emails. (complete / finished)
I'd *been seeing* him for ages before he asked. (unfinished)
I'd *seen* the film before. (complete)
He *must be waiting* outside. (I imagine now / unfinished)
He *must wait* outside. (general obligation)

Duration

You can use continuous or simple forms to show how long something happened with little or no difference in meaning. With the present perfect and past perfect, the continuous is usually preferred. Otherwise, simple forms are standard.

I've *been working* / I've *worked* here for six years. (both cases unfinished)
It wasn't a sudden success. I'd *been trying* / I'd *tried* for ages. (both continuing up to the success)
I *worked* / *was working* there for a year. (both finished)
I *work* five hours every day. (generally)
I'm *working* all the hours God sends. (at the moment)

Future meanings

We can use the present continuous for future arrangements.
I'm *meeting* a friend this evening.

Use the future continuous for a future activity based on an earlier decision (not a decision made now).
I'll *be seeing* John later, so I'll give the money to him then.
He'll *be waiting* outside so you won't need to park.
Call me on my mobile tomorrow. I'll *be helping* Keith move.

If you are uncertain whether the activity will go ahead – or want to avoid doing it – use *be supposed to be -ing*.
I'm *supposed to be going out* later, but I'm too tired.

Non-continuous verbs

Some verbs are not used in the continuous form (*agree, believe, belong, doubt, matter, own, seem,* etc.) or don't use the continuous with certain meanings (*have, see, mind,* etc.).

Exercise 1

Complete the pairs of sentences using the words in **bold**. One sentences requires a continuous form, the other requires a simple form.

1 *draw up*
   a I .... the contract. You just need to sign it.
   b I .... the guidelines for the new project and I've got a couple of issues I need your input on.

2 *lose*
   a They had to make huge cuts because they .... so much money.
   b It was strange but when I .... my job, it actually gave me a new lease of life.

3 *deal with*
   a On this new project, Molly .... finance, so any queries about that go to her.
   b I .... Martin if you want. I know how awkward he can be.

4 *have*
   a We .... so many problems with him that in the end we decided to let him go.
   b I was really upset to lose that watch because I .... it since I was a kid.

5 *process*
   a Over 200,000 orders .... in this plant every week.
   b My visa application .... as we speak, so hopefully I'll receive it sometime in the next week or so.

6 *not sit*
   a If it hadn't been for that chance meeting, I .... here now.
   b I .... there if I were you. That's the CEO's chair!

7 *interview*
   a It was mildly embarrassing because I got a bout of hiccups while I .... I had to ask for some water.
   b Before I ...., I did some meditation to calm myself down.

Exercise 2

Find six mistakes and correct them.
1 I wouldn't be asking you if I knew the answer!
2 He must've done at least 80km/h when he crashed.
3 We can't meet in the office at the moment because it's doing up.
4 We're actually supposed taking on some new people soon, but I don't know when.
5 I'm seeing you're reading the new Dan Brown book. Is it any good?
6 She's been coming up with three possible solutions to the problems we've been having.
7 The company was going bankrupt when we took over.
8 I'll be sorting out those files later if you just leave them on my desk.

10 HEALTH AND ILLNESS

MODAL VERBS

We can use modal verbs like *should, could, might / may, must, can't* and *would* to comment on both the past and the present. To talk about the past, the form is modal verb + *have* + past participle (or + *have been -ing*). To talk about the present, the form is modal verb + verb (or + *be -ing*).

should

I *should've gone* earlier. (= it was a good idea to go, but I didn't)
You *shouldn't have been drinking* if you were on antibiotics. (= it was wrong of you to be drinking)
You *should get* some rest. (= it's a good idea for you)
You *shouldn't be walking* around yet. (= it's wrong of you to be walking around now)

could

I *could've died*! (= it was possible for me to die, but I didn't)
They *couldn't have done* any more than they did. (= it was impossible to do more)
You should have that looked at. It *could be* broken. (= it's possible that it is broken)
He *couldn't have examined* me properly. (= I am 95% sure he didn't examine me properly)
In the third sentence, *might* is possible instead of *could*.
In the last sentence, we can use *can't* instead of *couldn't*.

might / may

It *might've been* something I ate. (= maybe it was)
My grandmother *may have had* a similar condition. (= maybe she did. I'm not sure)
He *might / may be walking* again in a matter of weeks. (= it is possible he will be walking again soon)

must

You *must've felt* relieved. (= I'm 95% sure you felt relieved)
He *must've been working* for 24 hours or more. (= I'm 95% sure he was working for 24 hours or more)
That *must hurt*. (= I'm 95% sure it hurts)
He *must be feeling* awful. (= I'm 95% sure he's feeling bad)

can't (and couldn't)

Can't (and *couldn't*) is the opposite of *must*. Use *couldn't* to talk about the past. Use *can't* for past and present.
He *can't / couldn't* have been taking his medicine if he's had a relapse. (= I'm 95% sure he wasn't taking it)
The junk food *can't / couldn't* have helped. (= I'm 95% sure it didn't help)
It *can't cost* that much. (= I'm 95% sure it doesn't)

would

I *would've screamed* my head off! (= definite result if I had been in that situation)
I*'d ask* for a second opinion. (= definite result now if I was in your situation)

Exercise 1

Rewrite the sentences using modal verbs in place of the words in *italics*.

1 *I am 95% certain that that was* painful.
2 *It's wrong that he didn't stop* smoking earlier.
3 *I'm 95% sure it's not* that hard to do.
4 *It was impossible for them to do* any more to help.
5 *I am 95% certain that it wasn't* cheap.
6 *It's a bad thing that he was* taking those pills.
7 *It's possible that you will* need three or four operations.
8 *I am 95% sure he was lying* about his diet!
9 *It's possible that she* picked up the bug from my son.
10 If he managed to get to hospital in time, *I am 100% sure that everything was* fine.

Exercise 2

Complete 1–6 using the correct modal verbs given and the correct form of the verbs in brackets. The modal verbs are not necessarily in the order you will need to use them.

1 **would, might**
   I know it's too late to worry about now, but it .... a good idea to talk to a few different doctors. They .... something your doctor didn't. (be, see)

2 **should, would, may**
   They think he .... a heart attack. If you ask me, they .... the autopsy earlier. That .... at least .... all the speculation that's been going on in the press. (suffer, carry out, stop)

3 **could, must, should**
   That .... very painful. It looks really bad. Maybe you .... and get it X-rayed. It's probably just badly bruised, but you never know – it .... broken. (be, go, be)

4 **would, should, could**
   You .... in the road! What were you thinking? You .... killed! If a car had come round that corner, you .... time to get out of its way! (not / play, be, not / have)

5 **might, must, can't**
   All that medication .... good for you. It .... your immune system slowly. Seriously, you .... better quicker if you just stop taking that stuff altogether. (be, weaken, get)

6 **would, must, could**
   I don't know how you got through it! You .... a very strong stomach! I .... my head off if I'd been in your shoes. How you .... calm all the way through is beyond me! (have, scream, remain)

11 PLAY

LINKING WORDS

so / then
So shows the reason for / result of doing an action, whereas *then* simply shows what happens next.
Keep your cards close to you *so* no-one can see them.
Shuffle the cards. *Then* deal three to each player.

so / so as (not) to / in order (not) to
So as to and *in order to* also show purpose. They are more formal. We usually use *to* + infinitive.
Switch off the console when not playing ... *so* you save energy.
Switch off the console when not playing ... *so as to / in order to / to* save energy.

if / whether
These both link a condition. Use *whether* for choices. *Whether* can be followed by *to* + infinitive.
The need to decide *whether / if* they'll play. (or not).
The manager is deciding *if / whether (or not)* to play him.
If / ~~Whether~~ they play him, his injury might get worse.

provided / so long as
Provided is used to talk about rules and give permission. It means *only if the following happens*. It is often followed by *that*. We also use *providing*.
Two people can swap cards *provided* that everyone agrees.
So / as long as have a similar meaning.
You can go out s*o long as / as long as* you're back by ten.

unless / otherwise / until
Unless means *if you don't*. If you DO and want to show a resulting action, use *in which case*.
You can't move *unless* you throw a six, *in which case* you move six and throw the dice again.
Otherwise shows the alternative result if you don't do something.
I'd better go now, *otherwise* I'll miss my bus
Until links the action that continues and the point it stops.
You can't start the game *until* you throw a five.

even though / although / even if
Even though shows something that makes the main fact in the sentence very surprising. Note that *although* can also be used here, but *even though* is more common.
I beat him *even though / although* I'd never played before.
Although is also used in the same way as *but* – to show a contrast or contradiction between two things.
You can find cheats on the Internet for computer games, *although* I don't use them. I don't see the point.
Even if emphasises that something will remain true in the event of a hypothetical situation.
He won't score *even if* he gets an open goal.

Exercise 1
Choose the correct linking word.
1 He scored two goals *so / and then* he got sent off.
2 *Even if / Even though* they got a goal back now, it still wouldn't be enough.
3 I'll watch almost any sports, *even though / although* I'm not very keen on golf.
4 The game was postponed *so as not to / in order to* clash with the city's festival celebrations.
5 He's going to be banned from playing for two years *if / unless* the decision is upheld in the court.
6 He was running really well *until / unless* he faded on the last lap.
7 He was taking the drug EPO *in order to / so* boost his performance.
8 Even though he's the underdog, he can still win *so long as / whether* he plays at the top of his game.
9 They need to win their last game, *otherwise / unless* they get relegated.

Exercise 2
Complete the explanation of Blackjack with ONE word in each gap.
Blackjack is a game we play quite a lot. The aim of the game is to get rid of all your cards. Each player is dealt seven cards and the rest of the deck is placed face down [1].......................... you can't see the cards. You then turn the top card over and place it next to the deck. The player next to the dealer has to try to put down a card that follows suit or is a card of the same rank, [2].......................... they pick up a card from the deck and play moves to the left. You can place a run of cards down, such as five, six and seven – [3].......................... that they are of the same suit. You could also put down several cards of the same number, say three sixes, assuming you have them. There are a number of special cards. For example, [4].......................... you put down a black jack, the next person picks up five cards from the face-down deck, unless they have the other black jack, in which [5].......................... the person after them picks up ten, unless they have a red jack which they can play so [6].......................... to avoid picking up anything. Actually, people often still win [7].......................... if they do pick up ten cards. The other special cards are eights – miss a go; twos – pick up two; kings – change direction; and queens, which you have to cover with a card from the same suit. It's quite complicated, [8].......................... it only takes a couple of rounds to get the hang of it.

> ## Glossary
>
> **clash:** if two events clash, they are happening at the same time and may disrupt each other
> **get the hang of:** if you get the hang of something, you begin to be able to do it more easily through practice

12 HISTORY

DRAMATIC INVERSION

Inverting a sentence by putting the adverb and / or auxiliary before the subject is a way of adding emphasis to certain pieces of information. If there is no auxiliary, we add *do / does / did*.

Inversion is more common in literary or journalistic writing than in spoken English, but it can be used in conversation to make descriptions more dramatic.
No sooner had we begun to recover *than* the war began.
No sooner did the troops arrive *than* the war ended.
No sooner was the castle finished *than* it was attacked.

Here are some other ways of inverting sentences. All are more common in writing and formal speech. Informal ways of saying each one follow in brackets.
Not only was he saved *but* so were thousands of others. (He was saved as well as thousands of others).

Never before had one nation controlled so much of the world.
(It was the first time that one nation had controlled so much of the world.)

Nowhere else in the country *will* you get a better impression of what it was like in the old days.
(It's the best place to see how things used to be.)

Not until 2002 *was* independence finally gained, after more than 30 years of waiting.
(We gained independence in 2002, after more than 30 years of waiting.)

Only when the national bank went bust *did* the size of the financial crisis we were facing become apparent.
(When the national bank went bust, we all started realising just how serious the financial crisis really was.)

Only after a public enquiry had been held *were* we able to comprehend the full horror of what had occurred.
(We didn't really know quite how bad things had been until after the public enquiry.)

It was made very clear to us that *under no circumstances were* we supposed to be out on the streets after nightfall.
(We were warned not to go out onto the streets at night.)

At no time in history *have* our kids been more overweight.
(Kids are fatter than they've ever been.)

In no way did the Occupation lead to the end of the Resistance movement. If anything, it strengthened it.
(The Occupation certainly didn't crush the Resistance!)

Diplomats made it clear to him that *on no account was* he to use such inflammatory language again.
(He was warned not to use that kind of language again.)

Exercise 1

Rewrite the sentences using the beginnings provided.

1 He only admitted his involvement in the scandal when it became obvious it could no longer be contained.
   Only when it ....
2 It really was the first time we'd witnessed an international relief operation on such a scale.
   Never before ....
3 The first women's team didn't come into existence until 1996.
   Not until 1996 ....
4 Nobody tried at any point to prevent the tragedy.
   At no time .... prevent the tragedy.
5 It's the best place in the world to combine business and pleasure.
   Nowhere else in the world .... quite so well.
6 They basically said that if I moved, they'd shoot me.
   They made it very clear that under no circumstances ....
7 After America rebelled against the high import taxes imposed on tea, coffee become more popular.
   Only after ....
8 He was an artist and a poet as well as being a military leader.
   Not only ....
9 The government put taxes up almost as soon as they took office.
   No sooner ....
10 We've only had one honest leader in the whole of our recent history.
   Only once in our recent history
   ....

Exercise 2

Correct the mistake(s) in each sentence.

1 Never before so few people did so much for so many.
2 Not only she campaigned against injustice of all kinds, but she was also the first female minister.
3 Only when a society refuses to acknowledge its past failings it starts to lose its moral authority.
4 No sooner the truce had been called than peace talks began in earnest.
5 Only after tighter checks were introduced corruption finally was tackled.
6 A law was passed saying that on no account foreigners would be allowed into the city centre.

Glossary

contain: if you contain something harmful, you stop it from spreading to other people / places
in earnest: if you do something in earnest, you do it with great energy and determination

13 NEWS AND THE MEDIA

REPORTING AND VERB PATTERNS

Verb + (that) clause

acknowledge	announce	argue	boast
claim	confess	confide	confirm
declare	grumble	guarantee	insist
reiterate	state	vow	

Verbs in the '(that) clause' use past forms unless the facts / actions are still relevant / true now – or are yet to take place.
He *reiterated that he had never seen* the victim before.
He *confirmed he was / is going to compete* in the Olympics.

Verb + object + (that) clause

assure	confirm	convince	notify
promise	remind	tell	warn

The party *assured voters* (that) they would not raise taxes.
The verbs *admit, announce, confide, confess, point out* and *report* use *to* before the object with this pattern.
He *admitted to police* he'd been drinking.
Note: He *(dis)agreed with me* that it had been a mistake.

Verbs + *to*-infinitive

demand	guarantee	promise
refuse	threaten	vow

I *volunteered to do* the work.

Verbs + object + *to*-infinitive

advise	beg	encourage	instruct	invite
order	persuade	remind	urge	warn

He *warned us not to invest* in that project.
Note: He *pleaded with them to* help.

Verb + noun phrase

cite	confirm	criticise	declare	praise	reject

Many people have *voiced their anger* over the incident.
The union *criticised the president* for not helping.
We sometimes use noun forms of verbs to report:
My parents gave me *encouragement* to study harder.

Verb + preposition + *-ing*

apologise for	blame on / for	criticise for / over
forgive for	insist on	threaten with

Some verbs have prepositions connected to them.
Verbs that follow will use the *-ing* form.
He was *accused of* murder.   She *accused* me *of lying*.

Exercise 1
Choose the correct verb.
1 The President *cited / stated* his father as a source of inspiration.
2 The party leaders *urged / reiterated* everyone who could to go out and vote.
3 The two parties have *rejected / refused* to cooperate.
4 The government *criticised / blamed* the stalemate on the opposition.
5 Our landlord suddenly *announced / notified* that he was putting up the rent.
6 He's *instructed / demanded* his lawyers to evict us if we don't pay.
7 My son *begged / pleaded* with us to buy him a car and in the end we gave in.
8 I heard him *boasting / praising* that his parents were rich.

Exercise 2
Complete the reports of the direct speech with no more than six words including the word in **bold**.
1 'I can't believe they have decided to put up taxes.'
   anger
   He voiced .... rises.
2 'I haven't told anyone before, but I was terrified.'
   me
   She confessed .... been terrified.
3 'I'll definitely have it ready by Friday.'
   done
   He guaranteed .... by Friday.
4 'You two should really visit sometime.'
   urged
   He .... sometime.
5 'We have worries regarding a possible deterioration in the situation.'
   concern
   They .... might deteriorate.
6 'If you don't do as I say, I could get you sacked.'
   with
   He .... if I refused.
7 'The plan was flawed. I never denied that.'
   acknowledged
   The minister .... flawed.

Exercise 3
Complete the reports using noun forms of the verbs in *italics* and the other words given.
1 The school provides ....
   encourage / students / apply for university
2 The president has come in for ....
   criticise / his decision
3 We turned down ....
   invite / work with them on the project
4 They made ....
   announce / they / get married last week

14 BUSINESS AND ECONOMICS

RELATIVE CLAUSES

There are two kinds of relative clause: defining and non-defining. Defining relative clauses identify who or what we are talking about and are an essential part of the meaning of the sentence. No commas are needed at the beginning or end of the relative clause.

To add information about a person, use *who* or *that*. To add information about a thing, use *that* or *which*. For places, we use *where* or *that* (+ a preposition). For times, use *when* or *that*. In all examples, *that* is more commonly used.

It's nice to meet someone *who / that* says what they think!
It was the banking crisis *that / which* led to the bankruptcy.
Peru is the country *where* we're doing most business.
Peru is the country *that* we're doing most business in.
The 90s was a time *when* house prices rocketed.
They were years *that* I look back on very fondly.

We tend not to use a relative pronoun in defining relative clauses if it is the object of the clause that follows. In these cases, the noun that follows the relative pronoun is the subject of the clause.
Can I talk to *the person (that) I spoke to earlier*, please?
It's *a place (that) we're looking to expand into* in the future.

Where the relative pronoun is the *subject* of the clause, make sure you don't add another subject pronoun!
The local branch became simply a tiny part of a much bigger beast, a beast *that it̶ fed off your hard-earned cash.*

Prepositions in defining relative clauses usually go at the end of the clause, except in formal texts.
Banks became *places (that) you went to* for a whole range of financial services. (rather than *to which you went*)
This does not cover theft of your mobile phone when left unattended in *a place to which the public has access.*
The person I wrote to last time told me to contact you.
The person to whom all subsequent correspondence should be addressed is Mr James Mason.

Non-defining relative clauses add extra – non-essential – information to a sentence. These clauses always follow a comma and are more common in written English. They start with words like *which, most of which, by which time, where, when, whose, who*, etc. We cannot use *that* in these clauses.
Our cash-flow situation worsened, *which* caused serious problems. We waited a full six months for one major payment, *by which point / time* we were almost bankrupt.

Some abstract nouns often occur with clauses introduced by *where, when* or *why* – or as part of prepositional phrases with *which*.
It was a *situation where* we lost sight of our basic goals.
The *ways in which* the situation could change are numerous.

Exercise 1

Rewrite each of the pairs of sentences below as one sentence. Start each sentence with the underlined words. You will need to leave some words out.

1 Improvements can be made in some areas. <u>We</u> have to identify these areas.

   ....

2 <u>My boss</u> heard everything. Her office is next to mine!

   ....

3 We borrowed 10,000 euros <u>in January</u>. Most of it has already been spent.

   ....

4 The way in which you approach negotiations is incredibly important. <u>Deals</u> can depend on this.

   ....

5 We chose 2004 <u>for the starting point of our study</u>. Our president submitted his first budget that year.

   ....

6 To some extent, large corporations influence the economic health of nations. <u>I</u> wanted to explore this.

   ....

7 In retrospect, <u>the meeting in 2008</u> was a very important year. We realised then we could no longer work as allies.

   ....

8 <u>We</u> have over 9,000 employees. The vast majority are based in China.

   ....

9 It was a very difficult situation. <u>We</u> found ourselves expected to pay large bribes to local officials.

   ....

10 <u>We've</u> reached a crucial point. We can't cut costs any further without having to lay people off.

   ....

Exercise 2

A Join the sentence halves using *which* or *whom* after a suitable preposition.
1 Our founder was Mr Johnson,
2 We're lucky enough to have an incredible team,
3 After much research, we've come up with a prototype
4 We're conducting research into the Kazakh market,
5 I'd like to say thanks in particular to my boss,
6 Naturally, we are all influenced by the things

a we currently know very little.
b I've learned a huge amount.
c we are all very satisfied.
d we surround ourselves.
e we would never have survived this difficult year.
f the company is named.

B Rewrite the six sentences above in a less formal way, putting the prepositions at the end of the relative clauses.

15 FASHION

PREPOSITIONS

Prepositions can be followed by nouns, pronouns or *-ing* forms. Below are some common confusions.

as / like

As shows the job, use or duty something actually has. We use *like* to make comparisons. It's followed by a noun.

As ~~Like~~ *an actor,* he was great; *as a parent,* he was awful.
We were very close. She was *as* ~~like~~ *a mother* to me. (= she's not my mother)

from / of

From shows the origin or the condition before it changes.

He was sacked ~~of~~ *from a design company.*
It's a translation ~~of~~ *from German.*

into / to

Into shows what someone or something becomes – or a movement entering or hitting something.

It's grown ~~to~~ *into the biggest company* in the country.
He crashed ~~to~~ *into the car in front.*

up to / until

Up to shows the maximum amount possible (how much). *Until* shows when something stops.

The temperature can reach ~~until~~ *up to 45 degrees.*
I can work ~~until~~ *up to six hours* without a break.
I have to work *until* ~~up to~~ *ten o'clock tonight.*

for / during / throughout

For shows how long. *During / throughout* goes with dates, events, etc. and shows when. *Throughout* shows that the action didn't stop; with *during*, it maybe happened just once.

Hats were essential clothing ~~during~~ *for centuries.*
~~For~~ *During the 20th century,* hats went out of fashion.
The prime minister was booed *throughout / during the rally.*

Collocations

Prepositions may collocate strongly with some nouns, adjectives and verbs – or be part of a set expression.

on purpose	fond of	owe to
by yourself	prior to	rely on
in debt	effect on	hint at
at random	reaction to	account for
in the long term	the same as	bombard with
with regard to	on a ... basis	amount to

Linking sentences

Prepositions can link two parts of a sentence.

With the heatwave, sales of swimsuits took off. (= because)
On finishing college, he got a job at Dior. (= when / after)
In improving the design, SPM have leapt ahead of their competitors. (= as a result of)
Besides having a nine to five job, I write novels. (= also)

Exercise 1

Complete the story with a preposition in each space.

The accident happened during my daily run. I usually drive to some woods near here and run [1]...... 30 or 40 minutes or [2]...... to eight kilometres. [3]...... this particular occasion, though, I was [4]...... a rush so decided to just go for a quick jog round our small local park. Maybe I was a bit distracted [5]...... everything I had to do that day, but I ran [6]...... a small wire fence and fell over. I was a bit shaken and my knee was a bit sore, but I basically thought I was OK, so I walked back home and went to work.

However, my knee went [7]...... being a bit sore to incredibly painful. I tried to ignore it, but it was agony and [8]...... the rest of the day, I was taking painkillers to try and ease the pain. [9]...... waking the next morning, I was in absolute agony again. I decided to drag myself to the hospital to get it checked out. Apparently, I'd torn a ligament and I'll need an operation and physiotherapy. I've got a note [10]...... my doctor saying I should be [11]...... work for at least a month, so I may not be back [12]...... the new year.

Exercise 2

Rewrite sentences 1–7 using the words in **bold** and between two and five other words.

1 They deliberately lost the game to win a bet.
 purpose
 They lost .... win a bet.
2 I think it's good in terms of the overall design.
 regards
 I think .... it's fine.
3 The company was in a terrible state before he arrived.
 his
 Prior ...., the company was failing.
4 We've made it more accessible as a result of the reduction in costs.
 enabled
 In .... more people to buy it.
5 Every day I have to check the stock
 basis
 I have to check the stock ....
6 It's fine for the time being, but it won't last forever.
 term
 It's fine now, but .... it'll need replacing.
7 23% of our exports are connected to fashion.
 accounts
 The fashion industry .... a quarter of all our exports.

Glossary

agony: agony is extreme pain or distress
casualty: casualty is the department in a hospital that deals with accidents and emergencies

16 DANGER AND RISK

OTHER FUTURE FORMS

There are lots of ways of talking about the future in English. You have already studied the most common at earlier levels. Certain forms, though, are often used in particular contexts, such as journalism and the media.

Be set to is often used in news reports when something is likely to happen. We also use *be set for* and *looks set to*.
Campaigners *are set to challenge* the decision in court.
The sector *is set for explosive growth* this year.
The strike *looks set to intensify* after talks broke down.

Be to is commonly used in the news to talk about actions that have been officially arranged or scheduled.
The Queen *is to meet* the president in private tomorrow.
Peace talks *are to begin* early next month.

Be due to is used in formal English to show something is planned to happen at a particular time.
The next train *is due to arrive* on platform 3 in six minutes.
I'm *due to start* back at work next Monday.

We can also use other prepositions with *be due*.
Your car insurance *is due for renewal* imminently.
All three films *are due for release* this month.
The baby *is due in December*.
I'm *due at a meeting* in a minute or two.

Be likely is often used for making predictions.
The offer *is highly likely to be rejected* by shareholders.
Critics claim the legislation *is not likely to / is unlikely to stop* the problem.
It *seems likely that* the two parties will form a coalition.

Be bound to shows you're sure something will happen.
He's *bound to hear* about it sooner or later.
If you ask me, e-books *are bound to fail*.

We also use *be sure / certain to* with a similar meaning.
They're *bound / certain / sure to* check all the figures.

There are several nouns and noun phrases used to talk about future events and to show how sure we are of things happening.
He's *on the verge of* signing a new contract.
(= He's about to sign a new contract)
To be honest, I'm *on the point of* giving up my diet.
The chances of it happening are slim / pretty good.
There's *no / a slim / a good chance of* it working.
The odds / chances are that the police will crack down hard.
The odds of it happening are pretty high / low.
In all probability / likelihood, it'll soon be forgotten about.
The probability / likelihood is that it'll require surgery.
There's a *distinct / definite possibility that* it won't sell.

Exercise 1

Decide if one or both choices are possible in each sentence. Delete any incorrect options.

1 There's a *distinct / probable* possibility that you'll experience side effects from the medication.
2 He's *about to be / on the point of being* kicked out of school for good.
3 We are *due to / about to* hold meetings on the matter in a couple of months' time.
4 There's a *slim / slight* chance we might be late.
5 It seems *probable / likely* that the election will be held in June.
6 In all *chances / likelihood*, we'll be done by tomorrow.
7 They're *set to announce / on the verge of announcing* record profits.
8 The odds of things going wrong are pretty *high / likely*.

Exercise 2

Complete the sentences by adding the correct prepositions.

1 The likelihood .... them listening is pretty low.
2 He's due .... court tomorrow.
3 The stage is set .... a thrilling race.
4 I'm .... the point of quitting, to be honest.
5 Apparently, I'm due .... a tax refund.
6 What does 'payment is due .... the time the service is rendered' mean?

Exercise 3

Rewrite the sentences using the words in **bold** so they have a similar meaning.

1 Arrangements have been made for the work to be overseen by a team of international inspectors.
   is
   The work ....
2 In all probability, the news will damage his reputation.
   sure
   The news ....
3 Police believe they're close to finding the killer.
   point
   Police ....
4 We're on the verge of being evicted.
   about
   We ....
5 Where there's passion, it is inevitable that success will follow.
   bound
   Where there's passion, ...
6 Prices will almost certainly rise this year.
   highly
   Prices ....

FILE 1

Unit 1, p. 10, Reading

Group A

Tangshan

Tangshan had been a major industrial city until 28th July 1976, when an earthquake with a magnitude of 8.3 struck the city, devastating 80% of the buildings. It was the biggest natural disaster in the 20th century in terms of cost to human life. The official death toll was just short of a quarter of a million people – or one in four of the population – with a further 160,000 serious casualties. Some, though, put the death toll as much higher. At the time, China was a very closed country and the government refused all foreign aid, ordering Chinese troops to lead the relief efforts. The operation was a huge undertaking, but the victims of the quake were quickly provided with temporary shelter and the coalmines were put back into operation.

However, the rebuilding of the city was then stalled for three years, in part because of political disputes among government leaders. In some ways, the quake and its aftermath marked a turning point in China's history, and ushered in the modern era and the country's emergence as a global economic power. Tangshan is now a symbol of that change, having been completely rebuilt since 1980. It has become a thriving industrial city again, based on both steel and technology, and is home to three million people. In China, it is widely known as 'the brave city' and it takes great pride in its self-reliance and the will of its people to shake off the painful experience – or to 'walk out the pain' as the Chinese saying goes.

Glossary

death toll: number of people dead
troops: soldiers
undertaking: difficult thing to take charge of doing
shelter: a place to protect or live in often temporary
stall: to stop / fail to make progress
aftermath: the effects of something bad / important
usher: lead to
thriving: successful, flourishing
will: determination, desire

FILE 2

Unit 3, p. 25, Speaking

Student A

Two good friends of yours have fallen out badly. You are having a few friends over for you birthday and would like them both to come, but you don't want a scene or bad atmosphere between them to spoil the evening.

Your father is looking after your mother, who is very frail and unsteady on her feet, but he himself has become very absent-minded and is struggling to cope.

Your son takes a very laid-back attitude to his studies, and although he's taken things in his stride so far, you're worried he might fall behind and fail.

Glossary

a scene: if someone makes a scene, they shout or argue or cause a disturbance
take it in your stride: if you take something in your stride, you cope with new things or difficulties easily

FILE 3

Unit 6, p. 43, Conversation Practice

Conversation 1

You share a house with Student B and three other people. For some time now, you've felt that Student B doesn't really fit in. He / she is always complaining about the noise and about everyone else's inability to stick to the rota of household chores, yet doesn't seem to realise his / her own failings. He / she has a short temper, and frequently ends up screaming and shouting or slamming doors after rows. You feel he / she needs to lighten up and relax – or else leave!

Start the conversation by saying *Good morning* to Student B and asking *How are you?*

Conversation 2

You work for an import-export company. Student B is your immediate superior and has asked to have a word with you after work. You're worried it may be about a piece of gossip you passed on to a couple of friends. You've felt for some time that Student B is victimising you – and you once reported what you felt had been bullying behaviour to the regional manager. You fear Student B still holds a grudge against you for this.

FILE 4

Unit 12, p. 85, Developing Conversations

Student A

Bryan Ward-Perkins

He is an archaeologist and historian. He has written *The Fall of Rome and the End of Civilization*. Oxford: Oxford University Press (2005)

External pressures

The Romans came under attack from a variety of external tribes and competing empires such as the Huns and the Persians. The Empire was eventually overrun in the west by the waves of Germanic tribal armies, because, it is claimed, its military resources were too stretched.

Christianity

Christianity was incorporated into the Roman Empire and then became the established religion. Rome became the church's centre, with the Pope at its head. It is argued that this not only created an alternate powerbase that undermined the emperor's authority, but also ran counter to imperial expansion. Basically, the people were content to wait for the riches of heaven, rather than attempting to gain more power in the here and now.

Lead poisoning

Some academics have asserted that lead was consumed through lead water pipes and the preparation of a common syrup used to flavour wine. They point to statistics that suggest that the intake of lead was likely to have been many times higher among the ruling classes and claim this caused early deaths and lower birth rates. This theory has been widely challenged, though.

Economics

High inflation, unemployment and a devalued currency have all been seen as weakening the imperial economy and undermining military power.

FILE 5

Unit 4, p. 29, Speaking

Student A

Joke 1

One day a florist goes to a barber for a haircut. After the cut, he asks about the bill and the barber replies, 'I can't take any money from you. I'm doing community service this week.' The florist was delighted and skips out of the shop.

When the barber goes to open his shop the next morning, there's a 'Thank you' card and a dozen roses waiting for him at the door.

Later that day, a college professor comes in for a haircut, and when he tries to pay his bill, the barber shakes his head and waves him away - 'I can't take any money from you. I'm doing community service this week.' The professor is very pleased and strolls off.

The next morning when the barber opens his shop, there is another 'Thank you' card and a bundle of books including *How to Improve Your Business* and *Becoming More Successful*.

Then, a politician comes in for a haircut, and when he goes to pay his bill, the barber again lifts his hand and says, 'I can't take any money from you. I'm doing community service this week.' The politician can't believe his luck and races out of the shop.

The next morning when the barber goes to open up, there are a dozen other politicians all lined up, waiting outside.

Joke 2

For her homework one day, a schoolgirl was asked by her teacher to write an essay entitled 'Why I love our Great Leader.' The girl went home and asked her father sweetly, 'Dad, why do you love the Great Leader?'

'I don't,' her father shouts. 'I hate the man and everything he represents.'

The little girl then went into the bathroom and asked her mum and then her brother and her grandma – and she got the same answer from every single person!

Then she went up to her room and did her homework. 'I love our Great Leader,' she wrote, 'because nobody else does!'

FILE 6

Unit 8, p. 59, Reading 2

Group A

The Wild Bactrian camel is found in the Gobi desert of Mongolia and China, which ranges from boiling sand dunes to frozen hills and mountains. It has evolved to withstand the extremes of heat and cold as well as the arid landscape. It has thick eyelashes that close to form a full barrier against sandstorms and it can also completely close its thin, slit-like nostrils to prevent dust entering. It eats snow in the winter months and unlike any other camel can also drink salt water. It is still unknown how it processes the salt water.

Excess water is stored not in its humps, but in the bloodstream. The humps are largely made up of fat. The camel draws upon these reserves at times of drought and famine. Like other camels, it reduces water loss by hardly sweating or urinating. It also has an incredibly tough tongue, capable of eating the sharp thorns of desert shrubs. These camels are also incredibly resistant to disease, which may surprise people considering their numbers are dwindling.

The Wild Bactrian camels roam widely in small herds of two to fifteen members and are threatened from a number of angles. They were heavily hunted in previous years, and continue to be so where there is competition for water sources from domestic herds. They have also suffered poisoning as a result of the use of dangerous chemicals in illegal mining activities. Finally, they often interbreed with domestic Bactrians, which leads them to lose the capability to drink salt water.

Despite efforts to crack down on illegal mining and hunting, the Wild Bactrian camel has become one of the rarest mammals in the world. There are now captive breeding programmes aimed at restoring populations.

FILE 7

Unit 4, p. 29, Speaking

Student B

Joke 1

A flock of sheep are trying to sneak across the border when a guard stops them.

'Why do you want to leave the country?' the guard asks them.

'It's the secret police,' the terrified sheep explain. 'They've been ordered to arrest all the elephants.'

The guard scratches his head and points at them. 'But you're not elephants. You're sheep'.

The sheep let out a laugh. 'Ha! Try telling that to the secret police!'

Joke 2

A desperate man was crouching in the shadows on a back street near the parliament building in the capital city. Suddenly, he saw a wealthy-looking man in a suit and tie strolling towards him. He noticed the expensive leather briefcase and pulled his knife out of his pocket. Just as the man was passing, he leapt out and screamed, 'Give me all your money.'

'You can't do this to me,' his victim wailed.

'I'm a member of parliament!'

'Well, in that case,' the mugger replied, 'give me MY money!'

Joke 3

A senior politician went on a visit to the country's biggest car factory. The manager went out of his way to show him around and at the end of the tour he offered the politician a free car. 'Oh, no,' came the response,

'I couldn't possibly accept anything like that.'

'Well, in that case, I'll sell it to you for 100 euros,' said the manager.

As quick as a flash, the politician pulls out two 100 euro notes, hands them over and says 'That's very kind. I'll take two of them.'

FILE 8

Unit 7, p. 49, Conversation Practice

Student A

Article 1

Two male penguins are rearing a chick together after they were given an egg to look after. The male pair had previously been seen mimicking heterosexual behaviour and zookeepers wanted to see how they would react to real fatherhood. The pair immediately sheltered the egg and saw it hatch. They have since continued to look after it and behave as a normal mother and father. Zoologists say that homosexual-type behaviour is quite prevalent in animals of all kinds.

Article 2

A company, Antiquity Perfumes, is producing fragrances based on the DNA of famous dead people such as Marilyn Monroe, Elvis Presley, Einstein and Michael Jackson. The DNA has been extracted from locks of hair that have been acquired by John Reznikoff, who has the world's largest collection of hair from famous people, dating back to the 16th century. The company says that the resulting fragrance is the 'essence' of the star, rather than being their actual smell, but that the process is entirely scientific. The perfume varies in price, but on average costs around $90.

Article 3

Scientists in Japan have devised a way to produce pictures based on brain activity. The process uses a magnetic resonance imaging machine to measure blood flows in the brain as the subjects are shown a series of random black and white images. Sophisticated computer software was then used to associate new brain activity with different images so that the machine was able to display letters spelling 'neuron', which was what the participant was thinking of. The images are still very basic, but it is believed that the process will have the capability of, for example, reading dreams in the not-too-distant future.

FILE 9

Unit 12, p. 85, Developing Conversations

Student B

Edward Gibbon

He was a historian and MP in the 18th century and is most famous for writing *The History of the Decline and Fall of the Roman Empire*, now considered a classic of English literature.

Decadence

The Romans are still famous for their lust for life and lavish lifestyles, born of the great wealth that was generated by the empire. However, some contend that this emphasis on leisure over work amongst the elite led to the army being less well-trained and more reliant on foreign mercenaries. It was also seen as contributing to economic problems.

Division

Not only was power divided between emperor and the Pope, but the empire itself was divided between the west in Rome and the east based in Constantinople (now known as Istanbul), which was headed by a separate emperor. This created competition and denied funds to the west. The Eastern Empire was more efficiently run and survived the collapse of Rome. In addition to this, the west was plagued with infighting and civil war among army leaders staking their claim to the throne.

Environmental degradation

It is claimed that the demands for fuel, agriculture, construction and the like led to widespread deforestation during the times of the Empire. This in turn led to soil degradation, problems with flooding and reduced crop yields. Doubts have been cast on the theory because of a shortage of reliable data and some assert that the theory is the result of more modern environmental concerns.

FILE 10

Unit 6, p. 43, Conversation Practice

Conversation 1

You share a house with Student A and three other people. It's Tuesday morning and you haven't slept very well because someone was playing music and chatting loudly until 2 a.m. You have exams next week and feel your housemates are being inconsiderate. You are also generally fed up with how messy everyone else is and are really reaching your limit!

You've come down to the kitchen to make some coffee.

Student A will start a conversation with you.

Conversation 2

You are the departmental manager for an import-export company. You are very concerned about the behaviour of Student A, who works under you in the company. You have reason to believe he / she has passed on information about a forthcoming deal to some rival companies. You also feel he / she has an attitude problem, and have not forgotten that last time you had words, Student A then went over your head and complained about you to the regional manager.

Start the conversation by discussing Student A's attitude problem.

FILE 11

Unit 8, p. 59, Reading 2

Group B

The Aye-Aye resembles a cross between a small monkey and a rat because of its rodent-like front teeth. It lives in the canopy of trees in the Madagascan rainforest, usually nesting in a fork of the tree. As well as fruit and vegetation, it also eats small worms and insects living in the trees, which it finds in a similar way to a woodpecker. It taps on the trunk until it detects a hollow sound, then gnaws away at the bark with its teeth to make a hole, before inserting its elongated middle finger in through the hole to pull the grubs out. There is only one other animal that uses this technique.

When foraging for food, Aye-Ayes may cover over four kilometres a night as they leap from treetop to treetop. Aye-Ayes are generally solitary creatures that only socialise in order to mate, with the female of the species being dominant. The males will often aggressively compete for a female's attention.

The Aye-Aye is endangered because of a number of factors. Firstly, its habitat is being destroyed, increasingly forcing it to raid villages for food. It is quite fearless in approaching humans. Unfortunately, humans aren't quite so friendly to it. Villagers not only kill Aye-Ayes because they are a nuisance and eat farm crops, but also because they are believed to be evil – capable of sneaking into homes and puncturing a person's heart while they sleep.

Although laws exist against killing them and several reserves in the jungle have been set up, their numbers continue to dwindle. Captive breeding programmes are also working to preserve them.

FILE 12

Unit 1, p. 10, Reading

Group B

New York

New York may have been a major city for many years, but it has still had to overcome many problems in its time, not least its reputation as a violent city of muggings, shootings and murder. By the late eighties, large swathes of the city had effectively become no-go areas for tourists and residents alike. In 1990, the murder rate peaked when it reached 2,245, while there were also thousands and thousands of other serious crimes such as rape and armed robbery.

Since then, however, murder has fallen more than fourfold and some believe it will have dipped below 400 a year by the next election. Other types of crime have fallen even more dramatically. The reasons for the fall are hotly debated, as other cities now want to replicate New York's success. There was an economic boom and a fall in the number of young adults who predominantly commit crime, but these changes were widespread throughout the country.

Three factors of policing seemed to differentiate New York at the turn of this century: firstly, there was an increase in the police force with more officers on the street; secondly, there was a more aggressive 'broken windows' policy that didn't tolerate minor offences; and thirdly, a computerised statistics model was introduced to manage and target policing more effectively. Alongside this, the city hall pumped money into improving housing in the poorest neighbourhoods and those with the highest crime. This mix of changes brought about the falling crime rate, and then having less crime in itself is thought to have helped by creating a 'virtuous circle': lack of crime allows for stronger communities, which in turn deter crime.

Glossary

overcome: defeat / recover from
swathes: large area
peak: reach the highest value
dip: fall
fourfold: four times
predominantly: mainly
offence: a type of crime
target: direct money or action towards a place or people
pump into: invest a lot of money in

FILE 13

Unit 10, p. 74, Reading

Group B

I swear I can't help it

Tourette's syndrome is an inherited neurological disorder estimated to affect around 1% of the population. Interestingly, it is more likely to occur in boys than girls. Onset is usually during childhood and the most common symptoms are repetitive, rapid movements, known as tics. Tics can be both physical and verbal, and range from the mild (repeated shrugging of shoulders, blinking of eyes, clicking of the tongue, clearing of the throat, sniffing, etc.) to the more extreme (jumping or spinning around, inappropriate sudden swearing and repetition of words or sounds heard recently). There may also be a tendency towards other forms of obsessive-compulsive behaviour, attention deficit disorder, sleep disorder and learning disabilities.

Tourette's syndrome in itself, however, has no negative impact on either intelligence or life expectancy, and symptoms generally decrease as sufferers pass out of adolescence. The symptoms tend to be beyond the control of the sufferer and attempts to suppress them for any length of time can cause stress, which ends up making a severe bout more likely. Nowadays, though, the condition can be treated effectively through the use of therapy or drugs.

The most important factor in dealing with the disorder seems to be the support and understanding of friends and family. Due to the odd nature of the symptoms, sufferers frequently find it hard to integrate fully into society, and feelings of rejection can lead to psychological damage.

FILE 14

Unit 3, p. 25, Speaking

Student B

Your neighbours seem to be going through a very rough patch and are constantly shouting. You've just heard several things being smashed and a woman screaming 'Stop it. Stop it' at the top of her voice.

You've had a few problems with a project at work – through no fault of your own – but you think a colleague has been going behind your back in order to undermine you and get your job.

The doctor wants to discharge a member of your family from hospital, but you aren't convinced they are ready to come home and you're not sure if you'll cope.

Glossary

rough patch: a period where you suffer a lot of problems
behind your back: if something is done behind your back, people do something you don't want without you knowing

FILE 15

Unit 7, p. 49, Conversation Practice

Student B

Article 1

Japanese scientists are making see-through frogs commercially available. The frogs, which will be sold for around $100 each, were bred for educational purposes. Rather than getting killed for dissection in class, the transparent frogs allow students to see all the internal organs in action.

Researchers in Boston had previously created transparent fish to study the development of cancer. The fish, which are genetically similar to humans, have cancerous cells inserted in their bodies so researchers can watch them grow. Studies on normal animals only show cancer development via autopsy. It is hoped a greater understanding of cancer growth will pave the way for new treatments.

Article 2

An online survey has revealed that one in five scientists have used so-called brain-boosting drugs to help them work better – many on a regular basis. The drug Ritalin, which is generally used to treat children suffering from Attention Deficit Disorder, can, in normal brains, heighten concentration.

The revelation has opened a debate in scientific circles with some defending the drug use. They argue that, while more research needs to be done, if drugs are shown to have insignificant long-term side effects, they could offer a way to improve educational performance.

Article 3

A nuclear physicist who had had funding requests for research into time reversal rejected has raised $40,000 from the public to carry out his experiment. Professor John Cramer, a leading scientist in quantum mechanics, is setting out to solve a famous paradox in quantum theory, which allows split sub-atomic particles to travel faster than the speed of light and 'communicate' instantaneously. It may seem far-fetched, but one theory for this paradox is so-called 'retrocausality': in other words, that the future can affect the present or past. His proposed experiment is a first step towards testing the theory and, if successful, he hopes to attract funding from government.

FILE 16

Unit 15, p. 105, Conversation Practice

FILE 17

Unit 3, p. 25, Speaking

Student C

You have been assigned to do an assessed project with a new classmate and you're finding her quite hard work. She doesn't contribute much to discussions and you feel she's not pulling her weight in other ways.

Your best friend has started going out with someone who from the first moment rubbed you up the wrong way. It's difficult to put your finger on why you just don't like him / her but recently you've had the feeling that maybe he / she fancies you!

You think your husband / wife is too soft with your children and far too indulgent. You often refuse to buy the children things and you set clear rules, but then they go to your husband / wife and he / she gives in immediately and undermines you.

Glossary

pull your weight: if you don't pull your weight, you don't do your share of the work

rub you up the wrong way: if someone rubs you up the wrong way, they annoy you

put your finger on it: if you put your finger on a problem or reason, you identify exactly what it is

FILE 18

Unit 1, p. 10, Reading

Group C

Dortmund

As a city, Dortmund in Germany bears little relation to what it was like 50 years ago, even if much of the architecture has remained the same. Before the 1960s, the region in which it is situated had been a centre for heavy industry, in particular coal mining, steel and brewing, but these industries went into decline from then on. Dortmund was hit by high unemployment and could easily have gone into economic meltdown with the associated breakdown in society.

However, rather than giving up and moving elsewhere to look for work, its residents reinvented themselves and their city for the future, and now Dortmund is an affluent place, internationally renowned for innovation in science and technology and a model for regeneration. The city has had support from EU funding as well as grants from central government, but its successful transformation is largely seen as the result of a unified and long-term commitment to regenerate the city between local government, businesses and the citizens of Dortmund through the so-called 'Dortmund Project' and the establishment of Dortmund University, which specialises in technology.

It is also worth noting that the people did not choose to completely rebuild the city and forget their industrial heritage. Instead of being demolished, many of the old steel plants and breweries have been converted into centres of research or for dance and theatre. In fact, a vibrant arts scene has long flourished in Dortmund and it was designated the European Capital of Culture for 2010.

Glossary

bear: have the quality of
brewing: process of making beer and similar drinks
meltdown: complete collapse
breakdown: situation where something fails / stops
renowned: well known
regenerate: develop again
heritage: buildings, traditions, art, etc that are important to a culture
demolish: deliberately destroy
flourish: be successful / thrive

FILE 19

Unit 7, p. 49, Conversation Practice

Student C

Article 1

French researchers have discovered that sufferers from autism who inhale the hormone Oxytocin are better at noticing facial signals and maintaining eye contact. The so-called 'love' hormone is found in high levels in breast milk and is thought to be responsible for encouraging bonding between mother and child. Previous studies have also shown those with autistic conditions may have a deficit of Oxytocin. The experiment focused on those sufferers who did not have highly impaired language skills. Currently, other drugs are prescribed to deal with symptoms such as anxiety, but researchers believe this could be a breakthrough in dealing with more underlying causes of the condition.

Article 2

Dogs that can glow in the dark have been successfully reproduced by inserting a gene that produces a fluorescent pigment in the dogs' skin into a cell. The cell is then cloned and implanted into the mother. The scientists had previously done the same with cats. The research is seen as a step towards finding cures for genetic disorders in humans. If genes can be introduced into animals without adverse effects, then it could pave the way to inserting missing genes or repairing damaged ones that are the root cause of various congenital conditions.

Article 3

A study by vets in Britain has revealed that on average cat owners are more intelligent than dog owners, as cat owners typically had a higher level of education. The researchers suggest that this is not down to any transference through the interaction of cats with their owners, but rather is due to the fact that cats are more independent and tend to require less attention. As highly educated people are likely to have longer working hours in more high-powered jobs, they do not have the time to dedicate to a dog's upkeep. This is just one finding of a census undertaken by the Department of Clinical Veterinary Science at the University of Bristol.

UNIT 01

🎧 1.1
Conversation 1
A = Woman, B = Man

A: How was your trip?

B: Great. Really amazing. Have you ever been there?

A: No. What's it like?

B: It's really wild. It took me by surprise, actually.

A: Yeah?

B: Yeah. I don't know what I expected, really. I just thought it'd be quieter, but the nightlife is totally mad

A: Really?

B: Honestly. The people there party like there's no tomorrow. We went out with these people and ended up in a place at about four in the morning and it was absolutely packed.

A: Yeah?

B: Seriously. You couldn't move. In fact, the whole city was still buzzing. You can still get stuck in traffic at that time of night.

A: Wow!

B: Actually, that was a bit of a downside, the congestion.

A: Really? Is it bad?

B: Unbelievable! You just spend hours and hours in your car crawling along, with everyone honking their horns. You'd be quicker walking, really.

A: So did you?

B: No, it's unbearably humid, so you can't, really. Honestly, you only have to walk out of your hotel and you're dripping in sweat. It's just like a thick wall of heat that hits you.

A: There must be a fair amount of pollution, then.

B: That as well. There's this appalling cloud of smog that constantly hangs over the city. You nearly choke on the fumes when you're outside.

A: Sounds pretty grim. Are you sure it's so great?

B: Well, you know, it does have its drawbacks but, as I say, it just has a real buzz – especially downtown with the skyscrapers and the neon lights flashing and the people and the noise. It's just a very vibrant place.

Conversation 2
C = Man, D = Woman

C: What's your hometown like? It's supposed to be nice, isn't it?

D: It is, if you like that sort of place.

C: What do you mean?

D: It's just very conservative. You know, it's very affluent – you see loads and loads of people in fur coats and posh cars, and the streets are spotless, but it's also just incredibly dull. There's not much going on.

C: Right.

D: I know it's a bit more run down here, but at least it's more lively. There's more of a music scene, you know.

C: Yeah, I know what you mean. So you wouldn't consider going back to live there?

D: Maybe. I mean, don't get me wrong, it is a good place to live if you're bringing up kids – everything works very smoothly and, as I say, there's not a speck of litter on the streets. So if I were to settle down, I might move back. It's just not what I want right now.

C: Fair enough.

🎧 1.2
I = Interviewer, L = Lloyd Jones

I: Following the latest hurricane to hit the Caribbean, we're here talking with Lloyd Jones, an expert on disaster recovery. Lloyd, this has been a particularly devastating storm. How long can we expect the city and region to take to overcome this crisis?

L: Well, in very basic terms – getting rubble cleared away, providing basic shelter, getting services up and running and so on – very quickly. Even with some of the logistical problems we've been seeing, I'd expect it to have happened in a matter of weeks, if not days, but, of course, real long-term recovery can take years.

I: Several politicians are already talking of this in terms of an opportunity – to rebuild a city which had suffered economic and social problems for years.

L: Hmm, yes. I always slightly worry when I hear that.

I: Really?

L: Well, it very much depends what you mean by 'opportunity' and who the opportunity is for. For example, in a number of fishing villages struck by the Asian tsunami some years ago, what emerged from the recovery was not a flourishing fishing industry, but rather hotels and tourism. This was seen by many as a positive step in developing the economy by those investing, but for the fishermen it meant losing a way of life and control over their own income.

I: Right.

L: Unfortunately, throughout history it's often the rich who define recovery and the poor who lose out. For example, going back to the 19th Century, most of the city of Chicago was devastated by fire. There was a huge push to reconstruct the city driven by an image of the future. Skyscrapers sprung up to replace what had been there, and you know what, during the construction more people died than in the fire itself!

I: So what should happen?

L: I think the best projects are those that fully involve the affected community – in fact, that are led by them. Where we're talking of very deprived areas with social problems, that can certainly be difficult, but outsiders often underestimate poor people's capabilities. People are resourceful.

I: Lloyd Jones, we have to leave it there. Thank you very much.

🎧 1.3
Speaker 1
A really terrible thing happened to a woman I used to work with. One day, she woke up and found her car had been stolen from outside her house, so she called the police and reported it, but when she got back home from the office that night, the car had been returned. It was in the driveway. It'd been completely cleaned and there was a note on the driver's seat apologising for taking it. Whoever had written the note said that his mum had been taken ill and he'd had to drive her to the hospital. Next to the note there were a couple of tickets for a concert the following day. The woman, she was really thrilled you know – so happy – her car back, two free tickets – fantastic. So she called a friend and they both went to the concert and had a really fantastic time.
Once she got home though, …

Speaker 2
Someone told me a story about a guy from Tokyo who'd gone on a golfing holiday. On the third or fourth day, he suddenly collapsed and had to be rushed to hospital for treatment. Eventually, they diagnosed him as having been poisoned and they reported the incident to the police. The detective in charge of the case questioned the man, but he couldn't think of any reason why anybody would want to poison him. It was something really silly in the end. They worked out …

Speaker 3
This mad thing happened to a guy that a friend of my brother knows. Apparently, one day, he went to a supermarket to buy a few bits and pieces and as he was looking for the bread, he noticed this elderly woman just staring at him with these desperately sad eyes.

He turned away, grabbed a loaf and went off in search of some milk. Once he'd found the milk, he turned round only to see the same woman there again – still just staring like mad at him. Anyway, he was getting a bit freaked out by this – as you would – so he rushed off to pay, but then he remembered that he'd run out of toilet paper and so he went back to get some. When he got back to the cashier, there was the old woman again – in front of him in the queue and her trolley was almost full to the brim. This time she turns to him and she says: 'I'm really sorry for staring, but the thing is, you're the spitting image of my son who died last year.' She's wiping her eyes, getting all tearful, and she says 'You've got the same eyes, the same hair. It's incredible.' As she was packing all her stuff away, she whispered to the guy and said: 'Could you do me a tiny little favour? Could you just say "Goodbye, Mum" when I leave? It'd mean the world to me. ' Well, what was he going to do? This little old lady and her tragic story, trying to hold back the tears – so as she's leaving the store, struggling with all her shopping, he shouts out 'Goodbye Mum.' He felt like he'd done his good deed for the day, but then …

💿 1.4
Speaker 1
Once she got home though, she discovered she'd been burgled and all her valuables had been stolen. Then to top that, about a week later, the police called her and told her that her car had been used as the vehicle to get away from a major bank robbery on the day that it had gone missing. That is so unlucky, no?

Speaker 2
It was something really silly in the end. They worked out that the man had actually poisoned himself by accident. Apparently, when he was playing golf he used to hold the tee – that plastic thing you put the golf ball on – between his teeth as he was walking round between the holes, but the golf course had been sprayed with pesticide, so he was basically just sucking in toxic pesticide.

Speaker 3
He felt like he'd done his good deed for the day, but then the cashier told him his bill was like 300 pounds. He said there must've been a mistake as he'd only bought a few things, but then the cashier explained. She said, 'Yes, I know, but your mother said you'd pay for all of her shopping as well!'

UNIT 02

💿 2.1
Conversation 1
A = Woman, B = Man
A: So, how long were you there for?
B: Just under a month, so long enough to get a feel for the place.
A: I really admire the fact you went there. It must've been fascinating, but also very challenging, I'd imagine.
B: Challenging in what way?
A: Well, I mean, it's a very male-dominated society, isn't it?
B: I don't know about that. It may have that reputation, but that wasn't really my experience of the place.
A: No?
B: No, not really. I mean, it's all very close-knit, but I didn't feel women there were any worse off than in many other places. In fact, the family we stayed with, the wife seemed to more or less run the show, to be honest.
A: Oh, OK. That's interesting. And how was the traffic? Do people really drive as badly as the stereotype has it?
B: Well, they're not the best drivers in the world, it must be said, and it does get quite congested, but to be honest, it wasn't that that really bothered me. It was more just the total lack of any decent

public transport. There's no tube or anything and the buses were always so crowded that you ended up driving yourself and then you become another part of the problem.

Conversation 2
C = Man, D = Woman
C: One thing that's surprised me here is the music scene. I've been to some amazing gigs – and people seem to really go for it! They're usually so formal and polite, but put them in front of a live band and they go absolutely crazy.
D: I know. Actually, I think the arts scene in general seems to be thriving. There are some great young film directors coming up as well.
C: Yeah, yeah. What amazed me was how much they get away with. I'd expected a lot more state control, because you hear about all the censorship before you arrive, but some of the topics they tackle are very politically sensitive.
D: Absolutely. I saw a film the other week that was basically dealing with corruption and the fact that people are always having to pay bribes.
C: Yeah? That sounds pretty close to the bone. Someone was telling me the other day, actually, that one thing making a big difference right now is the fact that the economy is doing so well. It just means there's a bit more money floating around, and so people are happy to invest in new projects, and all that's fuelling this freedom of expression.

💿 2.2
1 I'm not sure about that.
2 Isn't that a bit of an exaggeration?
3 I wouldn't go that far.
4 That's a bit over the top, isn't it?
5 Well, that's one way of looking at things.
6 That's a bit of an overstatement, isn't it?
7 I don't really see it like that myself.

💿 2.3
1 Vaughan
What bugs me is the way people use 'British' and 'English' interchangeably. Wales is a separate country, with a distinct cultural heritage and language to the English. In fact, sometimes I think the English are jealous because they haven't maintained their own cultural traditions like us or the Scots. I mean, not many people celebrate St George's Day in England.

I'd personally like the Welsh to gain even more autonomy from the UK. That's not because I'm very nationalistic or consider myself super-Welsh, because I'm not. I don't actually speak Welsh that well. Nor am I a big fan of flag-waving because I think that can lead to narrow-mindedness and can even breed racism.

No, I want independence for political reasons. Traditionally, the Welsh have been more left-wing, but that's not really reflected in the British government. Also, I don't understand why we still have royalty. The only 'God Save the Queen' I'll sing along to is an old anti-royalist punk song! In some ways, I'd like to be seen as a republican and citizen of the world first, then European, and Welsh, or even British – but never English!

2 Amir
I guess some people don't expect to see someone like me running a fish and chip shop, but for 99% of my customers, it's just not an issue. I was born here and my parents were born here and I'm as British as anyone else. I just happen to be Muslim as well, that's all. It's no big thing. I do get the occasional comment about it, but it doesn't bother me.

The only time I ever feel vaguely conflicted about my identity is when England play Pakistan at cricket. I can't help it, but I always want Pakistan to do well. There's always a bit of banter about that with the local lads, but as I always say, I'm sure most English blokes living on the Costa del Sol still support England if they ever play Spain at football. It's human nature, isn't it?

3 Emily

Last week I went to a ceremony where a friend of mine, Nyasha, gained British citizenship. She's originally from Zimbabwe and came here as a refugee, so it was a big day for her. To become a British national, she had to pass a test, which meant learning things most British people don't even know about – like the year that 18-year-olds first got the vote!

I have to say, the more I thought about it, the harder it became to really say what being British means to me. You meet some foreigners who still believe we all wear bowler hats and shop at Harrods and can recite Shakespeare, and others who stereotype us as all being madly into football, drinking too much lager and eating curry or kebabs, but apart from liking curry, I don't fit into either group! I'm more into car boot sales and baking cakes. I don't know ... I think everyone has their own idea of what British culture really means. For my son, it'd be hip hop! It's a very personal thing.

UNIT 03

🎧 3.1
Conversation 1
A = Man, B = Woman

A: So how's it all going? Any better?

B: I'd say things are worse if anything, to be honest. He doesn't seem to have a clue how the department should work or what's expected of him – and he's dragging the rest of the team down with him. I've tried to talk to him about it, but he always just gets really defensive and puts up this great big barrier. What really drives me mad, though, is the man's arrogance. He's so full of himself! He's one of those people who'll just never accept they've done anything wrong. He just blames it all on everyone else.

A: Sounds like an idiot to me! Maybe you need to go over his head and talk to someone else about it.

B: I would do, but our line manager isn't very approachable. And even when you do get to talk to him, he's not exactly the best listener in the world.

Conversation 2
C = Woman, D = Man

C: I can't stand him.

D: Really? I've always thought he comes across as a really decent guy.

C: You're joking, aren't you? He's so fake!

D: Do you think so? In what way?

C: All that rubbish about saving the world and helping the starving millions that he's always going on about.

D: What's wrong with that? I quite admire the fact he's prepared to stand up for what he believes in. He doesn't have to do all that charity work, does he? He could just keep his mouth shut and keep his millions and carry on making music.

C: Yeah, but it's all just self-promotion, really, isn't it? It's just to sell more CDs. If he was really bothered, he'd give all his money away and really help people. He just likes to be seen to be doing good.

D: I just think you've got him wrong. He's done a lot to raise awareness of various different causes and he works really hard to make a difference. You're just a cynic.

C: And you're just naïve!

Conversation 3
E = Man, F = Woman

E: So what're they like? Are you getting on OK with them all?

F: Yeah, more or less. I haven't really seen much of the guy next door. I've passed him once or twice in the corridor, but he keeps himself to himself, really.

E: OK.

F: But the girl opposite is great. She seems really nice and bright and chatty. We hit it off straightaway.

E: That's good, then.

F: The only problem is she kind of hogs the bathroom. I mean, she's in there for hours every morning, doing her hair and her make-up. It's really annoying because we've only got the one bathroom.

E: Oh no! Really? That'd drive me mad, that would!

F: And the other guy, in the little room upstairs, seems pleasant enough, but he strikes me as a bit of a slacker. I mean, he's not working at the moment and he just seems ... well ... extremely laid-back about it.

E: To the point of horizontal, then, eh?

🎧 3.2
Conversation 1
A = Woman, B = Man

A: It's a bit worrying actually, I haven't seen her around for a bit.

B: How old is she?

A: Well, she must be getting on because she mentioned going to university in the sixties and occupying the Chancellor's office during a protest.

B: A bit of a radical, then.

A: Oh yeah, and she's still very with it – she hasn't lost any of her faculties at all. She's one of these people who are always writing to their MP – calling them to account.

B: Maybe she's away visiting family.

A: I'm not sure she has any to speak of. I know she had a sister, but she told me they'd had a major falling-out. I just would've thought she'd have mentioned going away, asked me to water her plants or something.

Conversation 2
C = Woman, D = Man

C: What's up?

D: It's Connor. He's got another detention. I actually had a phone call this time from Miss Jones.

C: You're joking.

D: She said he's just constantly answering back.

C: I think she just overreacts. I know he has a tendency to be a bit cheeky – but let's face it, it's a bit of a family trait, wanting to have the last word – but it's just harmless banter really: disagreeing for the sake of it.

D: It didn't sound like it.

C: She's just singling him out for punishment, if you ask me.

D: You should've heard what he said to her. He can be very hostile, you know.

C: He's going through a slightly more rebellious phase, but that's perfectly normal. She should be used to it, and this isn't going to help.

D: We should put our foot down with him or he's going to go completely off the rails.

C: Oh, don't exaggerate. It'll all blow over.

Conversation 3
E = Woman 1, F = Woman 2

E: We've obviously both got a strong competitive streak, but I wouldn't call it sibling rivalry, would you?

F: No, not at all. I think it's all <u>channelled into</u> the tennis. We can both be pretty ruthless with each other. I mean, Sal showed no mercy when she thrashed me, in the Open last year, but after the match – well, obviously I was disappointed – in bits, really – but Sal comforted me, and once I got over the disappointment, I was really pleased for what she'd achieved – there was no jealousy or anything.

E: That's right. I think it's very much down to the way we were brought up, which was always very much share and share alike, and very loving

F: Absolutely.

Conversation 4
G = Man, H = Woman
G: Apparently, they were quite close at school, but nothing really <u>came of</u> it and then they just drifted apart and lost touch, as you do, you know, and then suddenly, completely out of the blue, he got this email and that's how they got back in touch. Like she'd been carrying this flame for him all this time.

H: Aww! That's so sweet.

G: The really amazing thing is that as it turns out, she has a couple of kids already from a previous marriage.

H: No!

G: Yeah, but he seems to have taken it all in his stride and it seems to be really working out for them.

H: Oh, I'm so delighted for him. He's such a lovely bloke.

Conversation 5
I = Woman, J = Man
I: I sometimes feel we're just on a conveyor belt and she's just ticking boxes.

J: I know what you mean.

I: I mean, I was feeling really under the weather, but she wouldn't listen, she just dismissed it as a slight bug.

J: I wouldn't <u>put up with</u> it – you should register with someone else. Why don't you try at my place? They're very good there. They're always very sympathetic if I need a sick note or to take time off work.

UNIT 04

4.1
Conversation 1
A = Woman 1, B = Woman 2
A: Personally, I'm in favour of curbing the salaries of people like bankers and executives.

B: How would you do that, though?

A: I don't know. I'm sure it's not without problems, but there must be a way. I just find some of these salaries are <u>obscene</u> – especially when they have people in the same company earning peanuts.

B: Hmm. I know what you mean.

A: And it twists everything else, because if they're earning that much, **it encourages other people to ask for more**, and it <u>pushes up</u> prices.

B: Curbing salaries may be OK in principle, but in practice? It's going to be unworkable, isn't it?

A: I don't see why. We have a minimum wage so why not a maximum one?

B: Well, how are you going to decide the maximum? And **what would you include in pay**? **What if they were given a boat or whatever, instead of money**?

A: Well, **they'd just declare it as part of their income** in the normal way, no? And **it could be, say, ten times the lowest wage.**

B: Only ten? **I'm sure they'd be able to find ways round it**. And you don't think it'd discourage people from doing those jobs?

A: **Some, maybe,** but I don't see that as a bad thing. I mean, maybe they'd think about doing other jobs that are more useful. Anyway, I thought you said it was a good idea in theory.

B: I did. I'm just playing devil's advocate. And, as I said, I do have major doubts about how it'd work.

A: Well, personally I think the benefits far outweigh the difficulties.

Conversation 2
C = Man, D = Woman
C: Did you hear about this proposal to <u>bid</u> to hold the Olympics here?

D: Yeah. You don't sound happy about it.

C: No, absolutely not! I'm totally opposed to it. It's a complete waste of money. Aren't you against it?

D: I'm not sure where I stand, really. **Won't the games make a lot of money** if we get them?

C: No. They always talk about them leaving a good <u>legacy</u> and boosting the economy, but it's all rubbish.

D: Really? I can't pass judgement. I don't know enough about it.

C: Have a look on the Internet. Apparently, in Montreal they're still paying taxes on the debt – and they held them in 1976!

D: Really?

C: I tell you, it's lucky we don't have a hope in <u>hell</u>, so **they'll only waste the money on the bid.** Imagine if we actually won it, though! **It'd be a recipe for disaster. It'd probably bankrupt us.**

4.2
Joke 1
Two friends are strolling down the road when one turns to the other and asks 'So, what do you think of our president?' And the other guy looks around. 'I can't tell you here. Follow me'. And he sneaks off down a side street. 'Now tell me what you think' he asks again. 'No, not here. It's not safe'. And they tip-toe down the stairs of an old block of flats and into the deserted basement. Having checked that there is no-one around, the friend tries a third time: 'So, now you can tell me what you really think about our leader.' The other one glances around nervously. 'Well,' he whispers, 'I actually really like him!'

Joke 2
A middle-aged couple have a son who's still living at home with them. They've started getting a bit worried because the boy seems quite unable to decide on a career, so they decide to do a little test. They take a 20-dollar bill, a Bible and a bottle of whisky and leave them on the kitchen table. They then hide, pretending they aren't at home.

The dad's theory was that if his son took the money, it meant he'd become a businessman; if he took the Bible, he'd become a priest; and if he went for the whisky, he'd probably end up as a no-good drunk.

So anyway, the parents hide away under the stairs and wait, expectantly. After a while, the son arrives home and they peer out to watch him. First, he picks up the money, holds it up to the light and then slips it into his pocket. Next, he picks up the Bible, flicks through it and then pockets that as well. Finally, he grabs the bottle, opens it and sniffs it to check it's good quality, before sticking it into his bag. He then happily skips up the stairs to go for a nap.

'Oh no!' the father exclaims. 'Our son is going to be a politician!'

Joke 3
A man is walking down the street muttering to himself, cursing the government and the poverty that's ravaging the country. 'We have no food, no warm water, nothing!'

As it happens, a group of plain-clothes policemen come past in the opposite direction and overhear him. They all suddenly leap on him and drag him down to the station, where they throw him into the interrogation room. They make him sit on a chair in the middle of the room and take a gun and fire blanks at him. The man's scared stiff and curls up in fear. The police, seeing him so terrified and, thinking he's learned his lesson, let him go.

As the guy trudges off home, he starts moaning to himself again: 'Stupid country! No food, no warm water. We haven't even got any bullets. Stupid!'

4.3

Speaker 1
I used to like watching *Star Quality*, but since this scandal has erupted, I've lost interest in it. This story leaked out that they were encouraging people to phone in even though they'd already decided the result. They were manipulating things so that one guy didn't get voted off because it helped the programme's ratings if they had a kind of hate figure. I might not have minded so much if the calls were free, but they're making a fortune on them.

Speaker 2
We only called a vote because negotiations were going absolutely nowhere, and despite the massive support we've received from our members, the management is persisting with a derisory offer that will see wages fall in real terms next year. If it hadn't been for their intransigence, we would not be taking this action now. We understand the public's frustration – we share it – but the blame for this dispute should be laid firmly at the door of the train company.

Speaker 3
I'm totally in favour of a vote on the issue. The way the current system works, some parties get a seat with only 100,000 votes, while others who poll more than twice that don't get any. In the run-up to the election, the New Party had promised to hold one if they got into power, but in the event all that talk has faded away. I guess if they hadn't won a landslide victory, they'd be keener to bring about electoral reform, but I truly believe the vast majority of the electorate still wants to see a change and would vote yes, whatever their reservations.

Speaker 4
On another day I wouldn't have taken part, but I was at a bit of a loose end when the researcher called and she caught me off guard. It took about half an hour and I have to admit I quite enjoyed it – moaning about the government. Mind you, when the results were published in the paper, I was a bit taken aback. It seems I'm in a small minority! People must be mad!

Speaker 5
I know in some places it's just tokenism with no real power, but that isn't the case here. In these days of voter apathy, it's important that young people learn that democracy can give rise to positive change. Apart from deciding things like the end of term trips, pupil reps can decide on policy. It's unlikely we would've abolished uniforms if we didn't have a body like this. Voting isn't obligatory, but nearly everyone does.

REVIEW 01

R 1.1

Speaker 1
When I saw him on telly during the campaign, he came across as quite humble and down-to-earth, you know, but then they won that landslide victory and, I don't know, I think it must've gone to their heads. Since then he's just behaved with such arrogance. Honestly, I doubt he knows the meaning of the word 'principles' – he's certainly stabbed a few colleagues in the back. There's just no substance. I wish I'd never voted for him.

Speaker 2
Don't get me wrong. I'm generally in favour of the changes. I think the positives outweigh the negatives. Salazar's been in decline for years – neglected by successive governments – and I like the arts scene which is now emerging. I also think we're managing to maintain our close-knit community. What I'm opposed to though is demolishing buildings with historic value. I just don't believe that they couldn't've been done up.

Speaker 3
When I first met her, I have to say I thought she was a bit of a snob. She didn't really say anything, but her face and manner ... well, I just thought she was looking down on me. Anyway, it was ridiculous really, but we got stuck in a lift one day for about half an hour and I was getting in a state and she calmed me down and made me laugh. That's really how she is – laid-back and cheerful. In fact, it turned out that the day we first met she'd had an upset stomach, which is why she wasn't exactly chatty.

Speaker 4
At the start of the campaign, I was definitely going to vote yes. I thought the reforms would benefit the country and strengthen workers' rights, but it's difficult to totally ignore the no lobby. I'm sure the idea that the reforms will devastate the economy is an overstatement, but it has undermined my confidence in the proposals and now I don't know where I stand.

Speaker 5
One hears many people voicing concerns about the negative impact globalisation is having on local traditions. I would argue that those people are propagating a myth about culture. A closer inspection of how so-called traditions came about will often reveal that they are relatively recent and were often adopted from other countries that were influential at the time. The changes we are undergoing now are real, but they are not new and may in fact create future local traditions.

UNIT 05

5.1

Conversation 1
A = Woman 1, B = Woman 2
A: Hey Maddy. You look a bit rough.
B: I know. I'm exhausted. I didn't get to bed till three.
A: How come?
B: Oh, this friend of mine, it was her 25th and we organised a surprise party.
A: I bet she was pleased.
B: Yeah, she was, although she actually burst into tears when she first came in.
A: Oh!
B: Ah, she's been through a lot recently, which is partly why we planned the do.
A: Cheer her up?
B: Yeah, exactly. Anyway, she obviously found it a bit overwhelming at first, but she got over it pretty quickly.
A: That's good. Where was it?
B: In this bar. They'd hired a room and they had a band. I think they were friends of hers too.
A: Any good?
B: Yeah, brilliant. They played this old school rock and roll, but really well. Honestly, everyone was up dancing. Actually, it was hilarious – you know Finley, don't you?
A: Vaguely – only really by sight.

B: You've never seen him strutting his stuff then?

A: No, why?

B: He's awful. Honestly, he dances like a crippled chicken! We were in stitches watching him.

A: Poor bloke. He'll probably never dance again.

B: Nah. I mean I would've been mortified, but he's one of those people – he's so full of himself, I don't think he even registers when people are taking the mickey!

A: You won't be saying that when he comes and guns you all down in revenge!

B: Trust me, he's very thick-skinned. Anyway, talking of dancing, are you still going to those tango classes?

A: Yeah – on and off.

B: You must be getting quite good.

A: I wouldn't go that far. I'm still a bit prone to treading on toes.

Conversation 2

C = Woman, D = Man

C: Hi, glad I caught you. Have you sorted everything for the big meeting?

D: Yeah, yeah, it's all in hand. I've also booked a table at 'Eugine's'.

C: Excellent. I didn't mean to hassle you. I'm just stressing about it.

D: That's all right. I'm sure it'll be fine.

C: Yeah, it will. I could just do without it at the moment. Just too much on.

D: Tell me about it! I was tossing and turning all night! I just couldn't switch off.

C: I know. Perhaps you should take up meditation.

D: Yeah.

C: Anyway. Thanks for being so on top of things.

D: No problem.

C: By the way, how was your meal the other night?

D: Oh, great. We went to this place, 'Porchetta'?

C: Oh yeah. How was the food?

D: Gorgeous, but there was so much – you have six or seven courses. I lost count.

C: You must've been stuffed by the end.

D: I thought I'd burst – all a bit too much really. Actually, there was a bit of a scene while we were there. This guy just burst out shouting at a waiter – really ranting about something stupid, like there was a dirty fork or something.

C: It sounds like he was off his head.

D: I don't know. But they got him to leave.

C: Strange.

🔊 5.2

1 A: That must've been pretty dull.
  B: Awful. I couldn't stop yawning.

2 A: You must be glad you didn't go now.
  B: Absolutely. It obviously doesn't live up to the hype.

3 A: He must've been a bit disappointed.
  B: Actually, he was kind of expecting it.

4 A: You must be feeling a bit rough now.
  B: Actually, I feel surprisingly fresh.

5 A: You must've been mortified.
  B: I wouldn't go that far, but it was a bit embarrassing.

6 A: She must've been quite upset.
  B: Oh, she was in bits – just in floods of tears.

🔊 5.3

When Oprah Winfrey added a book club section to her phenomenally popular American talk show back in 1996, she could surely never have envisaged the impact she would have – not only on the reading habits of the nation, but also on the publishing industry itself.

Winfrey personally chose all the books she endorsed and didn't benefit financially from any of her selections. In terms of sales, endorsement by Oprah is worth anywhere between 20 and 100 times the recommendation of any other public figure in the United States and has sufficient clout to fundamentally alter Amazon rankings, best-seller lists and author royalty payments. Her club now boasts over two million members and has a website that provides tips on different approaches to reading, celebrities discussing favourite pieces of literature and ample space for users to share their own thoughts on featured titles.

In the wake of all this highly visible public enthusiasm, book clubs have started springing up everywhere. In Britain alone, there are now an estimated 40,000 reading groups, with people meeting to discuss their latest literary loves in private homes or in cafés, in libraries and bookstores or simply online. This phenomenon has spawned such specialist gatherings as the Vegan Book Club and a Socialist Feminist group, as well as meetings specifically targeted at lovers of crime novels and even comics!

The remarkable surge in the popularity of book clubs seems to be down to a number of different factors. Cultural commentator Rosalie Nicholson:

'We live in hectic times. As we all become ever busier and ever more bombarded with an overload of information, reading groups clearly represent a craving for trustworthy recommendations. They act as a kind of filter. In addition, book clubs seem to tap into some kind of desire for community in an age of increasing social fragmentation. Ironically, it seems that the solitary activity of reading can help provide a sense of shared experience.'

However, not everyone sees the trend in such a positive light. Here's critic Bryan Sewer:

'Let's face it, most reading groups are little more than gossiping circles or else simply a literary guise for dating clubs! And I know from my own observations that when they do finally get round to discussing books, the discourse is generally coarse and displays limited insight or intellect. I also fear that the whole nature of the set-up has created a tendency towards a certain kind of sentimental autobiographical writing, which one can only suppose must be easier for a mass audience.'

Bryan Sewer's opinion, though, seems to have little impact, and certainly hasn't halted the spread of communal reading. Indeed, one recent book club favourite, *Reading Lolita in Tehran*, by Azar Nafisi, details the transformational experience of reading and discussing frequently banned Western books in the Iranian capital in the 1990s. The appeal, it would seem, is universal.

On top of the multitude of reading groups now thriving, other innovative projects have also been conceived. Book Crossing is a free online book club that aims 'to make the whole world a library'. After having registered with the site, which connects users and attempts to track the movement of items donated, users are encouraged to leave books they've finished reading in public spaces, where they may then find new admirers.

Seattle, meanwhile, instigated the now globally popular idea of One City, One Book – a community reading project designed to give everyone within a specific geographical location the opportunity to read and then talk about one book at one particular time. As the idea has spread, different cities have added their own twists: bookstore talks by authors here, related arts programming there and sometimes even integration with school curricula. The city of Liverpool went so far as to celebrate its year as European Cultural Capital by funding 20,000 free copies of the year's chosen book, *The Savage*, by David Almond.

UNIT 06

6.1
Conversation 1
A = Woman, B = Man 1, C = Man 2

A: Ricardo! Ricardo!

B: Yeah. What's up?

A: Look! I wish you wouldn't do this! Really! It's not fair on the rest of us.

B: Do what?

A: Leave everything in such a state in here! Look at it. It looks like a bomb has exploded in here and it means I now have to tidy everything up.

B: I'll give you a hand if you want.

A: That's not the point! You used it last – you should've cleaned it up. That's the rule.

B: OK, OK. There's no need to bite my head off about it. I just forgot. I'm sorry. I've just been really busy, all right?

C: So busy you've not managed to clear all your debts yet!

B: Meaning what?

C: Meaning you still haven't paid Kathrin back the 40 pounds she lent you for the gas bill three weeks ago.

B: Not this again, Owen. I wish you'd stop going on about it. I've told her like a thousand times I'll sort it out when I get paid. That's on the 21st. Which is five days from now. OK?

C: What is it with you? How come we never have a proper conversation? Why are you always so defensive all the time? And why do you always have to exaggerate everything?

B: Who's the one exaggerating? You should listen to yourself – never, always, always, never.

A: Can both of you just stop it? Please! Honestly, I wish I'd never mentioned it now! You're like a couple of kids.

Conversation 2
D = Man, E = Woman

D: Miriam, could I have a word?

E: Can't it wait?

D: Not really, no.

E: It really is a rather awkward moment.

D: Look, I don't think I would bother you like this if it was only something trivial. I do think it would be better if we sorted this out now.

E: What do you mean? Sort what out?

D: The small matter of the parcel for Milan ... which they still haven't received yet.

E: Have they not? That's weird.

D: I thought I expressly asked you to send that parcel recorded delivery.

E: I did! You can ask Kate if you don't believe me. She saw me hand it over to Shane.

D: Woah! Stop right there. You did what?

E: I gave it to Shane. He was on his way and he said he'd do it for me.

D: Listen, Miriam, I don't mean to be rude, but when I said I wanted YOU to send it, that's precisely what I meant. It's not someone else's responsibility, it's YOURS. Have you any idea what is riding on this deal? If we can't show we're capable of the most basic things, how on earth are they going to trust us with their account?

E: I'm really sorry. Honestly, it won't happen again.

D: It won't because to be frank with you, I'm really not sure there's a future for you here at all.

E: No. I do understand I made a mistake.

D: And not for the first time, I hasten to add.

E: No, I know. It was stupid of me, really stupid. I don't know what I was thinking ...

D: That's as maybe, but it's a bit late for all that now.

6.2
A man working for a soft drinks company is standing trial today accused of spying on its biggest rival. Dan Craddock is said to have infiltrated Jazz Drinks on behalf of its competitor Pit-Pots. Over recent years, the two companies have been engaged in a fierce battle to capture market share, pouring money into ever more extravagant advertising campaigns in an effort to outdo each other. Last year was Jazz Drinks' best ever, and, as Pit-Pots was losing ground, it is claimed they secretly recruited Mr Craddock, who held a high-level post in Jazz Drinks, to pass on information on marketing and pricing strategy for the coming year. Mr Craddock denies any wrongdoing. The case continues.

The TV presenter Jonas Bakeman is fighting to salvage his career following revelations of his affair with a researcher on his programme, *Justice Fight*. As reporters laid siege to his home, he released a statement expressing regret over the affair, but defended himself against allegations that he'd pursued and harassed the woman, Petra Campbell. He claimed it had been a case of mutual attraction and he had surrendered to weakness during a momentary lapse of judgement. However, Ms Campbell has made available evidence that she had been bombarded with text messages and emails of a personal nature and that the affair had been more than 'momentary'. Bosses of the TV company are to meet tomorrow to consider Mr Bakeman's future.

Campaigners have claimed victory in their battle against full body scanners in airports following a court decision supporting a woman who refused to accept a scan. A number of civil liberties groups had joined forces to back the woman in an attempt to defeat the government's proposals that everyone travelling by plane should have to pass through the machines. The campaigners say it is a gross invasion of privacy as the scanners can see through clothing. The government has said that it will not retreat in its policy and believes the scanners are an important part of its armoury in the war on terror. They plan to get the decision overturned.

And finally, peace has now broken out in the village of Paulston. A dispute had been raging over a statue of St John of Bidshire, the multi-prize-winning pig of local farmer Tim Langford. The three-metre pink sculpture, which had been standing at the entrance of the village for over a year, had split the village into two camps, with half saying it was a hideous eyesore, while supporters of Mr Langford said it stood as a proud symbol of the local produce for which Paulston is famous. Protesters had marched onto Mr Langford's land and sprayed the statue with paint. Reprisals against the vandals then followed. Now the local council has stepped in as peacemaker to broker an agreement between the two sides. The statue is to be relocated to a nearby sculpture gallery, but will be moved back to the village during the three-day summer festival.

6.3
Speaker 1
As a man of the church, I believe the Commission has been immensely important and has gone a long way towards healing a wounded, traumatised nation. It's only by learning about the wrongs of the past that we can ensure these mistakes will never be repeated.

Obviously, though, it was not a perfect process. I was appalled at the evil that was uncovered. Bearing witness to such awful suffering takes its toll on you and, more often than not, a day spent listening to testimony ended with tears and profound, soul-searching questions about the Higher Purpose. I understand how these revelations stoked anger within the country, though I don't condone acts of vengeance against perpetrators.

One thing that exacerbated the situation was the fact that perpetrators were given instant amnesty, whilst victims were required to wait before receiving compensation, payment which invariably failed to recognise the true degree of suffering experienced.

Speaker 2

I've tried to forgive and to forget, I truly have, but it's beyond me. My son was murdered by the police and I had to collect his bruised and bloodied body from the morgue. I went before the Commission to recount my experiences, yet rather than walk away healed, I left feeling worse than ever before. All I felt was that I was re-living his death all over again. That's why I rejected the sum that they offered me. It would've been like taking blood money! How can I put this behind me when I still don't know who did this to my boy or why it happened? I want justice.

Speaker 3

After years of being seen as a pariah state, as the lowest of the low, the Commission has at least shown the world we can draw a line under the past and move on in a civilised manner. In that respect, it's been a great success. When the old system collapsed, I was desperately worried there'd be a wave of revenge attacks, and although there's been a bit of that, by and large the transition has worked.

The Commission has been key in shaping the national mood and moving people away from revenge and towards a place where we can all see the wrongs that were committed by both sides and the pain that was inflicted on all.

UNIT 07

🔊 7.1
Conversation 1
A = Woman, B = Man

A: Did you read that thing about transplanting the nose of mosquitoes?

B: What? Are you serious? I didn't think mosquitoes even had noses!

A: Yeah, well, it's obviously not a nose in the sense of our noses, but apparently it was like the smelling receptors on the antenna and what they do is they somehow get these receptors to grow on frog's eggs so that they can do tests on them.

B: How on earth do they do that?

A: To be perfectly honest, I'm not sure. They extract the DNA of the receptors or something and then inject it into the eggs. It's a bit beyond me really. I just thought it was amazing.

B: It sounds a bit dubious, if you ask me. I mean, what's the point?

A: Well, apparently, they use them to see what smells trigger the receptors.

B: And?

A: Well, it's to stop the spread of malaria. Obviously, mosquitoes are strongly attracted to the smell of human sweat, but if they can find odours which create a bigger stimulus or which produce no trigger, then they could use those smells to manufacture traps to draw the mosquitoes away from humans, or spray-on repellents to mask human smells.

B: OK. I suppose that makes sense. I have to say, though, I still find all that gene manipulation a bit disconcerting.

A: What do you mean?

B: Well, it's a slippery slope, isn't it? One moment it's mosquito noses, the next they'll be engineering babies.

A: Come off it! It's hardly the same thing!

Conversation 2
C = Man, D = Woman

C: Did you read this thing about building a sun shield in space to prevent global warming?

D: No. It sounds a bit unlikely, though. I mean, how big would it have to be?

C: Apparently about 60,000 miles long!

D: 60,000! That's ridiculous! I mean, how on earth are they going to build something that big, let alone get it up there? They struggle to build a stadium here on time and on budget.

C: Well, that's it – the idea with this is it's not like one big structure, it's millions of little reflectors which form a massive 'cloud'.

D: But how many would you need?

C: Trillions. They reckon if they deploy a stack of these things every five minutes it'd take ten years to make.

D: Hardly an instant solution then!

C: No.

D: And what about the cost?

C: I've no idea, to be honest, but they claim it's all quite feasible. Anyway, this guy's got a grant to look into it further.

D: You're joking! What a waste of money! Are you sure it isn't just a scam or some made-up story?

C: It was on a fairly reputable website.

D: Pah! Mind you, I sometimes wonder whether the whole climate change thing is a scam. It's all just about vested interests and people out to make a buck.

C: You're not serious, are you?

D: Yeah, why not?

C: Because the evidence is pretty incontrovertible.

D: Says who?

🔊 7.2
1 What on earth for?
2 Why on earth would they want to do that?
3 What on earth's that?
4 Who on earth would buy something like that?
5 Where on earth are they going to get the money for that?
6 What on earth is he going on about?

🔊 7.3
1 It's difficult to interpret this story without knowing the number of accidents per mile travelled. If there were twice as many journeys in fair weather, then the snowstorm has indeed increased the accident rate. Furthermore, more evidence is needed over a period of time to establish a correlation. It could be that bad weather really does reduce incidents due to people driving more carefully.

2 The statistics themselves in this study were accurately collected and described. However, the lobby group who commissioned the study were so-called 'stay-at-home mums' and in the interpretation and the narrowness of the time frame for the study, there was a strong element of twisting the data to fit a conclusion they'd set out to find.

   The truth, which was excluded from the analysis, is that aggression is a normal developmental stage, where children test boundaries. Not only is aggression normal, it doesn't usually last. The study failed to measure the stay-at-home toddlers' behaviour when they were mixed in groups, where the same levels of aggression can be observed. Indeed, a follow-up study by different researchers discovered that those kids who had been kept at home exhibited more aggression later at school, than those who'd been in nursery, i.e. it simply appeared at a later stage.

3 This statistic seems counter-intuitive, but only if you ignore other evidence. The statistic fails to mention that the number of fatalities plunged. As more survive accidents, more are treated for injury. Of course, the statistic also tells us nothing about the severity of the injuries.

4 The group are self-selecting, so we might imagine those strongly against animal testing will be more inclined to phone.

Furthermore, the poll is biased because it followed a report on cruelty and mistreatment in one laboratory.

5 The base numbers are all true. However, the starting point that was chosen was the year when there had been a terrorist bombing in the city, which obviously inflated the figures. In previous years, the figures had actually been 94 and 98. Of course, whether that correlation can be attributed to government policy is another thing. There could be a number of underlying causes.

7.4

Speaker 1
There's a popular notion that we're a peculiarly nocturnal breed that stays up all night glued to our telescopes, but the reality is far more mundane. Most of the time, we work normal nine-to-five hours and are busy analysing visual data or working on computer programmes that'll help us process the abundance of information we receive. Where we differ from the vast majority of other scientists is in the fact that we do not have direct contact with our object of study. We are obviously unable to weigh, touch or dissect stars and so observation and reasoning skills become paramount.

Speaker 2
The job can involve anything from conservation to genetics, and you may end up being employed in museums or schools, by state or local governments or even by private companies. Broadly speaking, though, the profession splits into two main camps: there's the research side of things, based mainly in the lab, carrying out experiments to help determine the wellbeing of animals. Then there are those of us such as myself who work in situ. What we do is direct the activities that animals should go through, study behaviour patterns, advise on habitat and so on.

Speaker 3
As a rule, I don't discuss my own particular line of work, though in essence the field I am involved in is one that remains vital for national security. We study the techniques, psychology and practice of war and other forms of armed conflict. We're responsible for developing new prototypes; we aim to increase the effectiveness of concepts and systems; we develop new training regimes; and we come up with strategies to enable us to maintain status in an ever-changing world. Obviously, this also means we play a very active role in advising central government on how best to ensure full capability.

Speaker 4
As with many other kinds of scientists, my work divides between fieldwork and office work. Generally speaking, what I do is I analyse, assess, forecast and report on the water environment. The work I do feeds directly into and helps underpin the work the Environmental Agency does. I mainly work with rainfall and river flow data – looking at the flood risk side of things, of course, but also looking at potential damage to the environment in low-flow areas and the like. It's incredibly rewarding knowing my endeavours may well lead to positive environmental outcomes.

Speaker 5
The stereotype is that we all spend our time in exotic locations around the globe, analysing mating rituals and spiritual beliefs, and there may once have been a grain of truth in those assumptions, but nowadays things are very different. Take me, for instance: I tend more towards the cultural side of things. I mean, my first research project was a study of reggae music around the world and I've also spent time in the UK studying pub etiquette. My partner, on the other hand, works freelance as a personal trainer, assisting business people with transitions from one culture to another during relocations on a global scale.

UNIT 08

8.1
Conversation 1
A = Woman 1, B = Woman 2
A: So how was your holiday? Did you have a good time?
B: Yeah, it was amazing, it really was.
A: Where were you again? France somewhere, wasn't it?
B: Yeah, Jura, right near the Swiss border. It's an amazing bit of the country. We started off in the southeast, where it's really mountainous, with all these gorges dropping down into the valleys and these winding rivers, and then we slowly worked our way northwards, to where all the vineyards are, because it's a big wine-making region up there.
A: Wow! It sounds great. So were you driving, then?
B: No, we weren't, actually. We were hiking.
A: Seriously?
B: Yeah, it was a group thing. We booked it over the Internet.
A: It must've been pretty strenuous.
B: To be honest, it wasn't that bad. I mean, it's pretty rugged in places, but you soon get into the swing of it. It was great exercise, I can tell you! I haven't felt this fit in years.
A: I bet! And what were the other people on the tour like? Did you all get on OK?
B: Yeah, they were all great. What was weird, though, was that there was a couple there from my hometown.
A: Yeah? That's a bit spooky.
B: Yeah. Look. That's them there in the photo. Marçin and Monica.
A: Oh, OK. They look nice – and that's an amazing view behind them!
B: Yeah, stunning, isn't it? That's Mont Blanc you can see in the background.

Conversation 2
C = Man 1, D = Man 2
C: So what is it that you do, then?
D: I'm a geologist.
C: Oh, OK. And where are you based?
D: I work all over the place, really, but the last six months I've been in Venezuela. I actually only got back the other day, so I'm still getting back into the swing of things a bit.
C: I imagine it must take a while. So what were you doing there? I mean, what was your project?
D: Oh, I was doing some research on a big glacier there, Glacier Los Perros, seeing what kind of impact global warming has had on it.
C: That sounds amazing, it really does.
D: Yeah, it was wonderful. It's a breathtaking place, Venezuela. Have you been there?
C: No, never, no.
D: Where we had our HQ was right on the edge of all this dense woodland, looking out over the ice, with these snow-capped mountains off in the background, and every morning when I got up, my heart just leapt to see it all. It was something else.
C: And what are its prospects? I mean, how did it come out after the research?
D: Well, nothing's conclusive as yet, but it does seem that there's definitely some melting going on, unfortunately.

8.2
1 I wouldn't drive it if I were you, I really wouldn't.
2 The views were just stunning, they really were.
3 The scenery takes your breath away, it really does.
4 I just love it there, I really do.
5 It made no difference whatsoever, it really didn't.
6 He'll never change, he really won't.
7 I've never been anywhere like it, I really haven't.
8 That sounds amazing, it really does.

8.3

It's common knowledge that men and women do things differently, isn't it? The male of the species, we're told, retreats into a cave to brood at the slightest sign of stress, whilst the female reaches out and shares her feelings. After all, women are better communicators, aren't they? Well, aren't they?

That's certainly how we've been conditioned to see things over the last 20 years or so. The glut of self-help books that have followed in the wake of *Men are from Mars, Women are from Venus* have served to perpetuate the myth of difference and, I would argue, have had a profoundly negative effect on our culture.

It's easy to assume these books must be based on valid scientific research, but in reality very few are. Indeed, even a cursory inspection of the literature of the field reveals that in fact men and women communicate in remarkably similar ways. Take the notion that women talk more – and use more words to do so. Despite being widely reported as fact, research actually shows that both sexes tend to talk equally as much and use as many words per day while doing so – around 16,000.

Then there's the belief that men interrupt more. Evidence actually suggests that women interrupt at least as much as men. Whilst some men do interrupt far more than the vast majority of women, this is atypical, and such actions are often tied in to a position of power. Ultimately, when and how people interrupt has far more to do with social status and power than it does with genetic make-up and 'nature'. Linguistic studies have shown there's an overlap of more than 95% in the way the sexes communicate. Yet still myths of Venus and Mars prevail. Given this, it's surely worth asking why!

Well, firstly, such sweeping generalisations as 'Women are more in touch with their feelings' appeal because they match the stereotypes we already have. As such, we recall occasions on which evidence backed this idea up – and forget examples that might contradict it!

A more significant reason for the continuing appeal of such theories, though, may well lie in the fact that gender roles have changed dramatically over recent years. Both women and men now frequently aspire to an education, a career, a decent income – and both often act, talk and maybe even dress in similar ways. For many people, these changes have happened too quickly and are deeply unsettling. What better way to comfort yourself than a return to the traditional gender roles and stereotypes of the past?

Should you require any further proof that difference is rooted in nurture far more than nature, consider the village of Gapun in Papua New Guinea, where the men pride themselves on their ability to speak indirectly and never say what they mean, whilst the women frequently give voice to their anger by launching into lengthy swearing sessions. Does this prove that sometimes it is women that are from Mars? I suspect not. Personally, I see this as proof that we are all from Earth and need to start dealing with this fact rather better than we have been!

8.4

1 Unusually for this species, it can swim underwater as well as burrow underground, which is handy as it inhabits low wetland areas. Its long claws are adapted for digging through the earth and its water-resistant fur allows it to remain submerged in water. The long thick tail is thought to store extra fat to draw upon during the mating season. The mole is functionally blind, which is why it has developed the distinctive star-shaped set of feelers.

The feelers are incredibly sensitive to movement. Uniquely, the mole can also smell underwater. It does this by blowing out tiny bubbles through its nose in order to capture scents that are sucked back in. These adaptations are highly efficient and the star-nosed mole is apparently the fastest eater in the animal kingdom, being able to identify, snatch and consume its prey all in a matter of milliseconds.

2 The sparrowhawk is most commonly found in woodland. Its short, broad wings and long tail allow it to manoeuvre quickly through the trees. The light striped markings on its breast and its darker upper parts help it to blend into the background, which allows it to lie in wait for its prey before shooting out. It has relatively long legs that enable it to kill in mid-flight. The long slender central toe is adapted to grasp with a small protuberance on the underside enabling it to grip and hold on to its prey. Its small hooked beak is used for plucking and tearing flesh rather than killing. It also sometimes hunts on foot through vegetation. In recent years, it has encroached more and more into cities where it has no predators and where it is often seen as a pest damaging garden bird populations.

REVIEW 02

R 2.1

I = Interviewer, L = Leila

I: So, joining us in the studio now is the photographer Leila Flannagan, who's going to be chatting with us about her latest book 'Predators and Prey' as well as her life in photography, so any questions or comment remember you can e-mail us on cope@gbs.com. Love to hear from you. So Leila, welcome to the show.

L: Hi, thank you for inviting me.

I: You've had a hectic schedule.

L: Yeah, loads of interviews presenting the book and last night we had the opening of the exhibition at the Gagosian, so a late night!

I: Feeling a bit rough?

L: A little, not too bad, just a bit overwhelmed with it all, to be honest – as a photographer, I hide behind my camera. I'm not used to being the focus. And for some reason the book and exhibition have just been phenomenally successful wherever we've been.

I: Well, it certainly lives up to any hype, because there are some stunning photos in there and some incredibly moving ones, because of course it mixes photojournalism and nature.

L: Thanks. Yeah, I was very much trying to challenge and blur those traditional boundaries between styles of photography – you know, why should you have to stick to one genre – sports, fashion or whatever. Make new connections! Get insights.

I: Absolutely. But presumably, you started out in one genre.

L: Yeah, sure. I actually started out working for an engineering magazine, so it was kind of architecture – taking photos of construction projects. And on one assignment they were building a dam in a gorge to create a reservoir and I got caught in unrest and fighting. The project was threatening wetland which sustained several tribes, as well as destroying the gorge itself, but the government simply crushed all dissent and broke up any protests. It was quite brutal and, for me, very unsettling. So then I became interested in the conflicting stories of these projects and how the so-called benefits didn't always stand up to scrutiny – you know, vested interests and corruption often twisted things. It took my photography in a different direction and, ultimately, paved the way for this book.

I: So what about the wildlife – how did that come about?

L: Well, whenever I undertook any assignment my primary concern was to portray the impact on people. These massive projects – airports, industrial estates, dams, etc – they often hit minority communities who find themselves under siege. And then you have workers' struggles and so on. But of course, mixed in with all that are adverse affects on the environment and species becoming endangered. So I started taking photos of animals as an addition to the main story, but frankly, also as a way of relaxing. Some of the human stories can be pretty heart-wrenching.

I: I'm sure. Though I'm not sure how relaxed I'd be watching a crocodile leap out of the water to grab an antelope in its jaws – it's pretty gory.

L: Yeah, I guess. I remember getting a shot of this lion and it suddenly let out an enormous roar – that was pretty terrifying.

I: Rather you than me. So do you have a favourite?

L: Well, I guess amongst the wildlife it'd be the blue diamond iguana puffing up to try and scare off something. I always think it's what people are doing when they protest against these projects.

I: Right.

L: And the other thing with that was I was actually waiting to get a glimpse of a puma. I'd covered myself with leaves and stuff to blend into the background and I was waiting in this spot for hours. I never saw the puma, but I captured this great picture. Wildlife photography's like fishing: you need enormous patience and you're never sure exactly what you'll catch.

UNIT 09

9.1

H = Harry, T = Tasneem, B = Bianca

H: Hi, I'm looking for Tasneem.

T: That's me. You must be Harry.

H: That's right.

T: Nice to meet you. Did you find us OK?

H: Yeah, yeah. Well, I came here before for my interview.

T: Right. So where do you live? Does it take you long to get here?

H: I've just moved to Redditch, but it was quicker than I expected. I've actually been hanging around in the coffee bar over the road for the last hour.

T: Really? You were eager to get here, then.

H: Well, I didn't want to be late and, you know, first-day nerves and all that.

T: Sure. Anyway, I'm sure you'll settle in quickly. We're a pretty good bunch. Nobody bites. Well, almost nobody!

H: Right.

T: So, raring to go, then?

H: Absolutely.

T: OK, well, just dump your stuff down here for the moment and I'll show you the ropes.

H: OK.

T: I should've said, we'll be working alongside each other on this new project. I liaise with our external service providers. I was just emailing one of them to schedule a time for us all to meet when you arrived. Anyway, as you can see, the office is mainly open-plan. We'll sort you out with a spot later.

H: Right.

T: It's a bit chaotic at the moment with all the changes. We've been rushed off our feet so it'll be good to have more people.

H: I'm not the only one who's being taken on now, then.

T: No. Three or four more are supposed to be joining in the next couple of weeks.

H: That's good. There'll be some others in the same boat.

T: Yeah. This is Bianca. She's our main admin assistant. She'll sort out any travel or bookings and other stuff. Bianca, this is Harry.

B: Hiya. Nice to meet you. Hope Taz is treating you well. She's a real slave-driver, you know.

H: Really?

B: Oh yeah, she's probably being all kind and helpful now, but wait till you get started.

H: That sounds ominous.

T: Take no notice. She's just pulling your leg. You need to watch her!

B: I don't know what you mean! Actually, Harry, can I just take a quick photo while you're here? I'm just sorting out your entry card and setting up your e-mail.

H: Sure.

B: OK. ... Say cheese ... Lovely – very handsome. That's it. Anything you need or you're not sure about, don't hesitate to ask.

H: Thanks. I'll get the card later, then, yeah?

B: If that's OK.

T: OK, let's move on. That lot over the far side are the sales team. We won't disturb them now. I can introduce you later. To be honest, you won't be having that much to do with them in your day-to-day dealings.

H: OK. What about these rooms? Are they offices?

T: Um, the last two are the boardrooms for meetings. The near one is Mary's office. She's the managing director.

H: OK. What's she like?

T: She's OK. She comes across as being quite down-to-earth ... the few times we've talked.

H: She's not in the office that much, then.

T: No, she's here most days, but as I said, I guess we've all been so busy that everybody just sticks to their own tasks. Anyway, just going back to the rooms – that one with the door open is the photocopier room. I'd better show you how it works. It's a bit temperamental. It has a tendency to jam if you don't treat it with tender loving care.

H: OK.

T: So how come you moved to Redditch? It's not that close to here.

H: No, but I'd been thinking about moving out there for a while and I happened to get the house just before I got this job.

9.2

1 I've actually been hanging around in the coffee bar over the road for the last hour.

2 I should've said, we'll be working alongside each other.

3 I was just emailing one of them to schedule a time for us all to meet when you arrived.

4 I'm not the only one who's being taken on now, then.

5 Three or four more are supposed to be joining in the next couple of weeks.

6 She's probably being all kind and helpful now, but wait till you get started.

7 To be honest, you won't be having that much to do with them in your day-to-day dealings.

8 I'd been thinking about moving out there for a while and I happened to get the house just before I got this job.

9.3

Is David Bolchover's experience a freak occurrence? Well maybe, but only in the sense that he was allowed to stay at home to not work. Bolchover argues that much of the workforce in many big companies is badly under-employed at work and backs up his arguments with a barrage of statistics. One in three of all mid-week visitors to a UK theme park had phoned in sick. In one year, there were nine million dubious requests for sick notes from the doctor. That's about a third of the working population! Two-thirds of young professionals have called in sick because of a hangover, and on it goes.

Once at work, things don't improve: on average, employees spend 8.3 hours a week accessing non-work-related websites and 14.6% of all so-called 'working' Americans say they surf the net constantly at work. 18.7% send up to 20 personal e-mails a day and 24% said they had fallen asleep at their desk, in a toilet or at a meeting.

Bolchover argues that there's a conspiracy of silence over this workplace slacking. Workers have no vested interest in saying they do nothing, while businesses want to maintain their image of being highly efficient.

Under-employment happens, he suggests, because workers feel a disconnection with big companies. Unlike with small companies, employees don't see how their small contributions fit into the whole picture. Furthermore, managers typically fail to develop or motivate workers because, he claims, in large corporations people progress not by looking down, but by looking up. Instead of managing effectively and getting the most out of those under you, the way to get ahead is by advertising yourself and networking with those above you. People below you don't give promotions.

With smaller companies, slacking happens less because workers see how failure to pull your weight can directly impact on colleagues and the company. Bolchover suggests the solution, therefore, is to break up large companies into smaller competitive units. From a worker's view, doing nothing might seem fun at first, but in the end it's soul-destroying and a waste of talent.

9.4

1 A 27-year-old man has been arrested and fined for stealing biscuits from a colleague's desk. While working a night shift in a call centre, Michael Campbell thought no-one would mind if he helped himself to the remains of a biscuit tin abandoned in a corner. The following day, however, a co-worker returned to find her £7 gift selection gone – and decided to trawl CCTV footage to find the culprit. Campbell was then arrested and hauled in front of a magistrate, who ordered him to repay the cost of the biscuits as well as £150 court costs. He was also dismissed from his job as a result of the incident and is currently retraining as a bar manager.

2 A postman who was sacked after taking a week off work to mourn the death of a pet has won over ten thousand pounds' compensation. David Portman had a history of taking numerous weeks off work because of unfortunate 'accidents', and was absent for a total of 137 days in just five years, an employment tribunal heard. In his defence, Mr Portman claimed the majority of his injuries were incurred during the course of his duties at work. However, when he took further leave following the demise of his dog, his bosses decided enough was enough. The tribunal felt this was a step too far and they insisted he be awarded compensation, especially as the manager had failed to tell the postman he could have applied for compassionate leave.

3 A new study released this week shows that paternity leave schemes in Iceland are now among the most generous in the world – and suggest that this is to the immense benefit of society. Last year, nearly all new Icelandic fathers took their full entitlement of three months off work at 80% of their salaries. Since legislation to ensure such leave in 2002, gender roles have been transformed and the divorce rate has dropped sharply – while the birth rate has risen. The director of one of the country's biggest firms recently went on record to state he wanted all fathers on his staff to take their full 12 weeks leave on full pay as they provided positive role models which could benefit both company and country in the long run.

4 Budget airline Quickjet is cutting costs even further by banning its staff from charging their mobile phones at work. Passengers with the no-frills firm do not get pre-assigned seats and all food and drink is charged for, while cabin crew have to pay upwards of a thousand pounds for initial training and are then expected to buy their own uniforms. Now, however, the company has decided that any use of mobile phone chargers at work is unacceptable, and amounts to theft of the company's electricity. A spokesperson claimed yesterday that all savings will go towards lowering fares for European consumers.

5 A new research project has begun in New Zealand to explore whether the country's rapidly ageing one-million-plus generation of over-65s is planning to slip awkwardly into its golden years as a burden on the state or whether there will be a reinvention of the way society views older people and the workforce. Many signs seem to suggest the latter is the most likely option. All the indications are that many of this generation are not eagerly anticipating retirement. Instead, they plan to work, contribute to social causes and continue to influence society, as they have all their lives. However, they want to do so on their own terms and with more time for leisure, travel and their families. This could revolutionise the workforce as employers begin to offer sabbaticals, part-time work, flexible hours and other incentives to retain experienced staff.

UNIT 10

10.1
Conversation 1
A = Woman, B = Man

A: You look so different without your glasses on. I almost didn't recognise you there.

B: The glasses have gone! They're a thing of the past. I had my eyes done the other day, with laser surgery.

A: Really? That's brave of you. Didn't it hurt? I've always imagined it must do.

B: No, not really, but it is quite scary because what they do is they numb your eyes and then they kind of clamp them open so they can slice this tiny little flap in the front of the eye – and you kind of have to watch as the whole thing happens.

A: Sounds horrendous! How do they administer the anaesthetic? Is it an injection or something?

B: No, they just pour in a bucketful of these eye drops and they do the job. Oh, and they dosed me up with a couple of Xanax as well, just to calm me down.

A: And how long does the whole thing take?

B: It's over in a matter of minutes. After they cut the eye open, you have to stare at this laser for a few seconds and that reshapes the inside of your eye – and then you're done.

A: And how long does it take to recover from?

B: To be honest, the next day I woke up and I pretty much had perfect vision. They're still a bit sore, and I have to go back a few times for the after-care, but it's all very quick. I should've got it done years ago, really!

A: Right. Wow! I still think I'll stick with contact lenses for the time being, though, personally.

Conversation 2
C = Man, D = Woman

C: So why did you have to rush off to the dentist's the other day, then?

D: Oh, haven't I told you? Well, about a week or so ago, I got this excruciating pain in my upper jaw and I went along to get it looked at and he told me that one of my teeth had died somehow and that I'd need a root canal.

C: Died? How did that happen?

D: He said I must've taken a knock. I'm not sure, but I think it might've been my daughter, actually, thrashing her arms and legs around while I was changing her nappy one day.

C: Kids, eh! All that work and that's the kind of thanks you get.

D: Yeah. And then today I went in and he drilled a hole in the back, cleaned everything up and then stuck some kind of temporary filling in, to prevent any bacteria or anything getting in.

C: That can't have been much fun! Did it hurt at all?

D: No, not really. I mean, I was conscious of what he was doing, but I couldn't feel anything.

C: Do you have to go back again sometime?

D: Yeah, next week. They'll remove the temporary filling and put a more permanent thing in, but then I'm done.

C: How much is all that going to set you back, then? It must be quite expensive.

D: It's not that bad, but it's not cheap either. I won't see much change from five hundred pounds.

🔊 10.2

So, coming to sit now. We'll be sitting for a while so make yourself comfortable on your chair, but also moving forward so your back is not leaning against the chair, but is supporting itself, and your back, neck and head are in line in an erect posture, but not stiff. Let your shoulders drop and relax so your posture embodies a sense of dignity, a sense of taking a stand, of being awake, aware, in touch with this moment. And now letting your eyes close, relaxing your facial muscles, not frowning or feeling tension there and now we're coming to focus on our breathing. Focusing on wherever you notice the breath moving most distinctly in and out of your body. And this might be at the tip of your nose, at the back of the throat, or in your chest or belly, noticing how it rises with the in breath and falls on the out breath. And noticing precisely the sensations that accompany each in breath and each out breath. Each breath is unique, with its own sensations. Simply tune in to each one in its own time, giving each one its own attention. This breath coming in ... this breath going out .... Allowing the breath to anchor you in the present moment. And whenever you notice your mind wandering, bring it gently back to your breath, back to the present moment. And the mind may wander many times. Sometimes it may wander for a short time, sometimes a longer time, and you may find yourself judging and criticising yourself for the wandering mind, but that's what minds do. If you have a mind, it will wander. So the task of meditation is not to still the mind or banish thoughts and feelings, but simply to notice its patterns, to be aware of what it's doing, and then as soon as you notice that it's wandered, to acknowledge where it's wandered to and then gently bringing it back. So if it happens many times, bring it back many times. Beginning over and over again with the next in breath ... or the next out breath. And then using the stretches of silence to carry on this work by yourself.

And now at a certain point expanding your awareness around the breath so that you're aware of the whole body as you sit here. Aware of the space that your body takes up and the space around the body and the boundary between these two spaces, the skin. Aware of sensations in your body. And if there are any intense sensations, then breathing into them, directing the breath to the edge of that intensity and into the centre to explore what's here, right now. Allowing yourself to be open, to soften around the intensity instead of tightening or clenching as we so often do. Opening yourself up to experience the sensations you're feeling here right now, in this moment ... and in this moment ... and in this moment. ... And now letting go of any intention to focus on anything – the breath or the body – and allowing yourself to sit here, resting in awareness itself. Whatever comes up.

And taking this sensation of spaciousness, of awareness of this present moment, into your day and remembering that this moment of presence is always available to you any time by simply reconnecting, through your breath, to your mind and body.

🔊 10.3

The dedicated parents of an eight-year-old boy who had been suffering from a blood disorder so rare that it doesn't even have a name have amazed doctors by finding a cure for him.

Dexter Austen-Brown's illness had been likened to living with a permanent hangover, but after a period of painstaking research, his parents Stephen and Anne discovered that the condition could be relieved with the aid of ordinary dietary protein supplements.

Incredibly, doctors now believe that the treatment could also prove to be a breakthrough for sufferers of cancer and other diseases and have commissioned official research.

Before being treated, Dexter had required regular painful blood transfusions because of his low red blood cell count. As he was growing up, his immune system was so weak that he often suffered from ailments such as asthma and eczema. He was weak, frequently fatigued and struggled with speech. In terms of his all-round development, he was at least a year and a half behind other children. His heart was having to work much harder to compensate, leaving him vulnerable to heart attacks.

After countless tests, his parents were informed that there was nothing doctors could do to help their son. This did not deter them, however, and they turned to the Internet in a hunt for alternative therapies. They toyed with the idea of acupuncture before coming across nutritional consultant Richard Wright.

Mr Wright discovered Dexter suffered from a shortage of vital proteins in his body. He was thus put on a special diet of additional dietary supplements, which cost around £10,000 a year. The new diet has been incredibly successful. His last blood count revealed an average number of red cells and his height has shot up. Mr Austen-Brown, a teacher, said, 'We're obviously delighted about the result of all our hard work, though I have to say it's no thanks to many in the medical profession. The doctors can't have considered Dexter's condition as thoroughly as they should've done and they clearly should've looked into other options themselves, but having said that, I also wish we'd started our research earlier. We could've come to our own conclusions sooner and that way Dexter wouldn't have had to go through all this trauma.'

UNIT 11

🔊 11.1
Conversation 1
A= Woman 1, B = Woman 2

A: How was the tennis?

B: Good.

A: Who won?

B: Mena, but it was pretty tight actually.

A: What was the score?

B: 6–3, 6–2, I think.

A: Hmm, right. Very close!

B: No, honestly, it was! I mean, most of the games were quite even – lots of deuces. She just did some great shots at the crucial moments.

A: She's quite good, then.

B: Well, neither of us are exactly pros. I mean, we both have a tendency to serve double faults, and if anything I probably actually have a better technique, but she's just fitter and stronger. I tend to fade towards the end.

A: Oh, right.

B: We're both getting better, though. We had some pretty long rallies. A couple of shots down the line, you know.

A: So I'll be expecting to see you at Wimbledon soon.

B: Not quite!

Conversation 2
C = Man, D = Woman

C: How was the weekend?

D: Don't ask?

C: Oh dear. What happened?

D: Well, Hannah took us for a little 'stroll' which involved trudging up some 2,000-metre mountain in the pouring rain.

C: Hmm, sounds very relaxing!

D: Honestly, I could've killed her at one point, because she was so enthusiastic and jolly and I was like 'This is just awful. I'm exhausted, I'm soaked and I'm close to getting hypothermia'. And we couldn't see a thing because it was shrouded in mist from about 1,000-metres. I felt like bursting into tears, not grinning like an idiot!

C: Oh dear. So what happened?

D: Well, in the end, I just bit my tongue and we continued to the top. And funnily enough, when we got there, the clouds suddenly broke, the sun came out and we got this amazing view. I mean, it only lasted for about five minutes, but it was stunning!

C: It made it all worthwhile, then.

D: Well, I wouldn't quite go that far. I won't exactly be raring to go if she suggests something like that again.

Conversation 3
E = Man 1, F = Man 2

E: How was the game last night? I missed it.

F: Incredible. Arsenal were lucky to draw. Honestly, it could've been about five–nil after the first 20 minutes. The Arsenal keeper made some great saves and then Manu missed a ridiculously easy goal. He managed to kick the ball over the crossbar when he was literally only a metre from the line.

E: Ah, Manu ... he's so overrated. There's no way he's worth 60 million or however much he cost. He's rubbish.

F: You're right. He's totally useless. ... that's why he scored those two fantastic goals after that!

E: OK. OK. He IS good, just not THAT good!

F: No, I do know what you mean – and actually for his first goal the Arsenal keeper made a right cock-up to let them score.

E: Right. So, how did Arsenal manage to get back in the game then?

F: Well, they made some substitutions and brought on Wallace, who made a huge difference.

E: Really?

F: Yeah, really. He scored a great goal, which got the whole team going. Then Arsenal got a slightly dubious penalty and a Barça defender got sent off.

E: It wasn't a penalty, then.

F: Well, it wasn't exactly the strongest tackle I've ever seen, let's put it that way. Anyway, it was an amazing game. Really open.

E: Sounds it. I'll have to watch the return game next month. We'll thrash them at home!

F: I don't know. Two of your defenders are suspended, and you have a couple of other people injured. And Arsenal will be the underdogs so they won't have any pressure on them. Honestly, I wouldn't be surprised if Barça got knocked out.

E: By Arsenal? Not a chance.

11.2

Playing cards are popular the world over, but their origins and development are far from clear. It's possible they originated from Chinese paper dominoes, China having invented paper some thousand years before its use in Europe. However, the multitude of designs that existed in the past suggests they are an amalgam of various traditions.

There are three types of deck widely used today. The 52-card deck is the most widespread, particularly with the popularity of poker. The four suits – hearts, clubs, spades and diamonds – each have 13 cards: numbers two to ten followed by jack, queen, king, and ace as the highest-ranking card.

Then there's the Spanish *baraja*. These decks use different suits which supposedly represent different power groupings in the Middle Ages. There are coins which represent merchants, clubs representing peasants, gold cups for the church and swords symbolizing the military. There are only 40 cards: that's one to seven plus a jack, a knight and a king.

Finally, there are the East Asian flower cards. They have 12 suits, one for each month of the year, with four cards each. They don't have numbers, just pictures. These cards originally came into existence in the 17th century to avoid a ban on gambling with 'Western' cards that had been introduced from Portugal.

Playing cards are still so popular because they offer an infinite variety of games. In some games, you have to collect sets of cards, while others require you to shed the cards in your hand so you have none left. Alternatively, you may sometimes have to accumulate points or the whole pack. They range from simple games of chance to ones with complex rules and strategy, using trumps, which are a suit or cards that have an added value, or jokers, cards which can replace any other, as well as the opportunity to bluff or team up with other players. And all that varied entertainment for less than the price of a cinema ticket.

11.3

Speaker 1

We used to play this game me and my brother made up for long journeys, but it kind of spread through friends at school. The aim was to spot a particular kind of car and be the first to shout out, say, 'yellow car, no returns'. The one who was first then had the right to punch the other on the shoulder and the 'no returns' meant that they couldn't punch you back. It sounds a bit brutal, but in practice you didn't do it that hard because you knew they could get their own back at any moment and you didn't want to get hurt.

Speaker 2

We used to play *Parchís* at home. It's a board game where you move your counters all round the board and back home to win. The people playing can capture each other and send each other back to the start. My parents actually banned it for a while because it kept ending in fights. My brothers used to gang up on me ... you know, they wouldn't capture each other so they could catch me! I remember once, I was on the point of winning – I was two places short of safety – and Miguel landed on my square. My brothers all burst out laughing and teased me and I just tipped over the board and stormed out of the room.

Speaker 3

I can't play any card games now, because it just triggers that desire. It's a shame because there are some great games that don't involve gambling and games really bring families or friends together. There's always a bit of banter around it. It's educational even. The problem lies when there are stakes involved. I started off with blackjack for small change with my mates, but it escalated when I played poker online. I kept thinking I'm bound to win next time and I became ever more desperate – bluffing badly when I couldn't win.

Speaker 4

I woke up this morning and my shoulders were really stiff. I could hardly raise my arm or even clench my fist. I felt like I'd been beaten up, but then I remembered I'd been playing boxing with my son on this sports game. You have to punch madly at the screen with the controller to try and knock the other figure out and I guess I'm just not used to using those muscles. I had to take the day off!

Speaker 5

On one level, you look at it and you just wish the roles they take on weren't so awful – gunning down cops, mugging people for cash and the like. It's hardly a good example for life. And you do hear negative stories in the press. Then again, it's a very open game. You know, you can choose the tasks or quests you undertake and it involves different skills and a bit of strategy and you can team up with other players. I mean, my son plays with people in Korea, Mexico, all over. It's amazing, really. And my son's pretty level-headed and has reached the age of 16 without becoming a mass murderer or gang leader, so I guess he distinguishes fact from fiction OK.

UNIT 12

12.1

A = Man 1, B = Man 2

A: So how did it go with Sara's parents, George?

B: Oh, it was surprisingly good, actually. The whole visit passed off far better than I'd dared to hope it would.

A: Yeah? Even with her father?

B: Yeah. It turns out his bark is much worse than his bite. We had a long talk over dinner on Saturday and got on really, really well. He's a pretty amazing guy, actually.

A: Yeah? In what way?

B: Well, he's just had an incredible life. I mean, he's from a first-generation immigrant family, grew up in a very strict, very close-knit immigrant community, not really speaking the local language, and basically living in total poverty. Then when he was 13 his dad passed away and as the oldest son he found himself having to support the family.

A: Seriously? Is it a big family?

B: Yeah, colossal. Twelve brothers and sisters! So he had to drop out of school and start working.

A: That's VERY young to be working. What was he doing?

B: He started off selling ice creams on the street of the town he was living in, and then moved on to selling textiles door-to-door, and by the time he was about 17 he was going off all round the island selling and making deals.

A: That's amazing. I was still living at home stressing about my end-of-school exams at that age.

B: Yeah, exactly. Then when he was about 21 he decided that if he really wanted to get ahead, he'd have to move to the capital, and so he set off to make his fortune. He got there, somehow managed to start up his own company selling outboard motors for boats and then just slowly built things up until he got to where he is today, where he can afford to have all his kids educated in the States and go off on holiday whenever he feels like it.

A: So he really is a proper self-made man, then.

B: Yeah, completely, but what was great about him is that he's still quite rough around the edges. I mean, he eats like a peasant still and burps after dinner and everything, all of which I found strangely endearing.

A: And what did he make of you and the idea of his daughter dating an artist, then?

B: Well, he's still coming to terms with that, obviously, trying to get his head round it all, but his eyes lit up when I told him how much I got for that portrait I sold last year. Basically, I think he just wants to see that she'll be provided for.

A: Despite the fact she's earning twice as much as you are already!

B: Yeah, well. I didn't dwell on that fact too much.

12.2

1 You cited someone called Edward Gibbon. Could you provide us with a reference for that?

2 When you were talking about changes in construction techniques, you mentioned thatching. Could you just explain exactly what that is?

3 You referred to a theory that lead poisoning contributed significantly to the demise of the Empire. Could you elaborate on that a little?

4 You mentioned some findings that suggested that environmental degradation was a cause. Do you have any statistics available on that?

12.3

1 Back in 2003, I came home from college one day and turned on the TV – and saw that Anna Lindh had been attacked. She was the Swedish minister for foreign affairs and a woman I'd always admired. She'd taken a strong stand against injustice and had campaigned against apartheid and the arms trade and that kind of thing. She'd even started being talked about as a possible future prime minister. Then one day – it was September the 11th, I remember, because it was the second anniversary of the World Trade Center attacks – she went out shopping in Stockholm and was stabbed in the chest and the stomach by this random guy with a history of mental illness. She was rushed to hospital, but they were unable to save her.

It was just such a senseless murder and it kind of sounded the death knell for this notion we'd had of Sweden being a safe country where even leading politicians could go out during their lunch break without fear of abuse or assault.

2 For many Poles of my generation, joining the European Union was a huge event. It represented the moment we moved closer to the west in all manner of ways – mentally, economically, politically. It symbolised a kind of rite of passage, a moment when we were finally recognised by the elder statesmen of Europe, by Germany and the UK and France and so on. It implied we were somehow mature enough now to be accepted into the unifying structure, and after so much bad blood between so many European countries all through the 20th century, it felt like we were drawing a line under the past and moving on into the future. In the referendum, over three-quarters of the population voted to join the EU and the changes since then have been enormous.

One of the most remarkable phenomena was the number of people who went to live overseas. No sooner had we been granted full membership than literally hundreds of thousands of young Poles headed off abroad. I spent three years living in the north of England, and while I loved it and learned a lot there, it was also good to come home. I had money in the bank, my language skills had improved and I'm now proud to help develop my nation's economy. The freedom of movement that our accession to the EU allowed me has really helped me kick-start my business back home.

3 Probably the most significant event of recent times in my country, Azerbaijan, was the opening of the Baku–Tbilisi–Ceyhan pipeline back in 2005. It's a pipeline transporting oil over one thousand miles from our capital, Baku, to Ceyhan, on the Mediterranean coast in Turkey. It was a very historic event for us because it signalled a kind of financial and economic independence. Because the Caspian is a landlocked sea, all the movement of oil in the past went through Russia, but this pipeline bypasses the old trade routes and goes through Georgia instead. It's placed us closer to the heart of the global oil market, and of course it gives Turkey greater geo-political clout as well. The income that's been generated is so substantial that it's forced us to allow greater transparency and to introduce tighter checks against corruption as well. All of that can only be for the good.

4 For me, the standout event of recent years was the apology issued to the aborigine community a few years ago. A motion was passed in Parliament, followed by a speech from Prime Minister Rudd, and it was the first time that we as a nation had really acknowledged the mistakes of the past with regard to the treatment of our indigenous population.

I don't know how much you know about it, but over the years successive governments carried out a kind of cultural genocide. Just to give one example, throughout most of the 20th century, any mixed-race kids were forcibly removed from aborigine communities and basically forced to live in white-only communities, thus losing all knowledge of their cultural heritage. A lot of the kids who were removed didn't get properly educated and so face higher levels of unemployment today and plenty of them suffered chronic abuse in care as well. The apology for all of this was long overdue, but at least it was an attempt to start removing the stain that's been left on the whole nation.

REVIEW 03

R 3.1
Speaker 1
I've seen people with third-degree burns and met people who've lost limbs, so no, I'm really not willing to stand here today and say standards haven't deteriorated. There's been a chronic neglect of the workforce and accidents that have occurred have been somehow reclassified or else simply met with a conspiracy of silence. Now I know you may have me down as some extremist militant, but I warn you I speak with the full backing of my colleagues.

Speaker 2
Technically, it was never a penalty. To be honest, it was a complete and utter dive, but the referee didn't hesitate to blow his whistle. The guy taking it looked incredibly confident as he placed the ball on the spot, but as he was running up, he slipped and landed flat on his backside. The shot was slow enough for me to anticipate its direction and I managed to tip the shot over the crossbar. The rest of the guys went wild and then we held on for a thoroughly deserved draw.

Speaker 3
I think my decision to go stemmed from the death of my brother a couple of years back. When something like that happens, it really highlights your own mortality. I got trapped in a bit of a downward spiral for quite some time afterwards, and that culminated in me spending a few months in a kind of hospital. Anyway, we set off on a Monday and it was pretty tough, but we made it to the ruins by Thursday. The whole site is incredible. Seeing it just gave me a whole new outlook on life.

Speaker 4
I went into the event as a bit of an underdog, but it was a surprisingly tight contest. I don't want to say my opponent was overrated, but she certainly wasn't as good as I'd been fearing! Anyway, we had a couple of great rallies and I felt she was starting to fade when suddenly it happened. I fell badly and somehow managed to slice my forehead open on the side of my racket. They stitched me up a bit, but basically the opportunity had gone.

Speaker 5
One of the claims that many scholars have advanced over recent years is that the massacre was some kind of attempted genocide, but I think that these new findings establish once and for all that this can't have been the case. I highlight the role played by the assassination of the king and assert that this essentially gave rise to the atmosphere in which the subsequent atrocities were allowed to occur.

UNIT 13

13.1
Conversation 1
A = Man 1, B = Man 2
A: Have you seen the news today?
B: Yeah. Did you see that MP got off?
A: Well, what did you expect? It's one rule for us and another for them, isn't it?
B: It makes me sick. It was so obvious he's been lining his own pockets. I don't know how he's got away with it.

A: Apparently, the case was dismissed on some kind of technicality.
B: Typical. As you say, if it'd been someone lower down, they'd have been convicted.

Conversation 2
C = Woman 1, D = Woman 2
C: What do you think of this story about cutting back the public sector workforce?
D: I'll believe it when it happens.
C: You don't think it will?
D: No. I mean, look at it from the government's point of view. Why would they? What do they have to gain? There's an election coming up in just over a year. It'd be a disaster for them.
C: That's true. Maybe the opposition is just stirring up trouble.
D: More likely. I don't think they've said the source of the story.

Conversation 3
E = Man 1, F = Man 2
E: I can't believe they're still going on about this guy and his affair. It's such a fuss about nothing.
F: I don't think she'd see it like that!
E: No, I know. It's obviously a big deal for her, but I don't see how having it all over the papers will help. What's it got to do with us? And what's it got to do with playing tennis?
F: Nothing. It's all to do with money and sponsorship, isn't it?
E: Exactly. As if anyone cares. It's such nonsense.

Conversation 4
G = Man, H = Woman
G: Did you see that thing about the Secretary of State and what he said?
H: Yeah. I can't believe he's refusing to resign!
G: I don't know. Put yourself in his shoes. Can you imagine the pressure politicians are under when there's so much news coverage? It amazes me they don't make more slips.
H: I know, but it's not the first time and I think it undermines our standing in the world. What are other countries going to think?
G: Ah, it's just a storm in a teacup. It'll all blow over quickly enough.
H: You think so?

Conversation 5
I = Man 1, J = Man 2
I: Did you see that business with the Hampton supporters?
J: Yeah, it was a disgrace. They're just animals. They should do something about them.
I: Didn't you hear? They have! A whole load of them have had their season tickets confiscated.
J: Well, it's about time, though why on earth aren't they being prosecuted? The amount of damage they caused! Not to mention the intimidation.
I: I know. They're thugs. They should be locked up.

13.2
It would obviously be absolute folly for newspaper owners and publishers to ignore current technological developments, but it should also be acknowledged that newspaper companies are still alive and well and doing quite nicely, thank you. Whilst it's obviously true that technology has changed potential modes of delivery, the fact remains that there is no content without a news organisation to gather and edit news.

Indeed, Internet-only sites that have attempted to publish solely their own content have struggled, while the online news sites that *have* thrived have done so almost entirely as a result of others' labours. Newspapers are still very much the main news-gatherers as well as being the primary suppliers of news to Internet-based companies, and the bottom line is that this will continue to be the case until online journalism becomes as profitable as print-based media. Even bearing in mind reduced delivery and printing costs, such parity is probably still many, many years away.

Another important factor in the continued survival of newspapers has ironically been the new income generated from advertising placed on the companies' websites. The vast majority of newspaper websites are still free to access, as efforts to monetise them have had decidedly mixed results. As a result, they are attractive to advertisers keen to hit as wide a range of potential customers as possible. Most companies have strong brand identities, are in healthy financial positions and have access to a deep well of content, all of which suggests that rumours of the death of the newspaper have been somewhat exaggerated!

🎧 13.3

This is the six o'clock news with SBC. I'm Natalie Davis. The headlines this evening: Finance Minister Carol Dixon announces her retirement; medal awarded to sniffer dog; two dead as rioting continues in Manova; interest rates to rise; Jermaine Johnson is out of the final World Cup qualifier; and Simon Crouch and Jennifer Ponting win their libel case against *News Enquirer*.

🎧 13.4

N = Newsreader, CD = Carol, I = Interviewer, HC = Hassan, NS = Nico, FH = François, AK = Anita, L = Lawyer

N: In an interview with SBC, Finance minister Carol Dixon has confirmed rumours that she is to retire on health grounds. She categorically denied that her retirement was connected to recent criticism of the government's decision to build two new nuclear power stations, although she acknowledged there had been division on the issue.

CD: Of course there was a dispute over nuclear energy. I've been a long-term opponent and I've never hidden that, but I lost that argument. On broad policy – hand on heart – I remain totally behind this government.

N: However, she refused to comment further on the health reasons for her departure.

I: And will you be giving more details on your health? Otherwise, it's bound to fuel speculation.

CD: No. I really think that's a private matter between my family and me.

N: A sniffer dog has received a medal for bravery for its work in a bomb disposal unit. Bodge has worked in several war zones over the last six years and has helped find over 200 bombs and mines to be deactivated. His handler, Corporal Hassan Cleaver, said it was a proud day and praised the work of the whole unit.

HC: It's just fantastic. We're so proud of him. And he deserves it, as do lots of the dogs we work with. What they do is just unbelievably important. They're fantastic.

N: Rioting over government reforms has continued in Manova, with two men being killed. Crowds throwing missiles confronted police armed with batons in the main square and conducted running battles in the surrounding streets throughout the day. Nico Smith reports.

NS: There are conflicting reports about the deaths. A police spokesman assured reporters that the men died when a car exploded after being set alight by a petrol bomb that had been thrown by rioters. Meanwhile, demonstrators claim they were crushed when police fired tear gas to disperse the crowd in the square, forcing people down narrow side streets. As the news of the deaths spread, protesters rampaged though the surrounding area, smashing things

in anger. The rioting lasted most of the day until an uneasy calm fell upon the city this evening. Addressing the country on television, the president blamed the rioting on subversive groups trying to destabilise the country and rejected demands for the government to change tack. He urged what he termed a silent majority to make their voices heard. However, there are no signs that that call will be heeded. Nico Smith, Manova.

N: Interest rates are set to rise half a percent, taking the base rate to a ten-year high of 4%. The central bank refused to rule out further increases this year as it bids to control inflation.

Sport, and the national football team have been dealt a further blow in the run up to their crucial World Cup qualifying match against Russia. The goalkeeper and team captain Jermaine Johnson has been ruled out with a thigh strain. The team have struggled and must win if they are to go through to the finals next year. The manager, François Houllier, expressed confidence in Johnson's replacement, Paul Harrison.

FH: Obviously it is not the ideal preparation, but Paul is a great keeper and has been on good form, so I am not so worried.

N: The Hollywood couple Simon Crouch and Jennifer Ponting have won their libel action against the paper *News Enquirer*, following allegations that theirs was a sham marriage. Anita Karaji reports.

AK: During the compelling three-day hearing, the court heard claim and counter-claim about the state of Crouch and Ponting's marriage, but in the end the judge found in their favour, awarding £560,000 damages. Outside the court, in a statement read by their lawyer, the couple thanked supporters and vowed to donate the money to charity.

L: Simon and Jen would like to thank all those fans who sent well wishes and never doubted the outcome of this case. They would also like to make clear that all the proceeds from this decision will be given to good causes, because this case was never about personal gain, only about personal truth.

AK: *News Enquirer* said it disagreed with the decision and was considering an appeal.

N: And that's the news from SBC. It's five past six.

UNIT 14

🎧 14.1

Conversation 1

M = Maria, D = Delphine

M: Hello. InTech Corporation. Maria speaking. How can I help you?

D: Oh hello there, Maria. It's me, Delphine.

M: Oh, hi. How're you?

D: Not too bad, thanks. Listen, I'm just calling to check whether the delivery we sent out on Monday has reached you yet.

M: It has, yeah. It came in this morning, I believe.

D: Oh, that's good. I was just panicking over nothing, then.

M: Well, better safe than sorry, isn't it?

D: Exactly. Anyway, how're you? How's things your end?

M: Oh, you know. We're hanging in there. Sales have actually picked up a bit this quarter, so that's good, and we've actually taken on a couple of new people, so can't complain, you know. How's life with you? How's the little one?

D: Oh, she's good. She's just coming up to one now and she's crawling around everywhere and babbling away to herself all the time.

M: Oh!

D: Yeah. I'll send you pictures if you want.

M: That'd be lovely, yeah. And how's Mark?

D: He's OK. He's been away a lot with work recently, actually, which has been a bit of a pain, but hopefully that'll ease off a bit soon.

M: And how was your holiday? Didn't you go away somewhere recently?

D: Yeah, that's right, we did. Two weeks in Crete. It was lovely. Over far too quickly, of course, but much needed.

M: Oh, that's good, though.

D: Yeah.

Conversation 2

M = Matt, D = Dietmar

M: Hello. CNC.

D: Hi, is that Matt?

M: Yeah. Dietmar. Hi. I was just thinking of you, actually. I saw the draw for the European Championships.

D: Oh yeah. I'm sorry, but England have to lose to someone.

M: Don't count your chickens yet! Let's wait and see.

D: I admire your optimism.

M: Well, you have to look on the bright side, don't you – especially in our line of work.

D: Tell me about it! How're things, anyway?

M: Oh, not too bad, all things considered.

D: And what's happening with the relocation?

M: Well, it's still on the cards, apparently. We've told them it's a bad idea, but they just won't listen!

D: Well, just think of all the savings you'll make on your overheads.

M: And on wages if half the staff who're threatening to walk actually do!

D: A lot of that's just talk, I'd imagine. They'll soon come round.

M: I hope you're right. Anyway, what can I do for you today?

D: Well, I was wondering if we could maybe sort out a time for a meeting during the trade fair next week. It'd be good to talk through Mexico with you.

M: Yeah, of course. ... Is Thursday any use to you?

D: I could squeeze you in in the morning, if you want. Say 10? 10.15?

M: Yeah, 10.15 should be fine. I'll pencil it in.

♨ 14.2

K = Katrin, P = Peter, H = Henry, R = Rachel, A = Alex

K: I've also been approached by the unions, but perhaps that can wait till Any Other Business at the end of the meeting.

P: Right. Let's move on to the next item on the agenda.

H: OK. Well, I've handed out the spreadsheet of current figures and, as you can see, we're set to make a substantial loss this year.

R: We've exceeded our sales targets in Eastern Europe.

A: Yeah, this is a prototype of what we're calling the Shoe Saver.

♨ 14.3

K = Katrin, P = Peter, H = Henry, R = Rachel, A = Alex

K: I've also been approached by the unions, but perhaps that can wait till Any Other Business, at the end of the meeting.

P: Right. Let's move on to the next item on the agenda. We've already touched on the background to this, but perhaps, Henry, if you could just restate the situation.

H: OK. Well, I've handed out the spreadsheet of current figures and, as you can see, we're set to make a substantial loss this year. Obviously, it's been a volatile year for everyone in the industry, but we can't simply blame economic problems. We've also underperformed.

R: Not entirely! We've exceeded our sales targets in Eastern Europe.

H: Yes, that offers some hope Rachel, but that was starting from quite a low base. I know Alex sees great possibilities with his new product, but I really feel the way forward is to cut back on costs.

K: Cutting costs? I would've thought we were at the limit, to be honest. People are already overstretched.

H: It doesn't have to mean more work. We could renegotiate deals with suppliers and then scale back operations.

K: You mean layoffs?

H: Some redundancies, maybe, but hopefully they'd be voluntary.

K: Really? I can't imagine ...

P: Oh, OK. Katrin, I think we're getting ahead of ourselves here. Let's see what Alex has to say first and we'll take it from there. Alex.

A: Yeah, this is a prototype of what we're calling the Shoe Saver. As you see, it's basically a compact box. This is a basic design, but we're planning others. Essentially, you pop your shoes inside and give it a blast to remove all the smells. I've brought along a pair of my son's trainers to demonstrate.

R: Oh, they smell dreadful!

A: Yeah. They've been left damp in a bag to show you just how effective the box is. So I put them in ... and switch it on. It takes a minute. Yes, Rachel?

R: How does it work?

A: It uses tiny particles of silver, which have anti-bacterial properties once ionised. They essentially kill the microbes that cause the odours.

R: Right. OK. I'm not sure what 'ionised' means, but isn't the silver expensive?

A: Yeah, but we're talking tiny amounts. ... OK. ... There. Done. Have a sniff.

R: Wow! That's amazing.

K: Very impressive.

H: Very. So what margins are we looking at with this?

A: Well, unit costs are between 35 and 45 euros and we're looking for it to retail at between 100 and 120 euros.

R: That'd certainly improve our bottom line.

H: Why such uncertainty about production costs? That's quite a big range you've given.

A: Well, we're looking at a deal to outsource production, which could bring significant savings. The higher figure would be if we used our own factories and that's also very much erring on the side of caution.

H: Sure. And what kind of sales projections do you have?

A: We've estimated something in the region of 10,000 units in the first year, followed by 30,000 in year two, 100,000 in year three and quarter of a million by year four.

R: Gosh.

P: I know it's ambitious, but we really are excited about this product. Henry, you don't look convinced.

H: Yeah, I don't want to be the bad guy, but have you really thought this through? You know, there's already a range of products that can solve this problem. Will people really want to pay 120 euros for this?

A: Fair question. I think the first point is that this is far more effective than the sprays and insoles currently on the market. We estimate it could extend a shoe's life by up to 50%, so it'd pay for itself. Secondly, our initial market is not actually homes, but health clubs and gyms. Longer term, growth would come from high-end consumers and we've already had some positive feedback from focus groups.

P: I think Katrin wants to come in.

A: Sure.

K: Yes. What about patents? Is this original technology?

A: Well, no. In fact, the technology's been around for a while, so that's not something we control, but we have patented a couple of the manufacturing processes that we think will give us an edge over any competitors. Plus, of course, we'll have a head start in establishing the brand.

UNIT 15

🔊 15.1

Conversation 1

G = Gail, T = Tatiana

G: Hey, Tatiana!

T: Gail! Gosh! I hardly recognised you. It's a bit radical, isn't it?

G: You don't like it?

T: No, no, you look fantastic. It's just that it's so different. What brought that on?

G: Oh, I just fancied a change. I was getting sick of it, especially with the summer, and I've taken up running again. I mean, you can have it in a ponytail or tie it up but ... I don't know ...

T: No, I know what you mean. I wish I could get away with it short like that – it'd be so much easier.

G: You don't think you could?

T: No – my face is too round. I'd look like a lollipop!

G: That's a bit of an exaggeration! You could have it a bit shorter – a wavy bob like just above the shoulders. That'd work.

T: You think?

G: Yeah, definitely. Not that you need to change.

Conversation 2

C = Colette, D = Diana

C: How do I look?

D: Hmm.

C: You don't like it. I have to say I'm not sure about the sleeves. They're a bit frilly.

D: No, I think they're OK, I just think you need something else. ... I don't know – some beads or something to set it off. Here, try these ... And maybe these bangles.

C: OK.

D: Let's see. Yeah, that's better. What do you think?

C: Yeah, they work well together.

D: It's great. It really shows off your curves.

Conversation 3

E = Ella, F = Fiona

E: Oh, my gosh! Look at her outfit.

F: You don't like it?

E: A flowery dress with a checked shirt? And the ribbon in her hair – and then those army boots!

F: Hey, it wouldn't work for me, but I think she pulls it off. It's quite a funky look. I might lose the ribbon, but those kind of clashing patterns are really in at the moment.

E: Well, it's not a trend I like. And the boots?

F: Well, they kind of show off her legs in a funny way.

E: I think they make them look like sticks. She'd be better off in some strappy heels or some wedges.

Conversation 4

G = Gunilla, H = Harry

G: Are you going like that?

H: Why? What's wrong with it?

G: Nothing. You look very smart. It's just that I don't think it's going to be that kind of do.

H: Oh, right. Shall I lose the tie, then?

G: Yeah, I mean, I'm just going to wear these jeans and that green top.

H: Right, so you want me to change then?

G: Well ... I just don't want you to feel awkward, because you're sticking out. So, ...

H: OK.

🔊 15.2

We live in an age of unprecedented visual saturation. We are bombarded with more images than ever before, images transmitted by an ever-growing range of technologies, and because of the explosion of such technologies, the phenomenon is no longer unique to developed countries, but is penetrating every corner of the world. I shall be arguing that this is not a neutral occurrence and shall be attempting to give you an overview of some of its results.

There are two slightly different ways we can conceptualise the growth in visual representation. On the one hand are those who argue that what is going on is simply an attempt to represent reality, to depict or show the world – or at least portions of it – as it really is. However, it can also be argued that these images shape our reality. They stand in for us in the way that our political representatives do, and so become symbolic of some kind of idealised or perfected parallel world.

Obviously, a large number of the images that confront us on an hourly basis are produced and disseminated by the fashion industry and over recent years what this has meant is that a particular kind of image of beauty has dominated our consciousness: that beauty is predominantly young, white, and almost impossibly thin! Driven by the big fashion houses' need to sell clothes in a cut-throat market, models become little more than human hangers – something stick-thin and lovely that products are 'hung' from. I'm sure we're all familiar with the kind of thing I mean here.

Now obviously cause and effect are nigh-on impossible to prove conclusively, but it seems to me to be no coincidence that this has coincided with a huge rise in the incidence of eating disorders – and what we've seen in particular is anorexia and bulimia among teenage girls, the main consumers of fashion magazines. However, as images of men have also multiplied, and in particular since the move towards thinner and thinner models, as opposed to the more muscle-bound images of a previous generation, we've also started seeing a rise in what's being termed 'manorexia'.

On top of all that, both sexes are increasingly turning to cosmetic surgery and we're seeing younger and younger people opting for procedures such as Botox that were once the preserve of much older patients. As if this wasn't disturbing enough, there's growing evidence that young black and Asian girls are so deprived of role models in the world of high fashion that they are undergoing extreme procedures such as skin bleaching and eyelid reshaping operations in an attempt to simulate what they see as Western standards of beauty. It's a kind of deracialisation process and verges on the obscene.

The degree to which images of the body beautiful have become the norm can best be demonstrated by the fact that token alternative representations can now be used as a selling point. Brands such as Dove had huge success with their 'real beauty' campaign, which uses a far broader range of women in its advertising, and which seems to have struck a chord with women fed up with the pressure on them to be young and slim. Similarly, singer Beth Ditto, who weighs in at around a hundred kilos, has attracted massive amounts of publicity as she has launched her fashion range for sizes 14 to 32. Nevertheless, as refreshing as it may be to see such images reach the mainstream, it should not be forgotten that they only have impact due to the fact they swim so strongly against the dominant tide.

UNIT 16

🔊 16.1

Conversation 1

A = Annabel, B = Belinda

A: Well played. I thought I might stand a chance after you blew that second set, but you thrashed me!

B: Oh, you played OK ... you just need to work on your serve!

A: And my backhand and my footwork and everything else!

B: Yeah, well … maybe a bit! By the way, I hope you don't mind me asking, but what happened to your leg? That's one hell of a scar!

A: What? This?

B: Yeah?

A: Oh, it's a long story.

B: Go on, then. I've got time!

A: Oh, it's stupid, really. It happened when I was in my final year at university. You know I did architecture, right?

B: Yeah.

A: Well, we had to make a lot of models and present them and one time I was up half the night trying to finish off this one particular model and it was about four in the morning and I was more dead than alive and my hand slipped and I somehow managed to cut a huge great big slice out of my thigh with the scalpel I'd been using.

B: Oh! Nasty.

A: Yeah, but I was so out of it that I was just staring at this gaping great hole, half in shock, half in complete exhaustion, and in the end I just wiped the blood off with a tissue, tried to super-glue it all together and crashed out. Next morning, I woke up early, went along to A and E to get it cleaned up and stitched – and still managed to present my model in the afternoon.

B: And who said students are lazy, eh!

Conversation 2

C = Chloe, D = Doug

C: How did you get that scar, if you don't mind me asking?

D: Which one? The one on my chin?

C: No, I meant the one on your forehead. It's pretty nasty.

D: Oh, that. Yeah, well, I was smart enough to somehow walk straight into a head-height shelf when I was 18. I was working at this summer camp in the States and I'd been out to a party with some friends one night, stumbled home and whacked myself when I got back to my cabin. I decided that, while it hurt a bit, it'd probably be OK and that what I really needed was my bed. I woke up in the morning to find there was blood everywhere – all over the bed, the floor – and most shockingly, when I looked in the mirror, I realised my face was covered in dried blood, which I really hadn't been expecting! The doctor said he could've stitched it if I'd seen him right away, but that it was unstitchable the following day! Just my luck.

C: Oh, that's awful.

D: Yeah, well, it's my own stupid fault, really.

C: And … um … I'm scared to ask now, really, but what about that other one?

D: You won't believe me when I tell you. Honestly.

C: Um … OK. Is it gruesome?

D: Not really. Just odd. I don't know if you remember, but a couple of years ago, there were all these reports of people getting blown off their feet by high winds, and even someone getting killed by being blown head first into a door.

C: No! That must just have completely passed me by somehow.

D: Yeah? Well, it was pretty crazy. What happened with me was that one night I just got totally blown down the drive at the side of my house, completely out of control! I somehow managed to go head first between two parked cars, whacking my head on both of them and landing on my chin in the middle of the road.

C: Ouch!

D: Yeah – and when I came to, I found my chin completely split open … and my wisdom teeth weren't too happy either!

C: Woah! You're fairly accident-prone, really, aren't you?

D: I've got another one, actually, if you want to hear about it …

🔊 **16.2**

1 Wow!

2 Fff! Ouch!

3 Yuk!

4 Gosh!

5 Phew!

6 Mmm!

7 Ahem!

8 Mmm

9 Umm

10 Oi!

11 Sshhh!

12 Oops!

🔊 **16.3**

1 A: She speaks six different languages.
  B: Wow! That's impressive.

2 A: I was running and I heard something in my knee just snap!
  B: Fff! Ouch! Painful!

3 A: His false teeth fell out onto the floor and he just picked them up and put them straight back into his mouth again.
  B: Yuk! That's disgusting!

4 A: I've still got a scar. Look.
  B: Gosh! That's awfully big!

5 A: The doctor I went to for a second opinion said I'd been given the wrong diagnosis and it wasn't as serious as they'd thought.
  B: Phew! That's a relief, then.

6 A: Mmm! This is delicious! What's yours like?
  B: Yeah, not bad.

7 A: Ahem!
  B: What? … Oh, sorry.

8 A: And then she said, like, you know, that she thought it was a bit too revealing, but I wasn't sure so … are you listening to me?
  B: Mmm. Yeah. Course.

9 A: So how come you decided to do that, then?
  B: Umm. That's a good question, actually. I'd have to think about that.

10 A: Oi! What do you think you're doing?
   B: Quick! Run!

11 Sshhh! The baby's sleeping.

12 A: And then I realised I'd copied my boss in on the email by mistake!
   B: Oops! That wasn't very clever.

🔊 **16.4**

I = Interviewer, EC = Eva Chakrabati

I: So I'm here in a school in Chipping Sodbury where I'm talking to Eva Chakrabati, who's a health and safety officer. Now I have to say, Eva, I was a bit surprised to see what you were doing there. You were holding bubbles of methane and setting them alight. Exploding gases in front of children isn't what we expect from people like you.

EC: No? Well, that's very much the kind of misconception we're trying to combat here. Health and safety is not about removing all risk from life. Personally, I'm into rock climbing and I'm all for people having fun and excitement. Society relies on people doing hazardous jobs, whether it be working in quarries, on oil rigs or in farming, but there's a difference between risks and recklessness. We analyse risk and set legal guidelines to reduce it.

I: OK, but that's the issue – those guidelines. We constantly hear stories of the reams of paperwork involved in setting up, say, a school trip. Doesn't it turn basic pleasures and education into a bureaucratic nightmare?

EC: I wouldn't deny some forms are excessive, but I would query whether that's really down to us. We've produced templates for risk assessment for school trips that are just three pages long. However, some bodies in charge of implementation produce one form covering every type of assessment, with the result that they're overlong and contain much that's irrelevant to individual events.

I: Why don't you force the use of your forms, then?

EC: Well, they are widely available and we're running a campaign on health and safety myths, but really we're caught between a rock and a hard place. On the one hand, we have these hysterical stories in the media that we're imposing a nanny state, but then here you're saying we should override local people on the ground. Actually, I think we should stick to our policy, which is providing standards that generally have the caveat that common sense should apply and changes only made where the cost is appropriate to the benefits.

I: So you're saying that many of the stories we hear – banning snowballs; stopping clowns blowing bubbles; punishing staff for moving chairs round a room– all those are essentially nonsense.

EC: Well, yes! They may have a grain of truth, but they're usually over-generalised or wrongly blamed on us. It's possible some schools have banned snowballs, but I think that's likely to have been a response to a particular incident and maybe fears of litigation. It's certainly not the result of anything we've said. The clown story is something similar. He was using a bubble-making machine and he couldn't get insurance – we didn't stop him. Actually, there IS a risk there because the machines create lots of soapy liquid and on smooth surfaces they're a hazard, but we'd say used on grass, gravel or some other non-slip surface they're great fun – go ahead! As for the furniture in our office, we have chairs and desks fitted with lockable wheels that can be moved by anyone, but yes we do have porters to shift other, heavier furniture.

I: And you don't think that's excessive?

EC: No, as I say, we're raising awareness and giving workers options. Literally thousands of people are injured at work because of disregard for safety standards. Helping avoid that saves heartache and millions in lost revenue.

I: Eva Chakrabati, thank you very much.

🔊 16.5

M = Michael, J = Joyce, N = Nigel

M: With the news that the Internet penetration rate is set to reach 80% sometime in the next month coming hot on the heels of revelations that children as young as eight are now receiving treatment for Internet addiction, today we're turning our attention to this most modern of phenomena and asking whether the Internet has become more of a curse than a blessing. As ever, if the show is to work, we need you to call up and tell us what's on your mind.

And I think we have our first caller, on line one. It's Joyce in Crawley. Joyce, hello.

J: Oh hello, Michael. Thank you. Yes. Well, I've been a secondary school teacher for some 40 years now and I'm on the verge of retiring. I'm due to stop work in the summer, and I must say I'm awfully glad about it.

M: Why's that, then, Joyce?

J: Well, to be frank, I think the Internet has ruined childhood and created a generation of idiots and I honestly don't think things are likely to get any better in the foreseeable future.

M: Well, that's a fairly bleak appraisal. What is it about the Web that particularly concerns you?

J: Well, the first thing is simply the ease of access it provides. I'm obviously not opposed to people being able to access useful information, but most students nowadays have lost the ability to construct their own essays or think their own way through a question. They simply cut and paste and hand things in, which

appalls me.

M: So, plagiarism, in short?

J: Exactly. And in addition to that, the Internet basically dangles all manner of temptation in front of young people, often very vulnerable young people, and that's bound to cause problems.

M: I'm guessing that you're talking about pornography and the like here, Joyce?

J: Well, of course that's a worry, but there's so much more to it than that. I've heard tales of students getting sucked into white supremacist sites and religious extremist sites. Then there are sites offering assistance with weapon-making and I've had students of my own get involved in online gambling. They run up huge debts and end up having to be bailed out by their parents. And to put it mildly, none of this exactly helps them perform academically.

M: The chances of it helping are pretty slim, I'd imagine. Anyway, Joyce, thanks for that. Next up is Nigel, in Manchester. Hello.

N: Hello there, Michael. Nice to be with you. Long-time listener here. What I wanted to say was it's time we got tough and cracked down more on the Web.

M: And how do you propose we do that, then?

N: Well, if it were up to me, I'd arrest anyone caught looking at banned websites. I mean, they must know who these people are, mustn't they, the government.

M: That's a huge online policing presence you're suggesting there, Nigel, and in all likelihood, most offenders are actually pretty harmless when it comes down to it.

N: Yeah, OK, but maybe we should make an example of one or two people, then, you know. Hit them with the toughest sentences we can. Like spammers and online fraudsters and what have you. Do that and the odds are you'll put the others off.

M: Or, do that and there's a distinct possibility you'll end up embroiled in a lengthy legal dispute about proportionate punishments, I would've thought, to be honest.

🔊 16.6

1 The Internet penetration rate is set to reach 80% sometime in the next month.
2 If the show is to work, we need YOU to call up and tell us what's on your mind.
3 I'm due to stop work in the summer.
4 I honestly don't think things are likely to get any better in the foreseeable future.
5 The Internet basically dangles all manner of temptation in front of young people, and that's bound to cause problems.
6 I'm on the verge of retiring.
7 The chances of it helping are pretty slim, I'd imagine.
8 In all likelihood, most offenders are actually pretty harmless.
9 Hit them with the toughest sentences we can. Do that and the odds are you'll put the others off.
10 Do that and there's a distinct possibility you'll end up embroiled in a lengthy legal dispute.

REVIEW 04

R 4.1

C = Clive, V = Victoria

C: Well, it's that time of year again when glitter and glamour take over and our woman on the ground, Victoria Cohen, has all the latest from the film industry's big annual award night. Victoria, what's your assessment of things from your ringside seat?

V: Thanks, Clive. Well, yes, here I am on Main Street and what a night it's been. Obviously, these events are a real morale-booster for the industry in times of economic hardship, and that desire for escape and fantasy has perhaps been reflected in some of the outfits we've seen on the red carpet. Just a few moments ago, Lady Za-Za came past in a remarkable pinstripe suit, the kind of thing that was once the preserve of the city gentleman, but very tailored to show off her magnificent curves and – you're gonna love this – sprayed completely gold! Interestingly, her famous silver bob that we've all become so familiar with is no more and in its place is a spiky blonde look that stunned the crowds gathered here.

C: Perhaps she decided the silver and gold would clash, Victoria.

V: Who knows, Clive? It was brave, that's for sure, and it's hard to think of many other celebrities who could pull off such a look. Anyway, before that we'd seen Kyleen McClose making her first public appearance since her former PA accused her of bullying ...

C: Accusations, we should add, that Ms McClose categorically denies.

V: Indeed. Kyleen tonight went for a simple, slightly faded linen outfit, which many observers felt left her looking worn down by her recent troubles, but which I felt was a refreshing change from the norm, given the predominant styles on display.

C: And I understand there was some drama earlier on in the evening.

V: That's right. The model Noella Cartwright appeared around seven, towering over most of us in the most incredibly high heels ... and then managed to fall head first as she stepped onto the red carpet. She picked herself up OK, but for a second or two there looked to be in absolute agony.

C: And I hear there's talk of a possible lawsuit, Victoria.

V: Incredibly, that's true, yes. Noella's agent has informed us that she may well be seeking damages from the designer for endangering her career.

C: Fantastic. You couldn't make it up.

CREDITS

Although every effort has been made to contact copyright holders before publication, this has not always been possible. If notified, the publisher will undertake to rectify any errors or omissions at the earliest opportunity.

Text
The publishers would like to thank the following sources for permission to reproduce their copyright protected texts:

Pages 66–67: from The Living Dead by David Bolchover, copyright © Capstone, Wiley-Blackwell; Listening 10.3: based on recording on Mental Health Foundation website http://www.bemindful.co.uk/about_mindfulness/experience_mindfulness;
page 106: from Adorned in Dreams by Elizabeth Wilson, copyright © Elizabeth Wilson.

Photos
The publishers would like to thank the following sources for permission to reproduce their copyright protected images:

Alamy – pp8 (Jon Arnold Images Ltd), 9 (Jon Arnold Images Ltd), 10l (Iain Masterton), 10r (Index Stock), 15 (Kevin Foy), 18b (Janine Wiedel Photolibrary), 18t (Johnny Greig people), 23bl (Image Source), 23br (David Lyons), 24bl (Catchlight Visual Services), 24c (Jenny Matthews), 24tl (LatinStock Collection), 26bl (Justin Kase), 26l (Purestock), 26tl (Index Stock), 26tr (Li Ding), 28t (RichardBaker), 30 (Dean Shults), 36l (Peter Dench), 40 (UpperCut Images), 53bl (Adam Seward), 53tl (Megapress), 58tcr (vario images GmbH & Co.KG), 64 (Johner Images), 66 (Peter Scholey), 73 (LOOK Die Bildagentur der Fotografen GmbH), 76b (Action Plus Sports Images), 76t (Image Source), 78bl (Radius Images), 78br (Luis C. Carvalho), 78cc (Daisy Images), 78cl (Didi), 78tc (Nikreates), 81b (Rob Snow), 81t (Agencja FREE), 82 (Ryan McGinnis), 83 (Thomas Cockrem), 85 (Iconotec), 87l (Neil Cooper), 87r (Daniel Dempster Photography), 92 (David Young-Wolff), 95 (TH Foto), 95b (Mikko Mattila), 95t (Allstar Picture Library), 98c (David Hancock), 101b (The Art Gallery Collection), 101t (40260.com), 104tl (Allstar Picture Library), 104tr (Ulana Switucha), 112r (DC Premiumstock), 112tl (Neil Harris), 124c (Roger Bamber), 124t (D. Hurst), 130(1) (Hugh Threlfall), 130(2) (Buzzshotz), 130(3) (Motion Picture Library), 130(4) (Adams Picture Library), 130(5) (Joe Fox), 130(6) (Miguel Angel Munoz Pellicer), 132t (Ingram Publishing), 134 (David Gee), 158tc (Frenk Kaufmann), 158tl (George Impey); **Cartoonstock** – 25 (Mike Baldwin), 29t (Randall McIlwaine), 29b (Baloo/Rex May), 44bl (W. B. Park), 77bl (Jonny Hawkins), 93br (Mike Baldwin), 97br (Fran), 103 (Nick Kim), 105bl (Joseph Farris), 111bl (Simon Bond); **Chicago Review Press** – p41r; **Corbis UK Ltd.** – pp16tl (Andreas Schlegel/Fstop), 17tl (Rubberball), 17tr (Daniel Attia), 24br (Moment/Cultura), 46r (Peter Turnley), 53r (Stefan Sauer/Epa), 55 (Lance Nelson), 67 (Jose Luis Pelaez, Inc./Blend Images), 86 (Peter Turnley); **Frank Lane Picture Agency** – p58br (Frank W Lane); **Getty Images** – pp3 (Ivan Piven/Flickr), 11 (Simon Lim/AFP), 17bl (Ivan Piven/Flickr), 31b (Per-Anders Pettersson), 31t (Robert Nickelsberg), 36r (Visions Of Our Land), 39b (th.egilson/Flickr), 44 (Nabil Mouzner/AFP), 46bl (Jane Sweeney/Robert Harding),

58bcr (Paul Nicklen), 58bl (Art Wolfe), 58tcl (David Haring), 59c (Christophe Simon/AFP), 69 (Image Source), 74 (CMSP), 98t (Ian Waldie), 108bl (Jun Sato); **iStockphoto** – pp8–9t (Justin Horrocks), 12 (Stefanie Timmermann), 14–15t (Robert Churchill), 20–21t (Aldo Murillo), 23t (© Sandra O'Claire), 26–27t (Franky De Meyer), 27br (MaleWitch), 28b (Chan Pak Kei), 36–37t (Dirk Freder), 37b (Mlenny), 42–43t (Rahul Sengupta), 45 (Anthony Brown), 48–49t (mbphoto, inc), 49 (ABDesign/Vetta Collection), 50 (enot-poloskun), 51 (andreas Reh), 52 (dra_schwartz), 54–55t (Markus Seidel), (56 (blindtoy99), 58 (ooyoo), 64–65t (Catherine Yeulet), 67bg (Uyen Le), 70–71t (Steve Cole), 76b (Nekada). 76–77t (Boris Katsman), 82–83t (Knud Nielsen), 84 (Arne Thaysen), 92–93t (Danil Melekhin), 97t (Murat Giray Kaya), 98b (Natalia Bannykh), 98–99t (Ricardo Infante Alvarez), 101bg (eyeidea), 102 (James Steidl), 104–105t (mbbirdy), 109 (Larysa Dodz), 110–111t (Mutlu Kurtbas), 114 (tanika84), 120–121t (Nikada), 122–123t (Mark Goddard), 124b (Renee Keith), 124–125t (Kati Molin), 126–127t (Evgeny Kuklev), 128–129t (Mark Goddard), 130–131t (Monika Adamczyk), 132–133t (Axaulya), 134–135t (Mike Clarke); **Karen Grainger** – p39t; **Photolibrary Group** – pp14 (Oliver Gutfleisch/imagebroker.net), 19 (David Muscroft/age fotostock), 58bcl (Tsuneo Nakamura), 58tl (Michael Habicht), 58tr (Tony Tilford/Oxford Scientific), 71 (Medicimage), 72–73 (Johnson Derek/Monsoon Images), 123 (W Cody/Flirt Collection), 158bl (Liane Cary/age fotostock), 158br (Bruce Talbot/DK Stock); **Press Association Images** – pp46rl (Gavin Barker/Sports Inc), 104bl (Julien Behal), 104br (LaPresse Italy), 108tc (Hahn-Nebinger-Orban/ABACA), 108tl (Stephane Kossman/ABACA USA), 108tr (Maxa/LANDOV); **Rex Features** – pp96b (Richard Austin), 112bl (Michael Runkel/Robert Harding), 132b (Ken McKay); Science Photo Library p48 (Victor Habbick Visions); **Shutterstock** – pp16bl (HomeStudio), 16br (Bragin Alexey), 16tr (Rudy Umans), 17br (Monkey Business Images), 24tr (Piotr Marcinski), 26br (Monkey Business Images), 65 (Denis Babenko), 78tl (vblinov), 108bo (Martina Ebel), 158tr (Claires); **Sort of Books** – p41l; **Zooid Pictures** – p78bc.

Cover photo: iStockphoto (Kenneth C. Zirkel)

Ilustrations: pp 33, 61, 89, 117 – Mark Draisey; all others – KJA Artists

INTRODUCTION TO *OUTCOMES VOCABULARY BUILDER*

Learning vocabulary in collocations and phrases will develop your fluency. And doing a little revision regularly is the best way to learn vocabulary. That's what the *Outcomes Vocabulary Builder (OVB)* will help you with.

It has been written to provide you with the important vocabulary in the Student's Book and to show you how these words are commonly used. It does not include easier words which you should know from lower levels such as *boring*, or unusual words, which you probably don't need to remember at this level.

What each entry contains

- Each entry has a short explanation of the word's meaning and often gives information on other forms or opposites.
- There is then a list of up to six typical collocations and phrases that the word is used with.
- Regular language boxes provide extra information on the idioms found in each unit.

How the *OVB* is organised

It is organised to make it quick and easy to use in class and to revise at home.

- Each unit in the **OVB** contains the most important new words from exercises, texts and listenings in the unit of the Student's Book.
- The units are then divided according to each double page of the Student's Book and the words within those pages are written in alphabetical order.
- At the end of each unit there are exercises to do.
- There is an answer key at the back of the book.

Ways you can use the *OVB*

- Read the word list *before* you study the unit in the book.
- Translate all the words you don't know based on the explanation. Check the collocations for each word. Do they make sense? Are any different to your language?
- In class, if you have forgotten a word, look it up again. Write out the collocation list and add one of your own.
- Cover words in the list and say or write phrases with the word. Then compare with the collocation list.
- Choose five to ten words from the list to learn each day.
- Put eight new words in a story using the collocations listed.
- Do the exercises at the end of each unit some time *after* you've done it in class. Then check the answers in the key.
- Write a list of the words you find difficult to remember and write sentences using the words.

01

CITIES

PAGES 8–9

affluent someone who is affluent is very rich. The noun is **affluence**: *a fairly ~ area / an ~ family / an ~ businessman / an ~ lifestyle / the relative affluence of the south-east*

appalling something that is appalling is extremely bad. **Appalled** is also an adjective: *an ~ crime / live in ~ conditions / it's absolutely ~ / I was absolutely appalled*

buzz if there is a buzz in a place, it is lively and exciting. The adjective is **buzzing**: *the area has a real ~ / there's a real ~ in the city / the whole place is buzzing*

choke if you choke, you feel as though you cannot breathe: *you sometimes ~ on the fumes / ~ on a piece of meat*

congestion if there is congestion, a place is too crowded with people or vehicles. The adjective is **congested**: *measures to curb ~ in the city centre / severe traffic ~ / it led to ~ in the centre / reduce the ~ / the roads are heavily congested*

crane a crane is a tall machine that is used for lifting heavy objects and building tall buildings: *see hundreds of ~s from our hotel window / a ~ driver*

crawl if you crawl, you move very slowly. **Crawl** is also a noun: *the cars ~ along / I ~ed into bed / the days seem to ~ by / the traffic slowed to a ~*

crumble a building that is crumbling is in very bad condition and starting to fall down: *the buildings were crumbling / the house was beginning to ~ / a crumbling old house*

derelict a derelict building is empty and in bad condition: *a ~ building / ~ houses / the building now stands ~ / ~ land*

downside a downside is a disadvantage. The opposite is **upside**: *what are the ~s? / the ~s of where you live / a big ~ / one of the upsides of living in London*

drawback a drawback is a disadvantage: *the main ~ of living here / a major ~ of the scheme*

dump a dump is a dirty and untidy place. It is also a place where rubbish is taken: *the city is a ~ / the house is a ~ / take it to the rubbish ~*

fumes fumes are smoke or gas with an unpleasant smell: *a factory which produces nasty ~ / choke on the ~ / traffic ~ / toxic ~ / noxious ~*

mugging a mugging is a crime in which someone is attacked in the street and their money is stolen. The verb is **mug**: *there are a lot of ~s and shootings / I was mugged on my way home*

ridiculously ridiculously means in a way that is very extreme and not sensible. The adjective is **ridiculous**: *houses are ~ expensive / ~ cheap / it was ~ easy / prices around here are ridiculous*

run-down a run-down building or area is in bad condition: *the building was very ~ / extremely ~ / it's a bit ~ now / a ~ area of the city*

smog smog is polluted air that is a mixture of smoke and fog: *a cloud of ~ hangs over the city / heavy ~ / urban ~ / the ~ levels in the city / a ~ alert*

smoothly if something works smoothly, it works quickly and well. The adjective is **smooth**: *everything works very ~ / let's hope everything goes ~ / it's all running ~ / a smooth changeover to the new system*

spotless something that is spotless is completely clean. The adverb is **spotlessly**: *the house is always ~ / a company with a ~ reputation / a ~ record / the room was spotlessly clean*

sprawling a sprawling city covers a large area in an untidy way. The noun is **sprawl**: *a large, ~ city / miles and miles of urban sprawl*

vibrant something that is vibrant is lively and exciting: *it's an incredibly ~ place / a ~ city / a ~ community / a ~ economy*

PAGES 10–11

capability if you have the capability to do something, you have the ability or resources to do it: *the company has the ~ to expand / it's beyond my capabilities / the country's military ~ / the nuclear ~*

decline if something declines, it becomes worse. **Decline** is also a noun: *the area has ~d / standards in education are declining / the economy has ~d sharply / ~ steeply / ~ significantly / a sharp ~ in living standards*

demolish if you demolish a building, you destroy it deliberately. The noun is **demolition**: *a lot of the old buildings were ~ed / the old cinema has been ~ed / the building is due for demolition*

dip if a number or amount dips, it becomes lower. **Dip** is also a noun: *the number of murders has dipped below 400 / profits dipped by 4% / prices* dipped sharply / a ~ in prices / a sharp ~ in inflation / a slight ~ in house prices

downturn a downturn is a reduction in economic activity. The opposite is **upturn**: *a ~ in the economy / a sharp ~ in demand for oil / a serious ~ / a slight ~ / an upturn in the economy*

earthquake when there is an earthquake, the ground shakes: *an ~ hit the city last month / a massive ~ / a huge ~ / a small ~ / a devastating ~ / the ~ measured six on the Richter scale / buildings that were destroyed in the ~*

emerge if you emerge from a place or a situation, you come out from it: *a strong community spirit ~d from the disaster / he finally ~ed from the building / the country is emerging from a recession*

flooding when there is flooding, water from rain or a river covers the land: *the city suffered serious ~ last year / the rain caused ~ in many areas / the risk of ~ / the effects of ~*

flourish if something flourishes, it is very successful: *many businesses are now ~ing / a ~ing community*

-fold something that increases or decreases three-fold, four-fold, etc., increases or decreases by three times, four times, etc.: *unemployment has risen three-fold / murders have fallen four-fold / a three-fold increase in the price of petrol*

grant a grant is an amount of money that a government or organisation gives to someone for a particular purpose: *the city received a £50 million regeneration ~ / they provide ~s for people starting up new businesses / a large ~ / a small ~ / student ~s / apply for a ~ / get a ~ / be awarded a ~*

hurricane a hurricane is a storm with extremely strong winds: *the city has been hit by a ~ / the houses destroyed by the ~ / the whole area was devastated by the ~ / ~ Katrina*

lose out if you lose out, you do not get an advantage that other people are getting: *the city lost out on development grants / worried we might ~*

overcome if you overcome a problem, you deal with it successfully. The past tense is **overcame** and the past participle is **overcome**: *the city has ~ a lot of problems / managed to ~ my fears / he successfully overcame his disabilities*

rate the rate of something is how many times or how quickly it happens: *the crime ~ has fallen / a falling birth ~ / the unemployment ~ / the ~ of inflation / rising ~s of unemployment / the ~ of change / prices are increasing at an alarming ~*

recruit if you recruit someone, you get them to join a company or organisation. A **recruit** is someone who has recently joined a company or organisation: *they want to ~ more police officers / the company ~s large numbers of graduates / he was ~ed as a sales rep / they were ~ed into the army / the new ~s / army ~s*

regenerate if you regenerate a place, you develop it and make it successful again. The noun is

regeneration: *the area has been ~d / a plan to ~ the city centre / a £50 million regeneration grant*

renovate if you renovate something old, you repair it and make it look new again. The noun is **renovation**: *they've ~d the old cinema / plans to ~ the historic city centre / it's been completely ~d / a £20 million renovation scheme*

resourceful someone who is resourceful is good at finding solutions to problems: *a ~ community / she's very ~*

rough a rough place is not pleasant because it has a lot of crime: *the area used to be quite ~ / a ~ housing estate / a ~ neighbourhood / some very ~ areas / some parts of the city are a bit ~*

rubble rubble is the stones and bricks from a building that has been destroyed: *the house was reduced to a pile of ~ / a heap of ~ / people are still trapped in the ~ / buried under the ~ / searching through the ~ for survivors*

shelter shelter is a place where people are protected from bad weather or danger: *thousands of people still have no ~ / we need tents to provide ~ for people / we ran to find ~ / ~ from the rain / seek ~ in a doorway*

step a step is one action in a series of actions: *this is the first ~ to recovery / an important ~ forward / a ~ in the right direction / what's the next ~? / we need to take things ~ by ~*

thrive if something is thriving, it is successful. If someone is thriving, they are happy and healthy: *the business is now thriving / a thriving economy / the city is thriving / most plants ~ with plenty of water and heat / the baby's thriving*

underestimate if you underestimate something, you think it is less important or less serious than it really is. The opposite is **overestimate**: *we ~d the problem / I ~d the cost / don't ~ the importance of a good diet / it's important not to overestimate children's abilities*

undergo if you undergo something, you experience it. The past tense is **underwent** and the past participle is **undergone**: *the stories ~ change over time / ~ an operation on my knee*

Pages 12–13

brim the brim of a cup or bowl is its top edge: *coffee cups full to the ~ / filled to the ~*

burgle if someone burgles a place, they go into it and steal things from it. A **burglary** is a crime in which a place is burgled. A **burglar** is someone who commits a burglary: *the house has been ~d three times / we've been ~d! / a series of burglaries in the area / an attempted burglary / the burglars stole all of my jewellery*

circulation the circulation of information is the way in which it is passed between people. The verb is **circulate**: *the ~ of urban myths / ~ of the report / the number of banknotes in ~ / circulate a document among colleagues*

decode if you decode something, you understand its meaning when the meaning is hidden: *scholars attempt to ~ the meanings of stories / trying to ~ the message / the meaning can be difficult to ~*

deed a deed is something that you do: *do a good ~ / brave ~s / perform heroic ~s / an evil ~ / the ~ is done*

deep-rooted a deep-rooted feeling or belief is very strong and difficult to change: *~ fears / ~ prejudice / a ~ hatred of politicians / their beliefs are very ~*

depth if you discuss something in depth, you discuss it in a lot of detail. **In-depth** is also an adjective: *we discussed the issue in ~ / analysed it in ~ / he's written in ~ about his experiences / an in-depth discussion / in-depth analysis*

desperately if you are desperately sad or unhappy, you are extremely sad or unhappy. The adjective is **desperate**: *I was ~ unhappy / ~ sad / ~ worried / a ~ sad situation / a ~ tragic event / I felt absolutely desperate*

diagnose when doctors diagnose an illness, they say that someone has that illness. The noun is **diagnosis**: *the doctors ~d cancer / I was ~d with cancer / the condition is difficult to ~ / can't make an accurate diagnosis yet / a firm diagnosis / early diagnosis is vital*

freak out if you freak out, you lose control because you are so angry or upset: *I ~ed out in the supermarket / ~ed out when she saw the police / I totally ~ed out*

grab if you grab something, you take hold of it quickly or roughly: *I grabbed my bag / grabbed me by the arm / someone tried to ~ my purse / grabbed hold of him*

merit the merits of something are its good points: *the literary ~ s of the stories / discussed the ~s of different voting systems / assess the ~s of both ideas / consider the relative ~s of each approach / it's of no ~*

pocket if you pocket something, you put it in your pocket or steal it: *~ the rest of the money / saw him ~ my phone*

poison if you poison someone, you kill them with poison: *the police think he was ~d / the best way to get rid of rats is to ~ them*

ring the ring of something you hear is how it seems to you: *the story has a ~ of truth about it / his name has a familiar ~ / a name with an old-fashioned ~*

shadow a shadow is a dark place where there is no light. If someone is in the shadows, they are in a difficult situation: *the garden is in ~ most of the day / deep ~s / the ~ cast by the house / people who live in the ~ of war / the country is emerging from the ~s*

small talk small talk is polite talk about things that are not very important: *I don't like making ~ / I'm not very good at ~ / after a few minutes of ~*

suck if you suck on something, you put it in your mouth and move your tongue around it: *~ing on a sweet / ~ing on a cigarette*

thrilled if you feel thrilled, you feel very happy and excited. **Thrilling** is also an adjective: *I was really ~ / absolutely ~ / ~ with my new car / ~ at the news / a thrilling experience / a thrilling adventure*

voice if you voice your ideas or feelings, you talk about them: *a chance to ~ your worries / ~ your fears / ~ your opinion / ~ your concerns*

wipe if you wipe a recording, you remove it. If you wipe something from your memory, you deliberately forget it: *sorry, I ~d the tape / I ~d the disk / ~d the incident from my memory*

IDIOMS

rolling in money if you are rolling in money, you have much more money than you need: *people who are obviously ~*

the spitting image if one person is the spitting image of another, they look completely identical: *he's ~ of his dad*

spread like wildfire if information spreads like wildfire, it spreads very quickly between people. A wildfire is a large, uncontrolled fire in the countryside, which spreads very quickly: *the news ~ / the rumours ~*

by and large if something is true by and large, it happens generally or usually: *~ the town is well-preserved / the system works well, ~*

give or take you say 'give or take' to show that an amount you are talking about is not completely accurate: *the population's ten million, ~ / I'll be there at ten, ~ five minutes*

here and there if something happens here and there, it happens in a few places but not in very many: *there are still pockets of deprivation ~ / I've lived ~ / there are a few houses ~*

long and hard if you think about something long and hard, you think in a detailed way for a long time: *I thought ~ about it before making a decision / need to think about this ~*

now and then if something happens now and then, it happens sometimes, but not very often: *I still like to party ~ / we visit them ~ / I see him ~*

EXERCISES

PREPOSITIONS

A Complete the sentences with the correct preposition.
1 You can see Central Park ...... the hotel window. *from*
2 I crawled ...... bed at 2 a.m. *into*
3 The pollution is a disadvantage ...... living there. *of*
4 There's been a slight drop ...... house prices. *in*
5 When can you pay me the rest ...... the money? *of*
6 She wrote a book ...... her experiences. *about*
7 He had an operation ...... his back. *on*
8 We found a bus stop to shelter ...... the rain. *from*

WORD FAMILIES

A Complete the expression with the correct form of the word in bold.

1 they **diagnosed** cancer	an early ....
2 a wide **circulation**	It was .... among colleagues.
3 a clever **burglar**	My house was ....
4 it was **demolished**	flats due for ....
5 **spotlessly** clean	a .... record
6 traffic **congestion**	a .... street
7 signs of **affluence**	an .... neighbourhood

IDIOMS

A Complete the idiom with the correct word in the list.

wildfire	long	here	rolling
image	large	then	take

1 He just bought a new car. He's .... **in money**.
2 It's about a six-hour drive, **give or** .... an hour.
3 Your brother is **the spitting** .... of someone in my office.
4 I've thought about it .... **and hard** and I've decided not to take the job.
5 News of the scandal **spread like** ....
6 It's a poor neighbourhood with some nice houses .... **and there**.
7 I still see my old classmates **now and** ....
8 A few people didn't like it, but **by and** .... the play was a success.

COLLOCATIONS

A Complete the sentences with the correct form of the verbs in the list.

take	attempt	live	buzz	voice	trap

1 People are still .... in the rubble of the collapsed building.
2 There was an .... burglary on my neighbours house.
3 It's a place where people are .... in the shadow of war.
4 Don't be afraid to .... your opinion.
5 I'm not going to rush things. I'm going to .... them step by step.
6 There is a great atmosphere inside. The place is ....

B Complete the missing adjectives.
1 a step in the r _ _ _ t direction
2 a h _ _ _ _ _ g estate
3 u _ _ _ n sprawl
4 a r _ _ _ h neighbourhood
5 a g _ _ d deed
6 f _ _ l to the brim
7 s _ _ _ l talk

C Match the two halves of the collocation.

1 it was absolutely	a) standards
2 it's in bad	b) officer
3 a decline in living	c) appalling
4 the rate of	d) thrilled
5 a police	e) inflation
6 a renovation	f) condition
7 I'm absolutely	g) rep
8 a sales	h) scheme

PHRASAL VERBS

A Complete the sentences with the correct form of the phrasal verbs in the list.

fall down	start up	freak out	lose out
come out			

1 That old house looks like it's ....
2 Some good ideas have .... of the seminar.
3 You need capital to .... a business.
4 We .... to a company with a better proposal.
5 I .... when I realised how late it was.

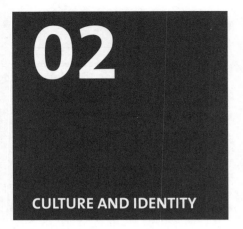

02

CULTURE AND IDENTITY

abolish if something is abolished, people get rid of it officially. The noun is **abolition**: *income tax should be ~ed / ~ school uniforms / they want to ~ it completely / ~ it altogether / vote to ~ capital punishment / the abolition of income tax*

bribe a bribe is an amount of money that you pay to someone illegally so that they will do something for you. **Bribe** is also a verb. The crime of paying bribes is **bribery**: *pay ~s to police officers / offer ~s / accept ~s / take ~s / pay £2000 in ~s / charged with attempting to ~ officials / ~d him to keep quiet / charged with bribery and corruption*

censorship if there is censorship, parts of books, films, newspapers, etc. are removed by people in authority because they are not acceptable. The verb is **censor**: *there's still a lot of ~ in the media / there is strict ~ of the press / concerned about the amount of ~ / government ~ / lots of films are heavily censored*

challenging something that is challenging is difficult in a way that you enjoy: *a ~ job / a ~ course / give children interesting and ~ work / a very ~ problem*

close-knit a close-knit group of people know each other well and help each other: *it's a very ~ town / a ~ community / a ~ family / a ~ group*

crack down on if people crack down on a problem, they take strong action to deal with it. The noun is **crackdown**: *they're ~ing down on fraud / ~ crime / ~ing down on bullying in schools / ~ down hard on drug dealing / a government crackdown on crime / launch a crackdown on tax evasion*

damp damp is wet weather. **Damp** is also an adjective: *a month of ~ and drizzle / a ~ day / ~ weather / a ~ climate*

devout someone who is devout has strong religious beliefs: *she's very ~ / a ~ Christian / a ~ Muslim / a ~ Hindu / a ~ Catholic*

dominate if someone dominates, they control something or have a lot of power. The noun is **domination**: *we live in a male-~d society / tends to ~ the conversation / she's completely ~d by her husband / the industry is ~d by large multinationals / male domination*

drizzle drizzle is light, fine rain. **Drizzle** is also a verb: *a month of damp and ~ / a light ~ fell all day / a fine ~ / a steady ~ / it drizzled on and off all day*

fraud fraud is the crime of saying things that are not true in order to get money or achieve power. The adjective is **fraudulent**: *they're cracking down on ~ / tax ~ / insurance ~ / credit card ~ / allegations of electoral ~ / fraudulent business activities / a fraudulent insurance claim*

fuel to fuel something means to make it stronger or worse: *government policies that could ~ inflation / ~ people's fears / ~ her anxieties / ~ his anger / ~ rumours that the president could resign*

get away with if you get away with a crime, you are not punished for it: *they won't ~ it / ~ murder / I'd do it if I thought I could ~ it*

heavily if something happens heavily, it happens a lot. The adjective is **heavy**: *films are ~ censored / he drinks quite ~ / smokes ~ / she's ~ involved in politics / a lot of families have borrowed ~ / a heavy drinker / his heavy involvement in the charity*

infuriating something that is infuriating is extremely annoying. The adjective is **infuriated**: *he found the traffic absolutely ~ / it's really ~ / I was absolutely infuriated*

isolated an isolated place is a long way from other places: *an ~ village / an ~ community / people lead quite ~ lives / feel ~ from other people / be socially ~*

mild mild weather is quite warm: *the winters are incredibly ~ / a ~ climate / ~ weather / the weather's turned ~*

overstatement an overstatement is a statement that expresses something too strongly. The verb is **overstate**. The opposite is **understatement**: *I think that's an ~ / a bit of an ~ / it's an ~ to say that he lied / I think he's overstating its importance / that's an understatement!*

red tape red tape is official rules that prevent things from happening quickly: *a lot of companies are trying to cut ~ / reduce the amount of government ~ / bureaucratic ~ / it takes ages to get through all the ~*

scene a scene is the people and places that are involved with a particular activity: *there's a thriving music ~ / involved in the political ~ / part of the local art ~ / the drug ~*

secular something that is secular is not controlled by a church or religious authority. The opposite is **religious**: *a ~ state / a ~ education system / a ~ society / a ~ ruler*

stereotype a stereotype is a fixed idea about what a particular kind of person is like. The adjective is **stereotypical**: *a ~ of a businessman / national ~s / the ~s about the country / the traditional ~s / challenge sexual ~s / he doesn't conform to the ~s / a stereotypical teenager*

tackle if you tackle a problem, you try to find a solution to it: *the film ~s some difficult issues / the government is determined to ~ this problem / ~ unemployment / firefighters are still tackling the fire*

PAGES 16–17

bemusement bemusement is a feeling of being confused. The adjective is **bemused**: *he reacted with ~ / a look of ~ on her face / complete ~ / look bemused / feel completely bemused*

bizarre something that is bizarre is very strange: *a ~ instrument / ~ behaviour / a ~ combination of clothes / it's a bit ~ / it was really ~*

brew when you brew tea or coffee, you make it. You also brew beer: *you ~ tea in it / leave the tea to ~ for a while / beer has been ~ed for centuries here*

bucket a bucket is a container with a handle for carrying water: *a ~ of water / a mop and ~ / fill the ~ with water / a full ~ / carrying a ~ of soapy water*

craze a craze is something that becomes very popular for a short time: *there was a real ~ for them at school / the latest ~ / a passing ~ / a new fashion ~ / a dance ~*

drill a drill is a tool that you use for making holes in things. **Drill** is also a verb: *an electric ~ / a power ~ / use a ~ / ~ a hole in the wall / ~ through the wood*

flush when you flush a toilet, you press a handle and water cleans the toilet: *~ the toilet / the toilet won't ~ / ~ everything away / ~ it down the toilet*

knot a knot is a place where rope or string is tied tightly. **Knot** is also a verb: *tie a ~ in the rope / I can't undo this ~ / a ~ in my shoelaces / a tight ~ / a loose ~ / the string was tightly knotted*

loads loads of something is a very large amount or number: *I bought ~ of things / ~ of money / ~ of people / ~ of time / I've got ~ to do*

mend if you mend something, you repair it: *need to ~ my shirt / ~ the TV / ~ the door / ~ the car / can you ~ it?*

pad a pad is a thick piece of cloth or rubber that you use, for example, to protect something: *knee ~s / elbow ~s / a ~ of cotton wool / a cleaning ~*

pin a pin is a thin, sharp piece of metal that you use for holding pieces of cloth together while you are sewing. **Pin** is also a verb: *the dress was held together with ~s / a safety ~ / stick a ~ in the map / ~ the two pieces of cloth together*

rant if you rant, you complain about something angrily for a long time. **Rant** is also a noun: *~ about the government / he used to ~ about it / kept ~ing on about the money / stop ~ing! / a long rant about injustice*

rinse when you rinse something, you wash it in clean water to remove soap or dirt. **Rinse** is also a noun: *I ~d my glass / ~ my face / ~ the dishes / wash your hair and then ~ it / give it a quick ~*

rip if you rip something, you damage it by tearing it. **Rip** is also a noun: *~ your jeans / ~ the map / ~ the letter open / careful you don't ~ your skirt / ~ my dress on a nail / my clothes were ripped to shreds / a ~ in my jeans*

soak if you soak something, you get it completely wet: *~ the jeans in warm water / leave the beans to ~ overnight / I was completely ~ed*

scope the scope of something is how many different things it covers or deals with: *there was no cooker, which reduced the ~ of my cooking / the ~ of the new legislation / broaden the ~ of the enquiry / increase the ~ / narrow the ~ / it's outside the ~ of this book*

spill if you spill water, you accidentally pour it out of its container. The past tense and past participle is **spilled** or **spilt**. The noun is **spill** or **spillage**: *~ some water on the floor / mind you don't ~ your coffee / ~ wine all over the table / ~ tomato ketchup on my shirt / an oil spillage*

stain if you stain something, you leave a dirty mark on it by accident. **Stain** is also a noun: *~ my shirt / ~ the carpet / my fingers were ~ed with ink / my shirt was ~ed green / a coffee ~ on my shirt / blood ~s / can't get this ~ out / use ~ remover*

steep a steep slope rises or falls quickly. The adverb is **steeply**: *a ~ hill / a ~ slope / a ~ climb to the top / most toilets have ~ sides / the path rises steeply*

straw a straw is a long thin tube that you can drink through: *a drinking ~ / a plastic ~ / a metal ~ / drink through a ~ / sip the lemonade through a ~*

strike if something strikes you, you suddenly think of it. The past tense and past participle is **struck**: *a couple of things struck me / the thought suddenly struck me / it ~s me that it might be best to keep quiet about this / the first thing that struck me was how old he looked / he struck me as being not very intelligent / does something ~ you as odd about this?*

struggle if you struggle to do something, you find it very difficult. **Struggle** is also a noun: *~ to understand the text / ~ with the heavy bags / ~ to bring up a family / ~ for survival / the ~ for political freedom*

sweep if you sweep something, you clean it with a brush. The past tense and past participle is **swept**: *~ the floor / ~ the path / I'll help you ~ up / swept the dirt under the carpet*

tap a tap is a device you use for controlling the flow of water or gas: *the water that comes out of the ~ / the cold ~ / the hot ~ / a mixer ~ / the bath ~s / a gas ~ / turn the ~ on / turn the ~ off / the ~'s dripping*

thread when you thread something, you put thread or string through a hole. **Thread** is also a noun: *can't even ~ a needle / ~ the rope through the gap / a long piece of ~ / cotton ~ / polyester ~*

widespread if something is widespread, it happens in a lot of places or affects a lot of people: *I don't know how ~ this is / a ~ problem / he has ~ support / ~ protests about the war / the birds are becoming more ~*

wring out when you wring out a cloth, you squeeze it tightly to remove most of the water. The past tense and past participle is **wrung out**: *~ out the cloth / ~ out my wet shirt*

PAGES 18–19

abuse abuse is cruel or unfair treatment of someone, for example by hitting them or shouting at them. **Abuse** is also a verb: *sometimes has to deal with ~ / a victim of ~ / physical ~ / sexual ~ / verbal ~ / suffered years of ~ / she was abused as a child*

acquire if you acquire something, you get it: *keen to ~ British nationality / ~ some books / ~ information / ~ a disease / ~ the skills you need*

ancestry your ancestry is all the members of your family who lived a long time ago. Individual members of your family who lived a long time ago are your **ancestors**: *they nourish a common delusion about their ~ / what do you know about your ~? / can trace their ~ back three hundred years / find out more about your ancestors*

assumption an assumption is something that you think is true although you have no proof. The verb is **assume**: *don't make the ~ that everyone agrees with you / it's a false ~ / we're working on the ~ that the game will go ahead / I assumed you wanted to come with us*

autonomy if an area has autonomy, it has the right to rule itself: *the regions have a lot of ~ from central government / want more ~ / fighting for more ~*

breed a breed of animal is a type of animal that has been created by people: *different ~s of dog / ~s of cattle*

comfort to comfort someone means to make them feel happier and less worried or upset. **Comfort** is also a noun: *I tried to ~ her / it's a very ~ing thought / religion can be a source of ~*

commerce commerce is the business of buying and selling things. The adjective is **commercial**: *the economy is driven by ~ / international ~ / the company's commercial interests*

diverse things that are diverse are of many different types: *a ~ group of people / they have ~ interests / from ~ backgrounds / a ~ range of subjects*

drive if something drives a process or system, it makes it work: *the economy is driven by commerce / the motivation that ~s me / what drove her to commit murder?*

elite the elite are the people in a country or organisation who have all the power: *the ruling ~ / a small political ~ / the governing ~ / top business leaders form an ~*

found when you found a country or an organisation, you form it: *my grandfather ~ed the company / ~ a new charity / ~ a newspaper / nations are partly ~ed on negatives*

heritage a country's heritage is all the traditions, beliefs, buildings, art, etc. that it has: *the need to protect our ~ / preserve our ~ / proud of their ~*

inhabit if people inhabit a place, they live there. The people who live in a place are the **inhabitants**: *the people who ~ this land / the island is not ~ed / the inhabitants of Greece*

nourish if you nourish something, you encourage it to develop or spread: *they ~ a common delusion about their ancestry / ~ young talent*

priest a priest is a religious leader in some Christian churches: *a Catholic ~ / the parish ~ / become a ~ / women ~s*

propagate if you propagate ideas, you make them spread to a lot of people: *the ideas ~d by Marx / traditions are ~d through education and the media*

ruling the ruling people in a country are the people who have political power: *the ~ elite / the ~ classes / the ~ party / Fifa, football's ~ body*

retain if you retain something, you keep it. The noun is **retention**: *~ a sense of family roots / wants to ~ her independence / the company finds it difficult to ~ staff / want to ~ control of the organisation / their retention of power*

static something that is static does not move or change: *identity is not ~ / the economy is ~ / prices look set to remain ~*

wildly if something happens wildly, it happens a lot, or in an extreme way: *people's cultural identity can vary ~ / the statistics are ~ inaccurate / the show is ~ popular*

IDIOMS

close to the bone a remark that is close to the bone is very close to the truth in a way that can hurt or offend someone. The idiom comes from the idea of an injury that can be close to the bone and so is almost always extremely serious: *some of his comments were a bit ~ / some of her jokes are too ~*

EXERCISES

PREPOSITIONS

A Complete the sentences with the correct preposition.

1 Can you deal .... this problem?
2 We've had a month .... damp weather.
3 We live .... a male-dominated society.
4 Industry is controlled .... multi-national companies.
5 He was punished .... his crime.
6 The house is a long way .... here.
7 Soak the towels .... hot water.
8 It's best to keep quiet .... that.

WORD FAMILIES

A Complete the expression with the correct form of the word in bold.

1 the move to **abolish** conscription — the .... of slavery
2 **fraudulent** practices — be accused of ....
3 a **heavy** smoker — he smokes ....
4 a traditional **stereotype** — behaviour ....
5 a **bemused** reaction — a look of ....
6 a **steep** hill — the road rises ....
7 I **assume** that's correct — an incorrect ....
8 international **commerce** — a .... district

COLLOCATIONS

A Complete the sentences with the correct form of the verbs in the list.

soak	increase	struck	work	get
rip	tackle			

1 I need to .... rid of this old furniture.
2 We need new ways to .... this problem.
3 Argentina were .... to shreds by Germany in the World Cup.
4 We got completely .... in the thunder storm.
5 We plan to .... the scope of the enquiry.
6 It suddenly .... me how much she had changed.
7 We're .... on the assumption that the project will go ahead.

B Complete the missing adjectives.

1 I live in a c _ _ _ _ - _ _ t community.
2 She's always been a h _ _ _ y smoker.
3 He went on a l _ _ g rant about the government.
4 Give it a q _ _ _ k rinse under the tap.
5 He's suffered years of v _ _ _ _ l abuse.
6 My classmates come from d _ _ _ _ _ e backgrounds.
7 The Chinese c _ _ _ _ _ l government is in Beijing.
8 He was acting on a f _ _ _ e assumption.

C Complete the expressions with the words in the lists.

craze	pin	punishment	corruption
evasion	drill	elite	

1 the ruling ....
2 a safety ....
3 a power ....
4 the latest ....
5 bribery and ....
6 capital ....
7 tax ....

PATTERNS

A Complete the sentences with the correct form of the verbs in the list. Use *to-* infinitive or *–ing*.

happen	commit	protect	attempt	carry	rant

1 He's been charged with .... to bribe officials.
2 Red tape prevents things from .... quickly.
3 It's important .... your heritage.
4 Use a bucket for .... water.
5 He kept .... on about problems at work.
6 What drove her .... the crime?

PHRASAL VERBS

A Complete the sentences with the correct form of the phrasal verbs in the list.

wring out	get away with	get through
bring up	crack down	sweep up

1 I need to .... my wet T-shirt.
2 Can you .... this mess, please?
3 It's difficult to .... a family on my salary.
4 I'm trying to .... all my work before the weekend.
5 He thought he could .... not paying his income tax.
6 Police are .... on corrupt officials.

03

RELATIONSHIPS

absent-minded someone who is absent-minded often forgets things. The adverb is **absent-mindedly**: *she's quite ~ / he's getting a bit ~ / getting more ~ as she gets older / absent-mindedly put my keys down somewhere*

approachable someone who is approachable is friendly, so other people find it easy to talk to them. The opposite is **unapproachable**: *he's very ~ / important for teachers to be ~ / she's a bit unapproachable*

bitchy someone who is bitchy often says unkind things about other people behind their backs. The noun is **bitchiness**: *she's really ~ / a ~ comment / ~ remarks / a ~ conversation / a lot of bitchiness in the office*

cynic a cynic is someone who does not believe that people are good or honest. The adjective is **cynical** and the noun is **cynicism**: *you're just a ~ / a bit of a ~ when it comes to politics / people might call me a ~ / a hardened ~ / don't want to appear cynical / a bit cynical about her motives / listened to him with growing cynicism*

direct someone who is direct expresses their opinions and feelings in a clear and honest way: *she's very ~ / asked some very ~ questions*

hog if you hog something, you keep it or use it yourself rather than sharing it with other people: *he'd always ~ the remote-control / she always ~s the bathroom in the mornings*

incompetent someone who is incompetent does not have the ability to do a job well. The noun is **incompetence**: *she's completely ~ / an ~ teacher / accused the president of being ~ / grossly ~ / accused her of incompetence*

laid-back someone who is laid-back is very relaxed and doesn't get angry or upset easily: *she's very*

~ / ~ about everything / a ~ approach to life / a ~ attitude to exams

look down on if you look down on someone, you think that you are better than they are: *get the feeling he ~s down on me / ~s down on anyone who hasn't been to university*

principle the principle behind something is the general idea or plan that it is based on: *the idea is OK in ~ / the ~ behind the national health service / basic educational ~s / the ~ that everyone should pay the same amount*

prone if you are prone to something, you often do it, or it often happens to you: *I'm a bit ~ to treading on toes / he's ~ to forget things / ~ to coughs and colds / ~ to the disease / he's very accident-~*

stand up for if you stand up for something, you support it: *she ~s up for what she believes in / ~ your rights / ~ yourself / no one stood up for me*

strong-willed someone who is strong-willed is determined to do something even if other people do not want them to: *she's very ~ / quite ~*

thick-skinned someone who is thick-skinned is not easily offended or upset when other people criticise them. The opposite is **thin-skinned**: *she's quite ~ / incredibly ~ / try not to be so thin-skinned*

acrimonious something that is acrimonious involves a lot of arguing: *an ~ divorce / an ~ meeting / a rather ~ discussion*

amicable something that is amicable is done or discussed in a friendly way. The adverb is **amicably**: *an ~ divorce / an ~ relationship / an ~ agreement / an ~ discussion / it was all very ~ / it was all agreed quite amicably*

annulment if there is an annulment of an agreement or a marriage, it is stated formally that it no longer exists. The verb is **annul**: *seeking an ~ of the marriage / the ~ of the agreement / asked for the marriage to be annulled*

backdrop the backdrop to an event is the general situation in which it happens: *the news comes against the ~ of a series of celebrity divorces / negotiations took place against a ~ of continued fighting*

beg if you beg, you ask for something in a strong, emotional way: *I begged her father to open the door / ~ for mercy / ~ his forgiveness / I begged to go with them*

burden a burden is something that you are responsible for or have to deal with: *share the ~ of housework / shouldn't have to bear this ~ alone / shoulder the ~ / the ~ of care for young children / unemployment places a heavy ~ on the state*

chronically something that happens chronically continues to happen over a long period of time. The adjective is **chronic**: *~ high divorce rates / the* *health service is ~ underfunded / ~ ill / a chronic problem / a chronic illness*

comply if you comply with something, you do what it asks you to do: *the Pope would not ~ with Henry's wishes / ~ with her request / ~ with the regulations*

custody if someone has custody of a child, they have the right to take care of the child after a divorce: *get ~ of the children / be awarded ~ / a dispute over who should have ~ / fight for ~ / a ~ battle / sole ~ / joint ~*

distinction if someone has a distinction, they are different or special in some way: *Finland and Belarus share this dubious ~ / has the ~ of being the cleanest city in Europe / holds the ~ of being the first woman president*

dubious something that is dubious is not good, safe, or honest: *his alibi seemed a bit ~ to me / a rather ~ reputation / highly ~ / Finland and Belarus share this ~ distinction*

file if you file a legal case, you officially start it and ask for it to happen: *couples who ~ for divorce / ~ a complaint / ~ a lawsuit against the company*

go through if a legal decision goes through, it is accepted or approved: *when the divorce goes through / the agreement has gone through / a new law going through Parliament*

grant if someone grants something, they officially allow it: *persuaded an archbishop to ~ him his divorce / ~ her request / ~ his wish / ~ed him permission to build a house*

grounds the grounds for something are the reasons for doing it: *the ~ for divorce / had reasonable ~ for arresting him / good ~ for suspecting him / opposed it on moral ~ / on medical ~ / on environmental ~*

heir the heir to something is the person who will get it when someone else dies: *a male ~ to the throne / the ~ to the family fortune / the rightful ~ / the legitimate ~ / his son and ~*

high-profile something that is high-profile gets a lot of attention from the public and press: *a ~ divorce case / a ~ court case / a ~ environmental campaign / ~ celebrities / a ~ politician*

instigate if you instigate a process, you start it. The noun is **instigation**: *most divorces are ~d by women / ~ a programme of reforms / ~ a riot / ~ peace talks / done at the president's instigation*

maintenance maintenance is an amount of money that someone pays regularly to their former husband or wife after a divorce: *he refuses to pay ~ for the children / tried to claim ~ from him / gets £50 a week in ~ / ~ payments*

mutual something that is mutual is shared by two people: *get a divorce on the grounds of ~ separation / reach a ~ agreement / ~ respect / ~ trust / ~ understanding / an agreement that is of ~ benefit / a ~ friend*

phenomenon a phenomenon is something that happens. The plural is **phenomena**: *high divorce rates are a modern ~ / poverty is not a new ~ / a natural ~ / the growing ~ of youth crime*

sanction if you sanction something, you officially allow it or accept it: *all divorces have to be ~ed by the Pope / refused to ~ the marriage / the talks were officially ~ed / would never ~ violence*

split if there is a split between people or organisations, they officially separate. **Split** is also a verb and **split up** is a phrasal verb: *a ~ from the Church of Rome / the ~ between church and state / a major ~ in the party / led to a ~ between the two groups / after his ~ with his wife / the party ~ over the issue of tax cuts / she and her husband have now split up*

PAGES 24–25

answer back if a child answers back, they answer an adult rudely: *children who are cheeky and ~ / don't ~!*

blow over if an argument blows over, it ends: *I think it'll all ~ / it'll soon ~ / it's blown over now / these things usually ~ quite quickly*

channel if you channel something in a particular way, you direct or encourage it in that way: *the sibling rivalry is all channelled into tennis / ~ young people into higher education / ~ all his energy into writing / ~ more money into the health service*

cheeky someone who is cheeky is slightly rude to someone in authority: *children who are ~ and answer back / don't be ~! / it was a bit ~ of me / a ~ grin*

commitment a commitment is something that you have to do or have promised to do: *a time in your life when you have no ~s / have a lot of financial ~s / work ~s / family ~s*

drift apart if people drift apart, their relationship gradually ends: *they just ~ed apart / gradually ~ apart / ~ apart over the years / start to ~ apart*

faculties your faculties are your mental abilities: *she's starting to lose her ~ / still has all his ~ / still in possession of all her ~ / her mental ~*

frail someone who is frail is physically weak and not very healthy: *she's quite ~ now / very ~ / a very ~ old lady / getting a bit ~ / starting to grow ~ / old and ~*

home a home is a place where people are looked after: *she's in a ~ / going into a ~ / an old people's ~ / a residential ~ / a nursing ~ / a children's ~*

mercy if you show mercy to someone, you are kind to them and don't hurt or punish them: *she showed no ~ to me in the Open last year / begged for ~ / threw myself on his ~*

put up with if you put up with something unpleasant, you accept it: *I wouldn't ~ it / can't ~ this any longer / I don't know how you ~ it / refuse to ~ this behaviour*

register when you register for something, you put your name on the list for it. **Register** is also a noun: *you should ~ with another doctor / ~ as unemployed / ~ for the class / ~ to vote / put your name on the ~ / the electoral ~*

ruthless someone who is ruthless is determined to get what they want and doesn't worry about hurting or offending other people. The adverb is **ruthlessly**: *we can both be pretty ~ with each other / a ~ businessman / a ~ politician / ruthlessly pursued her own career*

sake if you do something for the sake of a person or thing, you do it to help that person or thing. If you do something **for the sake of it**, you do it for no particular reason: *they seemed to be disagreeing for the ~ of it / tried to keep the marriage together for the ~ of the children*

sibling your siblings are your brothers and sisters: *a lot of ~ rivalry between us / get on well with your ~s*

single out if you single someone out, you choose them and treat them in a different way: *I think she's just singling him out for punishment / be ~d out for special treatment / ~d out for an award / films that are ~d out as being particularly good*

tendency if there is a tendency for something to happen, it is likely that it will happen: *he has a ~ to be a bit cheeky / a ~ towards sentimental autobiographical writing / a ~ for women to get married later / a man with suicidal tendencies*

thrash if you thrash someone, you defeat them easily. The noun is **thrashing**: *she ~ed me in the Open last year / we ~ed them 7–0 / they absolutely ~ed us / gave them a 6–0 thrashing*

toddler a toddler is a young child who is just learning to walk: *a mother with a young ~ / a group for mothers and ~s*

trait a trait is a quality in someone's character: *what ~s are there in your family? / a personality ~ / character ~s / genetic ~s*

turn out the way something turns out is the way it is in the end: *it ~s out she has a couple of kids already / it ~ed out that we were all wrong / everything ~ed out OK in the end / hope it ~s out well*

unsteady if something is unsteady, it is not very stable and is likely to fall: *she's a bit ~ on her feet / the ladder looks a bit ~ / very ~*

wet if you wet the bed, you urinate in your bed: *she ~s the bed occasionally / worried about wetting the bed*

be getting on if someone is getting on, they are getting quite old: *she must ~ now / he's getting on a bit now*

be hard work if someone is hard work, you have to make a lot of effort to have a good relationship with them. A job that is hard work requires a lot of effort: *she's quite ~ / he's very ~ at times / it was ~ shifting all those stones*

cover a multitude of sins to cover a multitude of sins means to hide individual problems or faults. A sin is literally an action that is considered to be an offense against God: *the term 'unreasonable behaviour' can cover a ~*

full of yourself if you are full of yourself, you have a very high opinion of yourself: *he's so full of himself / she's really full of herself*

hit it off if people hit it off, they get on well with each other: *we ~ straightaway / I really ~ with him*

not lift a finger if you don't lift a finger, you make no effort at all to help someone with a job. The image is of someone who doesn't move even one finger of their hand to do something: *he never lifted a finger around the house / they don't lift a finger to help*

not mince your words if you don't mince your words, you say exactly what you think even if this might offend or upset people: *she doesn't mince her words / he didn't mince his words at all*

out of the blue if something happens out of the blue, it happens very unexpectedly. The image is of something that falls suddenly from the sky (the blue): *he got an email ~ / it was completely ~*

put your foot down if you put your foot down, you say very strongly that someone must do something: *we should put our foot down with him / it's time to ~*

set your heart on if you set your heart on something, you very strongly want to have it or do it: *once she's set her heart on something, there's no stopping her / he's set his heart on studying law*

stab someone in the back if you stab someone in the back, you say or do something that will harm them when they are not present. If you stab someone in the back literally, you stab them with a knife in their back: *she'll stab you in the back the minute you're not there / scared of being stabbed in the back*

take it all in your stride if you take something in your stride, you accept it and deal with it easily. A stride is literally a step that you take, so if you take something in your stride, you keep walking and don't struggle or fall: *he seems to have taken it all in his stride / she takes everything in her stride*

EXERCISES

PREPOSITIONS

A Complete the sentences with the correct preposition.

1 She's a bit .... a cynic.
2 He has a laid-back approach .... life.
3 Can I go .... you to the shops?
4 Have you registered .... the cooking class?
5 I'm worried .... losing my job.
6 You haven't complied .... the regulations.
7 The government has started a programme .... reforms.

WORD FAMILIES

A Complete the expression with the correct form of the word in bold.

1 that's a bit **cynical**   a hardened ....
2 accused of **incompetence**   he's completely ....
3 an **amicable** arrangement   it was agreed ....
4 an **annulment** of the marriage   try to .... the contract
5 a real **thrashing**   we .... them 5-0
6 **instigate** change   done at the .... of the president
7 a **chronic** situation   we're .... understaffed

IDIOMS

A Complete the idiom with the correct word in the list.

back	blue	finger	off	heart	on

1 I trusted him, but he stabbed me in the ....
2 I introduced them and they hit it .... immediately.
3 I'm not sure how old he is but he's getting .... a bit.
4 I do all the cooking. He never lifts a ....
5 He's really set his .... on being a pilot one day.
6 It was really unexpected. Completely out of the ....

COLLOCATIONS

A Complete the sentences with the correct form of the verbs in the list.

shoulder	file	drift	has	hold
award	throw	pay		

1 He .... himself at the mercy of the court.
2 You don't have to .... the burden on your own.
3 The mother was .... custody of the child.
4 He .... the distinction of being the youngest president.
5 Her parents are .... for divorce.
6 The father .... maintenance every month.
7 They were good friends but then they .... apart.
8 She's old but she still .... all her faculties.

B Complete the missing nouns.

1 Negotiations took place against a b _ _ _ _ _ _ p of violence.
2 There are no reasonable g _ _ _ _ _ s to charge the suspect.
3 My colleague and I have a mutual f _ _ _ _ d.
4 Sibling r _ _ _ _ _ y can be a real issue in families.
5 Would you put your parents in a nursing h _ _ e?
6 Some depressed people have suicidal t _ _ _ _ _ _ _ _ s.
7 My sister and I share many character t _ _ _ _ s.

C Match the two halves of the collocation.

1 do something for   a) custody
2 on moral   b) agreement
3 joint   c) the sake of it
4 beg for   d) the throne
5 a heavy   e) grounds
6 the heir to   f) mercy
7 a mutual   g) burden

PHRASAL VERBS

A Complete the sentences with the correct form of the phrasal verbs in the list.

turn out	stand up	blow over	split up
look after	go through	single out	

1 It .... that you were right and I was wrong.
2 She was .... for praise by the boss.
3 Could you .... my plants while I'm away?
4 We had an argument but it's all .... now.
5 They .... after ten years together.
6 It's important to .... for your rights.
7 She's just .... a really difficult time.

04

POLITICS

PAGES 26–27

bid a bid is an attempt to get or achieve something: *a ~ to hold the Olympics here / a successful ~ / put in a ~ / launch a ~ to take over the company / a ~ for power / a takeover ~*

compound if something compounds a problem, it makes it worse: *it'll ~ the existing problems / ~ the difficulties*

curb if you curb something, you control it or limit it: *it might help to ~ drug addiction / ~ the spread of the virus / ~ inflation / ~ violent crime*

declare if you declare money that you earn, you state officially that you have earned it, so that you will pay tax on it: *they ~ it as part of their income / ~ all your earnings / only ~s half his income*

devastate if something devastates a place, it causes a lot of damage in it. The adjective is **devastating** and the noun is **devastation**: *the hurricane could ~ the area / the city was ~d by an earthquake / a devastating storm / the floods caused devastation in the area*

go ahead if you go ahead, you do something that you have planned to do. The noun is **go-ahead**: *they want to ~ with the proposal / ~ and arrange the trip / the plans have been given the go-ahead*

judgment an opinion you have about something: *I can't pass ~ on this / it's difficult to form a ~ / make a ~ / I'll reserve ~ for the moment / a personal ~*

legacy a legacy is something that a person or thing leaves after they have gone: *they say the Olympics will leave a good ~ / the ~ of poverty left by the war / leave an enduring ~ / a ~ from the last century*

obscene something that is obscene is completely unacceptable. Something that is obscene is also very rude or offensive. The noun is **obscenity**: *some of the salaries are ~ / ~ language / made an ~ gesture / shouting obscenities at us*

outweigh if one thing outweighs another, it is more important than the other thing: *the negatives ~ the positives / the benefits ~ the risks*

reservation a reservation is a feeling of doubt that you have about whether something is good: *I have some slight ~s / have a few ~s about the company / some major ~s / deep ~s / express his ~s / went ahead despite our ~s*

stand where you stand on a subject is your opinion on it. The noun is **stance**: *where do you ~ on this issue? / what's your stance on capital punishment? / adopt a stance against the agreement*

strain strain is pressure that is on someone or something. **Strain** is also a verb: *it would put an enormous ~ on finances / put a ~ on their relationship / the economy is under considerable ~ / the ~ of being unemployed / could strain the relationship between the two countries*

trigger if something triggers an action, it makes it happen: *the crisis could ~ an election / environmental factors that can ~ cancer / ~ violence / ~ demonstrations*

undermine to undermine something means to make it weaker or less successful: *it'll ~ relations between the two countries / could ~ the economy / ~ confidence in business / ~ his authority*

PAGES 28–29

charisma someone who has charisma has a quality that makes other people like and respect them. The adjective is **charismatic**: *you need ~ to be a political leader / a young businessman with a lot of ~ / she's got a certain ~ / he lacks ~ / a very charismatic leader*

compassion compassion is a strong feeling of sympathy for someone who is suffering. The adjective is **compassionate**: *have a lot of ~ for the victims / feel no ~ / spoke with ~ / acted out of ~ / a caring and compassionate person*

compromise if you compromise, you accept less than you really want in order to reach an agreement. **Compromise** is also a noun: *need the ability to ~ / both sides refused to ~ / prepared to ~ on the salary / in the end we reached a good ~*

curl up if you curl up, you sit or lie with your arms and legs bent close to your body: *he ~s up in fear / ~ up and go to sleep / sitting ~ed up on the sofa*

curse if you curse someone, you say bad things about them because you are angry: *walking along the street cursing the government / ~ him for being late / ~d myself for being so stupid*

defiance if you show defiance, you refuse to do something that someone has told you to do. The verb is **defy**: *an act of ~ against oppression / a gesture of ~ / people protesting in ~ of the government's orders / decided to defy his parents*

dictatorship a dictatorship is a country that has a ruler with complete power. The ruler is a **dictator**: *an extreme ~ / the country is a ~ / live in a ~ / a ruthless dictator*

drag to drag someone somewhere means to take them there by force: *they leapt on him and ~ed him down to the station / ~ myself out of bed in the morning*

flick through if you flick through a book or magazine, you read it or look at it quickly: *he picks up the Bible and ~s through it / ~ through the photo album / ~ing through a magazine*

futile if an action is futile, it is useless because there is no chance that it will be successful. The noun is **futility**: *think it's silly and ~ / a ~ attempt to win power / our efforts proved ~ / the negotiations proved ~ / the futility of war*

glance if you glance at something, you look at it quickly. **Glance** is also a noun: *he ~s around nervously / ~ at your watch / ~ in the mirror / ~d over my shoulder / had a quick ~ at the newspaper / gave an amused ~ in my direction*

humble someone who is humble does not think they are very important. The noun is **humility**: *she's very ~ and down-to-earth / a modest and ~ man / spoke with humility*

leap if you leap, you jump. The past tense and past participle is **leapt**: *~ into the air / they ~ on him and drag him down to the station / ~ over the wall / ~ out of bed in the morning*

misfortune a misfortune is something bad and unlucky that happens to you: *they laugh at their own ~s / make money from the ~s of others / had the ~ to be caught in the storm*

mock if you mock someone, you laugh at them in an unkind way. The noun is **mockery**: *~ing politicians' records in power / it's easy to ~ other people / there was mockery in his voice*

mutter if you mutter, you talk very quietly: *walking down the street ~ing to himself / ~ing under her breath / he ~ed something I couldn't hear*

peer if you peer at something, you look very carefully because you can't see very well: *they ~ out to watch him / ~ing through the window / ~ing into the darkness*

perception your perception of something is the way you think about it, and what you think it is like. The verb is **perceive**: *the public's ~s of politicians / need to change people's ~s of government / her ~ of the situation / he is perceived as a future leader*

regard the way you regard something is the way you think about it, and the opinion you have of it: *they ~ comedians as a threat / ~ it as immoral / he's widely ~ed as one of the best actors ever*

release if something is a release, it allows you to show your feelings and feel less worried or upset: *humour is a ~ for them / provides a ~ / a ~ from pain*

satirical something that is satirical criticises a person or institution by using humour. The noun is **satire**: *a ~ show / a ~ magazine / ~ humour / political satire / his clever use of satire*

shrewd someone who is shrewd is very clever at judging other people and situations: *a ~ politician / a ~ businessman / very ~ / extremely ~*

sneak if you sneak somewhere, you go there quietly and secretly: *he ~s off down a side street / ~ out of the room / ~ up to bed*

sniff if you sniff something, you smell it by breathing in noisily through your nose. **Sniff** is also a noun: *he opens the bottle and ~s it / the dog was ~ing around / had a ~ of the cheese*

substance if something has substance, it expresses good or important ideas: *a politician with no ~ / a lot of ~ in the speech / what he said was completely without ~ / it lacked ~*

track record someone's track record is all the things they have achieved in the past: *his ~ as a politician / a minister with a good ~ / has an excellent ~ / a very poor ~*

allege if you allege that something is true, you suggest that it is true although there is no proof. The noun is **allegation**: *the ~d vote-rigging / it is ~d that he accepted bribes / her ~d involvement in the plot / allegations of corruption*

apathy apathy is the feeling of not being interested or enthusiastic. The adjective is **apathetic**: *the problem of voter ~ / public ~ / felt apathetic about the election*

ballot a ballot is a way of voting in secret, in which each person writes their vote on a piece of paper and puts it in a box. **Ballot** is also a verb: *a strike ~ / holding a ~ on strike action / take part in the ~ / a secret ~ / your ~ paper / the ~ box / ~ the party members*

body a body is an official organisation: *an official ~ / the school's governing ~ / the professional ~ representing doctors*

carry out if you carry out something, you organise it or do it: *~ a poll / ~ research / ~ an investigation / ~ a survey / ~ repairs*

cast when you cast your vote, you give it: *go and ~ your vote / ~ a ballot*

counterpart your counterpart is someone who has the same job as you in a different organisation: *MPs earn more than their ~s abroad / the foreign minister is talking to his American ~*

cover up if people cover up something dishonest or embarrassing, they hide it. The noun is **cover-up**: *~ up a scandal / the affair was ~ed up / accused the government of ~ing up their mistakes / a government cover-up*

determine to determine something means to influence or decide it: *the number of seats they gain is ~d by the percentage of the vote they get / how hard you train will ~ how well you do*

devolve if a government devolves power, it gives it to people at a lower level. The noun is **devolution**: *~ power from central government / ~ more power to the local level / the devolution of power*

erupt if a situation erupts, it suddenly becomes more angry or dangerous: *the scandal ~ed / fighting ~ed on the streets / a political row ~ed*

hollow a hollow victory has no real value or worth: *a ~ victory / a ~ triumph / a ~ win*

irrespective irrespective of something means without taking it into account: *they ridicule all politicians, ~ of their track record / anyone can join, ~ of age*

lobby if you lobby a member of parliament, you try to persuade them that a law should be changed: *~ your MP / ~ politicians / they're ~ing for a change in the law / ~ing against the war*

long-standing something that is long-standing has existed for a long time: *a ~ MP / a ~ dispute / a ~ problem / a ~ agreement*

outspoken someone who is outspoken expresses their opinion openly, even if this annoys or offends other people: *an ~ politician / an ~ opponent of the war / an ~ critic of the government / she's very ~ / extremely ~*

overwhelming something that is overwhelming is very large or great. The adverb is **overwhelmingly**: *an ~ vote in favour / an ~ victory / their ~ defeat / an ~ majority of voters / they were overwhelmingly defeated*

petition a petition is a written request for something, which a lot of people sign. **Petition** is also a verb: *50,000 signatures on the ~ / organise a ~ / launch a ~ / support the ~ / present the ~ to the prime minister / ~ the council to improve bus services*

poll a poll is a way of finding people's opinions by asking a lot of people the same question. The **polls** are an election. A **polling station** is a place where people vote in an election: *an opinion ~ / conduct a ~ / carry out a ~ / thousands of people are going to the ~s / the polling stations open at seven o'clock*

prominent someone who is prominent is very important: *a ~ figure in the anti-war movement / a ~ politician / a ~ scientist / play a ~ role in the government*

pull off if you pull something off, you manage to achieve it unexpectedly: *~ a surprise victory / didn't quite manage to ~ it off / he'll never ~ it off*

referendum a referendum is a vote in which the people in a country make a decision about one particular question: *a ~ on independence / hold a ~ / win the ~ / lose the ~ / this triggers a ~*

rig if people rig a vote, they illegally arrange the result: *claim that the election was rigged / allegations of vote rigging*

run-up the run-up to something is the time leading up to it: *in the ~ to the election / the ~ to the World Cup*

stand if you stand in an election, you try to be elected: *~ as an MP / ~ as a candidate / ~ for Parliament*

standing someone's standing is how popular or respected they are: *have a low ~ in the polls / a politician of high ~ / improve her ~ in the organisation*

turnout the turnout in an election is the number of people who vote: *a ~ of only 40% / voter ~ / a high ~ / a low ~*

IDIOMS

at a loose end if you are at a loose end, you have nothing to do: *I was at a bit of a loose end when he called / I was ~*

landslide victory a landslide victory is one in which one party gets a lot more votes than the other parties. A landslide is a sudden fall of earth or rocks down a mountain, so a landslide victory is like a victory that pushes all opponents out of the way: *a landslide election victory*

play devil's advocate if you play devil's advocate, you pretend to disagree with someone in order to have a good argument with them. The devil is the main evil spirit in some religions, so when you play devil's advocate you represent the devil by putting forward deliberately opposite opinions or arguments: *I was just playing devil's advocate*

EXERCISES

PREPOSITIONS

A Complete the sentences with the correct preposition.

1 The building was damaged ...... an earthquake.
2 I have some concerns ..... the project.
3 He's a leader ..... a lot of charisma.
4 I have a lot of compassion ..... the victims.
5 She's standing ..... a Labour Party candidate.
6 I'm not ..... favour of that idea.
7 He's been the boss ..... a long time.
8 We need to stop the spread ..... the virus.

WORD FAMILIES

A Complete the expression with the correct form of the word in bold.

1 a **devastating** loss	the war .... the area
2 accused of shouting **obscenities**	an .... gesture
3 a neutral **stance**	where do you .... on this?
4 a **charismatic** leader	a performer with great ....
5 a **compassionate** nurse	he feels no ....
6 live in a **dictatorship**	ruled by a ....
7 act with **humility**	a .... person
8 clever use of **satire**	a .... article

COLLOCATIONS

A Complete the sentences with the correct adjective from the list.

enduring	widely	outspoken	obscene
governing	violent	hollow	capital

1 There's a lot of .... crime in this area.
2 The past president left an .... legacy.
3 He sometimes uses .... language when he's angry.
4 I don't believe in .... punishment.
5 His work is .... regarded.
6 She sits on the school's .... body.
7 Although we won it was a .... victory.
8 She's an .... opponent of compulsory military service.

B Complete the missing nouns.

1 I'll reserve j _ _ _ _ _ _ _ t for the time being.
2 His working hours are putting a s _ _ _ _ n on their relationship.
3 Some people in the office are undermining her a _ _ _ _ _ _ _ y.
4 He muttered something under his b _ _ _ _ h.
5 Their argument lacked s _ _ _ _ _ _ _ e.
6 She has a poor academic track r _ _ _ _ d.
7 The government expects everyone to cast their v _ _ e.
8 He's a prominent f _ _ _ _ e in the town council.

C Match the two halves of the collocation.

1 an opinion	a) government
2 central	b) compromise
3 the ballot	c) addiction
4 an act of	d) turnout
5 reach a	e) defiance
6 drug	f) poll
7 a low	g) box

PATTERNS

A Complete the sentences with the correct form of the verbs in the list. Use *to-* infinitive or *–ing*.

judge	peer	compromise	show
hold	represent		

1 A trade union is a body .... workers.
2 He's very good at .... situations.
3 It's unusual for him .... his feelings.
4 There are some people .... through the window.
5 France has put in a bid .... the Olympics.
6 Both sides are not prepared ....

PHRASAL VERBS

A Complete the sentences with the correct form of the phrasal verbs in the list.

flick through	go ahead	sneak out
curl up	pull off	cover up

1 I was really surprised when they .... the deal.
2 The police are accused of .... the evidence.
3 I managed to .... of the conference before the end.
4 I found this ad when I was .... a magazine.
5 I wish I was .... in bed.
6 You can .... and make the reservations.

05

NIGHT OUT, NIGHT IN

PAGES 36-37

burst if you burst out laughing or crying, you suddenly start laughing or crying. The past tense and past participle is **burst**: *I ~ into tears / ~ out shouting at a waiter / ~ out laughing / ~ out crying*

crippled if someone is crippled, their legs are injured and they cannot walk properly: *he dances like a ~ chicken / she's ~ with arthritis*

hassle if you hassle someone, you keep asking them to do something: *I didn't mean to ~ you / keeps hassling me for money / stop hassling me!*

hype if there is hype about something, people talk about it a lot and try to make people think that it is good: *a lot of media ~ about the new show / the film didn't live up to the ~ / fed up with all the ~*

mortified if you feel mortified, you feel extremely embarrassed or ashamed: *I was ~! / felt ~ / absolutely ~ / ~ to hear that her son was involved*

overwhelmed if you feel overwhelmed, you feel very strong emotions and cannot think or speak. Something that is **overwhelming** makes you feel overwhelmed: *I was a bit ~ / felt quite ~ / ~ at people's kindness / it was all a bit overwhelming*

rough if you feel rough, you feel slightly ill: *I was feeling a bit ~ / you look a bit ~ / really ~*

scene if there is a scene, there is a loud, angry argument in a public place: *there was a bit of a ~ / try not to make a ~ / cause a ~ / an angry ~*

stuffed if you feel stuffed, you feel extremely full after a meal: *I was ~ after the meal / feel ~ / absolutely ~*

tread if you tread on something, you stand on it. The past tense is **trod** and the past participle is **trodden**: *don't ~ on my toes / ~ on a piece of glass / ~ dirt into the carpet*

yawn when you yawn, your mouth opens and you breathe in deeply because you are tired. **Yawn** is also a noun: *I couldn't stop yawning / tried to stifle a ~ / suppress a ~*

PAGES 38-39

across-the-board if something happens across-the-board, it involves everyone or everything: *it received good reviews ~ / a pay rise ~ / prices are reduced ~*

awe-inspiring something that is awe-inspiring makes you feel great admiration or respect: *an ~ journey / ~ views / an ~ achievement*

bake when you bake something, you cook it in the oven. **Baking** is cooking bread and cakes: *~ a cake / ~ the fish for 15 minutes / ~d apples / some baking tips*

blur to blur something means to make it less clear. **Blur** is also a noun: *~s the boundary between art and reality / ~ the distinction between life and fiction / suffer from blurred vision / the boats were a ~ in the distance*

burial a burial is a ceremony at which a dead person is buried: *the ~ is next week / go to his ~ / a creepy ~ chamber*

creep if you creep, you move slowly and quietly. The past tense and past participle is **crept**: *~ into the burial chamber / ~ out of the room / ~ past the guards*

creepy something that is creepy makes you feel scared: *a ~ burial chamber / the place was a bit ~ / ~ music / he's really ~*

discard if you discard something, you throw it away: *people ~ their artworks in the bin / ~ the wrapping / some ~ed clothes*

display a display is an arrangement of things for people to look at. **Display** is also a verb: *a ~ of her work / a fantastic ~ of photos / some of the work of art on ~ / they go on ~ at the museum next week / the best way to ~ your art*

disposal the disposal of something is the process of throwing it away. The verb is **dispose of**: *a container for the ~ of works of art / the best way to dispose of old paint*

feature to feature something means to include it or give it special importance. **Feature** is also a noun: *users share their thoughts on ~d titles / a new exhibition featuring works by Rembrandt / violence ~s prominently in his works / one of the car's special ~s*

figure a woman's figure is the shape of her body: *exercise that helps you get a better ~ / she's got a good ~ / lose your ~ as you get older / have to watch my ~*

format the format of something is the way in which it is organised: *the ~ of the classes / use the same ~ for all the shows / change the ~ of the conference*

genre a genre is a type of writing, art, music, etc.: *the traditional landscape ~ / different music ~s / a new ~ of filmmaking*

gory something that is gory shows or describes a lot of blood and violence: *reveal the ~ secrets of surgery in the past / a ~ film / a ~ description / told me all the ~ details*

guidelines guidelines are rules about the best way to do something: *simple ~ for effective weight loss / a new set of ~ / follow the ~ / ~ on the treatment of patients*

hint a hint is a useful piece of advice: *~s and tips on baking / helpful ~s on how to bring up children*

host if you host a show or TV programme, you introduce it. **Host** is also a noun: *the show is ~ed by Kenny Clarkson / a game show ~*

legendary something that is legendary is very famous: *London's ~ Hard Rock Café / a ~ actor / a ~ tennis player / his music is ~*

mark if you mark an important date, you celebrate it: *a display which ~s the centenary of his birth / celebrations to ~ 20 years since the end of the war / ~ the occasion with a party*

onset the onset of something is the beginning of it: *the ~ of war / the ~ of the disease / the ~ of winter*

outstanding something that is outstanding is extremely good: *an ~ rhythm section / an ~ piece of work / an ~ performance / absolutely ~*

quest a quest is a long search for something: *his epic ~ to find his family / her ~ for happiness / the ~ for peace*

release to release a film or CD means to make it available for people. To **re-release** it means to release it again. **Release** and **re-release** are also nouns: *the film is due to be ~d next week / the re-release of the 80's film*

role the role of something is the way it is involved in a situation and the influence it has: *the ~ ice plays in the solar system / the ~ of diet in disease / have an important ~ in the programme's success / play an important ~ / a major ~ / a prominent ~*

shape to shape something means to change it or help to form it: *how ice ~s the landscape / your political beliefs are ~d by your experiences*

slavery slavery is the system of owning people and forcing them to work for you. A person who is owned in this way is a **slave**: *he was sold into ~ / abolish ~ / the abolition of ~ / buying and selling slaves*

soaring something that is soaring is extremely high. If something **soars**, it goes high into the air: *the ~ Gherkin building / ~ skyscrapers / ~ mountains / birds soared above us*

stunning something that is stunning is extremely beautiful: *a ~ church / a ~ building / a ~ painting / a ~ view / absolutely ~ / you look ~!*

take your take on something is the way in which you understand it or interpret it: *an extraordinary ~ on the traditional landscape genre / what's your ~ on this?*

tip a tip is a small piece of advice: *~s relating to baking and decorating / ~s on buying a computer / gave me some useful ~s / got some good ~ s from her*

twist a twist on something is a version of it which is different in a clever way: *a ~ on a classic film / an old story with a new ~*

venture if you venture somewhere, you go there even though it is dangerous: *~ along Brick Lane / didn't dare ~ out / ~ into the room*

wealth a wealth of something is a very large amount or number: *a ~ of hints and tips / a ~ of information*

PAGES 40–41

boast to boast something good means to have it: *the club ~s over two million members / it ~s the best museum in the country*

centre if something centres on an idea or subject, that is the main idea or subject in it: *the novel ~s on the lives of two artists / a debate centring on the cost of education*

coarse something that is coarse is rude and not refined: *the discourse is generally ~ / ~ language / a rather ~ man*

commentator a commentator is someone who gives a description of an event as it is happening. The verb is **commentate**: *a sports ~ / a football ~ / TV ~s / commentating on the game*

conquer if you conquer someone or something, you defeat them: *love ~s all / struggling to ~ his drug addiction / ~ her fears / ~ their enemies*

endorse if a famous person endorses something, they say publicly that they think it is good. The noun is **endorsement**: *agreed to ~ the book / ~ the product / a celebrity endorsement that could be worth millions to the company*

envisage if you can envisage something, you can imagine it happening in the future: *can't ~ him ever getting a job / never ~d the impact she would have / it's difficult to ~*

forum a forum is a place where people can discuss subjects and give their opinions: *an Internet ~ / a ~ for political discussion*

halt to halt something means to stop it. **Halt** is also a noun: *~ the spread of the disease / ~ the search / ~ the economic decline / ~ work on the project / bring the traffic to a ~*

heart-wrenching something that is heart-wrenching makes you feel very sad: *talks about her alcoholism in ~ detail / a ~ story / ~ photos*

hectic something that is hectic is extremely busy: *we live in ~ times / a ~ day / a ~ social life / a ~ lifestyle*

insight insight is an understanding of a difficult subject or situation: *her writing is full of ~ / the work displays limited ~ / gives us an ~ into her life / some fresh ~s into his mind*

instigate if you instigate something, you start it: *the person who ~d the idea / ~ the peace talks / ~ the violence / ~ reforms*

memoir a memoir is an account that someone writes of their own life and work: *a moving ~ / a political ~ / writing her ~s / publish his ~s*

minimal if something is minimal, there is only a very small amount of it: *there is ~ dialogue in the novel / caused only ~ damage / hope the delay will be ~ / the cost will be ~*

narrator the narrator in a novel is the person who tells the story: *the ~ is a fourteen-year-old boy*

overload if there is an overload of something, there is too much. **Overload** is also a verb: *an ~ of information / suffering from information ~ / feeling ~ed with work*

portrayal a portrayal of something is the way in which it is shown or described. The verb is **portray**: *a vivid ~ of love / the ~ of the president in the press / the film portrays him as proud and arrogant*

protagonist a protagonist is one of the characters in a film or book, or one of the people taking part in an event: *a dialogue between the two ~s / the main ~s in the war*

ranking something's ranking is its position on a list which shows the best things of its kind: *the Amazon ~s / currently third in the world tennis ~s*

revolve around to revolve around something means to have that thing as the most important part: *her life ~s around the children / their lives ~ around food / thinks the world ~s around her*

royalty a royalty is an amount of money that is paid to an author or composer depending on how many of their books or songs are sold: *~ payments / pay him a ~ / gets millions in royalties*

sparse if something is sparse, there is only a very small amount of it. The adverb is **sparsely**: *the ~, minimal dialogue / a ~ population / a sparsely populated area*

spawn to spawn something means to cause it to start: *the phenomenon has ~ed some interesting new groups / the book ~ed an excellent TV series*

surge a surge is a sudden large increase in something. **Surge** is also a verb: *the ~ in the popularity of book clubs / a ~ of interest / a sudden ~ of anger / petrol prices have ~d*

tale a tale is a story: *an uplifting ~ / folk ~s / fairy ~s / the ~ of a young soldier / told me his ~*

trace if you trace the development of something, you study or describe it: *the book ~s the history of the feminist movement / ~ your ancestry / ~ the development of trade unions*

track if you track something, you follow it so that you can find where it is: *users can ~ the movement of items / ~ an animal through the woods / ~ing the criminals / ~ your parcel*

vivid a vivid description or memory is very clear and real: *a ~ portrayal of love and politics / a ~ memory of that day / a very ~ picture in my mind / has a very ~ imagination*

IDIOMS

in bits if someone is in bits, they are extremely upset and cannot think clearly. If an object is in bits, it is broken into a lot of pieces: *she was ~ / I was ~ after my divorce / the radio was lying on the floor ~*

in stitches if you are in stitches, you are laughing a lot and cannot stop. A stitch is a pain that you get in your side, which you can get by running or laughing a lot: *a routine that will have you ~ / we were all ~ / I couldn't run anymore because I had a stitch*

off your head if you are off your head, you are very drunk or have taken drugs and cannot think clearly: *he was off his head / completely off her head*

on top of things if you are on top of things, you have a situation under control: *thanks for being so ~ / feeling a bit more ~ now / trying to get ~*

take the mickey if you take the mickey, you say things to make people laugh at someone: *stop taking the mickey out of me! / there's no need to ~*

too much on if you have too much on, you are too busy: *I've got ~ at the moment*

toss and turn if you toss and turn, you keep moving around in bed because you cannot sleep. To toss something literally means to throw it: *I was tossing and turning all night / toss the letter into the bin*

EXERCISES

PREPOSITIONS

A Complete the sentences with the correct preposition.

1 There's a lot of hype .... his new film.
2 She suffers .... diabetes.
3 The gallery has his art .... display.
4 The German football team is ranked 3rd .... the world.
5 What's the format ...... the show?
6 What are your thoughts .... the issue?
7 We live .... interesting times.
8 I think this is the onset .... winter.

WORD FAMILIES

A Complete the expression with the correct form of the word in bold.

1 a bit **overwhelming**   I felt ....
2 how was she **portrayed**?   an accurate ....
3 he **endorsed** the product   a good ....
4 who is **commentating**?   a rugby ....
5 the building **soared** above us   .... mountains
6 he works like a **slave**   the abolition of ....

IDIOMS

A Complete the idiom with the correct word in the list.

bits	head	stitches	turning

1 I couldn't sleep. I was tossing and .... all night.
2 He was in .... after he lost his job.
3 She's really funny. She always has me in ....
4 He's drunk and off his ....

COLLOCATIONS

A Complete the sentences with the correct form of the verbs in the list.

revolve	due	take	halt
burst	write	play	make

1 My daughter dropped her ice cream and .... into tears.

2 He .... a scene and embarrassed everyone.
3 His life .... around his work.
4 Their new album is .... to be released next week.
5 Exercise .... an important role in physical health.
6 What's your .... on this article?
7 We need to .... the spread of the disease.
8 He's busy .... his memoirs.

B Complete the missing nouns.

1 There will be salary cuts across-the-b _ _ _ d.
2 How do you keep such a good f _ _ _ _ e?
3 Please spare me the gory d _ _ _ _ _ s.
4 He's a good game show h _ _ t.
5 Jupiter is the biggest planet in our solar s _ _ _ _ m.
6 He has very right wing political b _ _ _ _ _ s.
7 My daughter has a very vivid i _ _ _ _ _ _ _ _ _ n.
8 There's recently been a surge of i _ _ _ _ _ _ _ t in Asian stocks.

C Complete the expressions with the words in the lists.

union	all	overload	protagonist
display	information	tale	

1 a trade ....
2 a fairy ....
3 go on ....
4 the main ....
5 information ....
6 love conquers ....
7 a wealth of ....

PHRASAL VERBS

A Complete the sentences with the correct form of the phrasal verbs in the list.

bring up	burst out	live up to
fed up	venture out	throw it away

1 It's a dangerous neighbourhood. Don't .... of your car.
2 They did a good job of .... their children........................... .
3 I don't need this. You can ....
4 Some players didn't .... their reputations.
5 I'm .... with this bad service.
6 I told her the news and she .... laughing.

06

CONFLICT

PAGES 42–43

bitterly if you feel something bitterly, you feel it with great anger or sadness: *I ~ regret what I did / was ~ disappointed / the two sides are ~ opposed / complain ~*

chore a chore is a small job that you have to do regularly: *household ~s / domestic ~s / do your ~s*

expressly if you expressly ask someone to do something, you ask them in a clear and definite way: *I ~ asked you to send it recorded delivery / ~ told him to wait for us / they are ~ forbidden to use the computers*

freely if you freely admit something, you admit it openly: *he ~ admits it / ~ acknowledges that she was wrong*

grudge if you hold a grudge against someone, you continue to feel angry with them because of something that they did in the past: *I don't hold a ~ against him / try not to bear a ~ / a long-standing ~ / an old ~*

make up when people make up, they become friendly again after an argument: *I hope we can ~ and put it all behind us / decided to kiss and ~*

slam if you slam a door, you shut it roughly and noisily: *storm off and ~ the door behind you / slammed the door in my face / ~ the door shut / the gate slammed shut in the wind*

storm if you storm off, you walk away from someone because you are very angry: *~ off and slam the door / ~ed out of the house / ~ed off in a temper*

sulk if you sulk, you show that you are angry by being quiet and refusing to talk to people. **Sulk** is also a noun: *stop ~ing / continued to ~ all day / go off and have a big ~*

PAGES 44–45

amends if you make amends, you try to make a situation better after you have done something wrong: *try to make ~ / determined to make ~ for my mistake*

bombard if you bombard someone with things, you give them a lot all at the same time: *advertisers ~ target groups / ~ed him with questions / ~ them with information*

break down if something breaks down, it ends and is not successful: *the talks ~ down / negotiations ~ down / the system broke down / their relationship broke down / my marriage broke down*

casualty a casualty is someone who is hurt in an accident or attack: *the explosion caused a lot of casualties / inflict heavy casualties on your enemy / they suffered heavy casualties / high casualties / a ~ of war*

ceasefire a ceasefire is an agreement between two groups to stop fighting: *the two sides have declared a ~ / negotiate a ~ / call for a ~ / sign the ~ / a ~ agreement*

coup a coup is an attempt by a group of people to take control of the government of their country, usually by force: *stage a ~ / plan a ~ / a military ~ / an attempted ~ / a failed ~ / a bloodless ~*

engage if you engage in an activity, you do it: *the two supermarkets are now engaging in a price war / ~d in discussions / they're still ~d in a dispute / ~ in regular exercise*

escalate if a situation escalates, it becomes worse or more serious: *if the conflict ~s / the tension could ~ / the dispute could ~ into war*

fatality a fatality is a death caused by an accident, fighting or disease: *the accident caused three fatalities / there have been 23 fatalities so far / the number of fatalities on the road each year*

fierce fierce fighting involves a lot of anger and determination: *a ~ battle / ~ fighting / a ~ argument / ~ criticism of the government / ~ opposition to the plans*

gross gross actions are very bad and serious: *a ~ invasion of privacy / guilty of ~ negligence / ~ mismanagement / ~ misconduct*

harass if you harass someone, you annoy or upset them repeatedly. The noun is **harassment**: *denied that he had pursued and ~ed the woman / she was sexually ~ed at work / ~ed by the police / guilty of sexual harassment*

hostile something that is hostile is unfriendly. The noun is **hostility**: *fight off a ~ takeover / very ~ towards us / feels ~ towards his teachers / a ~ attitude / her hostility towards me*

inflict if you inflict something on someone, you make them suffer it: *~ed damage on each other / ~ damage on the economy / could ~ serious injury / ~ pain / ~ suffering / ~ harm*

initiate if you initiate something, you start it. The noun is **initiation**: *claims she didn't ~ the affair / ~ talks / ~ discussions / ~ legal proceedings / the initiation of criminal proceedings*

intervention intervention is becoming involved in a fight or difficult situation. The verb is **intervene**: *international ~ in the country's affairs / government ~ in the dispute / don't usually intervene in private disputes*

lapse a lapse is an occasion when you do not do something well: *a ~ of judgement / a ~ of concentration / a memory ~ / a security ~*

offence if you cause offence, you upset or anger someone slightly by something you say or do. The verb is **offend**: *didn't mean to cause ~ / he took ~ / sorry, I meant no ~ / didn't mean to offend you*

outdo if you outdo someone, you do something better than they do: *companies pouring money into even bigger advertising campaigns in an effort to ~ each other / determined not be outdone*

overthrow if people overthrow their ruler, they remove them from power. The past tense is **overthrew** and the past participle is **overthrown**. **Overthrow** is also a noun: *a plot to ~ the president / an attempt to ~ the government / the ~ of the dictator*

overturn if you overturn a decision, you change it: *want to get the decision ~ed / the Appeal Court ~ed the verdict*

plot a plot is a secret plan to do something illegal. **Plot** is also a verb: *a ~ to overthrow the president / a ~ against the king / an assassination ~ / hatch a ~ / be involved in a ~ / police have uncovered a ~ to assassinate the president / plotting to overthrow the government*

rage if something rages, it continues with great violence: *war ~s / the storm was raging / the debate continues to ~*

resolution a resolution is a formal decision: *a UN ~ to ban whale hunting / passed a ~ to impose sanctions / vote on the ~ / propose a ~ / approve the ~ / a ~ on arms control*

retreat if you retreat, you change your mind and decide not to do something because it is not popular. **Retreat** is also a noun: *the government will not ~ in its policy / ~ from its plan to increase taxes / a government retreat on nuclear power*

sanction sanctions are official orders that prevent countries trading with a particular country as a punishment to that country: *impose ~s on the country / lift economic ~s / called for ~s against Iran / trade ~s / accused of breaking the ~s*

seek if you seek something, you ask for it or try to get it. The past tense and past participle is **sought**: *~ing a UN resolution / ~ re-election to Parliament / ~ political asylum / ~ revenge / ~ shelter from the rain / ~ compensation*

seize if you seize something, you take it by force: *they ~d control of the country / ~ power / the police ~d drugs worth £2 million / ~d my hand*

settlement a settlement is an official agreement to end a fight or dispute: *the two sides agreed a ~ / finally reached a ~ / trying to negotiate a ~ / a peace ~ / a divorce ~*

siege a siege is a situation in which soldiers or the police have surrounded a place to try and get control of it: *the town was under ~ for weeks / a long ~ / a police ~ of a house in London / a three-day police ~ / the ~ finally ended*

stage if you stage something, you organise it and do it: *~ a coup / ~ a demonstration / ~ a two-day strike / ~ a protest / ~ an opera*

submit to if you submit to something, you agree to accept it or do it: *people don't have to ~ body scans at airports / we have to ~ EU laws / submitted to police questioning*

surrender if you surrender to something, you allow it to control you: *she ~ed to weakness / ~ to temptation / ~ to grief / ~ to an illness*

takeover a takeover is a situation in which one company takes control of another. The verb is **take over**: *fight off a hostile ~ / the ~ of Cadburys by an American company / the company launched a ~ bid for its rival / tried to take over Ryanair last year*

target a target is someone you are trying to get as a customer. **Target** is also a verb: *advertisers bombard ~ groups / the ~ audience for the show / decided to ~ students*

track down if you track something down, you finally find it: *police are still trying to ~ down the terrorists / managed to ~ him down in the library*

trial a trial is an event at which a court decides whether someone is innocent or guilty of a crime: *standing ~ accused of corruption / he was put on ~ for murder / now faces ~ for murder / due to stand ~ next month*

troops troops are soldiers: *send in the ~ / withdraw the ~ / government ~ / American ~ / enemy ~*

truce a truce is an agreement to stop fighting a war for a period of time: *call a ~ / offer a ~ / propose a ~ / a temporary ~ / the three-day ~*

violation a violation is something that goes against a law or right. The verb is **violate**: *reports of human rights ~s / a blatant ~ of the peace treaty / a ~ of the law / their human rights were violated*

withdraw if you withdraw something, you take it back: *~ troops / ~ your offer / the drug has been ~n from the market*

PAGES 46–47

amnesty an amnesty is an order from a government which says that people can go free or will not be punished for something: *request ~ from prosecution / be granted an ~ / an ~ for political prisoners*

atrocity an atrocity is a very violent and cruel action during a war: *punish those who had committed atrocities / the people who carried out this ~ / a terrible ~ / atrocities against civilians*

break up if you break up a fight or demonstration, you stop it: *troops were sent in to ~ the protest / ~ the demonstration / ~ the fight*

call for if you call for something, you ask for it publicly: *~ a boycott / ~ the release of the prisoners / ~ an end to the war / ~ her resignation*

cold-blooded a cold-blooded act is one that you do without any emotion: *a ~ massacre / ~ murder / a ~ killer*

condone if you condone something bad, you say that you believe it is acceptable: *I don't ~ acts of vengeance / would never ~ violence / we don't ~ bullying*

crush if a government crushes opposition, it uses force to stop it: *~ the unrest / ~ the rebellion / ~ the protest / the uprising was swiftly ~ed*

entitled what something is entitled is what it is called: *a body ~ the Truth and Reconciliation Commission / a film ~ 'Summer Love'*

exempt if you exempt someone from something, you say that they do not have to do it or experience it. The noun is **exemption**: *the power to ~ people from prosecution / they're ~ed from paying tax / a tax exemption*

impose if you impose something, you force people to accept it. The noun is **imposition**: *~ sanctions on the country / the court can ~ a fine / ~ a ban on smoking / new rules ~ d by the government / the imposition of the ban*

issue an issue is a subject or problem: *the ~ of how to move the country forward peacefully / an important ~ / the main ~ / discuss the ~ / raise the ~ in the meeting / decide the ~*

loom if a problem looms, it is likely to happen soon: *the issue ~ed large / a crisis is ~ing / the ~ing industrial unrest*

obstacle an obstacle is something that prevents something from happening or developing: *the road to freedom was littered with ~s / ~s to peace / place ~s in the way of progress / remove the ~s to equality*

pardon a pardon is official forgiveness for a crime. **Pardon** is also a verb: *anyone wanting a ~ had to show remorse / was granted an official ~ / all political prisoners have been ~ed*

perpetrator the perpetrator of a crime is the person who committed the crime. The verb is **perpetrate**: *help for both victims and ~s / the ~ of the crime / the criminals who perpetrated this crime*

presence the presence of something is the fact that it is present: *their ~ on the global stage / don't require your ~ at the meeting*

profound something that is profound shows great knowledge and understanding: *asked some very ~ questions / a ~ thinker / a very ~ book*

proportionate if something is proportionate, it is the right size or at the right level in relation to other things: *was the troops' reaction to the demonstration ~? / were their actions ~? / increased costs will lead to a ~ rise in prices*

prosecute to prosecute someone means to officially charge them with a crime. The noun is **prosecution**: *the commission doesn't have the power to ~ people / the police decided not to ~ / not enough evidence to ~ her / he now faces prosecution for dangerous driving*

recount if you recount a story, you tell it to someone: *I ~ed my experiences / ~ed my story / ~ed how we first met*

remorse remorse is a feeling of being sorry for something that you have done. The adjective is **remorseful**: *anyone wanting a pardon had to show ~ / feelings of ~ / deep ~ / filled with ~ for what she had done / feeling remorseful*

sabotage sabotage is deliberate damage that you do to something, to prevent it from working properly. **Sabotage** is also a verb: *planning acts of ~ / industrial ~ / tried to ~ the peace talks*

set out if you set out to do something, you have it as your intention: *they ~ to focus on the victims / didn't ~ to hurt anyone*

testimony a testimony is a formal statement you make for a court: *listened to his ~ / had to give ~ in court / a reliable ~*

toll a toll is a bad effect that something has: *witnessing such suffering takes its ~ on you / smoking has taken a ~ on his health / the heavy ~ of war / a heavy ~ on the environment / the rising death ~*

wave a wave of something is a large amount of it that happens at the same time: *a ~ of social unrest / a ~ of violent attacks / felt a ~ of panic / a ~ of public anger*

IDIOMS

draw a line under if you draw a line under something, you say that it is completely finished. When you draw a line under a piece of writing, you put a line under it to show where the end is: *agreed to ~ the past / ~ the whole thing*

the writing is on the wall if the writing is on the wall, it is clear that something is going to fail or no longer exist: *the writing was very clearly on the wall / ~ for the old voting system*

EXERCISES

PREPOSITIONS

A Complete the sentences with the correct preposition
1 I'm waiting .... them to arrive.
2 The United Nations is calling .... a ceasefire.
3 I wasn't present .... the meeting.
4 There are still some obstacles .... peace.
5 The journalist bombarded him .... questions.
6 The army took control .... the town.
7 The Security Council voted .... the resolution.

WORD FAMILIES

A Complete the expression with the correct form of the word in bold.
1 feeling **remorseful**   he showed no ....
2 no evidence to **prosecute**   he faces ....
3 I felt **violated**   a .... of human rights
4 I meant no **offence**   he .... her
5 she **intervened** in the dispute   a case of government ....
6 sexual **harassment**   you're .... me
7 he's **exempt** from military service   tax ....

COLLOCATIONS

A Complete the sentences with the correct form of the verbs in the list.

kiss	negotiate	impose	overthrow
make	bear	stand	complain

1 He .... bitterly about the decision.
2 She's not the kind of person to .... a grudge.
3 They argue but they always .... and make up.
4 I sent some flowers to .... amends.
5 The two sides are trying to .... a ceasefire.
6 A rebel group has attempted to .... the government.
7 The United Nations has decided to .... sanctions.
8 A former politician will .... trial for corruption.

B Complete the missing adjectives.
1 The company is facing a h _ _ _ _ _ e takeover.
2 Enemy forces suffered h _ _ _ y casualties.
3 There has been f _ _ _ _ e fighting around the capital.
4 He was found guilty of g _ _ _ s misconduct.
5 Her lawyers have initiated l _ _ _ l proceedings.
6 Some captured soldiers have become p _ _ _ _ _ _ _ l prisoners.
7 Journalists are reporting on the rising d _ _ _ h toll.

C Match the two halves of the collocation.
1 social   a) trial
2 peace   b) asylum
3 nuclear   c) talks
4 human   d) power
5 put on   e) unrest
6 a takeover   f) rights
7 political   g) bid

PATTERNS

A Complete the sentences with the correct form of the verbs in the list. Use *to-* infinitive or *–ing*.

smoke	submit	become	stop	bully	drive

1 Years of .... has affected his health.
2 He was stopped for dangerous ....
3 I don't want .... involved.
4 We don't accept .... in this school.
5 The two sides have agreed .... fighting.
6 Everybody has .... to the law.

PHRASAL VERBS

A Complete the sentences with the correct form of the phrasal verbs in the list.

storm out	set out	call for
break down	break up	track down

1 She was angry and .... of the meeting.
2 Negotiations between the two countries have ....
3 Police are trying to .... the criminals.
4 The army was sent in to .... the riot.
5 People are .... new elections.
6 The government has .... to improve the economy.

07

SCIENCE AND RESEARCH

adverse something that is adverse is not good or favourable. The adverb is **adversely**: *the ~ side-effects of the drug / got a lot of ~ publicity / ~ weather conditions / your health could be adversely affected*

breakthrough a breakthrough is an important discovery or development: *a major ~ in the fight against AIDS / an important ~ / made a real ~ / when the ~ finally came*

deploy if you deploy something, you use it. The noun is **deployment**: *planning to ~ millions of reflectors / ~ nuclear weapons / ~ troops in the area / the deployment of chemical weapons*

devise if you devise a new way of doing something, you invent it: *scientists have ~d a way to detect seismic waves / ~ a new scheme / ~ a better method of communication*

diminished if something is diminished, it is smaller or less than it was before. The verb is **diminish**: *left him with ~ hearing / chances of survival are greatly ~ / found not guilty on the grounds of ~ responsibility / did nothing to diminish our fears*

disorder a disorder is an illness or medical condition: *suffers from a genetic ~ / a heart ~ / a bone ~*

duplicate if you duplicate something, you do the same thing a second time: *haven't managed to ~ the results under laboratory conditions / don't want to ~ our efforts*

feasible if something is feasible, it is possible: *they claim it's quite ~ / economically ~ / technically ~ / wasn't ~ to keep the factory open*

impaired if something is impaired, it is damaged and not as good as before. The verb is **impair**: *left him with ~ hearing / people who are visually ~ / could impair your ability to work*

insert if you insert something, you put it into something else: *they ~ probes into the skin / ~ the key into the lock*

prevalent something that is prevalent is common: *the genetic condition is quite ~ / drug abuse is very ~ / these attitudes are quite ~*

stack a stack of things is a pile or large number of them: *if they deploy a big ~ of these things / a ~ of papers on my desk / they've got ~s of money*

underlying an underlying problem or cause is one that is important but is not easy to see: *look for ~ problems with the data / the ~ causes of crime*

undertake if you undertake something, you do it: *~ a survey / ~ research / ~ a new project*

wave a wave is the form in which sound, light, and some other things travel: *seismic ~s / sound ~s / radio ~s*

anomaly an anomaly is something that is different from what is usual or expected: *the figures are a statistical ~ / find some anomalies in the results*

anonymously if you do something anonymously, you do it without giving your name. The adjective is **anonymous**: *published ~ on the Internet / wrote ~ to the newspaper / the police got an anonymous tip-off about the robbery*

armoury your armoury is all the skills and information you have to help you: *part of every citizen's ~ / DNA testing is a useful weapon in the police ~*

attribute if you attribute something to someone, you say that they are responsible for it: *not sure if the change can be ~d to government policy / the fall in the death rate is generally ~d to improved health services*

biased if something is biased, it favours one group rather than another. The noun is **bias**: *the poll is ~ / claimed the referee was ~ / ~ towards the government / ~ against the unions / a lot of bias in the survey*

bond when people bond, they form a strong relationship with each other. **Bond** is also a noun: *hormones which encourage ~ing / I ~ed with him immediately / the strong ~s between them*

borne if something is borne out of something else, it is caused by it: *the responses are probably ~ out of fear / crimes ~ out of frustration / social problems that are ~ out of poverty*

causal something that is causal causes something to happen: *a ~ link between gaming and bad behaviour / a ~ relationship between poverty and crime*

census a census is an official process of counting people or things: *a ~ undertaken by the department of veterinary science / carry out a ~ / a population ~ / a traffic ~*

commission if you commission something, you ask someone to do it for you: *who ~ed the research / a survey ~ed by the government / ~ed me to write a book / ~ed a series of paintings*

conflicting conflicting facts or opinions are different from each other: *there is ~ evidence / people gave me ~ advice / there are ~ opinions within the government*

correlation if there is a correlation between two sets of facts, there is a relationship between them: *some data show a ~ / a strong ~ between obesity and heart disease / a high ~ / a significant ~*

counter counter facts or opinions are opposite to other ones: *there is bound to be an argument with ~ statistics / a series of claims and ~ claims*

data data is information that you collect and then use to understand something: *statistics is simply a way of interpreting ~ / collect some ~ / study the ~ / analyse the ~ / produce some interesting ~ / reliable ~*

disguise to disguise something means to change it so it cannot be recognised. **Disguise** is also a noun: *the increase in profits may ~ the inefficiencies / tried to ~ his accent / ~d herself as a nurse / a bomb ~d as a parcel / he was wearing a ~*

ends your ends are your aims: *twisted the figures to suit his own ~ / do anything to achieve her political ~*

extract if you extract something, you remove it from something: *DNA can be ~ed from hair / ~ oils from plants / had to have a tooth ~ed*

figure a figure is an official number: *twisted the ~s to suit his own ends / the official unemployment ~s / isn't clear how the government arrived at this ~*

flawed if something is flawed, it is not perfect but has mistakes in it. The noun is **flaw**: *the research is seriously ~ / ~ logic / the idea is fatally ~ / a major flaw in the design*

fuzzy something that is fuzzy is confused and not clear: *the truth can be ~ / some of the concepts are a bit ~*

intake your intake of something is the amount you eat or drink regularly: *not clear what our salt ~ should be / reduce your ~ of fat / a high ~ of alcohol / a low ~ of protein*

link a link is a connection between two things. **Link** is also a verb: *trying to establish a ~ between attitudes and health / a close ~ / a strong ~ / a clear ~ / strengthen the ~ between higher education and business / pay is ~ed to performance*

manipulate if you manipulate something, you control it or change it in a clever way for your own benefit: *the figures can be ~d / I felt I was being ~d / tried to ~ me into giving him money*

plunge if something plunges, it suddenly decreases by a large amount: *the murder rate ~d by 30% / unemployment has ~d to a record low / ~d sharply*

random if something is random, it happens without any definite plan or system. The adverb is **randomly**: *the group was chosen at ~ / ~ drug testing of athletes / a ~ sample of students / chose the families randomly*

rear to rear an animal or a child means to look after it while it is growing: *two male penguins are ~ing a chick / ~ pigs on the farm / a good place to ~ children*

scrutiny scrutiny is looking at something very carefully. The verb is **scrutinise**: *the figures don't stand up to ~ / careful ~ of the accounts revealed some errors / the company has come under close ~ / scrutinise their activities*

severity the severity of something is how bad or serious it is. The adjective is **severe**: *the ~ of their injuries / didn't understand the ~ of the situation / a severe injury*

stand up if facts stand up, they are shown to be true when they are tested: *the figures don't ~ to scrutiny / evidence that will never ~ in court*

tighten if you tighten a rule or law, you make it stricter: *the rules on animal experiments ought to be ~ed / ~ security at the airport / ~ up the regulations*

time frame the time frame for something is the amount of time that is available for it: *only a narrow ~ for the study / need to finish within a very short ~ / what's the ~ for the project?*

twist if you twist facts, you change them slightly for your own benefit: *~ed the figures to suit his own ends / tried to ~ what I had said / ~ed my words*

upward something that is upward is increasing. The opposite is **downward**: *the figures are part of an ~ trend / the ~ movement of property prices / interest rates are moving in a downward direction*

validity the validity of something is how true and believable it is. The adjective is **valid**: *this interpretation has greater ~ / questioned the ~ of his argument / a valid idea / a valid argument*

variable a variable is something that might be different in a different situation: *there are a number of ~s in the results / there are too many ~s to predict the result accurately*

Pages 52–53

abundant if something is abundant, it exists in large numbers or quantities. The noun is **abundance**: *an ~ supply of food / jobs were ~ at that time / an abundance of wildlife*

bubble a bubble is a ball of air in a liquid. **Bubble** is also a verb: *it blows out tiny ~s through its nose / the ~s in champagne / soap ~s / the water was beginning to ~*

capability a country's capability is its ability to take military action: *advise the government on how to achieve full ~ / America's nuclear ~*

come up with if you come up with an idea, you think of it: *we have ~ new strategies / ~ a good idea / ~ a plan*

diversity if there is diversity, there are a lot of different things or people. The adjective is **diverse**: *the ~ of activities that scientists engage in / a ~ of opinions / cultural ~ / ethnic ~ / people from diverse family backgrounds*

drought a drought is a long period without rain: *study the harm the ~ can do / a severe ~ / the worst ~ for twenty years / a long ~ / suffering from a ~ / plants that will survive ~ conditions*

essence the essence of something is the most important part of it: *in ~ my work is to do with national security / the ~ of government policy / the ~ of education*

exploratory something that is exploratory is done in order to find out information. The noun is **exploration**: *an ~ mission / ~ surgery / ~ talks / space exploration*

feed into if one thing feeds into another, it helps the second thing: *my work ~s into the work of the Environmental Agency / ideas that can ~ into our publicity campaign*

frantically if you do something frantically, you do it very quickly because you are in a great hurry. The adjective is **frantic**: *they were ~ scribbling equations / ~ searching for his key / spent a frantic half hour looking for my wallet*

glamorous someone who is glamorous looks rich and beautiful: *the stereotype is more ~ than reality / ~ supermodels / looks incredibly ~ / a ~ lifestyle*

habitat the habitat of a plant or animal is the environment in which it naturally lives: *advise on the animals' ~ / their ~ is being destroyed / the forest is an important ~ for plants and animals / see them in their natural ~*

immensely immensely means extremely: *the Commission has been ~ important / ~ rich / ~ popular / ~ strong / ~ talented*

mundane something that is mundane is ordinary and not exciting or interesting: *the reality is far more ~ / a ~ job / a rather ~ life / talk about more ~ matters*

regime a regime is a programme of exercise or diet to improve your health or fitness: *a training ~ / follows a strict dietary ~ / a ~ of morning exercise*

scrap a scrap of something is a small piece of it: *scribbling equations on a ~ of paper / a few ~s of food / some old ~s of material / managed to find a few ~s of information*

scribble when you scribble, you write something quickly or untidily. **Scribble** is also a noun: *frantically scribbling equations on a scrap of paper / managed to ~ his phone number down / a ~d note / book was covered in ~s*

status your status is your position in society: *help us maintain our ~ in an ever-changing world / people with high social ~ / low social ~ / want to improve the ~ of nurses / a big car is still a ~ symbol*

vital something that is vital is extremely important. The adverb is **vitally**: *my work is ~ for national security / it's absolutely ~ that you're there / of ~ importance / vitamins play a ~ role in health / vitally important*

wellbeing your wellbeing is how healthy and happy you are: *we care about the ~ of the animals / a feeling of ~ / physical ~ / psychological ~ / the economic ~ of the country*

IDIOMS

full of holes something that is full of holes has a lot of mistakes or faults. A piece of clothing that is full of holes is old and has a lot of holes in it: *the figures are ~ / the theory is ~ / an old jumper that's ~*

it's beyond me if something is beyond you, you cannot do it or cannot understand it: *I've tried to forgive and forget, but ~ / ~ why anyone would want to go there*

pave the way for if one thing paves the way for another, it makes it possible. The image is of creating a paved road for something else to move along easily: *the findings could ~ new techniques / this could ~ further reforms*

slippery slope a slippery slope is a course of action that is difficult to stop once you have started it. The image is of someone on a slippery slope who cannot stop moving downwards: *the experiment represents a ~ / on the ~ to drug addiction*

thin end of the wedge if something is the thin end of the wedge, it is the start of something bad, which will get worse if you allow it to start. The image is of putting a wedge into something, where you put the thin end in first, and can then gradually push in the thicker end: *the experiment represents the ~ / these job cuts are just the ~*

vested interest if you have a vested interest in something, you have strong reasons for making it happen because you will benefit from it: *the government has a ~ in removing people from the unemployment figures / the company has a ~ in getting the project approved*

EXERCISES

PREPOSITIONS

A Complete the sentences with the correct preposition.

1 There's a problem ...... my computer.
2 The information is available ...... the Internet.
3 The survey was commissioned ...... the government.
4 They extracted DNA ...... her hair.
5 Do you care ...... social issues?
6 I'm looking ...... my car keys.
7 He manipulated me ...... giving him money.
8 It's the worst drought ...... 50 years.

WORD FAMILIES

A Complete the expression with the correct form of the word in bold.

1 it's **vitally** important	she plays a .... role
2 space **exploration**	an .... visit
3 an **abundance** of wealth	an .... supply
4 I question its **validity**	a .... argument
5 **flawed** research	we found some ....
6 a **biased** opinion	the argument shows his ....
7 an **anonymous** caller	I sent it ....
8 **adverse** publicity	we were .... affected

IDIOMS

A Complete the idiom with the correct word in the list.

holes	way	wedge	slope	vested

1 Your plan is full of .... It will never work.
2 He's on the slippery .... to bankruptcy.
3 Her research paved the .... to understanding the disease.
4 This tax increase is just the thin edge of the ....
5 She has a .... interest in getting the project approved.

COLLOCATIONS

A Complete the sentences with the correct adjectives in the list.

genetic	conflicting	cultural
underlying	upward	nuclear
important	visually	

1 Scientists have made an .... breakthrough in the fight against HIV.
2 She suffers from a .... disorder.
3 He can't drive because he's .... impaired.
4 Poverty is an .... cause of crime.
5 His lawyers claim there is .... evidence.
6 The .... trend in European stocks continues.
7 Some countries are trying to develop a .... capability.
8 We come from different .... backgrounds.

B Complete the missing nouns.

1 The experiment took place under laboratory c _ _ _ _ _ _ _ _ s.
2 Drug a _ _ _ e is a problem in this neighbourhood.
3 She's a student of veterinary s _ _ _ _ _ e.
4 This region is suffering from a severe d _ _ _ _ _ t.
5 I like to observe wildlife in its natural h _ _ _ _ _ t.
6 Police have established a l _ _ k between the two suspects.

C Complete the expressions with the words in the lists.

rates	action	paper
campaign	symbol	wellbeing

1 your physical ....
2 a status ....
3 a scrap of ....
4 a publicity ....
5 military ....
6 interest ....

PHRASAL VERBS

A Complete the sentences with the correct form of the phrasal verbs in the list.

feed into	come under	stand up
borne out of	carry out	come up with

1 My work .... a bigger research project.
2 We need to .... a new idea to reduce unemployment.
3 Some government officials are .... a survey.
4 Much crime is .... poverty.
5 Department expenses have .... close scrutiny.
6 That argument won't .... in court.

08

NATURE

PAGES 54–55

arid arid land is very dry because there is very little rain: *the area is very ~ / ~ land / an ~ climate*

barren land that is barren has no plants growing in it and is not good for growing crops. The opposite is **fertile**: *the land is ~ / a ~ desert / ~ soil / good fertile land*

conclusive if evidence or proof is conclusive, it shows that something is definitely true. The opposite is **inconclusive**: *the evidence isn't ~ / ~ proof of his involvement in the crime / the findings were inconclusive*

dense something that is dense has things that are very close together: *some ~ woodland / a ~ jungle / ~ vegetation / a ~ forest / ~ housing / a very ~ population*

deserted if a place is deserted, there is no one in it: *the place is completely ~ / the ~ streets / the village was ~ / the place looked ~*

dune a dune is a hill made of sand: *then we hit sand ~s / camped on the sand ~s by the beach / walking over the ~s*

fertile land that is fertile has a lot of plants growing in it and is good for growing crops. The opposite is **barren**: *the land's very ~ / a very ~ region / ~ soil / a barren desert*

fringe the fringes of a place are the parts furthest from the centre: *villages on the ~s of the desert / camped at the ~ of the forest / stood on the ~ of the crowd*

lush lush plants are strong and healthy: *the landscape is very ~ and green / ~ countryside / a very ~ island / ~ vegetation*

pedal a pedal is a control that you operate with your foot: *a ~ boat / bicycle ~s / the accelerator ~ / press the brake ~ / put your foot on the accelerator ~*

rolling rolling hills have gentle slopes that are not very steep: *an area of ~ green hills / gentle, ~ hills / the gently ~ countryside*

rugged land that is rugged is rough and uneven, with many steep slopes: *a ~ landscape of mountain peaks / a ~ coastline*

strenuous something that is strenuous is physically difficult and tiring: *it was pretty ~ / very ~ work / 30 minutes of ~ exercise*

thick something that is thick has a lot of things growing close together: *an area of ~ woodland / ~ undergrowth / her ~ dark hair / a ~ beard*

track a track is a narrow road with a rough surface: *we drove along a bumpy dirt ~ / a narrow mountain ~ / a dusty ~ / a muddy ~ / a cycle ~ / followed the ~ to the next village*

winding something that is winding has a lot of curves and bends: *a ~ river / a ~ stream / a ~ road / a narrow ~ path*

PAGES 56–57

appeal the appeal of something is how popular it is. **Appeal** is also a verb: *explain the continuing ~ of such theories / has great ~ for younger people / the film's immediate ~ to young audiences / holds no ~ for me / ideas that ~ to a lot of women*

articulate someone who is articulate can use language well to express their ideas and feelings: *he's not very ~ / a very ~ man / an ~ speaker / highly ~*

aspire if you aspire to something, you would like to have it or achieve it: *they ~ to an education / ~ to wealth / ~s to a career in law / ~s to study medicine*

back up to back someone up means to show that what they are saying is true: *the research ~s me up / can you ~ me up here? / what you're saying isn't ~ed up by evidence*

blunt someone who is blunt gives their opinion openly and honestly, even if this might upset other people. The adverb is **bluntly**: *he can be very ~ sometimes / I was hurt by his ~ words / to be ~, it's no good / 'I don't like it,' she said bluntly*

bridge if you bridge a difference between people, you make it less important: *how can we ~ this vast divide? / ~ the gap between rich and poor / trying to ~ their differences*

butt in if you butt in, you interrupt a conversation rudely: *don't ~ when someone else is talking / always ~ing into other people's conversations*

condition to condition someone means to make them think or behave in certain ways: *that's how we've been ~ed to see things / we're all ~ed by the society we live in / women are ~ed to be passive*

conform if you conform, you behave in the way that is expected by other people: *women who ~ to traditional gender stereotypes / he refused to ~*

contradict to contradict something means to show that it is not true. The adjective is **contradictory**: *it's easy to forget examples that ~ our ideas / the evidence ~s his theory / their statements ~ each other / a lot of contradictory evidence*

cursory a cursory look is one that you do very quickly and not carefully: *a ~ inspection of the literature / a ~ glance at the newspaper / had a ~ look at my papers*

defy to defy something means to deliberately refuse to follow it or obey it: *women who ~ gender stereotypes / people who ~ the law / ~ an order*

follow-up a follow-up is something that is done to follow something else. **Follow-up** is also an adjective: *published numerous ~s to the book / a ~ to the first survey / do some ~ research*

gender your gender is whether you are male or female: *~ stereotypes / ~ differences between men and women / ~ inequalities / discrimination on the grounds of race or ~*

glut if there is a glut of something, there is more than you need: *the ~ of self-help books in the shops / fruit farmers last year had a ~ of apples / a ~ of computers on the market*

nurture your nurture is the way in which you are brought up and educated: *is ~ more important than nature?/ the old ~ –nature debate*

overlap the overlap between two things is the parts of the two things that are similar. **Overlap** is also a verb: *an ~ of 95% in the way the sexes communicate / there's a big ~ between chemistry and biology / the two roles ~*

provocation a provocation is an action that makes someone angry or upset, especially when this is done deliberately. The verb is **provoke**: *he'll bite at even the slightest ~ / attacked me without any ~ / did it under extreme ~ / provoked him into a fight*

reach out if you reach out to someone, you show that you want to listen to them or help them: *the female ~es out and shares her feelings / try to ~ out to young drug users*

recall if you recall something, you remember it: *we ~ occasions when evidence backed up this idea / can't ~ his name / don't ~ it very well*

remarkably in a way that is unusual or surprising: *men and women communicate in ~ similar ways / did ~ well in his exams / it's in ~ good condition*

retreat a retreat is a safe, quiet place where people can go to relax or forget about their problems: *he runs residential ~s / a religious ~ / a rural ~*

sweeping something that is sweeping is very great or affects a lot of things: *a ~ generalisation / ~ changes to the tax system / ~ reforms / ~ tax cuts*

tie if one thing is tied to another, the two things are related or combined in some way: *such actions are often ~d into positions of power / the two economies are closely ~d / ~d together*

unsettling if something is unsettling, it makes you feel worried or nervous. The verb is **unsettle**: *the changes are deeply ~ / an ~ experience / these are ~ times / felt a bit unsettled*

wake if something happens in the wake of something else, it happens after it or as a result of it: *new book clubs have sprung up in the ~ of this enthusiasm / changes that happened in the ~ of the election result*

bark the bark of a tree is the hard covering on the trunk: *it gnaws through the ~ / tree ~ / strip the ~ off*

blend if something blends in, it looks similar to the things around it: *it ~s into the background / the house ~s in with the surrounding countryside / worried I wouldn't ~ in at the party*

dig if you dig, you make a hole in the ground: *it ~s down into the earth / digging in the garden / have to ~ quite deep / digging for coal / digging through the rubble*

ecosystem an ecosystem is all the animals and plants in an area, and the way in which they are all connected: *it exists in a delicate ~ / prevent more damage to ~s / the rainforest ~ / marine ~s*

elaborate something that is elaborate is very complicated: *animals have ~ ways of attracting a partner / an ~ pattern / an ~ plan / a very ~ design / looks very ~ / sounds a bit too ~*

expanse an expanse is a big open area of land: *vast ~s of the earth are deserted in terms of mankind / a huge ~ of desert / the cold ~s of the frozen north*

flock a flock is a large group of birds, sheep or goats: *a ~ of migrating birds / a ~ of pigeons / a big ~ of sheep / a small ~ of goats*

food chain a food chain is a series of plants and animals that are connected because each one in the chain is eaten by the next one in the chain: *we are at the top of the ~, with no predators / at the bottom of the ~ / part of the same ~*

forage to forage for food means to search for it: *foraging for food in the trees / street kids who spend their days foraging for food*

gnaw if an animal gnaws something, it bites it repeatedly: *it ~s through the bark / a dog ~ing on a bone / ~ a hole in the carpet*

grasp if you grasp something, you take hold of it. **Grasp** is also a noun: *their toes are adapted to ~ things / he ~ed my hand / ~ed me by the arm / ~ed the handle / released the bag from his ~*

grip if you grip something, you hold it tightly. **Grip** is also a noun: *it ~s onto its prey / gripped my hand firmly / gripped my arm / gripping onto the steering wheel / he tightened his ~ on my arm*

hatch when an egg hatches, a young bird or animals comes out of it: *the eggs ~ after five days / the young were beginning to ~ out / watched the baby chicks ~ out*

herd a herd is a large group of cows, deer or elephants: *huge ~s of caribou / a small ~ of cattle / a ~ of elephants / they graze in ~s*

high-pitched a high-pitched sound is very high. The opposite is **low-pitched**: *a ~ squeal / a ~ scream / a very ~ voice / a low-pitched voice*

ingenuity ingenuity is great skill at inventing new things. The adjective is **ingenious**: *marvel at the ~ of the human race / an ingenious invention / an ingenious device*

let out to let out a sound means to make it: *~ a high-pitched squeal / ~ a scream / ~ a cry of pain / ~ a loud roar*

manoeuvre to manoeuvre means to move with a lot of skill: *they can ~ quickly through the trees / ~ the car into the parking space / managed to ~ myself into the corner*

markings an animal's markings are the coloured marks on its skin or fur: *it has lightly striped ~ on its breast / has very distinctive ~ / brown and white ~*

mate when animals mate, they have sex to produce young: *they ~ in the spring / the males ~ with several females / a mating call / a mating ritual*

nest a nest is a place made by a bird or insect to lay eggs: *it builds a ~ in the spring / a bird's ~ / a wasp's ~ / time for the young to leave the ~ / when the young have flown the ~*

pluck if you pluck something, you pull it: *a hooked beak for ~ing and tearing flesh / ~ed an apple from the tree / ~ed out a few grey hairs*

predator a predator is an animal that hunts and kills other animals for food: *we are at the top of the food chain, with no ~s / a skilful ~ / tries to avoid its ~s*

prey a prey is an animal or bird that is hunted and killed by another animal: *quickly snatches its ~ / catches its ~ by making a sticky web / pounces on its ~ / swoops down on its ~/ stalks its ~ / hunts its ~*

puff up to puff up means to become bigger or make something bigger: *it ~s up its chest / ~s up its throat / the pastry had ~ed up nicely / her face was all ~ed up*

reserve a reserve of something is an amount that you keep in case you need it: *it stores ~s of fat / have some ~s of food / huge ~s of oil / coal ~s / draw on your ~s / use my ~s of strength*

roam to roam means to walk or travel in no particular direction: *the caribou ~ over the plains / dogs that ~ around the city / allowed to ~ freely / children who ~ the streets*

slender something that is slender is quite thin: *its long ~ central toe / she's tall and ~ / ~ legs / ~ fingers / quite ~ / very ~*

snatch if you snatch something you take hold of it roughly: *it leaps out and ~es its prey / ~ed the letter from my hand / someone tried to ~ my bag*

web a web is a net of thin threads that a spider makes to catch insects: *it catches its prey by making a sticky ~ / a spider's ~ / spin a ~*

withstand if you can withstand something, you are not harmed by it. The past tense and past participle is **withstood**: *it can ~ freezing temperatures / plants that can ~ drought / he managed to ~ all the criticism / couldn't ~ the pressure*

IDIOMS

beat around the bush if you beat around or about the bush, you avoid talking about a subject because it is unpleasant or embarrassing: *I wish he's stop beating around the bush and get to the point / don't ~ ~ just say what you want*

get a word in edgeways if you can't get a word in edgeways, you cannot say anything because someone else is talking all the time. The image suggests that there are so few gaps in what someone is saying that you could not even fit in a word if it you turned it sideways: *no one else can ~*

get into the swing of it if you get into the swing of something, you get used to doing it and become fully involved in it: *you soon get into the swing of things / I only got back to work yesterday, so I'm still getting back into the swing of it*

get to the point if you get to the point, you talk about the main thing that you want to say: *I wish he'd ~ / come on ~ ~ / she got straight to the point*

put words into my mouth if you put words into someone's mouth, you tell them what you think they are trying to say. The image is of physically putting words into someone else's mouth: *he's always trying to ~ / don't ~*

EXERCISES

PREPOSITIONS

A Complete the sentences with the correct preposition.

1 This land is good .... growing crops.
2 Do you have proof .... his involvement?
3 Follow this road .... the next town.
4 She aspires to a career .... journalism.
5 We're all conditioned .... society.
6 We don't discriminate .... the grounds of race.
7 Animals have elaborate ways .... attracting partners.
8 Bears forage .... food in the forest.

WORD FAMILIES

A Complete the expression with the correct form of the word in bold.

1 he's known for his **ingenuity**
   an .... solution
2 I felt **unsettled**
   it's a bit ....
3 extreme **provocation**
   don't .... him
4 a **contradictory** statement
   she sometimes .... herself
5 a **blunt** assessment
   can I talk ....?

IDIOMS

A Complete the idiom with the correct word in the list.

word	swing	straight	mouth	bush

1 Say what you mean. Stop beating around the ....!
2 He's very direct. He always gets .... to the point.
3 She did all the talking. I couldn't get a .... in edgeways.
4 It's difficult at first, but it's OK once you get into the .... of it.
5 That's not what I said! You're putting words in my ....

COLLOCATIONS

A Complete the sentences with the correct form of the verbs in the list.

fly	bridge	hold	stalk	roam

1 I don't like zoos. Animals should be able to .... freely.
2 Have you ever seen a lion .... its prey?
3 All the young chicks have .... the nest.
4 Education can help .... the gap between rich and poor.
5 Working for a big company .... no appeal for me.

B Complete the missing adjectives.

1 The place looked completely d _ _ _ _ _ _ d.
2 A coastline of r _ _ _ _ _ g hills.
3 We walked through some t _ _ _ k undergrowth.
4 The village is at the end of a w _ _ _ _ _ g road.
5 He's a highly a _ _ _ _ _ _ _ _ e speaker.
6 I gave the newspaper a c _ _ _ _ _ y glance.
7 The report made some s _ _ _ _ _ _ g generalisations.
8 He knows the m _ _ _ _ g calls of different birds.

C Match the two halves of the collocation.

1 the food   a) race
2 a spider's   b) books
3 a parking   c) chain
4 the human   d) stereotypes
5 a flock of   e) space
6 self-help   f) web
7 gender   g) sheep

PHRASAL VERBS

A Complete the sentences with the correct form of the phrasal verbs in the list.

let out	back up	reach out
spring up	butt in	blend in

1 She .... a cry of joy when she saw her results.
2 Wild animals are good at .... to their surroundings.
3 Korean restaurants have .... all over the city.
4 He .... to me when I was very unhappy.
5 She's always .... to other people's conversations.
6 He didn't .... his statements with facts and figures.

09

WORK

PAGES 64–65

deadline a deadline is a date or time by which you must finish something: *make sure that everyone meets their ~s / working to a tight ~ / set a ~ / the ~ is tomorrow / the ~ for applications / missed the ~*

dealings your dealings are the things you do as part of your work. If you have dealings with someone, you have a business relationship with them: *don't have much to do with them in my day-to-day ~ / his business ~ / her financial ~ / have no ~ with him*

delegate if you delegate work, you give it to someone who is more junior than you. The noun is **delegation**: *she ~s the work to others / need to learn to ~ more / need to learn effective delegation*

draw up if you draw up a plan or document, you prepare it: *I ~ all the contracts / ~ plans for a merger / ~ new rules / ~ proposals / ~ a list of candidates*

dump if you dump something in a place, you drop it there in a way that isn't careful or precise: *~ your stuff down here for a moment / ~ed my bags on the floor / ~ed the pile of clothes on the bed / don't just ~ it all on my desk*

eager if you are eager to do something, you are very keen to do it. The adverb is **eagerly**: *we're ~ to start doing something / seems ~ to learn / ~ for news / an ~ young executive / their ~ faces / eagerly awaiting news of his flight*

hesitate you say 'don't hesitate' when you want to encourage someone to do something: *don't ~ to ask for help / don't ~ to call me*

input when you input information, you put it onto a computer. The past tense and past participle is **input**: *~ information into the database / ~ all the figures / need to ~ all the data*

invoice an invoice is a document with details of work that someone has done and the payment that they want. **Invoice** is also a verb: *I process the ~s /*
send in an ~ / submit an ~ for the work / an ~ for £400 / haven't paid the ~ yet / I ~ the company once a month

leadership leadership is being in charge of something, or having the qualities that a leader needs: *she provides ~ to the team / strong ~ / good ~ / effective ~ / poor ~ / challenge his ~ / has no ~ qualities / his ~ of the party*

liaise if you liaise with someone, you talk to them and share information so that you can work together. The noun is **liaison**: *I ~ closely with our reps in Russia / we need to ~ more / need closer liaison with the police*

network if you network, you meet people and talk to them so that you can build up new contacts and improve your opportunities at work. The noun is **networking**: *I have to ~ a lot to attract new business / it's important to ~ and make new contacts / hoping to do some ~ing in the evenings / plenty of opportunities for ~ing*

ominous something that is ominous makes you feel that something bad is going to happen: *that sounds ~ / an ~ silence*

oversee if you oversee work, you watch it and check that everything is done well. The past tense is **oversaw** and the past participle is **overseen**: *I ~ everything / ~ the project / ~ the work*

process if you process a document, you deal with it: *I ~ the invoices / ~ any expenses claims / it takes time to ~ all the applications*

schedule if you schedule something, you plan or arrange for it to happen at a particular time. A **schedule** is a plan of what things will happen at particular times: *~ a time for us to meet / we've ~d the meeting for 2.30 / we're ~d to meet next week / look at next week's ~ / have a busy ~ tomorrow*

take on if you take someone on, you give them a job: *I'm not the only one who's being ~n on / aren't taking on new staff at the moment / they took me on as a junior reporter*

troubleshoot if you troubleshoot, you try to solve problems that occur. Someone who does this is a **troubleshooter**: *we ~ any problems / my role is as a troubleshooter*

PAGES 66–67

admiration admiration is the feeling of respecting someone a lot. The verb is **admire**: *perceive ~ in their voice / feel nothing but ~ for her / great ~ / full of ~ for him / I admire him a lot*

assess if you assess someone or something, you make a judgement about what they are like and how good they are. The noun is **assessment**: *he's brilliant at ~ing people / need to ~ the situation carefully / ~ its value / ~ the effect of the policy / give an honest assessment*

backing backing is support that someone gives to a person or a project. The verb is **back**: *with his ~, the process was a formality / had the ~ of my boss / you have my full ~ / won ~ from a large organisation / need financial ~ / decided to back the plan*

backside your backside is your bottom: *sitting on your ~ at home / slapped him on the ~*

blissfully blissfully means in a very happy way. The adjective is **blissful**. **Bliss** is a feeling of great happiness: *I'm ~ happy / ~ unaware of the dangers / remained in blissful ignorance of the plans to close the school / it was pure bliss!*

conspiracy a conspiracy is a secret plan to do something bad or illegal: *a ~ of silence over the sacking / a political ~ / involved in a ~ / part of a ~ / a ~ against the prime minister*

drain if something drains away, it gradually reduces until there is none left. If you feel **drained**, you feel that you have no energy left. Something that is **draining** makes you feel this way: *my vitality ~ed away / felt completely ~ed / physically and emotionally ~ed / teaching kids is emotionally ~ing*

drift if something drifts, it moves in an uncontrolled way: *my mind was ~ing off / my eyes ~ed to the audience / was beginning to ~ off to sleep*

formality a formality is an official process that you have to go through: *the process was a ~ / it's just a ~ / go through the formalities / get the formalities over with first*

impact to impact on something means to have an effect on it. **Impact** is also a noun: *failing to pull your weight can directly ~ on colleagues / the changes won't ~ on you / had a huge ~ on the whole community*

inherently if something inherently has a quality, it has that quality as one of its natural features or characteristics. The adjective is **inherent**: *it's ~ interesting / a job that's ~ boring / it's ~ dangerous / the work has some inherent risks*

lean when you lean, you bend forwards, backwards or sideways: *he ~s forward on the edge of his seat / just ~ back and relax / ~ing to one side*

nod if you nod, you move your head up and down to show that you agree with someone: *she nodded and sounded interested / nodded in agreement / nodded his head*

numb if part of your body is numb, it cannot feel anything. You can say that something that is extremely boring is **mind-numbing** or **mind-numbingly** boring: *my mind was ~ with boredom / my fingers were ~ with cold / I was ~ with shock / dong mind-numbing work in a factory / it was mind-numbingly boring*

occurrence an occurrence is something that happens. The verb is **occur**: *do you think it was a freak ~? / a common ~ / an everyday ~ / a rare ~ / an isolated ~ / it doesn't occur very often*

redundant if an organisation makes employees redundant, it tells them that it no longer has a job for them. The noun is **redundancy**: *they were going to make me ~ / thousands of ~ workers / the company has announced 200 redundancies / should get a redundancy payment*

remotely if something is not remotely true, it is not true at all. A **remote** chance or possibility is very small: *it's not ~ interesting / wasn't ~ interested / it isn't ~ like the first film / only a remote possibility that it will work / a remote chance we could still win*

screw if you screw someone, you cheat them and get money or work from them unfairly: *I wasn't ~ing the system / tried to ~ me out of £50*

slack if you slack, you try to avoid working hard. Someone who does this is a **slacker**: *accused me of ~ing / come on – stop ~ing / no place for slackers here*

slump if you slump, you sit or stand with your shoulders bent forwards, not straight: *I'd return with my shoulders ~ed and my mind numb / sitting ~ed over my desk / ~ed in front of the TV / came in and ~ed down on the sofa*

take off if something takes off, it becomes very successful and popular: *the Internet still hadn't ~n off / don't think the idea will ~ / hoping the product will really ~ now*

technically technically means in a way that involves complicated physical movements. The adjective is **technical**: *gardening is ~ difficult / he's ~ a very good player / her performance was ~ brilliant / a lot of technical ability*

utterly utterly means completely. The adjective is **utter**: *it's ~ draining / ~ impossible / ~ brilliant / ~ exhausted / a feeling of utter despair / utter exhaustion*

workforce the workforce is all the people who work in a country or area, or for a company: *much of the ~ is under-employed / 50% of the ~ / the company has a large ~ / a skilled ~ / a well-qualified ~ / need to reduce its ~ / cut its ~ by 200 / expand the ~*

PAGES 68–69

amount to if something amounts to another thing, it is the same as it or has the same effect it: *using mobile phone chargers ~s to theft / actions which ~ to fraud*

anticipate if you are anticipating something, you are looking forward to it. The noun is **anticipation**: *many of his generation are not eagerly anticipating retirement / eagerly anticipating his arrival / waiting with great anticipation / a buzz of anticipation in the building*

award to award something to someone means to give it to them officially. **Award** is also a noun: *he was ~ed compensation on the grounds of unfair dismissal / he was ~ed the Nobel Prize for Literature / the college ~s a few scholarships each year / won an ~ for her work / the ~ for best actor*

crèche a crèche is a place where babies and young children are looked after while their parents are at work: *are ~s common in workplaces? / dropped* the baby off at the ~ / she goes to a ~ every day / good ~ facilities

discriminate if you discriminate against someone, you treat them unfairly. The noun is **discrimination**: *her employers ~d against her on the grounds of her faith / ~ on the basis of race or gender / they face discrimination at work / discrimination against women / racial discrimination / sex discrimination / age discrimination*

dismiss to dismiss an employee means to tell them to leave their job. The noun is **dismissal**: *he was ~ed for stealing / ~ed from her job / awarded compensation on the grounds of unfair dismissal*

duty your duties are the things you have to do as part of your job. If you are on duty, you are working: *she was taken off front-line duties / carry out your duties / perform your duties well / I'm not on ~ this evening / go off ~ at six o'clock*

embrace if you embrace something, you accept it willingly: *~d their new rights / most workers have ~d the changes / ~ the reforms / ~d the idea of a female president*

harassment harassment is threatening behaviour towards someone. The verb is **harass**: *a victim of sexual ~ / racial ~ / complained about police ~ / accused him of ~ / claim they were harassed by the police / sexually harassed at work*

haul if you haul someone somewhere, you take them by force. If you haul something heavy, you pull it or carry it: *he was ~ed in front of a magistrate / ~ed the suitcase up to my room / ~ed myself up to bed*

incentive an incentive is something that makes you want to try harder because you know you will get it if you do well: *many employers offer ~s to retain staff / offering cash ~s / the government is providing tax ~s to businesses / a good ~ / a powerful ~*

leave leave is time when you do not have to work but you are still paid: *German women get 14 weeks maternity ~ / get 30 days annual ~ / entitled to paid ~ / he's on ~ at the moment / go on ~ next Friday*

legislation legislation is a law. The verb is **legislate**: *~ was introduced in 1992 / new ~ to protect children / a new piece of ~ / the ~ comes into effect next year / ~ on wildlife protection / ~ against discrimination at work / the government plans to legislate to prevent this happening again*

maternity maternity means to do with having a baby: *German women get 14 weeks ~ leave / ~ pay / ~ benefits / ~ services / ~ clothes*

mourn when you mourn, you feel very sad because someone has died: *took a week off work to ~ the death of a pet / still ~ing the death of her son / still ~s for her mother / hundreds of people turned out to ~ him / ~ the loss of a friend*

neglect if you neglect to do something, you do not do it although you really should do it: *someone ~ed to pass on the information / ~ed to tell me about the change of plan*

notice notice is a warning that something is going to happen: *I should get one month's ~ to leave / asked to leave without ~ / had to move out of the flat at short ~ / they didn't give us very much ~ / I handed in my ~ at work* (said I was going to leave)

perk a perk is something extra that you get from your job, as well as your pay: *subsidised travel is a nice ~ of the job / the job has quite a few ~s / one of the ~s of working for a large company*

privilege a privilege is a special benefit or advantage that certain people get: *the abuse of staff ~s / one of the ~s of working in a school / prisoners can earn special ~s*

retain if an organisation retains staff, the staff stay there and do not leave: *many employers offer incentives to ~ experienced staff / difficult to ~ good staff / want to ~ skilled workers*

subsidise if an organisation or government subsidises something, it pays part of the cost: *we get ~d travel / farming is ~d by the government / heavily ~d / the government no longer ~s public transport*

substantially substantially means by a large amount. The adjective is **substantial**: *the government is planning to raise the retirement age ~ / unemployment has increased ~ / share prices have fallen ~ / a substantial increase / a substantial decrease*

tribunal a tribunal is a court that can make decisions about one particular thing: *he took his employers to a ~ / an industrial ~ / an independent ~ / a war-crimes ~ / appear before the ~ / give evidence to the ~*

unanimous if a decision is unanimous, everyone involved in the decision agrees. The adverb is **unanimously**: *try to reach ~ decisions / a ~ vote in favour of the plan / a ~ verdict of guilty / voted unanimously to reject the offer*

IDIOMS

begs the question if something begs a question, it makes you want to ask the question: *this rather ~ why did they offer to fund me?*

pull your weight if you pull your weight, you do your share of the work. The image is of an animal pulling a heavy load with other animals and working as hard as the others: *failing to ~ can directly impact on colleagues*

pulling your leg if you are pulling someone's leg, you are joking: *take no notice – she's just ~*

set the wheels in motion if you set the wheels in motion, you start a process. The image is of starting a machine by making the wheels turn: *she said she'd ~*

show you the ropes if you show someone the ropes, you show them the things they need to do in order to do a job. The image is to do with showing someone all the ropes on an old sailing ship, so they know how to sail the ship: *dump your bags here and I'll ~*

EXERCISES

PREPOSITIONS

A **Complete the sentences with the correct preposition.**

1 We have a business relationship .... them.
2 I'm preparing a list .... candidates.
3 I left the report .... your desk.
4 You need to input the data .... the database.
5 He's part .... the management team.
6 I don't agree .... that statement.
7 Farming is subsidised .... the government.
8 I'm thinking of taking a week .... work.

WORD FAMILIES

A **Complete the expression with the correct form of the word in bold.**

1 effective **delegation**	you need to .... more
2 **eagerly** awaiting news	an .... employee
3 you need to **network** more.	a .... opportunity.
4 financial **backing**	did you .... them?
5 **redundant** workers	receive a .... payment
6 gender **discrimination**	the company doesn't ....
7 a **substantial** increase	prices have increased ....
8 he's **technically** brilliant	a .... problem

IDIOMS

A **Complete the idiom with the correct word in the list.**

question	weight	leg	wheels	ropes

1 My co-workers showed me the .... on my first day of work.
2 This begs the ....: Do we need to hire more staff?
3 Don't worry, I'm just pulling your ....
4 I have to work overtime because my colleague doesn't pull his ....
5 Let's schedule a meeting to set the .... in motion.

COLLOCATIONS

A **Complete the sentences with the correct form of the verb in the list.**

sound	haul	miss	don't	come	feel	hand

1 I've .... in my notice at work.
2 The new policy .... into effect next week.
3 The naughty pupil was .... in front of the headmaster.
4 Are you .... drained after your exam?
5 I thought the news .... a bit ominous.
6 .... hesitate to contact me if you have any questions.
7 I .... my deadline because I was too busy.

B **Complete the missing nouns.**

1 He appeared before a war-crimes t _ _ _ _ _ _ l.
2 Share p _ _ _ _ s have dropped significantly.
3 Two of my staff are on maternity l _ _ _ e.
4 He's seeking compensation for unfair d _ _ _ _ _ _ _ l.
5 The news had a huge i _ _ _ _ t on the company.
6 It doesn't mean anything. It's just a f _ _ _ _ _ _ _ y.
7 I need to submit an expense c _ _ _ m for my trip.
8 I work to very tight d _ _ _ _ _ _ _ s.

C **Complete the expressions with the words in the lists.**

occurrence	decision	leave	incentive
discrimination	notice	duty	

1 a freak ....
2 racial ....
3 on ....
4 a cash ....
5 annual ....
6 short ....
7 a unanimous ....

PHRASAL VERBS

A **Complete the sentences with the correct form of the phrasal verbs in the list.**

go off	drop off	draw up
take on	take off	passed on

1 I .... the information .... to my colleagues.
2 Can you .... these books .... at the library on your way to work?
3 I usually .... work at about 6 p.m.
4 That new song has really .... Every body's playing it.
5 We can't afford to .... new staff.
6 We need to .... a contract before we make a deal.

10

HEALTH AND ILLNESS

PAGES 70–71

administer if you administer a drug, you give it to someone: *~ the anaesthetic / ~ painkillers / ~ drugs to patients*

amputate if a doctor amputates someone's arm or leg, they cut it off. The noun is **amputation**: *he had part of his leg ~d / may have to ~ his foot / had two toes ~d / the first time he had performed an amputation*

anaesthetise to anaesthetise a patient means to give them a drug so that they cannot feel any pain. The drug is an **anaesthetic**: *he was given an injection to ~ him / was given an anaesthetic / administer the anaesthetic / a general anaesthetic / a local anaesthetic* (for one part of the body only)

degree the degree of something is the level of it: *suffered third ~ burns / enjoy a great ~ of freedom / players of varying ~s of ability / things have improved to some ~*

drip a drip is a piece of medical equipment that is used for putting liquids directly into someone's blood over a long period of time: *he was put on a ~ / an intravenous ~ / a saline ~ / attached to a ~*

excruciating if something is excruciating, it is extremely painful. The adverb is **excruciatingly**: *in ~ pain / the pain was ~ / it was ~ / excruciatingly painful*

fast if you fast, you do not eat or drink anything. **Fast** is also a noun: *had to ~ for twelve hours / ~ing during the month of Ramadan / break their ~ in the evening / decided to end my ~*

flap a flap is a small, loose piece of something: *a tiny little ~ in front of the eye / a ~ of skin / a ~ of leather*

graft a graft is a piece of healthy skin or bone that is taken from one part of your body and attached to another part. **Graft** is also a verb: *had a skin ~ / a bone ~ / some skin from her leg onto her neck*

limb a limb is an arm or leg: *got a prosthetic ~ / soldiers who lose ~s in combat*

lump a lump is a swollen area that grows on your body because of an illness: *found a ~ in her breast / had the ~ removed / a small ~ / a painful ~ in his knee*

malignant a malignant growth on your body is likely to spread and make you ill. The opposite is **benign**: *the lump was diagnosed as ~ / a ~ growth / a ~ tumour / ~ cancer cells / extremely ~ / highly ~ / a benign lump*

medication medication is drugs that you take to cure an illness: *takes ~ for his heart / are you on any ~? / the doctor can prescribe ~ / the side-effects of the ~*

procedure a procedure is a medical operation: *she was unconscious during the whole ~ / a complex ~ / a simple ~ / the surgeon who carried out the ~*

rehabilitation rehabilitation is the process of helping someone to get better after an illness or operation. The verb is **rehabilitate**: *a six-week ~ programme / ~ after a stroke / the process of rehabilitating patients after serious illnesses*

relapse if you have a relapse, you become ill again after you had been getting better. **Relapse** is also a verb: *had a ~ two months later / suffered a ~ / drugs to help prevent a ~ / a high risk of ~ / worried she might ~*

remission remission is a period during which a serious illness gets better: *the cancer went into ~ / the disease is in ~ / a period of ~*

scarring scarring is marks on your skin after you have had cuts or wounds. An individual mark is a **scar**: *had to wait for the ~ to heal / quite bad ~ / the cut left a scar on my face*

sew when you sew something, you mend it with a needle and some thread. The past tense is **sewed** and the past participle is **sewn**: *taught the girls how to ~ / ~ clothes by hand / ~ a button back on / a ~ing machine / he had the fingers sewn back on*

stitches stitches are pieces of thread that are used to close a deep cut or wound on your body: *had ten ~ in my head / had the ~ removed*

swell if part of your body swells, it becomes bigger than normal. The adjective is **swollen**: *my cheeks ~ed up / my knee was badly swollen*

PAGES 72–73

anchor if you anchor something, you fix it somewhere very firmly: *~ their minds in the present / make sure the tent is firmly ~ed*

beat when your heart beats, it moves in a regular rhythm. **Beat** is also a noun: *my heart ~s quite slowly / heart was ~ing fast / could hear her heart ~ / the regular ~ of the drums*

blink when you blink, you close and open your eyes quickly. When a light **blinks**, it flashes on and off: *~ing in the bright sunlight / made me ~ / the light on the phone was ~ing*

bout a bout of an illness is a short period during which you have the illness: *a ~ of depression / suffered from ~s of insomnia / got a nasty ~ of flu*

chronic a chronic illness is one that continues for a long time and cannot be cured: *a ~ degenerative disease / ~ skin conditions / suffers from ~ pain / ~ asthma*

clench if you clench a part of your body, you press it tightly together: *try not to ~ your muscles / ~ my fist / ~ed my teeth*

click if something clicks, it makes a short, sharp sound: *~ed my fingers / the door ~ed shut*

clutch if you clutch something, you hold it tightly: *~ my chest / fell to the ground ~ing his stomach / arrived ~ing a bottle of wine*

crouch if you crouch, you stand with your knees bent so that your body is very close to the ground: *~ down behind the sofa / ~ed over the fire*

dwell if you dwell on something unpleasant, you think or talk about it for a long time: *shouldn't ~ on the past / I often ~ on things / not something I want to ~ on*

eradicate if you eradicate something, you destroy it or get rid of it completely. The noun is **eradication**: *we have ~d many infectious diseases / smallpox has been completely ~d / want to ~ racism from sport / impossible to ~ inflation from the economy / aiming for the complete eradication of polio*

fatigue fatigue is tiredness: *get physical symptoms such as ~ / can lead to extreme ~ / physical ~ / mental ~ / suffering from ~*

flutter if something flutters, it moves quickly and gently: *~ your eyelashes / my heart was ~ing / flags ~ing in the breeze*

frown if you frown, you make your face look serious or angry by moving your eyebrows together. **Frown** is also a noun: *looked at the letter and ~ed / had a ~ on my face*

glare if you glare at someone, you look at them angrily. **Glare** is also a noun: *~d at me / ~d round the room / gave me an angry ~*

grin if you grin, you give a big smile. **Grin** is also a noun: *looked at me and grinned / grinning from ear to ear / gave a big ~*

harmony if there is harmony, things combine or go together well: *~ between mind and body / singing in ~ / live in ~ with each other / trying to achieve peace and ~ in the world / racial ~*

moan if you moan, you complain in a way that other people find annoying. **Moan** is also a noun: *I get grumpy and ~ a lot / always ~ing about something / ~ing about the food / wish you'd stop ~ing / having a ~ about the weather*

mortality the mortality rate is the number of people who die each year: *western medicine has been incredibly successful in improving ~ / ~ rates among young men / infant ~ rates*

pat if you pat something, you touch it in a gentle, friendly way: *patted the dog / patted my arm / patted me on the head*

proponent a proponent of something is someone who supports it. The opposite is **opponent**: *~s of the new law / a leading ~ of gay rights / mindfulness ~s*

punch if you punch someone, you hit them with a closed hand. **Punch** is also a noun: *~ed me in the face / threatened to ~ me / started throwing ~es at each other / landed a ~ on the side of my face*

put off if you put something off, you delay it until a later time: *we are successfully putting off death / ~ the meeting off until next week*

recur if something bad recurs, it happens again. Something that is **recurrent** keeps happening. The noun is **recurrence**: *the problem can ~ / is likely to ~ / suffers from recurrent bouts of depression / a recurrent skin infection / the recurrence of his illness*

scratch if you scratch a part of your body, you rub your hand over it roughly because it is itching: *~ing the insect bites on my leg / try not to ~*

set off to set something off means to make it start: *it's probably ~ off by stress / cold weather always ~s off my asthma / the news could ~ off panic in the financial markets*

shrug if you shrug your shoulders, you lift them up slightly to show that you do not know something or do not care: *he shrugged his shoulders and walked off*

shudder if something shudders, it shakes roughly: *my body ~ed / ~ing with cold / the truck ~ed to a halt*

spiral a spiral is a situation that gets worse and worse and seems to have no end. **Spiral** is also a verb: *therapies that allow sufferers to break this downward ~ / the downward ~ of drug abuse / an endless ~ of hate and violence / trying to stop the inflationary ~ / want to get into an upward ~ of economic growth / fears that inflation could ~ out of control*

stroke if you stroke something, you move your hand over it gently: *~d the cat / gently ~d my hair*

underpin to underpin something means to support it: *Chinese traditional medicine is underpinned by a philosophy / the wall needs to be underpinned*

PAGES 74–75

aggravate to aggravate something means to make it worse: *it can be ~d by repeated use of the hand / don't want to ~ the problem / sending in troops will only ~ the situation*

classify when you classify something, you decide which group it belongs in: *it is classified as an auto-immune disorder / documents which are classified as urgent / patients are classified according to age*

clog if something clogs, it becomes blocked. You can also say that something gets **clogged**: *it causes the arteries to ~ / the sink's got clogged again / the roads get clogged up with traffic in the summer / the drain's clogged with leaves*

deter if you deter someone, you discourage them from doing it: *this did not ~ them / using a burglar alarm to ~ burglars / ways to ~ young offenders from re-offending*

deteriorate if something deteriorates, it gets worse. The noun is **deterioration**: *your motor skills ~ over time / her health has ~d / fears that the economy is deteriorating / the weather was starting to ~*

disorder a disorder is an illness: *an auto-immune ~ / a common ~ / a genetic ~ / a blood ~ / an eating ~ / a physical ~ / a mental ~ / a personality ~ / suffer from a ~ / able to treat the ~*

ease to ease something means to make it slightly better: *the symptoms can be ~d by avoiding caffeine / should ~ the situation / ~ the pain / ~ the tension / ~ the pressure on staff / the pain has ~d slightly*

exacerbate to exacerbate something means to make it worse: *it can be ~d by repetitive use of the hand / might ~ the problem / don't want to ~ the situation / ~ the pain*

hereditary if something is hereditary, it is passed from parents to their children when they are born: *a ~ disease / a ~ title / ~ wealth*

intruder an intruder is someone who goes into a building illegally: *the police arrested the ~ / an ~ in the building / mistakes its own cells as ~s*

painstaking if you do something in a painstaking way, you do it very carefully. The adverb is **painstakingly**: *a period of ~ research / a ~ search of the area / the painting has been painstakingly restored*

patch a patch is a small area that is different in some way from the parts around it: *white ~es on the body / a ~ of grass / a few icy ~es on the road / some wet ~es on the carpet / a small bald ~ / a damp ~ on the wall*

pigment a pigment is a substance that gives something its colour. The **pigmentation** of something is its natural colour: *the cells which produce the ~ responsible for skin colour / the natural ~ in the leaves / the ~s used in modern paints / vitiligo is a chronic skin condition that affects pigmentation*

stem from to stem from something means to be caused by it: *psychological problems stemming from sufferers seeing their bodies as unhealthy / problems that ~ poverty*

stick to if you stick to something, you keep doing it or using it, and don't change it: *have to ~ a strict diet / ~ our original plan / ~ my initial decision*

thoroughly if you do something thoroughly, you do it in a very careful way. The adjective is **thorough**: *didn't consider the condition ~ / searched the building ~ / cleaned it all ~ / make sure the meat is ~ cooked / a thorough search*

tone a tone is a colour: *people with darker skin ~s / a lighter ~ / darker ~s / lovely rich ~s / warm ~s*

transmit to transmit something means to pass it from one person to another: *the disease can be transmitted by person-to-person contact / a sexually-transmitted disease / transmitted from mother to baby via the blood / ways of transmitting knowledge*

vulnerable if you are vulnerable to something, you are likely to suffer from it: *people who are ~ to heart attacks / extremely ~ to infections / areas that are ~ to drought / the villages are very ~ to attacks / airports are highly ~ to terrorist attacks*

EXERCISES

PREPOSITIONS

A Complete the sentences with the correct preposition.

1 Doctors can administer drugs .... patients.
2 It happened over a long period .... time.
3 The cut left a scar .... her face.
4 He suffers .... bouts of depression.
5 Muslims fast during the month .... Ramadan.
6 Why are you glaring .... me?
7 Everybody's moaning .... the weather.
8 He hit him .... his fist.

B Choose the correct preposition.

1 You shouldn't dwell *on / in* the past.
2 The condition is aggravated *on / by* sun exposure.
3 Those documents are classified *with / as* confidential.
4 Why do you have that frown *on / at* your face?
5 The disease can be passed *about / from* mother to child.
6 The intruder went *of / into* the building.
7 Many social problems stem *over / from* poverty.
8 She's weak and vulnerable *to / on* infection.

WORD FAMILIES

A Complete the expression with the correct form of the word in bold.

1 an **amputated** leg — doctors performed an ....
2 it was **excruciatingly** painful — in .... pain
3 a **rehabilitation** centre — he's .... very well
4 a **recurrent** problem — it's not likely to ....
5 his condition **deteriorated** — a slow ....
6 the report was **painstakingly** researched — a .... study
7 a **thorough** search — we checked it ....

COLLOCATIONS

A Complete the sentences with the correct form of the verb in the list.

> go grin shudder clench ease throw remove

1 The cancer has .... into remission.
2 I had my stitches ....

3 He was .... his fists in anger.
4 She was .... from ear to ear when she heard the news.
5 Who .... the first punch in the fight?
6 England's World Cup campaign has come .... to a halt.
7 I took an aspirin to .... the pain.

B Complete the missing nouns.

1 He suffered a sudden heart a _ _ _ _ k.
2 Doctors have put him on a strict d _ _ t.
3 You can't cure that. It's a genetic d _ _ _ _ _ _ r.
4 Young o _ _ _ _ _ _ _ s are sent to a rehabilitation centre.
5 Financial m _ _ _ _ _ s reacted badly to the news.
6 She's a leading p _ _ _ _ _ _ _ t of gay rights.
7 The operation was performed under general a _ _ _ _ _ _ _ _ c.

C Match the two halves of the collocations.

1 post-tramautic   a) drip
2 a personality   b) alarm
3 a burglar   c) mortality rate
4 infant   d) stress
5 racial   e) disorder
6 a bone   f) burns
7 an intravenous   g) graft
8 third degree   h) harmony

PHRASAL VERBS

A Complete the sentences with the correct form of the phrasal verbs in the list.

carry out	set off	put on
stick to	put on	cut off

1 He was going bald so he .... all his hair.
2 He's been .... a new weight-loss programme.
3 The procedure was .... successfully.
4 I'm really busy. Can we .... the meeting .... until Monday?
5 Pollen from plants .... my asthma.
6 I haven't changed my mind. I'm still .... my original idea.

11

PLAY

Pages 76–77

boo if people boo, they shout 'boo' to show that they do not like a person or performance. **Boo** is also a noun: *would the crowd ~? / the audience started ~ing / she was ~ed off the stage / there were a few ~s from the audience*

dirty something that is dirty uses unfair or illegal methods: *a ~ game / a ~ player / a ~ fighter / use ~ tactics*

drop if you drop someone from a team, you no longer have them in the team: *worried he would be dropped from the team / dropped from the World Cup squad*

fade if you fade, you start to start to gradually feel tired or weak. If something fades, it becomes weaker: *start to ~ towards the end of the race / the noise gradually ~d away / the colour in my jeans has ~d*

go wild if someone goes wild, they behave in a very excited way because they are happy: *the crowd went wild / ~ when they see the band*

knock out if you knock out another player or team from a tournament, you win against them so they are no longer in the tournament: *get ~ed out of the World Cup / get ~ed out in the semi finals*

open an open game or match is one that both teams or players could win: *a very ~ game / the first half was quite ~ / seems quite ~ at the moment*

overturn if you overturn a decision, you change it. The opposite is **uphold**: *hope the decision will be ~ed / the referee can ~ the decision / the verdict was ~ed by the Appeal Court*

reckless something that is reckless does not pay enough attention to possible dangers: *a ~ tackle / found guilty of ~ driving / show a ~ disregard for their safety*

relegate if a team is relegated, it is moved into a lower division of a league. If someone is relegated,

they are given a less important job. The noun is **relegation**. The opposite is **promote**: *they were ~d to division 2 / ~d to general office work / the club is fighting to avoid relegation*

scrape through if you scrape through, you succeed in something but only by a very small amount: *managed to ~ to the next round / ~ my exams / ~ my driving test*

substitute if a player is substituted, they are taken out of a game and another player takes their place. The player who replaces them is a **substitute**: *not very happy about being ~d / ~d at the beginning of the second half / bringing on a ~ / they're allowed three ~s*

suspend if someone is suspended, they are not allowed to take part in something because they have done something wrong or broken a rule: *~d from the tournament / ~d from school / two police officers have been ~d / he's been ~d for three games*

tackle if you tackle someone in a game, you try to win the ball from them. **Tackle** is also a noun: *~d him just outside the penalty area / a fair ~ / a reckless ~ / a bad ~ / a late ~ / booked for his ~ on Drogba*

tight a tight game is one in which the players or teams play equally well and it is difficult for one to win: *a very ~ game / the first half was very ~*

underdog the underdog in a game or competition is the one who is not expected to win. The opposite is **favourite**: *everyone wants the ~ to win / they go into this match as the ~s / the ~s of the competition*

uphold if you uphold a decision, you decide that it was right and should not be changed. The past tense and past participle is **upheld**. The opposite is **overturn**: *the decision was upheld / the Appeal Court upheld the original verdict*

Pages 78–79

accumulate if you accumulate things, you gradually get more and more of them: *you have to ~ points / have ~d a lot of books over the years / ~ wealth*

ammunition ammunition is bullets or other things you can fire from a gun. Ammunition is also anything you can use against another person: *running low on ~ / run out of ~ / live ~ / use the information as ~ against him*

beat up to beat someone up means to hurt them badly by hitting them: *it felt like I'd been ~en up / threatened to ~ me up / attacked him and ~ him up*

bluff when you bluff, you pretend that something is true. **Bluff** is also a noun: *I think you're ~ing / tried to ~ / ~ed my way through the interview / it was only a ~ / I was sure it was a ~*

bypass if you bypass something, you avoid it: *find cheats on the Internet in order to ~ some tasks / tried to ~ the security system / ~ the waiter and talk directly to the manager*

capture if you capture something, you get control of it. If you capture a person, you take them prisoner: *a fierce battle to ~ market share / enemy soldiers ~d the bridge / ~d the town / was ~d by the Russians / managed to ~ the elephant*

counter a counter is a small flat object that you move across the board in some games: *you're moving my ~! / the blue ~ / the red ~ / which ~ is yours?*

deal when you deal cards, you give them out to people at the beginning of a game. The past tense and past participle is **dealt**. The person who deals is the **dealer**: *~ six cards to each player / I'll ~ / ~ the cards out / dealt me an ace / whose turn is it to be the dealer*

dice a dice is a small block of wood or plastic with a different number of dots on each side: *hurry up and throw the ~ / roll the ~ / it all depended on one roll of the ~*

distinguish if you can distinguish between two things, you can recognise the difference between them: *I guess he ~es fact from fiction / can't ~ between right and wrong*

face up if something is face up, it has the front part facing upwards. If it is **face down**, it has the front part facing downwards: *leave the rest of the cards ~ down / lying ~ down on the ground / the body was lying ~ up*

gang up if people gang up on someone, they join together to attack them: *my brothers used to ~ on me / the kids at school ~ed up on me / felt that everyone was ~ing up on me*

hand your hand in a game of cards is the set of cards that you have been given: *this is a terrible ~! / haven't got a very good ~ / dealt me a good ~ / don't show your ~ to anyone*

infinite an infinite number or amount does not have a limit. The adverb is **infinitely**: *an ~ variety of games / an ~ number of possibilities / seems to have ~ patience / the universe is ~ / I'm infinitely grateful*

merchant a merchant is someone who sells something: *coins which represented ~s / a coal ~ / a wine ~ / a timber ~*

originate if something originates from a place, that is where it started or came from: *they ~d from Chinese paper dominoes / a dish which ~s from the Middle East / medicines which ~ from plants / the idea ~d in France*

peasant a peasant is a poor farmer who has a small farm: *clubs represented ~s / eats like a ~ / ~ farmers / a ~ woman*

reset if you reset something, you change it so that it is ready to be used again: *need to ~ the clock / the controller needs resetting / ~ the timer / ~ the alarm*

shed if you shed something, you get rid of it: *you have to ~ the cards in your hand / the company*

plans to ~ 200 workers / trying to ~ a few kilos / trees starting to ~ their leaves / most snakes ~ their skin once or twice a year

shuffle when you shuffle cards, you mix them so they are in a different order before you play a game: *~ the cards / give the cards a good ~*

spot if you spot something, you see it: *tried to ~ a particular kind of car / spotted one of my friends on the platform / the symptoms are quite easy to ~ / he was spotted with a woman / spotted buying cigarettes*

stake a stake is an amount of money that you risk in a game or bet: *the problem lies when there are big ~s involved / a £10 ~ / a low ~ / a small ~ / a high ~ / a big ~ / raise the ~s*

sword a sword is a weapon with a long sharp blade: *~s symbolising the military / a long ~ / a double-edged ~ / armed with a ~ / drew his ~ / a ~ fight*

symbolise to symbolise something means to represent it: *swords symbolising the military / a skull symbolising death*

tease if you tease someone, you laugh at them in a friendly or unkind way: *my brothers ~d me / ~d me about my weight / used to ~ me mercilessly / I was only teasing*

tip over if you tip something over, you turn it over: *I tipped over the board and stormed out of the room / nearly tipped the boat over / mind you don't ~ my drink over*

PAGES 80–81

adept if you are adept at something, you can do it well: *they become increasingly ~ at processing idiomatic usage / an ~ musician / most politicians are ~ liars*

chant a chant is a set of words that you repeat over and over again. **Chant** is also a verb: *~s, songs and other noises / religious ~s / ~s of 'Out, out, out!' / the crowd was ~ing his name*

encompass to encompass a lot of things means to include them all: *language play ~es everything from nursery rhymes to advertising slogans / the course ~es a range of subjects / ~es different aspects of student life*

exposure exposure to something is experiencing it. The verb is **expose**: *~ to nursery rhymes / ~ to the celebrity lifestyle / reduce your skin's ~ to the sun / children who are exposed to violence*

forge if you forge something new, you make it or develop it: *~ memorable slogans / ~ a relationship with them / ~ an alliance / ~ a career as an actor*

grasp your grasp of something is how well you understand it. **Grasp** is also a verb: *develop a sophisticated ~ of language / have a good ~ of the subject / beginning to get a better ~ of it / doesn't seem to ~ it very well / doesn't ~ it fully*

hurdle a hurdle is a problem that you have to deal with before you can achieve something: *had to overcome a lot of ~s / managed to get over the first ~ / a major ~ to progress*

impulse an impulse is a sudden strong desire to do something: *I can't help acting on ~ / had a sudden ~ to laugh / my first ~ was to run / the basic ~ to fight / tried to resist the ~ to hit him / bought it on ~*

innate if a feeling or quality is innate, you were born with it: *the desire to play with language is ~ in many people / her ~ ability to make people laugh / his ~ sense of fairness*

linguistic linguistic means to do with language: *a ~ study / a child's ~ development / ~ skills / ~ differences*

peer your peers are the people who are equal to you in age or social status: *use the language of their ~s / very popular with his ~s / her ~ group / started smoking because of ~ pressure*

proclaim if you proclaim something, you say it officially or publicly: *a headline ~ing 'Iraqi Head Seeks Arms' / ~ your innocence / the country ~ed independence*

rear the rear of something is the part at the back. **Rear** is also an adjective: *at the ~ of the bus / the ~ of the building / a ~ wheel / the ~ door of the car*

slogan a slogan is a short phrase that is used to advertise something or to persuade people about something: *a memorable ~ / an advertising ~ / a political ~ / a crowd chanting anti-war ~s*

sprint a sprint is a short race in which the runners run very fast. **Sprint** is also a verb: *it's a marathon, not a ~ / the 100 metres ~ / a short ~ / made a ~ for the door / ~ed to the bus stop*

witty something that is witty uses language in a clever and funny way. The noun is **wit**: *~ lines / a ~ slogan / ~ remarks / she's very ~ / extremely ~ / laughed at his wit*

the ball's in your court if the ball is in your court, it is up to you to decide what to do next. If the ball is in your court in a game of tennis, it is your turn to hit it: *~ now*

below the belt if something is below the belt, it is unfair. The expression comes from boxing and wrestling, where fighters are not allowed to hit each other below the belt: *some of the comments were a bit ~*

blow your chance if you blow your chance, you lose a good opportunity: *they've blown their chances now*

keep your cards close to your chest if you keep your cards close to your chest, you do not let other people know what you are thinking. The expression comes from cards, when players hold their cards close to their chest so that other players cannot see them: *he keeps his cards close to his chest*

a level playing field if there is a level playing field, everyone has the same chance of winning or succeeding. The expression comes from games such as football, where if the playing field is level no team has an advantage: *all we're asking for is ~*

move the goalposts if someone moves the goalposts, they change the rules in a situation so that it is more difficult for you to succeed. The expression comes from football, where if someone suddenly moves the goalposts it is very difficult to score a goal: *the boss keeps moving the goalposts*

neck and neck if two people or groups are neck and neck in a competition, they are level. The expression comes from racing, where if two racers are neck and neck they are equal: *the two main parties were ~ in the polls*

a pawn in a game a pawn in a game is someone who is used by a more powerful person. The expression comes from the game of chess, where the pawns are the least valuable pieces. Someone moves the pawns in order to gain victory for themselves: *the city has been a pawn in regional power games for hundreds of years*

saved by the bell if you are saved by the bell, you escape from a difficult situation because an event ends. The expression comes from fighting, where a bell is rung to mark the end of each round of the fight: *Phew! ~*

show his hand if you show your hand, you let your opponents know your intentions, and what possible advantages you have. The expression comes from cards, where you try to keep your cards hidden until your opponent has shown theirs: *recent events have forced the president to ~*

time on your hands if you have time on your hands, you have time available when you are not busy: *now have more free time on my hands*

a high stakes game a high stakes game is a situation in which you risk losing a lot of money. The expression comes from cards, where the stake is the amount of money you bet on each game: *currency trading is a very high stakes game*

EXERCISES

PREPOSITIONS

A Complete the sentences with the correct preposition.

1 He's been suspended ...... the tournament.
2 England go ...... the game as underdogs.
3 I found the information ...... the Internet.
4 Do you want to play a game ...... cards?
5 He teased me ...... my haircut.
6 She has a good grasp ...... the language.
7 I had to sprint ...... the bus stop.
8 He's accumulated a lot of wealth ...... the years.

WORD FAMILIES

A Which of the words are both nouns and verbs?

1 sprint ____
2 suspend ____
3 distinguish ____
4 grasp ____
5 tackle ____
6 merchant ____

IDIOMS

A Complete the idiom with the correct word in the list.

belt	level	hand	cards
time	goalposts	court	neck

1 His comments were rude and a bit below the
  ....
2 It's really close! Both teams are neck and
  ....
3 It's your decision. The ball's in your ....
4 You never know with him. He keeps his
  .... close to his chest.
5 We didn't have a chance. It wasn't a ....
  playing field.
6 I wish they would stick to the plan and stop
  moving the ....
7 I'm really busy now but next week I'll have more
  .... on my hands.
8 Be patient. He'll have to show his ....
  sooner or later.

COLLOCATIONS

A Complete the sentences with the correct form of the verb in the list.

run	boo	act	overturn	raise	go

1 The band was .... off the stage.
2 The crowd .... wild when their team
  appeared.
3 We're .... low on printing paper.
4 Striking workers have .... the stakes in
  the negotiations.
5 I wasn't thinking. I just .... on impulse.
6 The decision was .... by the match
  referee.

B Complete the missing adjectives.

1 It was a very d _ _ _ y game. Three players were
  sent off.
2 They played much better in the s _ _ _ _ d half.
3 He was penalised for a l _ _ e tackle.
4 She found maths a m _ _ _ r hurdle in high school.
5 There are h _ _ h stakes involved in the deal.
6 It was a t _ _ _ t game. Both teams played well.

C Complete the expressions with the words in the list.

slogan	test	ammunition	area	share	group

1 an advertising ....
2 a peer ....
3 market ....
4 live ....
5 the penalty ....
6 a driving ....

PHRASAL VERBS

A Complete the sentences with the correct form of the phrasal verbs in the list.

gang up	get rid of	scrape through
knock out	beat up	run out

1 He complained that his classmates were
  .... on him.
2 We've .... of time. We have to stop now.
3 He was .... and robbed by some
  gangsters.
4 I passed my exams but I only just ....
5 Germany was .... in the semi finals of
  the World Cup.
6 I need to .... all the junk in the garage.

12

HISTORY

PAGES 82–83

dare if you dare to do something, you are not afraid to do it: *went far better than I'd ~d to hope / I didn't ~ look inside the room / I hardly ~d speak to him*

deprived if someone is deprived, they are poor and do not have the things that are considered normal or necessary: *she's from quite a ~ background / a ~ childhood / a ~ area / ~ children / extremely ~ / economically ~ / emotionally ~ / children who are ~ of love*

evacuate if you evacuate people, you make them leave a place because it is not safe: *she was ~d during the war / ~ everyone from the building / they were ~d to safety / ~d from the war zone / ~ the area / ~ the building*

flee if you flee, you run away. The past tense and past participle is **fled**: *they had to ~ the country / had to ~ their homes / ~ across the border / ~ to safety*

orphan if a child is orphaned, both their parents die. **Orphan** is also a noun: *he was ~ed when his parents were killed in a car crash / a home for ~s*

privileged *she's from a very ~ background / ~ children / they're extremely ~*

radical something that is radical uses new and different ideas: *he was involved in ~ politics / a ~ politician / a ~ left-wing party / ~ ideas / a more ~ approach / very ~*

scholarship if you get a scholarship your study is paid for by the school or an organisation: *she won a ~ to study in the States / got a ~ / they offered him a ~ / a ~ to Oxford*

sheltered someone who is sheltered has not experienced any of the unpleasant things in life: *she had a very ~ upbringing / lived a ~ life / she seems very ~ / quite ~*

textile a textile is a cloth: *sold ~s from door to door / printed ~s / a ~ factory / a ~ designer*

upbringing your upbringing is the way in which you are brought up and educated by your parents: *he had a very sheltered ~ / a strict ~ / a middle-class ~ / a religious ~ / wanted to give their children a good ~*

PAGES 84–85

advance if you advance an idea, you suggest it: *he ~d the theory of the end of history / the scientist who first ~d the idea*

assert if you assert something, you state very firmly that it is true: *he ~s that the Roman Empire's decline stemmed from invasions / ~ed quite forcefully that it had been a mistake / ~ed his innocence*

cast doubt if you cast doubt on something, you say that you think it is not true. The past tense and past participle is **cast doubt**: *archaeologists have ~ on the claim / ~ on the theory*

challenge if you challenge something, you question it and refuse to accept it. **Challenge** is also a noun: *he ~d the status quo / ~d her ideas / ~d the conventional views of the time / ~d the government's authority / plans to ~ the decision / ~ the verdict / mount a legal ~ to the decision*

cite if you cite someone, you mention it as an example of something you are talking about: *you ~d Edward Gibbon / ~d the president as an example*

contend if you contend something, you argue that it is true. The noun is **contention**: *he ~s that governments play a minor role in the economy / ~s that political freedom is more important than wealth / his contention that individuals should take more responsibility for their own actions*

culminate to culminate with something means to end with it. The noun is **culmination**: *a series of suggestions culminating with the leader's cry, 'Oh, shut up!' / the culmination of a year's work / a series of disputes which ~d in a general strike*

decadence decadence is immoral behaviour. The adjective is **decadent**: *the ~ of the Roman Empire / sexual ~ / a decadent regime / a decadent period*

demonstrate if you demonstrate that something is true, you show it clearly. The noun is **demonstration**: *she ~s that the Roman Empire's decline stemmed from invasions / ~s the link between poverty and crime / ~ how the justice system works / ~ your determination to win / a clear demonstration of the need for more police*

findings findings are things that you find or learn: *some new archaeological ~ / the key ~ of the report / the survey led to some interesting ~ / they will report their ~ next month / present his ~ at the meeting*

establish if you establish something, you find facts that prove that it is true: *he ~ed that the arrival of democracy was the endpoint for conflict / trying to ~ the truth / want to ~ who was in the building at the time*

give rise to to give rise to something means to cause it: *the Roman Empire's decline gave rise to invasions / ~ an argument / ~ concerns about his health*

go by when times goes by, it passes: *hardly a year goes by without a new book on the subject / another year has gone by / as the days ~ / the time went by quite quickly*

heritage your heritage is all the beliefs, traditions and customs of your family or country: *their cultural ~ / need to preserve our national ~ / a World ~ site / buildings that are an important part of our ~*

highlight if you highlight something, you show that it is very important: *~s the importance of ordinary people in American history / the report ~s the problem of youth crime / ~ the dangers of consuming too much alcohol / ~ the difficulties of policing such a large area*

lead lead is a soft grey metal: *~ poisoning / use ~ on the roof / ~ pipes*

outlook your outlook is your general attitude and opinion about something: *the ~ of modern green movements / an optimistic ~ on life / have a positive ~ / events which changed my ~ on life*

parallel a parallel between two things is a similarity between them: *draw ~s with Germany's integration into the European Union / find ~s between the two poets / see a clear ~ between the two cases*

pottery pottery is objects made out of baked clay: *stopped manufacturing ~ / found some Roman ~ / a piece of ~ / a ~ bowl / hand-painted ~*

put forward if you put forward an idea, you suggest it: *~ a new theory / ~ some interesting ideas / ~ a suggestion*

rigorous something that is rigorous is careful and exact. The adverb is **rigorously**: *a new ~ scientific age / a ~ piece of research / work to ~ standards / carry out ~ safety checks / everything is rigorously checked*

ruin a ruin is a part of a building that is left after the rest has been destroyed. The adjective is **ruined**: *Roman ~s / searching through the ~s of the building / reduced the building to a ~ / a ruined castle*

sack if people sack a city, they attack it and destroy it: *Rome was ~ed by the Barbarians / they ~ed the city*

sanitation sanitation is the systems for taking away dirty water and human waste from a building in order to protect people from diseases: *the building has no modern ~ / modern standards of ~*

scarcity if there is a scarcity of something, there is very little of it. The adjective is **scarce**: *the ~ of evidence available / a ~ of clean water / food scarcities / jobs are scarce at the moment*

scholar a scholar is someone who is well-educated and knows a lot about a subject: *most ~s agree on this / a brilliant ~ / a distinguished ~ / a Latin ~ / a history ~*

significant something that is significant is important. The opposite is **insignificant**: *plays a ~ role in the economy / a very ~ achievement / some ~ findings / some very ~ changes / this is highly ~/ this might prove ~/ consider it extremely ~ / an insignificant amount of money*

tile a tile is a square of baked clay that you put on a wall, floor or roof. Something that is **tiled** has tiles on: *~d roofs / a ~d floor / bathroom ~s / roof ~s*

transition a transition is the process of changing from one thing to another: *the ~ between the fall of Rome and the invading German tribes / the ~ to a market economy / a rapid ~ / a peaceful ~ / make the ~ from junior school to secondary school / a period of ~*

uprising an uprising is an attempt by a large number of people to change their government by force: *the Romans were not defeated by popular ~s / an armed ~ / a mass ~ / a successful ~ / the failed ~ / could spark an ~ / provoke an ~ / the government put down the ~ / crushed the ~*

whip up if you whip up a strong emotion, you try to make people feel it: *their leader is trying to ~ anger / ~ support for the party / trying to ~ interest in the scheme*

PAGES 86–87

accession accession is the formal process of accepting something or joining something: *their ~ to the European Union / their ~ to the World Trade Organisation / his ~ to the throne / her ~ to power*

assassinate to assassinate an important person means to kill them. The noun is **assassination**: *the president was ~d / an attempt to ~ the king / an assassination attempt / an attempted assassination / the assassination of the king*

bodyguard a bodyguard is someone whose job is to protect an important person: *the president's ~s / never goes anywhere without his ~s / armed ~s / a lot of celebrities have personal ~s*

bombing a bombing is a situation in which bombs are used to attack a place: *a series of ~s on civilian targets / a wave of ~s / the ~ of the American embassy / a ~ campaign / a ~ raid*

bust if a business goes bust, it loses all its money and cannot continue operating: *the organisation has gone ~ / his company went ~ / the business went ~*

civilian a civilian is someone who is not a member of the police, army, etc.: *hundreds of ~s were killed / innocent ~s / unarmed ~s / accused them of targeting ~s / ~ casualties*

clout if someone has clout, they have the power to change things or influence people: *it gives them greater geo-political ~ / the company has a lot of ~ / have considerable ~ / use their ~ to influence the committee*

dent to dent something means to damage or hurt it: *it ~ed our pride / ~ her reputation / ~ his confidence / could ~ profits*

equalise if someone equalises, they score a point in a game so they have the same number of points as their opponents. The point they score is an **equaliser**: *Brazil ~d in the second half / Ronaldo scored the equaliser*

genocide genocide is the murder of a whole group or race of people: *the ~ in Rwanda / mass ~ / commit ~ / accused of ~ / accused them of cultural ~*

loot if people loot, they steal things from shops or houses that have been damaged: *the ~ing began soon after the earthquake struck / shops and offices were ~ed*

massacre to massacre a large number of people means to kill them. **Massacre** is also a noun: *over a hundred civilians were ~d / brutally ~d / a bloody ~ / a terrible ~ / carry out the ~ / the troops responsible for the ~ / accused of taking part in the ~ of innocent civilians*

militant a militant organisation is willing to use extreme or violent methods to achieve political change: *a very ~ trade union / a ~ group / ~ anti-abortionists / becoming more ~*

push for if you push for something, you try to get it: *~ing for accession to the European Union / ~ing for a pay increase / ~ing for a complete ban on whale fishing*

stand your stand on an issue is your opinion that you state firmly: *take a strong ~ against injustice / don't want to take a ~ on the issue / criticised his ~ on abortion / the conservative ~ on immigration*

tense a tense situation is one in which people feel worried about what might happen: *a time of ~ industrial relations / a ~ situation / a ~ atmosphere / a very ~ meeting / a ~ silence / situation is growing more ~ / things remain ~ / extremely ~ / rather ~*

IDIOMS

avoid something like the plague if you avoid something like the plague, you try very hard to avoid it. The plague is a disease that causes spreads easily between people and causes death: *I avoid him like the plague*

bark is worse than his bite if someone's bark is worse than their bite, they seem unfriendly or unpleasant but they are really quite nice. The expression comes from the idea of a dog that barks a lot but us unlikely to bite you: *it turns out his bark is much worse than his bite*

broken home a broken home is a family that does not live together because the parents are divorced: *he comes from a ~ / children from ~s*

lust for life a lust for life is a strong feeling of wanting to enjoy life as much as possible. Lust is a very strong sexual desire: *she's always had a real ~ / a young man with a real ~*

memory like a sieve if you have a memory like a sieve, you forget things very easily. A sieve is a kitchen tool like a bowl with a lot of holes in. You use it for separating liquids from solids: *I've got a memory like a sieve*

rite of passage a rite of passage is something that a boy has to do in some cultures in order to become a man. You can also describe any difficult action someone must take as a rite of passage: *it symbolised a kind of ~ / saw giving her first speech as a kind of political ~*

EXERCISES

PREPOSITIONS

A Complete the sentences with the correct preposition.

1 She comes .... a privileged background.
2 Poor education plays a role .... social issues.
3 You have to take responsibility .... your actions.
4 He's concerned .... his health.
5 The report highlights the problem .... unemployment.
6 She has a positive outlook .... life.
7 He drew parallels .... other products in his presentation.

WORD FAMILIES

A Complete the expression with the correct form of the word in bold.

1 the dispute **culminated** in war   the .... of the investigation
2 from **decadence** to decay   a .... government
3 he **demonstrated** with an example   a clear ....
4 results are checked **rigorously**   a .... study
5 ancient **ruins**   it was .... by the sun
6 a **scarcity** of doctors   .... resources
7 Kennedy was **assassinated**   an .... attempt
8 they **equalised** in the second half   Drogba scored the ....

IDIOMS

A Complete the idiom with the correct word in the list.

plague broken memory lust bark rite

1 I really don't like him. I avoid him like the ....
2 Don't worry about her. Her .... is worse than her bite.
3 It can be harder on children who come from .... homes.
4 She has a great attitude and a real .... for life.
5 He forgets everything. He has a .... like a sieve.
6 Getting a driver's licence is a .... of passage for young adults.

COLLOCATIONS

A Complete the missing nouns.

1 I'm doing a course in industrial r _ _ _ _ _ _ _ s.
2 She takes a strong s _ _ _ d against abortion.
3 Disgruntled workers are threatening a mass u _ _ _ _ _ _ g.
4 The Foreign Secretary played a significant r _ _ e in the peace talks.
5 The report outlined the key f _ _ _ _ _ _ s of the study.
6 Forensic evidence has cast d _ _ _ t over his claims.

B Match the two halves of the collocation.

1 a sheltered   a) tiles
2 a general   b) economy
3 your cultural   c) upbringing
4 bathroom   d) school
5 a market   e) strike
6 secondary   f) heritage

PATTERNS

A Complete the sentences with the correct form of the verbs in the list. Use to- infinitive or –ing.

change	study	challenge
consume	establish	manufacture

1 The factory has stopped .... that model.
2 His lawyers have decided .... the decision.
3 People's opinions are in the process of ....
4 She won a scholarship .... in Australia.
5 Engineers are trying .... the cause of the problem.
6 He knows the dangers of .... too much alcohol.

PHRASAL VERBS

A Complete the sentences with the correct form of the phrasal verbs in the list.

give rise to	whip up	put down
carry out	put forward	

1 The Industrial Revolution .... modern technology.
2 Scientists have .... new ideas about evolution.
3 Police are .... an investigation.
4 The military has threatened to .... the uprising.
5 The speaker tried to .... support from the crowd.

13

NEWS AND THE MEDIA

PAGES 92–93

bar if you bar someone, you officially say that they cannot do something or go somewhere: *the club has barred football fans / he's been barred from leaving the country*

bid a bid is an attempt to do something: *a takeover ~ / his ~ to become Wimbledon champion / a ~ for freedom / an unsuccessful ~ to become the party leader / launch a ~ to take over the company*

blast a blast is an explosion: *two men were killed in the ~ / a huge ~ / a powerful ~ / heard the bomb ~ / a huge bomb ~ rocked the city centre*

blow a blow is something disappointing that happens: *safety fears deal a ~ to car company's recovery / a big ~ to the industry / a major ~ / a serious ~ / a devastating ~ / deal a crushing ~ to his hopes of becoming president / the news came as a ~ to local businesses*

brink the brink is the point when something very good or bad is about to happen: *the win brings the team to the ~ of the league title / on the ~ of war / seemed on the ~ of death / on the ~ of disaster / bring them back from the ~ of defeat*

clash if you clash with someone, you fight or argue with them. **Clash** is also a noun: *police ~ with protestors / ~ with the opposition leader in a heated debate / ~ over how to spend the money / violent ~es between demonstrators and the police*

clear to clear someone means to prove that they are not guilty of something: *Sanders ~ed of bribery charges / ~ed of all charges / ~ed by the Court of Appeal / new evidence which helped to ~ him / trying to ~ her name*

convict if someone is convicted of a crime, they are found guilty. The noun is **conviction**: *he was ~ed of murder / ~ed on charges of bribery and corruption / a ~ed thief / had no previous convictions / difficult for the police to secure a conviction*

coverage if there is coverage of an event, it is mentioned in newspapers or on radio or TV: *a lot of news ~ of the event / press ~ / TV ~ / the speech received a lot of ~ / got a lot of ~ / live ~ of the game*

fuss if there is a fuss about something, it gets a lot of attention and people get excited or angry about it: *it's such a ~ about nothing / don't want a lot of ~ about the wedding / can't see what all the ~ is about / make a ~ / kick up a ~*

hail if you hail something, you say publicly that it is very good: *president ~s breakthrough in peace process / ~ed it as a victory for common sense / event was ~ed a success / ~ed as a hero*

leak a leak is a piece of secret information that someone deliberately makes public. **Leak** is also a verb: *email ~ reveals secret plan to slash jobs / a ~ from Downing Street / determined to find the source of the ~ / the information was ~ed to the press*

outburst an outburst is a sudden expression of strong anger: *Hector vows to continue despite ~ / a sudden ~ / an angry ~ / a violent ~ / a furious ~ against the minister*

pull out if you pull out of something, you stop being involved in it: *Kohl ~s out of Open / ~ out of the completion / threatening to ~ out of the talks / could ~ out if their demands aren't met*

raid if there is a raid, the police go to a place without warning to find something illegal: *police seize $10 million drugs haul in house ~ / a series of police ~s / a ~ on the house / a dawn ~ / a drug ~ / carry out a ~ / injured during the ~*

rally a rally is a large public meeting in the street to protest about something: *police clash with protestors at union ~ / a big ~ / a mass ~ / a public ~ / a political ~ / a protest ~ / anti-government rallies / hold a ~ / stage a ~ / take part in the ~*

rule out if you rule something out, you decide that it is not possible: *teachers ~ out strike action / ~ out the use of troops / police have ~d out murder / ~ out the possibility of further funding*

seize if the police seize something, they take it: *police ~ $10 million drugs haul in house raid / ~ illegal goods / have the power to ~ his assets*

slash if you slash something, you reduce it by a large amount: *a secret plan to ~ jobs / ~ prices / ~ the workforce / ~ government spending*

technicality a technicality is a very small detail: *the case was dismissed on a ~ / case was dropped because of a legal ~*

vow if you vow to do something, you promise to do it: *Hector ~s to continue despite outburst / ~ed that he would continue / ~ never to forget / ~ed he would never see her again*

accusation an accusation is a statement saying that someone is guilty of something. The verb is **accuse**: *~s of sexism / a serious ~ / false ~s / made ~s against him / now faces ~s of corruption / deny the ~s / cannot prove the ~s / accused him of lying / accused of murder*

advocate an advocate for something is a person who supports it. **Advocate** is also a verb: *a leading ~ for freedom of the press / a firm ~ of free university education / a staunch ~ of democracy / he ~s more investment in public transport*

broadsheet a broadsheet is a serious newspaper that is printed on large sheets of paper. The opposite is **tabloid**: *reads one of the ~s / a serious ~ / a ~ newspaper / in all the ~s*

circulation the circulation of a newspaper is the number of copies that are sold each day: *the ~ of most papers is falling / a large ~ / a small ~ / has a limited ~ / a daily ~ of 15,000 / ~ is increasing*

editorial the editorial in a newspaper is an article which gives the editor's opinion: *the left-wing bias is reflected in their ~ / read the ~ / a newspaper ~ / publish an ~ / run an ~ on prisons*

gather if you gather something, you collect it: *traditional ways of ~ing news / ~ information / ~ evidence*

imminent if something is imminent, it is about to happen very soon: *predicting the ~ demise of paper-based publishing / in ~ danger / an ~ threat to national security*

libel libel is the offence of writing something untrue about someone that could harm their reputation. **Libel** is also a verb: *the paper has frequently been sued for ~ / a ~ case / ~ laws / claim damages for ~ / the newspaper had libelled him*

loathe if you loathe something, you hate it. The noun is **loathing**: *the Sun is loved and ~d in equal measure / absolutely ~ it / looked at me with loathing*

outright outright means complete. **Outright** is also an adverb: *want ~ independence / an ~ victory / an ~ majority / an ~ ban on smoking / told an ~ lie / they won ~*

propaganda propaganda is false information that is given to make people believe something: *accused of disseminating ~ / government ~ / state ~ / political ~ / a ~ campaign*

renowned if you are renowned for something, you are well known for it: *it's ~ for its catchy headlines / he's ~ for his brilliant speeches / an island ~ for its wildlife / a world ~ scientist*

retract if you retract something that you said, you say that you did not really mean it: *papers are sometimes forced to ~ claims / later ~ed his statement / ~ your confession*

sensationalist sensationalist news is news that is made to seem extremely exciting or shocking.

The noun is **sensationalism**: *a lot of the tabloids are very ~ / ~ headlines / ~ reporting / accused the newspaper of sensationalism*

spectrum a spectrum is a complete range of different things: *to the right of the political ~ / cover the full ~ of subjects / a broad ~ of opinion / the entire age ~ / people at opposite ends of the ~*

staple a staple thing is one that you always use or have: *~ foods / the country's ~ export products / a ~ part of our diet / their ~ diet is rice / the paper's ~ diet is celebrity gossip*

subscription a subscription is an amount of money that you pay regularly to receive a newspaper or magazine. The verb is **subscribe**: *97% of the circulation is ~-based / pay a monthly ~ / an annual ~ / take out a ~ to the New York Times / renew your ~ / cancel your ~ / subscribe to a scientific journal*

substantiate if you can substantiate something you have said, you can prove that it is true: *forced to retract their claims if they are unable to ~ them / no evidence to ~ the claims / can't ~ their accusations*

sue if you sue someone, you make a legal claim against them: *the paper has frequently been ~d for libel / ~ him for negligence / ~ them for breach of contract / threatened to ~*

supplement a supplement is an extra part of a newspaper: *a weekly ~ / a monthly ~ / a colour ~ / a Sunday ~ / a special pull-out ~*

tabloid a tabloid is a newspaper that is printed on small sheets of paper and does not deal with serious news subjects. The opposite is **broadsheet**: *a lot of the ~s are very sensationalist / read the ~s / her face is all over the ~s / ~ newspapers / the ~ press / ~ journalism*

vicious something that is vicious is very violent and cruel: *a ~ personal attack / a ~ murder / a ~ killer / a ~ dog / ~ criticism / looks quite ~ / could turn ~ / started to get quite ~*

acknowledge if you acknowledge that something is true, you admit it. The noun is **acknowledgement**: *~d that newspaper companies are still alive and well / ~ that it is a serious problem / ~ the need for more spending on education / an acknowledgement that he was wrong*

aftermath the aftermath of something is the period of time after it: *the ~ of a bombing / the ~ of the storm / the ~ of the earthquake / in the ~ of war*

allegation if you make an allegation against someone, you accuse them of something. The verb is **allege**: *~s that he'd harassed the woman / ~s of fraud / serious ~s / false ~s / unfounded ~s / made an ~ of misconduct against him / strongly deny the ~s / it is alleged that he was involved in the corruption scandal*

appeal if you make an appeal, you ask a court to change its decision. **Appeal** is also a verb: *the newspaper is considering an ~ / lodge an ~ / make an ~ / an ~ against the ruling / an ~ against the conviction / win your ~ / lose your ~ / judge upheld the ~ / decided to appeal against the verdict*

assure if you assure someone of something, you tell them that it is definitely true: *~d reporters that the men died when the car exploded / ~d me that it would be OK / it's true, I can ~ you / rest ~d that we are doing everything we possibly can*

broad a broad idea is a general one, without specific details. The adverb is **broadly**: *I agree with the ~ policy / explained it in ~ terms / there is ~ agreement on the need for reform / a ~ outline of the plans / the ~ aims of the organisation / I agree with you, broadly speaking*

confirm if you confirm something, you say that it is definitely true: *she ~ed rumours that she is to retire on health grounds / further tests ~ed that he had the disease / this research ~s earlier findings / ~ed my suspicions / our fears were ~ed*

confront if you confront someone, you face them in a threatening way. The noun is **confrontation**: *crowds ~ed the police / ~ her with the truth / confrontations between demonstrators and the police*

crush to crush something means to press it so hard that it is damaged: *they were ~ed when police fired tear gas to disperse the crowd / his legs were ~ed / ~ed to death / the front of the car was ~ed / ~ed garlic*

deny if you deny something, you say that it is not true. The noun is **denial**: *she categorically denied that her retirement was linked to the scandal / ~ committing the crimes / ~ the allegations / ~ the existence of the letters / strongly ~ it / strenuously ~ it / can't ~ it / issued a strong denial*

disperse if you disperse a crowd of people, you send them away in different directions: *police fired tear gas to ~ the crowd / ~ the demonstrators / the crowd gradually ~d*

dispute a dispute is a disagreement or argument: *a ~ over nuclear energy / a serious ~ / a bitter ~ / a long-running ~ / involved in a ~ with their neighbours / find a way to resolve the ~*

hearing a hearing is a meeting of a court to make a decision about something: *heard evidence during the three-day ~ / a court ~ / a formal ~ / attend the ~ / hold the ~ in public*

praise if you praise something, you say that it is good. **Praise** is also a noun: *~d the work of the whole unit / ~ him for his bravery / ~ her warmly / was quick to ~ the police / full of ~ for the nurses*

proceeds the proceeds from something are the money that is gained from it: *all the ~ will be given to good causes / all the ~ will go to charity / the ~ from the sale / my share of the ~*

reject if you reject an idea, you do not accept it. The noun is **rejection**: *~ed demands for the government to change tack / ~ the idea / ~ his offer / firmly ~ed it / the motion was unanimously ~ed / good reasons for the rejection of the proposals*

tack a tack is a way of doing something: *rejected demands for the government to change ~ / switch ~ / try a different ~ / on the wrong ~ / on the right ~*

urge if you urge someone to do something, you suggest very strongly that they should do it: *~d them to make their voices heard / ~d her to keep going / ~ caution / ~ restraint*

hand on heart if you say something hand on heart, you really mean what you are saying. The image is that you put your hand over your heart to show that you are being sincere: *on broad policy ~ ~ ~ I remain totally behind this government / I promise, ~, that I won't let you down*

invasion of privacy an invasion of privacy is a situation in which someone talks about another person's private life in a way that is upsetting and wrong. An invasion is literally a situation in which an army enters another country by force: *stories about their private lives are an ~*

line your own pockets if you line your own pockets, you make yourself rich by taking money for yourself in a dishonest way. When you line a piece of cloth, you sew another piece of cloth on the back to make it stronger or warmer: *it's obvious he's been lining his own pockets*

the lowest common denominator the lowest common denominator is the least intelligent or least attractive part of people. Literally, the lowest common denominator is the smallest number that be divided exactly by all the bottom numbers in a set of fractions: *it's all designed to appeal to ~*

storm in a teacup a storm in a teacup is a big fuss about something that is not very important. A storm is a period of very bad weather, and a teacup is a small cup for drinking tea from: *it's just a ~ / think it's all a ~*

EXERCISES

PREPOSITIONS

A Complete the sentences with the correct preposition.

1 He's been barred .... entering the club.
2 Police have clashed .... protesters.
3 Nelson Mandela has been hailed .... a hero.
4 The information was leaked .... the press.
5 The two brothers are involved .... a property dispute.
6 Proceeds .... the sale were donated to charity.
7 The party leader is being sued .... libel.
8 Several businessmen have been linked .... the scandal.

WORD FAMILIES

A Complete the expression with the correct form of the word in bold.

1 she **rejected** the idea — a firm ....
2 a **confrontation** with police — have you .... him?
3 accused of **sensationalism** — a .... article
4 make an **accusation** — he was .... of lying
5 three previous **convictions** — a .... criminal
6 strong **loathing** — I've always .... this style
7 living in **denial** — he has .... receiving money

IDIOMS

A Complete the idiom with the correct word in the list.

| hand | lining | storm | invasion | common |

1 Concern about crime is the lowest .... denominator in this election.
2 It's true, really. I put my .... on my heart.
3 It's not a big problem. More of a .... in a teacup.
4 I'm tired of corrupt officials .... their own pockets.
5 She complained that the story about her was an .... of privacy.

COLLOCATIONS

A Complete the sentences with the correct form of the verbs in the list.

| take | make | lodge | slash |
| dismiss | change | clear | |

1 She's trying to .... her name of plagiarism charges.
2 Workers from all over the country are .... part in the protest.
3 I'm going to .... a fuss about their loud music.
4 The building industry is .... jobs because of low demand.
5 The case was .... on a technicality.
6 They've decided to .... an appeal against the ruling.
7 This plan isn't working. I think we need to .... tack.

B Complete the missing adjectives.

1 It was a m _ _ _ r blow when the proposal was rejected.
2 The town council had a h _ _ _ _ d debate about the new road.
3 Don't believe everything you read. Use your c _ _ _ _ n sense.
4 The Labour Party is holding a p _ _ _ _ _ _ _ l rally.
5 I don't like driving. I prefer to use p _ _ _ _ c transport.
6 The Conservative Party were not able to win an o _ _ _ _ _ _ t majority.
7 Rice is a s _ _ _ _ e food in many Asian countries.

C Match the two halves of the collocation.

1 a football	a) security
2 press	b) journalism
3 freedom of	c) fan
4 national	d) gas
5 breach of	e) the press
6 tabloid	f) contract
7 tear	g) coverage

PHRASAL VERBS

A Complete the sentences with the correct form of the phrasal verbs in the list.

| rule out | kick up | carry out | take out | pull out |

1 I've .... a subscription to the *New York Times*.
2 Two players have been .... of the next game through injury.
3 Police are .... a thorough investigation.
4 Some members are threatening to .... of the talks.
5 Restaurant owners are .... a fuss about the new licensing laws.

14

BUSINESS AND ECONOMICS

PAGES 98–99

cash flow the cash flow of a business is the amount of money coming in and going out each month: *manage your ~ / the ~ has increased / improve our ~ / have problems with ~ / due to ~ problems*

consolidate if you consolidate things, you combine them in order to make them cheaper or more efficient. The noun is **consolidation**: *having to ~ the range of services we provide / ~ our debts / ~ their business activities / working towards consolidation of our activities*

dire if something is dire, it is terrible: *the economy is pretty ~ at the moment / the situation is ~ / warned of ~ consequences / in ~ need of food and medicines / a ~ warning*

draw a draw is a way of choosing which teams or players will play against each other in a competition, by picking the names in a random way: *the ~ for the European Championships / pleased with the ~*

float when you float a company, you sell shares to the public for the first time. The noun is **flotation**: *~ the firm on the stock market / company will be ~ed on the stock market next year / planning a flotation next year*

flood if things flood into a place, they arrive in large numbers: *we've been ~ed with orders / we were ~ed with offers of help / refugees ~ing across the border / calls have ~ed into the office*

inundate if you are inundated with things, you get a lot of them at the same time: *we've been ~d with orders / ~d with offers of help / ~d with requests for information / ~d with calls from angry viewers*

lay off if you lay someone off, you stop employing them because there is no work for them. The noun is **lay-off**: *we've had to ~ off thirty people / the factory is ~ing off workers / I was laid off last month / the company is predicting even more lay-offs*

morale your morale is how happy or unhappy you feel: *building team ~ / ~ is very low / ~ is quite high / want to boost ~ / it's bad for ~ / help keep up ~ among staff / a pay rise is a great ~ booster*

overheads the overheads of a business are the amounts of money it has to pay regularly in order to operate: *move to an area where ~ are cheaper / want to reduce ~ / keep ~ down / ~ are quite low / have very high ~*

pick up if something picks up, it improves: *hope things will ~ up soon / the economy is beginning to ~ up / her health has ~ed up a bit*

pitch when you pitch, you try to sell something to someone or try to win business. **Pitch** is also a noun: *we're ~ing for a big contract / ~ for new business / ~ing the product to potential buyers / gave a very good ~ / a sales ~*

quarter a quarter is a period of three months: *the sales strategy for the next ~ / sales rose in the last ~ / the first ~ of this year / the fourth ~*

relocate if you relocate, you move to a different place. The noun is **relocation**: *we're relocating to a smaller town / ~ the business to Scotland / people had to be ~d / the costs of relocation*

sink if something sinks, it gets worse: *the economy is ~ing into recession / ~ing further into debt / ~ into depression / ~ into despair / ~ into chaos*

solid if something is solid, it is good or strong: *we have a ~ client base / good ~ advice / no ~ evidence against him / gave a ~ performance / a ~ worker*

take on if you take someone on, you give them a job: *had to ~ staff this year / ~ about 20 young people each year / ~ new workers*

terminate if you terminate something, you end it. The noun is **termination**: *want to ~ the contract / decided to ~ the pregnancy / ~ the military operation / a termination of pregnancy*

upturn an upturn is an increase or improvement. The opposite is **downturn**: *an ~ in sales / an ~ in the economy / an economic ~ / a slight ~ in the housing market / a sharp ~ in oil prices / an economic downturn*

PAGES 100–101

asset an asset is something that is useful. In business, an asset is something a company has that is worth money: *my local bank was seen as an ~ / a big ~ / a great ~ / a valuable ~ to any organisation / a company with ~s worth over £10 million*

authorisation authorisation is official permission. The verb is **authorise**: *money has left your account without your ~ / need special ~ to enter the building / written ~ / don't have ~ / refuse ~ / refused to authorise the visit*

bail out if you bail someone out, you give them money to solve their financial problems. The noun is **bailout**: *the bank needs to be ~ed out / my parents refused to ~ me out / the bailout of the banks*

bonus a bonus is extra money that you get once a year if you have done well in your job: *the ~ culture of the banks / got a $20,000 ~ / a big ~ / a huge ~ / get an annual ~ / receive a ~ / pay big ~es / award ~es*

default if you default, you do not make the regular payments that you need to pay: *you've ~ed on your mortgage / ~ on the payments / ~ on his child support payments*

deposit a deposit is an amount of money that you pay into a bank account: *make a ~ at the bank / a cash ~ / a large ~ / a small ~ / bank ~s*

deregulation deregulation is removing rules and controls on the way something works. The verb is **deregulate**: *~ allowed banks to expand / calling for ~ of the banks / promised to deregulate the financial sector*

exceed to exceed an amount means to go above that amount: *you've ~ed the pre-arranged figure / ~ your targets / claims ~ing £1000 / ~ing the speed limit*

feed off to feed off something means to use it to become stronger: *a beast that fed off your hard-earned cash / suspicions that ~ our own insecurities*

jeopardise if you jeopardise something, you risk damaging it. The noun is **jeopardy**: *taking risks that ~ the interests of shareholders / could ~ his research / an attack that could ~ the peace process / put his political career in jeopardy*

lax something that is lax is not strict enough: *~ mortgage lending / ~ security / ~ regulation / rules are too ~ / ~ morals*

legitimise to legitimise something means to make it seem acceptable: *banking is ~d theft / do these movies ~ violence?*

prompt to prompt something means to cause it to happen: *what ~ed this blog entry?/ what ~ed him to resign? / the decision ~ed demonstrations*

pursuit the pursuit of something is trying to get it or achieve it. The verb is **pursue**: *the reckless ~ of short-term gain / the ~ of wealth / the ~ of happiness / pursue a career in politics*

repayment a repayment is an amount of money that you pay regularly to give back money that you owe. The verb is **repay**: *you are able to meet your ~s / make regular ~s / the monthly ~s / can't keep up the ~s / mortgage ~s / ~s on a loan / struggling to repay their mortgage*

scale the scale of something is its size or level. **Scale** is also a verb: *it was small ~ and friendly / now we can see the ~ of the problem / horrified by the sheer ~ of the destruction / happening on a large*

~ / on a massive ~ / company wants to ~ down its operations / ~ up production at the factory

shareholder a shareholder is someone who has shares in a company: *recommend the offer to ~s / a big ~ in the company / a major ~ / small ~s*

stock market the stock market is the business of buying and selling shares in companies: *launch the firm on the ~ / buy shares on the ~ / prices on the ~ fell / the international ~s / the New York ~ / the London ~*

sum a sum of money is an amount of money: *an obscene ~ of money / a large ~ / a considerable ~ / offered me a generous ~ of money / received a ~ / pay back the ~*

taxpayer a taxpayer is someone who pays tax: *~s are having to pick up the bill / could cost the ~ millions of pounds / the way the government spends ~s' money*

PAGES 102–103

agenda an agenda is a list of things that are going to be discussed at a meeting: *the ~ for the meeting / the points on the ~ / the first item on the ~ / draw up an ~ / what's on the ~? / take it off the ~*

base a base is a point from which something can start or develop: *a low ~ / a sound commercial ~*

bottom line a company's bottom line is the amount of profit it makes: *could affect our ~ / looking for ways to improve the ~*

bulk if you buy things in bulk, you buy a large amount at a time: *buy in ~ / discounts for ~ orders*

chair the chair of a meeting is the person in charge who controls the meeting. **Chair** is also a verb: *what does the ~ of a meeting do? Was elected as ~ / address comments to the ~ / offered to ~ the meeting*

concession a concession is something you allow someone else to have in order to end an argument: *make ~s / offer ~s / win ~s / get ~s / some key ~s / important ~s / a major ~*

contingency a contingency is a situation that might happen in the future: *put some money aside for contingencies / have a ~ plan*

edge an edge is a small advantage that you have: *this will give us an ~ over our competitors / gain a competitive ~ / have an ~ over the other teams*

err if you err on the side of safety or caution, you are more safe or cautious than you really need to be: *~ on the side of caution / ~ on the side of safety*

feedback feedback is advice or comments that people give about how good something was: *got some good ~ / positive ~ / useful ~ / negative ~ / ~ on my work / gave us all ~ / provided ~*

focus group a focus group is a small group of people that a company questions about how good its products are: *conduct ~s / be part of a ~ / listen to ~s*

head start a head start is an advantage that helps you become successful before other people: *we'll have a ~ in establishing the brand / gives us a ~ over our competitors*

margin a margin is the difference between the amount it costs a company to produce something and the amount they sell it for: *what ~s are we looking at? / the ~s are very low / small ~s / tight ~s / the profit ~ isn't very good / increase the profit ~s / price reductions are squeezing the profit ~s*

minute minutes are an official written record of a meeting. **Minute** is also a verb: *take ~s of the meeting / write up the ~s / circulate the ~s / read the ~s / the ~s of the last meeting / no need to ~ this discussion*

ongoing something that is ongoing is still continuing: *~ negotiations / the discussions are still ~ / the ~ police investigation / this is an ~ situation*

outsource if a company outsources work, it arranges for it to be done outside the company in order to save money: *~ back office / ~ certain kinds of work / savings made by outsourcing*

patent a patent is an official document that gives you the right to make something that no one else is allowed to copy. **Patent** is also a verb: *apply for a ~ / get a ~ for the design / take out a ~ on the invention / protected by a ~ / the ~ office / trying to ~ the process*

project if you project an amount, you calculate what it will be in the future. The noun is **projection**: *the ~ed sales for next year / the company ~s an annual growth rate of 3% / costs are ~ed to rise / sales projections for the next five years*

prototype a prototype is a new product that is made to test what it is like, before large numbers are made: *a ~ of the new plane / build a ~ / test the ~ / product is still at the ~ stage*

retail if something retails at a particular price, that is the price it is sold for in shops. **Retail** is also a noun: *they ~ at €100 / ~ for £19.99 / the ~ value of the goods / the ~ price /~ outlets*

seal if you seal a deal, you agree it: *trying to ~ a major deal / ~ the pact / ~ a bargain*

spreadsheet a spreadsheet is a document that shows rows and columns of numbers: *hand out the ~ of the current figures / show it on a ~ / a computer ~*

stake if you have a stake in a company, you have money invested in it: *offered to raise their ~ / hold a 60% ~ in the company / a large ~ / a majority ~ / buy a ~ / sell your ~*

switch if you switch something, you change it. **Switch** is also a noun: *want to ~ suppliers / ~ jobs / ~ to a new electricity supplier / ~ sides in the debate / ~ from English to German / the ~ from analogue to digital TV*

volatile if a situation is volatile, it is likely to change suddenly: *it's been a ~ year for everyone in the industry / a ~ political situation / the markets are very ~ / highly ~*

IDIOMS

be in a hole if you are in a hole, you are in a difficult situation: *I'm in a hole / in a bit of a hole*

be on the cards if something is on the cards, it is likely to happen: *the relocation is still on the cards*

daylight robbery if something is daylight robbery, it is much too expensive. The image is of someone robbing you in a very obvious way, during the day: *the 20% rate is ~*

in light of this in the light of something means taking it into consideration: *in the light of all this, the news that the bank might need bailing out is not surprising*

make a killing if you make a killing, you make a lot of money very quickly. The image is of killing an animal and getting a large amount of food very quickly: *the big western banks ~ by loaning money to poorer countries*

not count your chickens (before they're hatched) if you don't count your chickens, you don't make plans that depend on something before it is certain that it will be successful. The image is of counting eggs and imagining that you will have a lot of chickens when in fact some of the eggs might not hatch: *the contract isn't signed yet, so we can't count our chickens just yet*

EXERCISES

PREPOSITIONS

A Complete the sentences with the correct preposition.

1 We've been flooded ..... orders for Spanish football shirts.
2 The office is relocating ..... Manchester.
3 Bad sales have put his career ..... jeopardy.
4 She doesn't understand the scale ..... the problem.
5 He's a great asset ..... the project.
6 I sold her my shares ..... the company.
7 You can see the figures ..... this spreadsheet.
8 The project is still ..... the planning stage.

WORD FAMILIES

A Complete the expression with the correct form of the word in bold.

1 a sales **projection**	what are the .... sales?
2 monthly **repayments**	has he .... you?
3 receive **authorisation**	I didn't .... that
4 debt **consolidation**	we should .... our efforts .... of
5 we **terminated** the position	employment
6 the peace talks are in **jeopardy**	don't .... the situation
7 in **pursuit** of freedom	always .... your dreams

IDIOMS

A Complete the idiom with the correct word in the list.

light	hole	chickens	cards	killing	robbery

1 We haven't won yet! Don't count your .... before they're hatched.
2 These bank charges are daylight ....
3 He made a .... by outsourcing production to cheaper countries.
4 In .... of the travel warning, I've decided to cancel my trip.
5 The trip is still on the .... I haven't decided against it.
6 I'm in a bit of a .... at work. It's a difficult time.

COLLOCATIONS

A Complete the sentences with the correct form of the verbs in the list.

sink	err	seal	put	boost	chair

1 The staff aren't happy. We need to .... morale.
2 Analysts say the economy is .... into recession.
3 A local businessman was asked to .... the meeting.
4 You should .... some money aside for your retirement.
5 I tend to .... on the side of caution.
6 We're still talking. We haven't .... the deal yet.

B Complete the missing nouns.

1 The company offers a wide range of s _ _ _ _ _ _ s.
2 We need to discuss our sales s _ _ _ _ _ _ y for the next quarter.
3 There's been a downturn in the housing m _ _ _ _ t.
4 My pay package includes an annual b _ _ _ s.
5 What's on the a _ _ _ _ a for the meeting?
6 We've received some positive f _ _ _ _ _ _ k from customers.
7 The product is available in retail o _ _ _ _ _ s.

C Complete the expressions with the words in the lists.

rise	limit	group	line
pitch	downturn	margin	market

1 the stock ....
2 a pay ....
3 a sales ....
4 an economic ....
5 the speed ....
6 the bottom ....
7 a focus ....
8 a profit ....

PHRASAL VERBS

A Complete the sentences with the correct form of the phrasal verbs in the list.

lay off	keep up	pick up
take on	pick up	keep down

1 We had to .... some workers .... because of bad sales.
2 Recycling paper helps to .... overheads ....
3 I think the economy will .... next year.
4 I can't .... any more work right now. I'm too busy.
5 A lot of people are struggling to .... their mortgage payments.
6 The company is .... the relocation bill.

15

FASHION

PAGES 104–105

awkward if you feel awkward, you feel embarrassed: *I don't want you to feel ~ / an ~ teenager / looks a bit ~ / painfully ~*

baggy baggy clothes are loose on your body: *~ silk trousers / a ~ jumper / a ~ T-shirt / it's a bit ~*

clash if colours or patterns clash, they don't look nice together. **Clash** is also a noun: *~ing patterns / the colours ~ / it ~es with your shirt / a ~ of colours*

collar the collar on a shirt or dress is the part that goes around your neck: *a flat ~ / a high ~ / his shirt ~ / his ~ was undone / loosen your ~*

faded clothes that are faded have lost a lot of their colour: *a pair of ~ jeans / a ~ denim jacket*

get away with if you can get away with wearing something, you can wear it and look nice: *I wish I could ~ it short like that / I'd never ~ wearing that colour*

heel the heel on a shoe is the part that makes it higher at the back: *wearing high ~s / low ~s / flat ~s / stiletto ~s (high and very thin)*

laces the laces on shoes are the strings that you tie to when you put the shoes on. The verb is **Lace**: *shoe ~ / do your ~ up / tie your ~ / your ~ are undone / teach him to lace his shoes*

lapel the lapels on a jacket are the parts that are folded back just below the collar: *wide ~s / narrow ~s / big ~s are back in fashion / a brooch pinned to her ~*

lining the lining is material inside a piece of clothing: *a silk ~ / a warm ~ / a fleecy ~*

pull off if you pull it off, you wear something unusual and look nice in it: *do you think they ~ it off well? / she manages to ~ it off*

ribbon a ribbon is a narrow piece of cloth that you use to tie something: *girls with ~s in their hair / silk ~s / tie the ~ / untie the ~*

set off to set something off means to make it look nice: *need some beads to ~ it off / it ~s your hair off nicely / the black really ~s off the red*

show off if a piece of clothing shows off your body, it makes it look nice: *it really ~s off your curves / colours that ~ off your tanned skin*

sleeve the sleeves on a piece of clothing are the parts that cover your arms. The adjective is **sleeved**: *a dress with short ~s / long ~s / wide ~s / rolled-up ~s / roll your ~s up / a short-sleeved shirt*

strap a strap is a thin piece of material that holds of fastens clothing. Straps on a dress or top are thin parts that go over your shoulders. A dress or top with no straps is **strapless**. **Strappy** shoes have a lot of straps: *a dress with narrow ~s / a strapless evening dress / a pair of strappy sandals / strappy shoes*

sturdy something that is sturdy is strong: *~ shoes / a ~ table / a ~ plant*

FASHION VOCABULARY

bangle: a bangle is a ring that you wear over your wrist

bob: a bob is a short haircut which goes to your chin and is the same length all the way round

flared: flared trousers or jeans become a lot wider at the bottom

frilly: frilly clothes are decorated at the edges with narrow pieces of cloth that are folded tightly together

frizzy: frizzy hair has a lot of dry wiry curls

highlights: if you have highlights, you give some of your hair a lighter colouring

linen: a light cloth

low-cut: a low-cut top or dress has a low neckline and shows part of the woman's chest

permed: permed hair is given a special treatment to make it curly

pinstripe: pinstripes are very thin stripes on cloth, especially in suits

ponytail: a ponytail is a bunch of long hair tied together at the back of your head so that it hangs down

shades: shades are sunglasses

shawl: a shawl is a large piece of material that a woman wears round her shoulders or over her head

spiked: spiked hair is hair that is gelled so it sticks up in points

tartan: tartan is traditional Scottish material with a large checked pattern

wedges: wedges are shoes where the soles are thin at the toes and become very thick at the heel

detachable something that is detachable can be removed. The verb is **detach**: *a ~ section that can be washed / a ~ collar / a ~ lining / you can detach the hood*

dress a style of dress is a type or style of clothes: *the Ottoman style of ~ / wearing military ~ / formal ~ / everyone was in evening ~ / modern ~ / traditional ~*

fabric a fabric is a cloth: *prohibited the use of British ~s / a cotton ~ / silk ~s / a knitted ~ / a thick ~ / a fine ~ / patterned ~s*

frown on if people frown on something, they disapprove of it: *the style was ~ed on when it first appeared / divorce is still ~ed on in some countries*

garment a garment is a piece of clothing: *~s which have been used to show status / a heavy ~ / a light ~ / woollen ~s / wearing a large black ~*

glittering a glittering event is one for rich, glamorous people : *a ~ Hollywood party / ~ events / a ~ ball*

gown a gown is a long dress for formal occasions: *the old ~s in the museum / an evening ~ / a ball ~ / a wedding ~*

grave a grave is a place where a dead person is buried: *people who have long since gone to their ~s / visit his ~ / body was found in a shallow~ / buried in an unmarked ~*

hold up as if you hold someone up as an example, you give them as an example: *she was held up as a fashion icon / the school should be held up as a model to others*

hint if you hint at something, you suggest it without mentioning it directly: *they ~ at something only half understood / what are you ~ing at? / ~ that more money might be available*

hood the hood on a piece of clothing is the part that you can pull up over your head: *wearing the ~ up / a coat with a ~ / put the ~ up*

inmate an inmate is a prisoner in a prison: *~s are refused belts / the ~s of the jail / get on well with his fellow ~s / a former ~ of the prison*

liberation liberation is becoming free. The verb is **liberate**: *the design symbolised freedom and sexual ~ / a feeling of ~ / a wonderful sense of ~ / political ~ / a war of ~ / women's ~ / gay ~ / liberate the prisoners / liberate women*

mount if something mounts, it gradually increases: *a ~ing sense of panic / tension in Middle East is ~ing*

ornate something that is ornate is decorated with a lot of small details: *the neckline was often ~ / very ~ / ~ wooden carvings / an ~ gold mirror*

outfit an outfit is a set of clothes that you wear together: *the ladies in court did not wear an ~ twice / buy a new ~ / a summer ~ / a new winter ~ / look really nice in that ~*

poignant something that is poignant makes you feel sad. The adverb is **poignantly**: *a ~ moment in the film / found it very ~ / extemely ~ / they wait ~ly for the music to begin again*

quarters 'in some quarters' means among some groups of people: *the design was banned in certain ~ / criticism from several ~ / offers of money from many ~*

reinforce to reinforce something means to make it stronger: *ruffs were often ~d with wire frames / made of ~d concrete / ~ the idea / newspaper headlines that ~ readers' prejudices*

seal if you seal something, you close it tightly: *the tomb was ~ed up / the windows were all ~ed shut / a ~ed envelope / the area has been ~ed off*

sinister something that is sinister seems bad or evil and makes you feel slightly scared: *sees the clothes as ~ / looks slighty ~ / something ~ about the building / nothing ~ about his death*

symbolise to symbolise something means to represent it. The adjective is **symbolic**: *the design ~d freedom and sexual liberation / the symbolic meaning of the drawings / they're symbolic of an idealised world / a symbolic gesture*

cutthroat a cutthroat situation is one in which people are competing with each other in a very determined and unpleasant way: *trying to sell clothes in a ~ market / the ~ world of advertising / a ~ business world / ~ competition*

depict if you depict something, you show it in a picture or describe it in words. The noun is **depiction**: *the way teenagers are ~ed on TV / a book ~ing life in pre-war London / ~s her as a strong independent woman / should curb the depiction of unhealthy models*

disseminate if you disseminate something, you spread it to a large number of people: *images that are ~d by the fashion industry / ~ the information / the report has been widely ~d*

enhance to enhance something means to improve it: *fashion is life-enhancing / ~ your appearance / ~ the flavour / ~ his reputation / ~ your chances of getting a job*

incidence the incidence of something is how frequently it happens: *a rise in the ~ of eating disorders / a fall in the ~ of heart disease / a high ~ of cancer / a low ~ of violent crime / increase the ~ / reduce the ~*

induce to induce something means to cause it to happen: *a fashion is nothing but an ~d epidemic / a drug which ~s vomiting / drugs to ~ labour / a stress-~d illness*

mainstream the mainstream is the generally accepted ideas held by most people in a country. **Mainstream** is also an adjective: *these images have now reached the ~ / the ~ of British politics / ideas that have now entered the ~ / ~ society / the ~ political parties / the ~ press*

norm if something is the norm, it is the normal and accepted thing: *these images of the body beautiful have become the ~ / life on welfare is now the ~ for many families / the accepted ~ / differ from the ~*

obsolete something that is obsolete is old and no longer useful or needed: *nothing is as hideous as an ~ fashion / ~ farm machinery / ~ computer hardware / new technologies that quickly become ~ / computers have made their work ~*

off-putting something that is off-putting is not attractive and discourages you from doing something. The verb is **put off**: *seeing overweight people modelling clothes is ~ / found the smell ~ / it put me off eating / the price put me off*

overview an overview is a short description of something: *give an ~ of some of its results / present an ~ of the situation / an ~ of the issues / a broad ~ of the situation / a general ~*

penetrate to penetrate a place means to reach it or start to have influence in it. The noun is **penetration**: *the phenomenon is penetrating every corner of the world / the company wants to ~ the South American markets / Internet penetration*

predominant something that is predominant is more common or more powerful than other things. The adverb is **predominantly**: *the ~ colour in the room / the ~ group in British society / beauty is ~ly young, white and impossibly thin / the population is ~ly black*

preserve a preserve of one group of people is something that is only done or used by that group: *procedures such as Botox were once the ~ of much older patients / golf is still a male ~ / the financial world is still the ~ of white men*

refreshing something that is refreshing is pleasant because it is new and different. The adverb is **refreshingly**: *it's ~ to see such images reach the*

mainstream / a ~ change / it's ~ to see so many young players / refreshingly new

stand in if you stand in for someone, you do their job for them for a short time: *these images ~ in for us / ~ing in for my boss next week / can you ~ in for me?*

vain someone who is vain has a very high opinion of their own appearance or abilities. The noun is **vanity**: *men are almost as ~ as women / he's becoming quite ~ / very ~ / accused her of vanity / the idea appealed to her vanity*

verge on to verge on something means to almost be that thing: *it ~s on the obscene / a lot of his activities are verging on illegal / an idea that ~s on the ridiculous*

IDIOMS

struck a chord with if something strikes a chord with you, you feel that it is familiar or right. A chord is literally a combination of musical notes that sound nice together: *the campaign seems to have ~ a lot of women*

swim against the tide if you swim against the tide, you do something that is different from what most other people are doing. The tide is literally the regular movement of the sea towards the land and away from it: *images which swim against the dominant tide*

wear and tear wear and tear is damage that is caused by using something regularly. To wear something means to have it on your body and to tear it means to pull it into pieces: *this avoided ~ at the neckline / a certain amount of ~ on the furniture / due to normal ~*

EXERCISES

PREPOSITIONS

A Complete the sentences with the correct preposition.

1 That scarf goes nicely .... your jacket.
2 There's something strange .... this place.
3 I need some smart clothes .... formal occasions.
4 I suddenly had a wonderful sense .... liberation.
5 I like the dress .... the long sleeves.
6 He's a former classmate .... mine.
7 The TV news is about tension .... the Middle East.
8 I don't like the pattern .... that shirt.

WORD FAMILIES

A Complete the expression with the correct form of the word in bold.

1 a **detachable** collar	can you .... the hood?
2 women's **liberation**	soldiers have .... the city
3 she spoke **poignantly**	a .... moment
4 religious **depictions**	she was .... as a hero
5 market **penetration**	police have .... the drug ring
6 the **predominant** culture	the religion is .... Hindu

COLLOCATIONS

A Complete the sentences with the correct form of the verb in the list.

get	enter	become	strike	swim

1 Do you .... on well with your classmates?
2 Video chat has now .... the mainstream.
3 Increasingly hot summers have .... the norm.
4 The *Don't drink and drive campaign* has .... a chord with the public.
5 He always .... against the tide and does things his own way.

B Complete the missing nouns.

1 He gave me a broad o _ _ _ _ _ _ w of the project.
2 She's receiving treatment for an eating d _ _ _ _ _ r.
3 After the war, many bodies were found in unmarked g _ _ _ _ s.
4 The two leaders shook hands in a symbolic g _ _ _ _ _ e of friendship.

5 This area has a low incidence of violent c _ _ _ e.
6 She arrived wearing a beautiful evening g _ _ n.

C Complete the expressions with the words in the lists.

dress	heels	disease
envelope	hardware	jacket

1 a denim ....
2 high ....
3 an evening ....
4 computer ....
5 heart ....
6 a sealed ....

PATTERNS

A Complete the sentences with the correct form of the verbs in the list. Use *to*- infinitive or *–ing*.

induce	get	try	wear	model	lace

1 Many of the girls .... clothes are too thin.
2 She was given drugs .... labour.
3 I taught him how .... his shoes.
4 Good interview skills increase your chance of .... a job.
5 I don't like .... fitted jeans.
6 .... to sell jewellery in a cutthroat market isn't easy.

PHRASAL VERBS

A Complete the sentences with the correct form of the phrasal verbs in the list.

get away with	hold up	frown on
seal off	show off	put off

1 Not everyone can .... a really short haircut.
2 That dress doesn't really .... your figure.
3 Wearing short skirts is .... in some counties.
4 Football stars are often .... as role models by young people.
5 Police have .... the crime scene.
6 I wanted to buy it, but the price .... me ....

16

DANGER AND RISK

PAGES 110–111

agony agony is very great pain: *I was in ~ / in absolute ~ / screaming in ~ / writhing around in ~ / operation left him in ~*

assessment an assessment is a judgement that you make about something. The verb is **assess**: *his initial ~ of the injury / do a quick ~ / your final ~ at the end of the course / carry out an ~ / a risk ~*

blow when the wind blows something, it makes it move. The past tense is **blew**: *people were getting ~n off their feet / the wind was ~ing the leaves around / the door blew shut / blew the roof off / trees were ~n down in the storm*

chin your chin is the part of your face below your mouth: *hit his ~ against the side of the car / a square ~ / a pointed ~ / his stubbly ~*

come to if you come to, you become conscious again: *when I came to, I found my chin completely split open / ~ after the operation*

freak out if you freak out, you become very frightened: *I totally ~ed out and started screaming / it completely ~ed me out*

gash a gash is a big deep cut. **Gash** is also a verb: *I ended up with a huge ~ on my arm / a deep ~ / had a nasty ~ on my leg / got a ~ on the side of my head / gashed my arm on the rocks*

gruesome something that is gruesome is horrible because it involves someone being killed or injured: *is it ~? / very ~ / a ~ murder / a particularly ~ attack / give me all the ~ details*

head first if you fall head first, you fall with your head before the rest of your body: *being blown ~ into a door / fall ~ down the stairs / dive ~ into the water*

initial an initial action is one that happens first. The adverb is **initially**: *his ~ assessment of the injury / the ~ response from the government / during*

the ~ stages of the enquiry / initially, the doctors thought he had flu

pass out if you pass out, you become unconscious: *I passed out on the train / nearly passed out with the heat / the sight of blood makes him ~*

profuse if something is profuse, there is a very large amount of it. The adverb is **profusely**: *made ~ apologies / I was bleeding profusely / sweating profusely / apologised profusely*

regain if you regain something, you get it back: *when I ~ed consciousness, I couldn't feel my hands / ~ your confidence / ~ your appetite / ~ control of the situation*

ruin to ruin something means to spoil it completely: *the accident ~ed the day / the Internet has ~ed childhood / the attack has ~ed my life / ~ his career / my shoes are ~ed*

scald if you scald a part of your body, you injure it with very hot water. **Scald** is also a noun: *I ~ed myself really badly / mind you don't ~ yourself / ~ your hand / a nasty ~ on your arm*

scar a scar is a mark that remains on your skin after an injury. **Scar** is also a verb: *I've got a little ~ on my thumb / left me with an unsightly ~ on my face / left a permanent ~ / emotional ~s / deep psychological ~s / his face was badly scarred / left her scarred for life*

slice a slice is a thin piece of something. To **slice** something means to cut it into slices: *cut a big ~ out of my thigh / a ~ of cake / a ~ of bread / ~ the bread / I ~d my finger open*

snap if something snaps, it breaks with a loud noise. **Snap** is also a noun: *I heard the bone ~ / the branch snapped / ~ a few branches off the tree / ~ the ruler in two / heard a loud ~*

stuffy a stuffy room does not have enough fresh air in it: *it was so ~ that I passed out / the room was hot and ~ / a bit ~ in here / starting to get a bit ~*

stumble if you stumble, you walk in an unsteady way and almost fall over: *I ~d home / ~ up the stairs / ~d out of the building / ~d and fell / stumbling around in the dark*

tear to tear something means to damage it by pulling it very hard: *the machine almost tore one of my fingernails off / ~ your jacket on an old nail / ~ the letter up / ~ it to pieces / ~ a hole in my jeans / my T-shirt was torn to shreds / ~ a muscle / ~ a building down*

PAGES 112–113

appeal an appeal is a request to a court to change a decision. **Appeal** is also a verb: *the ban was overturned following an ~ / his conviction was overturned on ~ / an ~ to the High Court / you have a right of ~ / make an ~ / lodge an ~ / win your ~ / lose your ~ / court dismissed his ~ / a successful ~ / her ~ failed / plans to ~ to the High Court / ~ against her conviction*

back down if you back down, you admit that you were wrong: *bureaucrats ~ on tan ban / the unions refuse to ~ / government was forced to ~ / finally ~ed down over pay cuts*

bow to if you bow to a demand, you finally agree to it: *the EU has ~ed to pressure and excluded sunlight from the directive / the government has ~ed to demands for a public enquiry*

caveat a caveat is a warning that something is not perfect: *the standards generally have the ~ that common sense should apply / offered treatment with the ~ that it might not be successful*

compensation compensation is money that is paid to someone because they have been injured or have suffered in some way. The verb is **compensate**: *the company agreed to pay ~ / pay full ~ / claim ~ / seek ~ / try to get ~ / receive ~ / offer him ~ / was awarded ~ / paid £10,000 as ~ / got £3000 in ~ / ~ for loss of income / offered to compensate her for her injuries*

conviction a conviction is a decision by a court that someone is guilty of a crime. The verb is **convict**: *his ~ was overturned on appeal / don't have enough evidence to secure a ~ / confident they can get a ~ / managed to avoid ~ / has three previous ~s / no criminal ~s / a ~ for murder / he was convicted of murder*

cut out if a machine cuts out, it stops working: *the machines automatically ~ / the engine suddenly ~*

damages damages is money that a court orders to someone to pay to another person for harming them: *he was awarded $200,000 in ~ / claim ~ of £20,000 / threatening to sue the company for ~ / heavy ~ / receive ~ of £30,000 / win ~ / company may be liable for ~*

directive a directive is an official order: *the EU has bowed to pressure and excluded sunlight from is health and safety ~ / a government ~ on health / issue a new ~ / adopt the ~ / implement the ~ / the ~ comes into force next month / work in accordance with the EU ~*

exceed to exceed a limit or amount means to be more than it: *~ the speed limit / working week should not ~ 40 hours / profits are likely to ~ $40 million / the results ~ed our expectations*

exclude if you exclude something, you do not include it. The opposite is **include**: *the EU has ~d sunlight from is health and safety directive / a diet that ~s meat and fish / the decision to ~ him from the team / include her in the group*

exploit if you exploit something, you use it and take advantage of it: *companies try to ~ loopholes that go against the spirit of the law / ~ the opportunity / ~ the situation / ~ other people's weaknesses*

handcuff handcuffs are metal rings that are joined together and put over someone's hands by the police when they are arrested. **Handcuff** is also a verb: *put ~s on him / was led away in ~s / all*

wearing ~s / took the ~s off him / a pair of ~s / she was ~ed and taken to the police station

implementation the implementation of an idea or plan is putting it into action. The verb is **implement**: *~ of the plan / ~ of the report's recommendations / ~ of the decision / given the job of implementing the new policy*

lawsuit a lawsuit is a complaint that someone makes against a person or a company in a court of law: *a number of high-profile ~s / bring a ~ against the company / involved in a lengthy ~ / now faces an expensive ~ / vowed to defend the ~ / won his ~ / lost his ~ / agreed to settle the ~*

legislation legislation is laws: *oppose the new ~ / support the ~ / an important piece of ~ / bring in new ~ / the current ~ / ~ on the carrying of guns / abortion ~ / ~ to protect the elderly / the new ~ comes into force next year*

legitimate if something is legitimate, it is acceptable and allowed by law. The adverb is **legitimately**: *his ~ business activities / claims that the government is not ~ / it's perfectly ~ / safety standards can sometimes be ~ly ignored / a ~ly elected government*

liable if you are liable for something, you are legally responsible for it and must pay the cost of it: *companies are held ~ for accidents at work / the court found the company ~ / criminally ~ / legally ~ / hold you ~ for the mistake*

loophole a loophole in a law is a small mistake that allows people to do something illegal: *it's a ~ in the law / companies try to exploit ~s that go against the spirit of the law / use the ~ / a tax ~ / government has promised to close tax ~s*

negligence negligence is failing to take enough care, with the result that you make a mistake. The adjective is **negligent**: *he admitted medical ~ / professional ~ / was guilty of ~ / gross ~ / accused him of ~ / sued him for ~ / admit ~ / deny ~ / a claim for ~ / court found him to be negligent*

pose to pose a problem or danger means to cause it: *he ~d no danger by exceeding the speed limit / ~ problems for teachers / ~ a risk to the public / ~ no threat to public health*

regulation a regulation is an official rule: *laws and ~s / too many rules and ~s / health and safety ~s / building ~s / fire ~s / introduce strict new safety ~s / government has promised tighter ~s on food hygiene / have to comply with the ~s / tighten the ~s / relax the ~s / accused of breaking health and safety ~s*

revenue revenue is money that a business or government receives: *accidents at work account for millions in lost ~ / the company's annual ~ / ~ from sales / an increase in the government's tax ~*

shift if you shift something, you move it: *they aren't allowed to ~ any chairs / help me ~ this desk*

tighten to tighten a law or rule means to make it more strict: *the union wants to see laws ~ed / ~ the regulations / ~ the rules / ~ up on underage drinking*

Pages 114–115

appraisal an appraisal is your opinion of how good or bad something is: *that's a fairly bleak ~ / my ~ of the situation / give a detailed ~ of the scheme / make an ~ / carry out an ~ of the security systems*

bleak something that is bleak gives you no reason to be cheerful or optimistic: *that's a fairly ~ appraisal / the future looks pretty ~ / prospects for an end to the dispute seem ~ / extremely ~*

blessing a blessing is something good that makes you happy or helps you: *the Internet has become more of a curse than a ~ / it's a ~ no one was hurt / having grandparents nearby is a real ~ / it's a ~ in disguise* (something that seems to be bad, but is in fact good)

block if you block something, you prevent it from happening: *want to ~ the newspaper from publishing the details / ~ the introduction of new legislation / ~ imports of foreign goods / trying to ~ the proposals*

civil liberties civil liberties are rights of citizens to act freely as long as they do not break the law: *we run the risk of restricting ~ / an infringement of ~ / claims it violates ~ / new laws to protect ~*

curse a curse is something that causes a lot of problems: *the Internet has become more of a ~ than a blessing / living near such a busy road is a real ~*

danger danger is the possibility that you might be injured or killed: *Internet dating is fraught with ~ / in serious ~ of becoming addicted / don't put yourself in ~ / in great ~ / in serious ~ / in grave ~ / children who are exposed to ~ / face ~ every day in their work / try to minimise the ~*

embroiled if you are embroiled in a difficult situation, you are involved in it: *~ in a lengthy legal dispute / don't want to get ~ in an argument*

fraught if something is fraught with difficulties or danger, it has a lot: *Internet dating is ~ with danger / the situation is ~ with difficulties*

hacker a hacker is someone who uses their computer to get access to another person's computer illegally. The verb is **hack**: *cyber ~s / a computer ~ / a ~ managed to get into the system / hack into government computers*

hazard a hazard is something that is dangerous because it could cause an accident. The adjective is **hazardous**: *wet floors are a ~ / a fire ~ / a safety ~ / a health ~ / pose a ~ to members of the public / an occupational ~* (to do with your job) */ a hazardous job / chemicals that can be hazardous to health*

menace something that is a menace is dangerous or annoying: *should do more to combat the ~ of spam emails / the ~ of illegal drugs / he's a ~ to society*

perform if you perform well or badly, you do something well or badly: *it doesn't help them ~ academically / most of the players ~ed well / often ~ very badly in exams*

peril peril is great danger: *put your life in ~ / they are in great ~ / in ~ of choking to death / ignore this at your ~*

plagiarism plagiarism is using something that someone else has written or said, and pretending it is your own work. The verb is **plagiarise**: *a lot of students are guilty of ~ / accused him of ~ / university wants to cut down on ~ / accused him of plagiarising her book*

revelation a revelation is an interesting fact that is made public: *celebrity ~s / ~s that children as young as eight are being treated for Internet addiction / ~s about his private life / some astonishing ~s / amazing ~s*

threat a threat is a possible danger: *cyber hackers pose a grave ~ to global security / a ~ to world peace / a considerable ~ to the economy / a significant ~ / a big ~ / a major ~*

witness a witness is someone who saw a crime. **Witness** is also a verb: *a key ~ in the Mafia trial / an important ~ / a ~ to the crime / did anyone ~ the attack?*

Idioms

caught between a rock and a hard place if you are caught between a rock and a hard place, you have a choice between two things but both are equally bad: *really we're ~*

crash out if you crash out, you fall into a deep sleep: *I just ~ed out / ~ed out on the floor*

hot on the heels if one thing comes hot on the heels of another, it follows a very short time afterwards. The image is of one person chasing another and being just behind their heels: *comes ~ of revelations about the dangers of the Internet*

nanny state a nanny state is a government that controls the lives of its citizens too much. A nanny is someone who looks after young children: *we have hysterical stories in the media that we're imposing a ~*

on the ground people who are on the ground are in the place where something is actually happening: *local people who are ~*

EXERCISES

PREPOSITIONS

A Complete the sentences with the correct preposition.

1 He fell and cut the side .... his head.
2 I have a childhood scar .... my forehead.
3 I really don't like the sight .... blood.
4 It's very cold .... here.
5 The ruling was overturned .... appeal.
6 The company may be liable .... damages.
7 The judge declared him a menace .... society.
8 The work of a fire fighter is fraught .... danger.

WORD FAMILIES

A Complete the expression with the correct form of the word in bold.

1 **initially**, I was confused / what was your .... reaction?
2 I apologised **profusely** / suffering from .... diarrhoea
3 receive **compensation** / I haven't been ....
4 we **implemented** the plan / the .... stage
5 a **legitimate** excuse / taxes were not filed ....
6 accused of **negligence** / .... behaviour
7 a computer **hacker** / thieves can ..... into the system
8 **hazardous** waste / a driving ....

IDIOMS

A Complete the idiom with the correct word in the list.

ground	crashed	heels	nanny	rock

1 I don't know what to do. I feel like I'm caught between a .... and a hard place.
2 The BBC was first to have journalists on the ....
3 I just .... out in front of the TV last night.
4 The earthquake comes hot on the .... of a major flood.
5 We have too many regulations. It feels like a .... state.

COLLOCATIONS

A Complete the sentences with the correct form of the verbs in the list.

go	tear	break	bow
hold	compensate	regain	come

1 Paramedics at the scene helped him .... consciousness.
2 I .... a muscle during football training.
3 Management has finally .... to union pressure.
4 The court ruled that she be .... for loss of income.
5 The new directive on waste disposal .... into force next year.
6 Negligent drivers must be .... liable.
7 Violent play .... against the spirit of the game.
8 If you .... the law, you will be punished.

B Complete the missing nouns.

1 It was in absolute a _ _ _ y after the accident.
2 The court awarded £50 000 in d _ _ _ _ _ s.
3 A high p _ _ _ _ _ e businessman has been arrested for corruption.
4 All club members need to follow the rules and r _ _ _ _ _ _ _ _ _ s.
5 Faulty gas heaters are a fire h _ _ _ _ d.
6 A key w _ _ _ _ _ s was unable to attend the trial.

C Match the two halves of the collocation.

1 a slice	a) loophole
2 the police	b) liberties
3 a tax	c) station
4 a blessing	d) of bread
5 civil	e) hazard
6 an occupational	f) in disguise

PHRASAL VERBS

A Complete the sentences with the correct form of the phrasal verbs in the list.

come to	back down	cut down
cut out	freak out	pass out

1 The doctor told him to .... on smoking.
2 I don't know what the problem is. The engine just ....
3 Mediators have persuaded both sides to ....
4 He drinks and drinks until he ....
5 I .... because I thought there was someone in the house.
6 When I .... after the accident, I didn't know where I was.

01 CITIES

PREPOSITIONS

A

1 from   5 of
2 into   6 about
3 of   7 on
4 in   8 from

WORD FAMILIES

A

1 diagnosis
2 circulated
3 burgled
4 demolition
5 spotless
6 congested
7 affluent

IDIOMS

A

1 rolling   5 wildfire
2 take   6 here
3 image   7 then
4 long   8 large

COLLOCATIONS

A

1 trapped
2 attempted
3 living
4 voice
5 take
6 buzzing

B

1 right
2 housing
3 urban
4 rough
5 good
6 full
7 small

C

1 c
2 f
3 a
4 e
5 b
6 h
7 d
8 g

PHRASAL VERBS

A

1 falling down
2 come out
3 start up
4 lost out
5 freaked out

02 CULTURE AND IDENTITY

PREPOSITIONS

A

1 with   5 for
2 of   6 from
3 in   7 in
4 by   8 about

WORD FAMILIES

A

1 abolition
2 fraud
3 heavily
4 stereotypical
5 bemusement
6 steeply
7 assumption
8 commercial

COLLOCATIONS

A

1 get
2 tackle
3 ripped
4 soaked
5 increase
6 struck
7 working

B

1 close-knit   5 verbal
2 heavy   6 diverse
3 long   7 central
4 quick   8 false

C

1 elite
2 pin
3 drill
4 craze
5 corruption
6 punishment
7 evasion

PATTERNS

A

1 attempting
2 happening
3 to protect
4 carrying
5 ranting
6 to commit

PHRASAL VERBS

A

1 wring out
2 sweep up
3 bring up
4 get through
5 get away with
6 cracking down

03 RELATIONSHIPS

PREPOSITIONS

A

1 of
2 to
3 with
4 for
5 about
6 with
7 of

WORD FAMILIES

A

1 cynic
2 incompetent
3 amicably
4 annul
5 thrashed
6 instigation
7 chronically

IDIOMS

A

1 back
2 off
3 on
4 finger
5 heart
6 blue

COLLOCATIONS

A

1 threw   5 filing
2 shoulder   6 pays
3 awarded   7 drifted
4 holds   8 has

B

1 backdrop
2 grounds
3 friend
4 rivalry
5 home
6 tendencies
7 traits

C

1 c
2 e
3 a
4 f
5 g
6 d
7 b

PHRASAL VERBS

A

1 turns out
2 singled out
3 look after
4 blown over
5 split up
6 stand up
7 been through

04 POLITICS

PREPOSITIONS

A

1 by   5 as
2 about   6 in
3 with   7 for
4 for   8 of

WORD FAMILIES

A

1 devastated
2 obscene
3 stand
4 charisma
5 compassion
6 dictator
7 humble
8 satirical

COLLOCATIONS

A

1 violent   5 widely
2 enduring   6 governing
3 obscene   7 hollow
4 capital   8 outspoken

B

1 judgement
2 strain
3 authority
4 breath
5 substance
6 record
7 vote
8 figure

C

1 f
2 a
3 g
4 e
5 b
6 c
7 d

PATTERNS

A

1 representing
2 judging
3 to show
4 peering
5 to hold
6 to compromise

PHRASAL VERBS

A

1 pulled off
2 covering up
3 sneak out
4 flicking through
5 curled up
6 go ahead

05 NIGHT OUT, NIGHT IN

PREPOSITIONS

A

1	about	5	of
2	from	6	on
3	on	7	in
4	in	8	of

WORD FAMILIES

A

1 overwhelmed
2 portrayal
3 endorsement
4 commentator
5 soaring
6 slavery

IDIOMS

A

1 turning
2 bits
3 stitches
4 head

COLLOCATIONS

A

1 burst
2 made
3 revolves
4 due
5 plays
6 take
7 halt
8 writing

B

1 board
2 figure
3 details
4 host
5 system
6 beliefs
7 imagination
8 interest

C

1 union
2 tale
3 display
4 protagonist
5 overload
6 all
7 information

PHRASAL VERBS

A

1 venture out
2 bringing [...] up
3 throw it away
4 live up to
5 fed up
6 burst out

06 CONFLICT

PREPOSITIONS

A

1 for
2 for
3 at
4 to
5 with
6 of
7 on

WORD FAMILIES

A

1 remorse
2 prosecution
3 violation
4 offended
5 intervention
6 harassing
7 exemption

COLLOCATIONS

A

1 complained
2 bear
3 kiss
4 make
5 negotiate
6 overthrow
7 impose
8 stand

B

1 hostile
2 heavy
3 fierce
4 gross
5 legal
6 political
7 death

C

1 e
2 c
3 d
4 f
5 a
6 g
7 b

PATTERNS

A

1	smoking	4	bullying
2	driving	5	to stop
3	to become	6	to submit

PHRASAL VERBS

A

1 stormed out
2 broken down
3 track down
4 break up
5 calling for
6 set out

07 SCIENCE AND RESEARCH

PREPOSITIONS

A

1	with	5	about
2	on	6	for
3	by	7	into
4	from	8	for

WORD FAMILIES

A

1 vital
2 exploratory
3 abundant
4 valid
5 flaws
6 bias
7 anonymously
8 adversely

IDIOMS

A

1 holes
2 slope
3 way
4 wedge
5 vested

COLLOCATIONS

A

1 important
2 genetic
3 visually
4 underlying
5 conflicting
6 upward
7 nuclear
8 cultural

B

1 conditions
2 abuse
3 science
4 drought
5 habitat
6 link

C

1 wellbeing
2 symbol
3 paper
4 campaign
5 action
6 rates

PHRASAL VERBS

A

1 feeds into
2 come up with
3 carrying out
4 borne out of
5 come under
6 stand up

08 NATURE

PREPOSITIONS

A

1 for
2 of
3 to
4 in
5 by
6 on
7 of
8 for

WORD FAMILIES

A

1 ingenious
2 unsettling
3 provoke
4 contradicts
5 bluntly

IDIOMS

A

1 bush
2 straight
3 word
4 swing
5 mouth

COLLOCATIONS

A

1 roam
2 stalk / stalking
3 flown
4 bridge
5 holds

B

1 deserted
2 rolling
3 thick
4 winding
5 articulate
6 cursory
7 sweeping
8 mating

C

1 c
2 f
3 e
4 a
5 g
6 b
7 d

PHRASAL VERBS

A

1 let out
2 blending in
3 sprung up
4 reached out
5 butting in
6 back up

09 WORK

PREPOSITIONS

A

1	with	5	of
2	of	6	with
3	on	7	by
4	into	8	off

WORD FAMILIES

A

1 delegate
2 eager
3 networking
4 back
5 redundancy
6 discriminate
7 substantially
8 technical

IDIOMS

A

1 ropes
2 question
3 leg
4 weight
5 wheels

COLLOCATIONS

A

1 handed
2 comes
3 hauled
4 feeling
5 sounded
6 Don't
7 missed

B

1	tribunal	5	impact
2	prices	6	formality
3	leave	7	claim
4	dismissal	8	deadlines

C

1 occurrence
2 discrimination
3 duty
4 incentive
5 leave
6 notice
7 decision

PHRASAL VERBS

A

1 passed [...] on
2 drop [...] off
3 get off
4 taken off
5 dropping off
6 take on
7 draw up

10 HEATH AND ILLNESS

PREPOSITIONS

A

1	to	5	of
2	of	6	at
3	on	7	about
4	from	8	with

B

1	on	5	from
2	by	6	into
3	as	7	from
4	on	8	to

WORD FAMILIES

A

1 amputation
2 excruciating
3 rehabilitated
4 recur
5 deterioration
6 painstaking
7 thoroughly

COLLOCATIONS

A

1 gone
2 removed
3 clenching
4 grin
5 threw
6 shuddering
7 ease

B

1 attack
2 diet
3 disorder
4 offenders
5 markets
6 proponent
7 anaesthetic

C

1 d
2 e
3 b
4 c
5 h
6 g
7 a
8 f

PHRASAL VERBS

A

1 cut off
2 put on
3 carried out
4 put [...] off
5 sets off
6 sticking to

11 PLAY

PREPOSITIONS

A

1 from
2 into
3 on
4 of
5 about
6 of
7 to
8 over

WORD FAMILIES

A

sprint, grasp, tackle

IDIOMS

A

1 belt
2 neck
3 court
4 cards
5 level
6 goalposts
7 time
8 hand

COLLOCATIONS

A

1 booed
2 went
3 running
4 raised
5 acted
6 overturned

B

1 dirty
2 second
3 late
4 major
5 high
6 tight

C

1 slogan
2 group
3 share
4 ammunition
5 area
6 test

PHRASAL VERBS

A

1 ganging up
2 run out
3 beaten up
4 scraped through
5 knocked out
6 get rid of

12 HISTORY

PREPOSITIONS

A

1 from
2 in
3 for
4 about
5 of
6 on
7 with

WORD FAMILIES

A

1 culmination
2 decadent
3 demonstration
4 rigorous
5 ruined
6 scarce
7 assassination
8 equaliser

IDIOMS

A

1 plague
2 bark
3 broken
4 lust
5 memory
6 rite

COLLOCATIONS

A

1 relations
2 stand
3 uprising
4 role
5 findings
6 doubt

B

1 c
2 e
3 f
4 a
5 b
6 d

PATTERNS

A

1 manufacturing
2 to challenge
3 changing
4 to study
5 to establish
6 consuming

PHRASAL VERBS

A

1 gave rise to
2 put forward
3 carrying out
4 put down
5 whip up

13 NEWS AND THE MEDIA

PREPOSITIONS

A

1	from	5	in
2	with	6	from
3	as	7	for
4	to	8	to

WORD FAMILIES

A

1 rejection
2 confronted
3 sensationalist
4 accused
5 convicted
6 loathed
7 denied

IDIOMS

A

1 common
2 hand
3 storm
4 lining
5 invasion

COLLOCATIONS

A

1 clear
2 taking
3 make
4 slashing
5 dismissed
6 lodge
7 change

B

1 major
2 heated
3 common
4 political
5 public
6 outright
7 staple

C

1 c
2 g
3 e
4 a
5 f
6 b
7 d

PHRASAL VERBS

A

1 taken out
2 ruled out
3 carrying out
4 pull out
5 kicking up

14 BUSINESS AND ECONOMICS

PREPOSITIONS

A

1	with	5	to
2	to	6	in
3	in	7	on
4	of	8	at

WORD FAMILIES

A

1 projected
2 repaid
3 authorise
4 consolidate
5 termination
6 jeopardise
7 pursue

IDIOMS

A

1	chickens	4	light
2	robbery	5	cards
3	killing	6	hole

COLLOCATIONS

A

1 boost
2 sinking
3 chair
4 put
5 err
6 sealed

B

1 services
2 strategy
3 market
4 bonus
5 agenda
6 feedback
7 outlets

C

1 market
2 rise
3 pitch
4 downturn
5 limit
6 line
7 group
8 margin

PHRASAL VERBS

A

1 lay [...] off
2 keep [...] down
3 pick up
4 take on
5 keep up
6 picking up

15 FASHION

PREPOSITIONS

A

1 with
2 about
3 for
4 of
5 with
6 of
7 in
8 on

WORD FAMILIES

A

1 detach
2 liberated
3 poignant
4 depicted
5 penetrated
6 predominantly

COLLOCATIONS

A

1 get
2 entered
3 become
4 struck
5 swims

B

1 overview
2 disorder
3 graves
4 gesture
5 crime
6 gown

C

1 jacket
2 heels
3 dress
4 hardware
5 disease
6 envelope

PATTERNS

A

1 modelling
2 to induce
3 to lace
4 getting
5 to wear / wearing
6 Trying

PHRASAL VERBS

A

1 get away with
2 show off
3 frowned on
4 held up
5 sealed off
6 put [...] off

16 DANGER AND RISK

PREPOSITIONS

A

1	of	5	on
2	on	6	for
3	of	7	to
4	in	8	with

WORD FAMILIES

A

1 initial
2 profuse
3 compensated
4 implementation
5 legitimately
6 negligent
7 hack
8 hazard

IDIOMS

A

1 rock
2 ground
3 crashed
4 heels
5 nanny

COLLOCATIONS

A

1 regain
2 tore
3 bowed
4 compensated
5 comes
6 held
7 goes
8 break

B

1 agony
2 damages
3 profile
4 regulations
5 hazard
6 witness

C

1 d
2 c
3 a
4 f
5 b
6 e

PHRASAL VERBS

A

1 cut down
2 cut out
3 back down
4 passes out
5 freaked out
6 came to

INFINITIVE	PAST SIMPLE	PAST PARTICIPLE
be	was/were	been
become	became	become
begin	began /bɪgæn/	begun /bɪgʌn/
bet	bet	bet
bite /baɪt/	bit	bitten /bɪtən/
blow /bləʊ/	blew /bluː/	blown /bləʊn/
break	broke	broken
bring	brought /brɔːt/	brought
build /bɪld/	built /bɪlt/	built
burn	burned/burnt	burned/burnt
buy	bought /bɔːt/	bought
catch	caught /kɔːt/	caught
choose	chose /tʃəʊz/	chosen
come	came	come
cost	cost	cost
cut	cut	cut
do	did	done
draw /drɔː/	drew /druː/	drawn /drɔːn/
dream	dreamed/dreamt	dreamed /dreamt
drink	drank/dræŋk/	drunk /drʌŋk/
drive	drove	driven
eat	ate /eɪt/	eaten /iː/
fall /fɔːl/	fell /fel/	fallen /fɔːlən/
feel /fiːl/	felt /felt/	felt
fight /faɪt/	fought /fɔːt/	fought
find	found /faʊnd/	found
flee	flew	flown
fly /flaɪ/	flew /fluː/	flown /fləʊn/
forget	forgot	forgotten
forgive	forgave	forgiven
freeze	froze	frozen
get	got	got [US: gotten]
give	gave	given
go	went	been/gone
grow /grəʊ/	grew /gruː/	grown /grəʊn/
hang /hæŋ/	hung /hʌŋ/	hung
have	had	had
hear /hɪə/	heard /hɜːd/	heard /hɜːd/
hide	hid	hidden /hɪdən/
hit	hit	hit
hold	held	held
hurt /hɜːt/	hurt	hurt
keep	kept	kept
know /nəʊ/	knew /njuː/	known /nəʊn/
lay /leɪ/	laid	laid
lead /liːd/	led /led/	led
learn /lɜːn/	learned/learnt	learned/learnt
leave	left	left

INFINITIVE	PAST SIMPLE	PAST PARTICIPLE
lend	lent	lent
let	let	let
lie	lay	lain
lie (not tell the truth)	lied	lied
lose /luːz/	lost	lost
make	made	made
mean	meant	meant
meet	met	met
pay /peɪ/	paid /peɪd/	paid
prove	proved	proven/proved
put	put	put
read /riːd/	read /red/	read /red/
ride	rode	ridden
ring	rang /ræŋ/	rung /rʌŋ/
run /rʌn/	ran /ræn/	run
say /seɪ/	said /sed/	said
see	saw /sɔː/	seen
sell	sold	sold
send	sent	sent
set	set	set
shoot	shot	shot
show	showed	shown
shut	shut	shut
sing	sang /sæŋ/	sung /sʌŋ/
sink	sank /sæŋk/	sunk /sʌŋk/
sit	sat	sat
sleep	slept	slept
slide	slid	slid
speak	spoke	spoken
spell	spelled/spelt	spelt
spend	spent	spent
spoil	spoiled/spoilt	spoiled/spoilt
spread /spred/	spread	spread
stand	stood	stood
steal	stole	stolen
stick	stuck /stʌk/	stuck
strike /straɪk/	struck /strʌk/	struck
swear	swore	sworn
swim	swam /swæm/	swum /swʌm/
take /teɪk/	took /tʊk/	taken /teɪkən/
teach	taught /tɔːt/	taught
tell	told	told
think	thought /θɔːt/	thought
throw /θrəʊ/	threw /θruː/	thrown /θrəʊn/
understand	understood	understood
wake	woke /wəʊk/	woken /wəʊkən/
wear /weə/	wore /wɔː/	worn /wɔːn/
win	won /wʌn/	won
write	wrote	written /rɪtən/

CENGAGE
Learning™

Outcomes:
Advanced Vocabulary Builder

Sheila Dignen and
Guy de Villiers

Publisher: Jason Mann

Senior Commissioning Editor:
John Waterman

Assistant Editor: Heidi North

Content Project Editor:
Amy Smith

Production Controller:
Denise Power

Compositor: Q2AMedia

Cover and text design:
Studio April

For product information and technology assistance,
contact **emea.info@cengage.com**.
For permission to use material from this text or product,
and for permission queries,
email **emea.permissions@cengage.com**.

British Library Cataloguing-in-Publication Data
A catalogue record for this book is available from the British Library.

ISBN: 978-1-111-21176-9

Cengage Learning EMEA
Cheriton House, North Way, Andover, Hampshire, SP10 5BE
United Kingdom

Cengage Learning products are represented in Canada by
Nelson Education Ltd.

For your lifelong learning solutions, visit **www.cengage.co.uk**

Purchase your next print book, e-book or e-chapter at
www.cengagebrain.com

Printed in China by RR Donnelley
3 4 5 6 7 8 9 10 – 15 14 13